Role motivation theories

John B. Miner

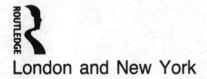

London and New York

First published in 1993
by Routledge
11 New Fetter Lane, London EC4P 4EE

Simultaneously published in the USA and Canada
by Routledge
29 West 35th Street, New York, NY 10001

First published in paperback in 1994

© 1993 John B. Miner

Typeset in Garamond by Intype, London
Printed and bound in Great Britain by
Mackays of Chatham PLC, Chatham, Kent

British Library Cataloguing in Publication Data
A catalogue record for this book is available from the British
Library.

Library of Congress Cataloging in Publication Data
A catalog record for this book is available on request.

Fig. 2.1 reproduced from *International Review of Industrial
and Organizational Psychology*, 1, (1986), with permission
of John Wiley & Sons, Ltd.

ISBN 0–415–11994–4

To my former and present students whose many contributions to this program of research are indicated in the references:

At the University of Oregon: Robert B. Bowin, Alfred W. Stoess.

At the University of Maryland: J. Frank Brewer, Jan P. Muczyk.

At Georgia State University: Michael Albert, Sandra F. Beldt, Frederic E. Berman, Cameron H. Black, Jeffrey S. Bracker, Bahman Ebrahimi, Aprile M. Holland, Louis F. Jourdan, Charles L. Lardent, John E. Oliver, John N. Pearson, M. Susan Pilgrim, John V. Quigley, Timothy M. Singleton, Lloyd J. F. Southern, Jeffrey M. Wachtel, Kay S. White.

At State University of New York at Buffalo: Saad A. Al-Kelabi, Chao-chuan Chen, Susan S. Doe, John N. O'del, Charles G. Porter, Celeste P. M. Wilderom.

John B. Miner is Professor of Human Resources at the State University of New York at Buffalo.

Contents

Figures and tables

Preface and acknowledgements

This book is a product of theory and research extending over a long time. The program really began in 1957 at The Atlantic Refining Company in Philadelphia, although it had roots extending back into the early 1950s at Princeton and Columbia. Over the years a number of students have worked with me and contributed through their own research – first at the University of Oregon, and then later at the University of Maryland, Georgia State University, and now the State University of New York at Buffalo. It has been a pleasure working with all of them. I have dedicated the book to them.

In addition there have been a number of faculty members at various institutions who have collaborated with me on research projects related to the role motivation theories in some way; we have published our work jointly. In order of the time of initial collaboration these are Norman R. Smith, Dorothy N. Harlow, John R. Rizzo, Donald P. Crane, Richard P. Butler, Max G. Holland, K. C. Yu, Robert J. Vandenberg, Alice Eagly, and Barbara Keats. Finally there is a group of individuals who have done or are doing work on role motivation theory and/or who have been very helpful to me through our discussions, even though we have not published together on the subject. In the early years this group included Robert J. House, Benjamin S. Gantz, and Abraham K. Korman; somewhat later Joseph A. Steger, Barry R. Nathan, Linda M. Calvert, Douglas W. Bray, and Ann Howard; and more recently Renato R. Bellu, Edwin A. Locke, Fred Dansereau, and Kenneth D. Mackenzie.

I would like also to acknowledge those who served as mentors to me in one sense or another during the 1950s when all this was coming together – Thelma G. Alper at Clark University, Silvan S. Tomkins at Princeton University, Russell Carrier at the Carrier Clinic, Eli Ginzberg at Columbia University, and George W. Taylor at the University of Pennsylvania. These people put a great deal of time and effort into my professional, and often personal, development; I appreciate it very much.

With regard to the present volume specifically, my professional debts are to Chao-chuan Chen who helped immeasurably with the literature search, and to Susan Doe who later took over his role. Sheldon Zedeck did the major review of the manuscript. It was thorough and penetrating. I appreciate his assistance very much. Subsequently Alan Bryman also reviewed the manuscript and provided a number of helpful suggestions. My secretary, Nancy Carrigan and my wife, Barbara Miner, prepared the manuscript for the publisher. Both exhibited their usual high levels of skill.

This book is not intended to be a final report on the role motivation theory research program. Rather it is a stock-taking and assessment at a point in time. It has been difficult, accordingly, to know when to stop. There have been repeated instances of delays occasioned by a desire to incorporate just one more piece of new research. Finally, however, this had to stop. Research on the task theory is continuing and new data arrive almost every day. A book on the subject should be forthcoming shortly. There are also several projects underway of an international nature dealing with both the hierarchic and task theories, and some work on the predictive potential of the professional theory.

There is an autobiographical piece prepared for Arthur Bedeian's project on the lives of contributors to the management field (Miner, 1992a). A good deal is said there that serves to explain how and why the role motivation theory research was initiated and continued. It would have been desirable to incorporate more from that piece here, but the two publications will have to stand as essentially supplementary. There is much more further back in the pipeline as well. Perhaps in another book, later on . . .

John B. Miner
Buffalo, New York

Chapter 1

The role motivation theories

This is a book about four types of organizations, and what makes them work. The four are not exhaustive of all possible organizational types, but they do represent the major forms found in the world today. If we wish to understand organizational functioning in modern society, it is necessary to have substantial insight into these four types of organizations. The four role motivation theories are intended to provide this insight.

DISTINGUISHING CHARACTERISTICS OF ORGANIZATIONAL TYPES

The four types of organizations are widely identified and described in the literature, although each one is usually considered independent of the other three. Thus Weber (1968) considers hierarchic systems, Vollmer and Mills (1966) treat professional systems, Collins, Moore, and Unwalla (1964) focus on entrepreneurial systems, and Herbst (1976) deals with socio-technical systems. Clearly these authors do mention other types of organizations beyond that which is their primary concern, but such references tend to be fleeting.

Although discussions of this kind in the literature provide useful inputs to an understanding of the organizational types, it seems preferable to rely on empirical data that distinguish among them. Data of this kind have been provided by Oliver (1981; 1982; Oliver and Fredenberger, 1987). The types are distinguishable in terms of their structures, the processes by which they operate, and the jobs that play a key role.

Hierarchic organization

In hierarchic systems management, being at the higher level plays the key role. The extent to which management is key is evident in the following list of defining characteristics:

1. Work rules and regulations are established by *management*.

2. Job results are evaluated by *superiors*.
3. Organizational changes are carried out by *management*.
4. Individual competence is judged by *management*.
5. Pay levels are based on seniority or *hierarchical position*.
6. Freedom of action is limited by *organizational* guidelines.
7. Organizational leaders are appointed by *management*.
8. Punishments are established by *management*.
9. Screening and selecting new employees is accomplished by a *personnel unit*.
10. Counseling of problem employees is carried out by *superiors*.
11. Replacement of absent employees is accomplished by *superiors*.
12. Job changes are initiated by *management*.
13. Risk of failure is assumed by top-level *managers*.
14. Resources for work accomplishments are allocated by *management*.
15. Meetings are called and conducted by *management*.

   Such an organization is large enough so that formalized, written communication is necessary, not merely face-to-face interaction (Stinchcombe, 1974). Management induces contributions down through the hierarchy by manipulating positive and negative sanctions. The energy thus generated is channeled to organizational goal attainment through the establishment of role prescriptions (division of labor) as specified in such documents as organizational charts and written job descriptions. General Motors, or any other large corporation, would be an example.

Professional organization

In professional or knowledge-based systems, role requirements derive from the values, norms, ethical precepts, and codes of the profession, rather than from the managerial hierarchy. They are transmitted through early professional training, by professional associations, and by colleagues. In professional organizations members of the core profession assume the key roles and perform many of the activities that managers perform in hierarchic organizations. In the conduct of their affairs the professionals use committees and voting procedures extensively. The overall structure tends to be flat with status differentiations based on professional expertise and experience. The law firm Alston and Bird based in Atlanta would be an example.

   That the dominant profession plays the key role in an organization of this type is apparent from its defining characteristics:

1. A large number of jobs are classified as *professions*.
2. Work satisfaction is based on enjoyment of one's *profession*.
3. Learning how to do the job is based essentially on *professional* training.
4. On-the-job training is intended primarily for *professional* development.

5. Long hours due to *professional* commitment are typical.
6. Important day-to-day communications are always with fellow *professionals* and clients.
7. Individual efforts are devoted to *professional* goals.
8. The benefits of work go to clients or *professional* colleagues.
9. Relationships with clients are based on *professional* knowledge and trust.
10. Career development is oriented toward *professional* development.
11. Primary loyalty is to the *profession*.
12. Leaders are selected on the basis of *professional* competence.
13. The *professional* job is central to one's life and part of one's individual identity.
14. *Professional* knowledge is more important than any other type.
15. Status is based on *professional* and occupational competence.

Task organization

In task systems the pushes and pulls of sanctions are built into the work itself. Instead of being mediated by higher managers or professional norms, they are part of the task. A prime example is the entrepreneur in an entrepreneurial organization, although profit center managers, corporate venture managers, straight commission sales representatives of the kind found in real estate, for example, and manufacturers' representatives among others may also serve in the key task system role. Much job enrichment appears to engage the task domain.

Taking the entrepreneur as a prototype, pulls or positive sanctions are inherent in the prospects for sizable financial rewards, community status, and personal gratification; pushes to stay in the entrepreneurial situation and to exert effort emanate from the threat of business failure and bankruptcy. These influences operate not only on the entrepreneur involved, but on family members and others who anticipate holding, or do hold, an ownership position. Entrepreneurs are generalists; they become engaged in every aspect of the business. They move to wherever the action is and whatever threats to the business appear, without regard for formal hierarchic channels. Communication is face-to-face and oral, rarely written. Forwarding Services Inc., a small but growing firm located in North Tonawanda, New York, provides an example of this organizational type.

Task systems operate on a personal or individual basis; the person involved is very close to the task, with no manager or profession or group mediating the definition of the job to be done. However, the person typically does establish goals to divide up the task in both scope and time; entrepreneurs do this frequently. The defining characteristics of task systems clearly emphasize the key role of the task performer and the goals set by that person:

1. Work rules and regulations are established by *oneself* to ensure goal accomplishment.
2. Rewards accrue consequent to effective *task* accomplishment.
3. Responsibility for daily work loads belongs to the *individual*.
4. Job results are evaluated by the *individual*.
5. Competence is judged by the *individual*.
6. Long hours are accepted to gain *personal* rewards and achievement.
7. Day-to-day work decisions are determined by *personal* job goals.
8. Job changes are made by the *individual* without permission from anyone.
9. *Personal* drive is the most valued characteristic of workers.
10. Risk taking is considered necessary for *personal* achievement.
11. Pay is based on successful *task* completion.
12. Daily work judgments are determined largely by *personal* goals.
13. *Personal* drive is directed to the achievement of *personal* goals.
14. Punishments are directly related to failure to achieve *personal* goals.
15. Advancement is based on *personal* goal accomplishment.

That the difference between task and hierarchic systems is not merely a matter of size may be illustrated with reference to a situation that developed at General Mills some years ago (Cox, 1982). General Mills had experienced a period of rapid growth through acquisitions of much smaller firms. The basic strategy was to buy up firms in a wide range of businesses that were still being run by their founder-owners and to make these same entrepreneurs division heads under the leadership of the executives in the company's general office in Minneapolis. Although the divisionalized structure was used, it actually operated with much more decentralization and many fewer controls from the top than are usually the case. The entrepreneurs retained much of their autonomy and continued to run all phases of their operations in the same personal but often autocratic manner that they had been used to in the past.

Ultimately a clash occurred between this entrepreneurial mode of operation and bureaucratic structure. Chief Executive Bruce Atwater felt it essential to introduce more structure and control over the division heads, in the interest of the company as a whole. Firm financial controls were introduced from the top. It was felt that continuing the independence that had existed for fifteen years or more would eventually lead to chaos. This shift from a cluster of task systems to a hierarchic structure led the entrepreneurs to claim that top management lacked understanding of their individual businesses. There were some bitter exchanges and a number of the entrepreneurs resigned. As so often happens in situations of this kind, the hierarchic system prevailed.

Group organization

In group systems decisions are made by consensus or majority vote and leadership is emergent, occurs at the will of the majority, and is often rotating. Communication tends to be face-to-face and the basic unit is the work group. These groups achieve goal-directed effort by exerting concerted pressure on members to behave in certain ways, as originally discovered in the Hawthorne research (Cass and Zimmer, 1975). For such a system to operate there must be a cohesive group with stable membership. The key performers are the group members in good standing. Although to an extent the energy of group systems is inherent in the process of participating in decisions and thus owning them, negative sanctions may also be invoked by the group in support of group norms.

A special problem for group systems is that groups often must be linked into a larger whole in some manner, even though there is no hierarchy or set of professional norms to accomplish this. One resolution is that the organization develops a pervasive ideology or culture, which ties the groups together. It is not uncommon for some group members to serve in more than one group, and thus operate as linking pins, spreading the organizational culture and coordinating the groups (Likert and Likert, 1976).

The key role played by work group members in good standing in these systems is evident in the defining characteristics:

1. Job learning is a consequence of *group* efforts to share skills and knowledge.
2. Responsibility for daily work loads is shared by *group* members.
3. Individual job results are evaluated by the *work group*.
4. Competence is judged by the *work group*.
5. Important day-to-day communications are with *work group* members.
6. Job rotation within the *group* is encouraged.
7. New worker selection is based on *work group* evaluations.
8. Individual daily work problems are a responsibility of the *work group*.
9. Sacrifices are made for the good of the *work group*.
10. Incompetence is judged by the *work group*.
11. Screening and selection of new employees is a responsibility of the *work group*.
12. Conflicts within the *group* are resolved by discussion and compromise.
13. Counseling of problem employees is a responsibility of the *work group*.
14. Replacement of absent employees is accomplished by the *work group*.
15. Housekeeping duties are performed by all *work group* members.

Clearly the work groups themselves take over many functions that in a hierarchic system would be carried out by management. Instances of group systems are autonomous work groups (Emery and Thorsrud, 1976) and voluntary groups (Wilderom and Miner, 1991). The autonomous work groups that exist in a number of plants at Mead Corporation would serve as an example.

Additional types

Although the hierarchic, professional, task, and group typology covers most organizational systems in modern society, it is not meant to be exhaustive. Weber (1968), for instance, gives considerable attention to patrimonial organizations, in which traditional authority is largely manifest, and to charismatic communities characterized by charismatic leader-follower relations. Weber considers both of these forms prebureaucratic, although both can be identified on occasion today.

Patrimonial systems lack the separation of private and official spheres that occur in bureaucracy, and allegiance is to an individual leader rather than to an office. Decisions are *ad hoc*, rather than according to a set of rational rules, and performance is evaluated relative to the degree of favor in which a person is held by the leader. Certain kingdoms and family undertakings are examples. In such systems leadership achieves its impact because it can draw upon, or play upon, a common set of early learning experiences among members. Such concepts as super ego, ego ideal, and positive transference from psychoanalytic theory (Freud, 1930) are particularly applicable. Because this type of system requires homogeneous and stable early socialization, it seems less likely to operate effectively in a world with as much mobility as we now experience. Groups of individuals who have been raised to honor and obey a particular person throughout their lives, and thus accept that person's commands whatever they may be, are no longer easy to find.

Charismatic systems require that supernatural, superhuman, or at the very least exceptional powers, be attributed to a leader. As in patrimonial systems, ties to this leader are highly emotional, but now the leader must prove the special powers repeatedly to induce continuing member contributions. Often there is a religious element involved, as in sects and certain communes. Empirical research on charismatic systems, which requires the development of an index of charisma, appears almost nonexistent. One reason appears to be that, just as when Maslow (1954) set out to study self-actualization, he found few subjects to draw on, efforts to study true charismatic systems face the difficulty that very few such organizations currently exist.

It is also possible to identify a factor labeled self-control (Miner, 1975) which represents the antithesis of a true organizational system. In certain cases an organization exists only nominally, perhaps after the disintegration of a previously existing organizational system. Where self-control rules there is very little if any power exerted by hierarchy, profession, task, or group. What exists is an interacting, largely self-motivated set of individuals. Only the individual conscience as a residue of early parental value training serves to constrain entirely self-serving behavior. Relying on self-control invites organizational anarchy, just as removing the force of law invites societal anarchy. Where self-control prevails, and external inducements to contribute to organizational goals are lacking, there really is no organization, only individuals. The situation is analogous to that Tannenbaum (1968) found under conditions where overall control levels throughout an organization are very low.

In emphasizing the concept of organizational types, several cautions need to be kept in mind. First, although some organizational boundaries encompass only one organizational form – a group medical practice might be an example – this is probably the exception. Many organizations hold within them several different types of systems. Thus a large manufacturing firm with hierarchy at the top may also include research and legal systems that are largely professional, new venture teams that are largely task systems, and autonomous work groups on the shop floor that are largely group systems. Most universities are professional systems at the bottom, but grade into hierarchies at the top.

A second consideration to recognize is that, although organizational systems have been treated to this point as discrete types, this is something of an oversimplification. Where a given organizational component exhibits many of the characteristics of one organizational form, say the professional, and few of the characteristics of the other three systems, it is useful to invoke the concept of type. However, underlying this classification are really four variables. Thus we may speak of the degree of hierarchy, the degree of professionalization, the extent to which a task system prevails, and the degree of groupness. Accordingly it is possible to have organizational systems that are mixed or composite, where no one type prevails; where, for instance, some features of the work context are largely hierarchic, but an almost equal number are professional. Many business school deans appear to face such organizational contexts (Hadley and Wilhelm, 1980). These composite systems may not be ideal from many perspectives, but they do represent organizational reality.

Mintzberg's parallel typology

Some sense of the pervasiveness of the organizational taxonomy developed by the author (Miner, 1975; 1980; 1982) may be gained by comparing it with a similar approach proposed by Mintzberg (1983; 1984; 1985). To the best of the author's knowledge, Mintzberg's views were developed entirely independently. Yet the parallels between the two typologies are striking. However, Mintzberg uses the term *power configuration* to describe the underlying dynamic of his classification system. Such a designation seems entirely appropriate for present purposes as well, but it was not used by the author in his earlier discussions; rather these discussions utilized terms such as *control processes* and *inducement systems*.

Mintzberg's system differentiates two types of bureaucracy – the *instrument* and the *closed system*; the latter tends to follow the former in time. Instruments are characterized by the fact that the primary power over them is external – in the hands of a single individual or a group of people who think alike. Often this power is mediated to the internal managers through a board of directors. The external power source may lie in one or more owners, in a corporation of which the organization is a subsidiary, or even in a single strong supplier or customer. In the closed system power resides directly in the line managerial hierarchy; the power is internal. The large corporation with widely diversified ownership provides an example. Both the instrument and the closed system fall within the author's concept of a hierarchic system.

Mintzberg's version of a professional system is the *meritocracy*. Here a group of experts or professionals with specialized knowledge have the power. These experts may work as a federation of single individuals or in what amounts to project teams. Within this knowledge-based form the Mintzberg and Miner formulations appear to occupy almost identical domains. A similar degree of overlap exists between Mintzberg's *autocracy* and the author's task system. An autocracy is a small, often newly founded, organization. Power resides entirely in the chief executive who is usually owner and founder as well. Mintzberg's *missionary* organization has a clear mission, and the ideology or culture supporting it are accepted by all members as guiding principles. Power really resides in the shared ideology. People do not become or stay members unless they hold to the ideology. Certain voluntary organizations, political movements, and religious groups are often of this kind. The basic structure is a set of groups or cells held together by the ideology. Although Mintzberg emphasizes the overarching ideology more and Miner the internal group dynamics, the two are clearly talking about much the same thing.

Mintzberg's sixth form is the *political arena* in which organizational politics captures the organization and its immediate environment. Although political arenas may represent transitory states that predate major changes, they can also capture an organization, hold it for long periods of time, loot it, and leave it devoid of assets and dying. This latter scenario most closely approximates the author's concept of a non-organization rooted only in self-control.

Of the two sets of organizational typologies, Mintzberg's clearly is the more useful in setting forth alternative structures, power sources, and transitions through the organizational life cycle. However, the author's approach has its major value in providing formulations regarding the intrinsic motive patterns which should guide the actions of key performers in the various organizational systems, to energize those systems and make them function effectively. Role motivation theory is essentially a normative theory of motivation–organization fit, or more properly at the present time, four parallel theories of motivation–organization fit (Miner, 1979). We have considered the organization aspect of this amalgam. Now we turn to the motivational component. It is important to recognize, however, that the Mintzberg–Miner parallelism is important not only in its own right, but because many other typologies appear to utilize a very similar format (Wilderom, Miner, and Pastor, 1991).

ROLES AND MOTIVATIONS

Role motivation theories deal with the relationships among organization types, role requirements for key performers (managers, professionals, entrepreneurs, or group members) that follow from these organizational forms, and motivational patterns that fit these roles. They are in effect *meso* theories which tie together the macro (organizational) and micro (individual) levels of organizational science.

The theories specify a set of informal role requirements that are derived logically (and in some cases empirically) from the form of organization involved and the relation of the key performers to that organization. A matching set of motive patterns is then specified, one for each role requirement. If the role–motivation match is good, the likelihood increases that the role requirements will be carried out and that effective performance will occur. On the other hand if the motive pattern of an individual does not fit the role, there is an increasing likelihood that the individual will be unsuccessful.

In specifying this concept of motivation–organization fit it is recognized that numerous questions have been raised regarding the fit approach in general, and that other than linear relationships may appear (Fry and Slocum, 1984; Schoonhoven, 1981; Van de Ven and Drazin, 1985). However, this nonsupportive literature has not been concerned with motivational variables. There are strong arguments for fit concepts as well (Ansoff, 1983; Galbraith and Kazanjian, 1986; Miles and Snow, 1984). When motivational variables are utilized, they do appear to exhibit linear relationships with performance factors within appropriate organizational domains (Miner, 1985).

When a particular organizational system is staffed appropriately (to achieve a motivational fit), it is activated, it runs smoothly and produces output. What was previously a static structure, becomes a dynamic, moving system. Should the staffing be motivationally inappropriate, the system may not run at all or if it does run, it will do so at markedly reduced levels of efficiency. The concept proposed is not unlike that of a machine which operates well only when the specific energy source or fuel for which it was built is utilized. An example is a boat engine constructed to burn a particular mixture of oil and gasoline. Should the mixture not fit the engine, in the same sense as motives fail to fit organizations, operating efficiency, or productivity, declines. If the gasoline is not enriched at all, system failure can be anticipated.

Machine analogies such as this tend to be unattractive simply because they seem to denigrate the dignity of the individual. Nevertheless, it is important to recognize that organizations need appropriate motivational inputs as an energy source to produce output. Organizations are systems contrived by humans to achieve objectives, just as machines are. This recognition of the tool property of organizations goes back at least to Weber (1968). What differs, however, is that organizations by their nature continue to use human motivation as their primary energy source; machines replace human motivation with some other type of energy.

Hierarchic roles and motivations

Figure 1.1 outlines the hierarchic role motivation theory. There are six role requirements and matching managerial motive patterns. This theory had its origins in the latter part of the 1950s; it was strongly influenced by the author's observations (as a psychologist in personnel research) of the cultural dynamics operating within the corporate headquarters of the Atlantic Refining Company in Philadelphia. However, there were contributions from the empirical literature as well. Sources include Kahn and Katz (1953), Pelz (1952), Fleishman, Harris, and Burtt (1955), Stogdill and Coons (1957), and a variety of studies into masculinity–femininity subsequently summarized by Harrell (1961). These sources influenced the role requirements and motivational patterns in ways that are apparent below.

Favorable attitudes to superiors match with the positive relations with authority role requirement. Managers are typically expected to behave in ways which do not provoke negative reactions from their superiors; ideally they will elicit positive responses. Managers must be in a position to represent their groups upward in the organization and to obtain support for their actions at higher levels. This requires a good relationship between manager and superior. It follows that managers should have a generally positive attitude toward those holding positions of authority over them, if they are to meet this particular role requirement. If managers do, in fact, like and respect their bosses, it will be much easier to work with the superiors in the numerous instances where cooperative endeavor is necessary. Any tendency to generalized hatred, distaste, or anxiety in dealing with people in positions of authority will make it extremely difficult to meet managerial job demands. Interactions with superiors will either be

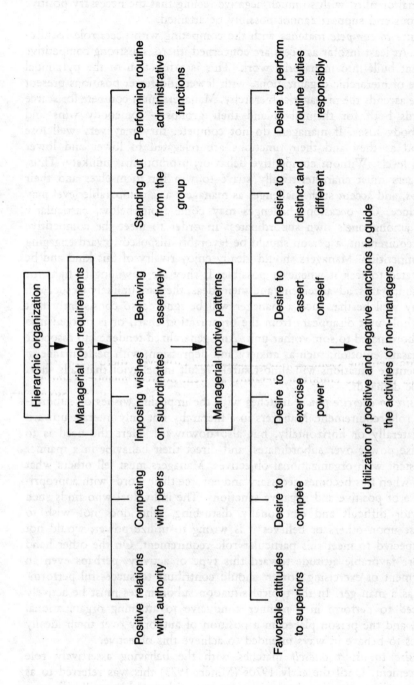

Figure 1.1 Outline of the hierarchic role motivation theory

minimal or filled with so much negative feeling that the necessary positive reactions and support cannot possibly be attained.

Desire to compete matches with the competing with peers role requirement. At least insofar as peers are concerned, there is a strong competitive element built into managerial work. This is a function of the pyramidal nature of hierarchic organizations, with fewer and fewer positions present as one ascends the managerial hierarchy. Managers must compete for scarce rewards both for themselves and their groups – somebody wins and somebody loses. If managers do not compete, they may very well lose ground as they and their functions are relegated to lower and lower status levels. Without competitive behavior, promotion is unlikely. Thus, managers must characteristically strive to win for themselves and their groups, and accept such challenges as managers at a comparable level may introduce. On occasion challenges may come from below, particularly from among one's own subordinates. In order to meet the competitive role requirement, a person should be favorably disposed toward engaging in competition. Managers should ideally enjoy rivalry of this kind and be motivated to seek it whenever possible. If they are unwilling to fight for position, status, advancement, and their ideas, they are unlikely to succeed. It may well be that such a manager will be ignored so consistently that the whole unit disappears from the organization chart, or is merged into or subordinated to some other unit. Any generalized tendency to associate unpleasant emotion, such as anxiety and depression, with performance in competitive situations will almost surely result in behavior that falls short of role demands.

Desire to exercise power matches with the imposing wishes on subordinates role requirement. Managers in a hierarchy not only interact upward and laterally or horizontally, but also downward. Here the need is to exercise power over subordinates, and direct their behavior in a manner consistent with organizational objectives. Managers must tell others what to do when this becomes necessary and enforce their words with appropriate use of positive and negative sanctions. The individual who finds such behavior difficult and emotionally disturbing, who does not wish to impose upon others or believes it is wrong to utilize power, would not be expected to meet this particular role requirement. On the other hand a more favorable attitude toward this type of activity, perhaps even an enjoyment of exercising power, should contribute to successful performance as a manager. In the typical situation subordinates must be actively induced to perform in a manner conducive to attaining organizational goals, and the person placed in a position of authority over them ideally desires to behave in ways intended to achieve this objective.

Desire to assert oneself matches with the behaving assertively role requirement. Until the early 1970s (Miner, 1973) this was referred to as the masculine role. The change in name was introduced because it became increasingly evident that many women possess this type of motivation at a high level, and thus a label which appeared to indicate a characteristic of males only was misleading. However, the conceptual foundation involved is the traditional male or father role as it existed in the United States during and prior to the 1950s. Although this masculinity–femininity aspect of motivation is less frequently noted in the literature of the 1960s and beyond, there are significant exceptions; see for example Ghiselli (1971) and Hofstede (1980). Clearly changing gender role patterns have had a significant impact over the past 35 years. Thus it is important to emphasize that the discussion of assertiveness here extends back to gender norms and expectations of an earlier period. This is the motive pattern, and role requirement, with which the theory is concerned. It appears to be less manifest today than in the past.

Taking, then, this pattern of a prior period, there appears to be considerable similarity between the requirements of the managerial role and the more general demands of the masculine, father role. Both sets of expectations emphasize taking charge, making decisions, taking disciplinary action when necessary, and protecting other members of the group (family). Thus, one of the more common role requirements of the managerial job is that the incumbent behave in this essentially masculine manner. In fact a major means of demonstrating masculinity has been to assume a position of managerial responsibility. When women are appointed to managerial positions, these same role expectations apply. Those individuals who prefer more characteristically feminine behavior patterns, irrespective of their sex, and those who become upset or disturbed at the prospect of behaving in this masculine manner would not be expected to possess the type of motivation that contributes to managerial success. The job appears to require an individual who obtains pleasure from performing as prescribed by this culturally defined male role, and who is therefore highly motivated to act in accordance with this particular behavior model. The behavior involved may well give the appearance of being somewhat macho. This motivation would be expected to arise out of a strong and stable father identification during the formative years, whether in males or females.

Desire to be distinct and different matches with the standing out from the group role requirement. The managerial job requires a person to behave in ways differing in a number of respects from the behavior of others in the same face-to-face group. An incumbent must in this sense stand out from the group and assume a position of high visibility. Managers cannot use the actions of the people with whom they are most frequently associated, their subordinates, as guides for their behavior. Rather they must deviate from the immediate group and do things which will inevitably invite attention, discussion, and perhaps criticism from those who report to them. The managerial role requires that an individual assume a position of considerable importance insofar as the motives and emotions of other people are concerned. When this prospect is viewed as unattractive, when the idea of standing out from the group, of behaving in a different manner, and of being highly visible elicits feelings of unpleasantness, then behavior appropriate to the role will occur much less often than would otherwise be the case. It is the person who enjoys being at the center of attention and who prefers to deviate to some degree from others in a group, who is most likely to meet the demands of the managerial job in this area. Such a person will wish to gain visibility and will have many of the characteristics of a good actor. Certainly a manager is frequently 'on stage.'

Desire to perform routine duties responsibly matches with the performing routine administrative functions role requirement. In this instance there is no specific reference to relationships with superiors, peers, or subordinates, although any of these may be involved on occasion. The basic concern is with communication and decision-making processes needed to get the work out and to keep on top of routine demands. The things that have to be done must actually be done. These functions range from constructing budget estimates to serving on committees, to talking on the telephone, to filling out employee rating forms and salary change recommendations. There are administrative requirements of this kind in all managerial work, although the specific activities will vary somewhat from one situation to another. To meet these prescriptions managers must at least be willing to face this type of routine, and ideally they will gain some satisfaction from it. If, on the other hand, such behavior is consistently viewed with apprehension or loathing, a person's chances of success in management would appear to be considerably less. A desire to put off or avoid the various more or less standard administrative duties of the managerial job can result in considerable deviation from role requirements.

Professional roles and motivations

Figure 1.2 outlines the professional role motivation theory. There are five role requirements and matching professional motive patterns. The theory was strongly influenced by the author's socialization experiences as a practicing industrial/organizational psychologist and as a university professor. However, the literature on the professions and professional organizations also played an important role. Included in this latter category are the theoretical and empirical work of Etzioni (1964), Satow (1975), Vollmer and Mills (1966), Hall (1967), Harrison (1974), and Sorensen and Sorensen (1974). While the hierarchic theory was first published in Miner (1960) and more fully elaborated in Miner (1965), the professional theory is a much later product. It was discussed as early as 1975, but the

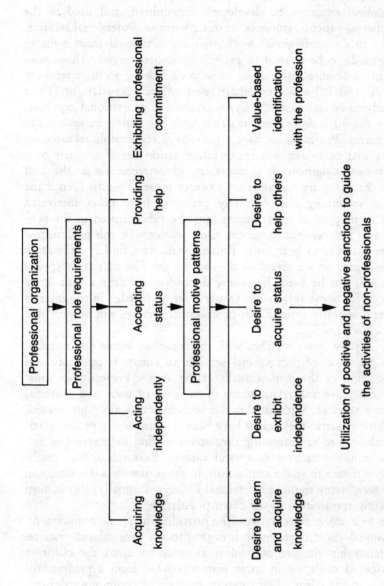

Figure 1.2 Outline of the professional role motivation theory

professional roles and motives were not fully explicated in print until 1980 (Miner, 1975, 1980).

Desire to learn and acquire knowledge matches with the acquiring knowledge role requirement. In the professions the essence of the work is that technical expertise be developed, transmitted, and used in the service of clients, patients, students, or other users of professional services. Accordingly to do professional work well a professional must want to learn what needs to be learned to provide an expert service. Those who do not want to acquire knowledge, or who find doing so distasteful for some reason, will fall short of others' performance expectations. Their work is likely to be lacking in the key ingredient of professional expertise.

Desire to exhibit independence matches with the acting independently role requirement. Professionals have a personally responsible relationship with clients that often requires independent action based on their own best professional judgment. It is necessary to determine what the best interests of the client are and then act to serve those interests, even if the client wants something else. Similarly pressures from other interested parties and in support of social norms must be subordinated to the professional's own independent judgment. Only in this way will professional expertise be brought to bear fully. Professionals who find it difficult to act independently, or are afraid to do so, run the risk that their special knowledge will not be used. Becoming dependent on others with lesser knowledge or for some reason not to use their knowledge in the interest of the client practically ensures that professional services will be provided at a level below capacity.

Desire to acquire status matches with the accepting status role requirement. The provision of professional services to clients is predicated on client recognition of the professional's expert status. Professionals must take steps to achieve and retain status in the eyes of users and potential users of their services. Without this the services will simply go unused, no matter how effective they might have been. Consequently professionals who are embarrassed at promoting themselves or find such activities distasteful are unlikely to have successful careers. Research and/or publication are one means to status acquisition. In the professions it is common practice to seek status among professional colleagues initially; this in turn is subsequently transmitted to the client population.

Desire to help others matches with the providing help role requirement. The professional–client relationship is central to any professional practice. In that relationship the professional is expected to assist the client in achieving desired goals, or in some instances what from a professional perspective is in the client's best interest, even if not consciously desired. As a consequence a professional must want to help others. In certain professions this role requirement is recognized by the designation 'helping profession.' However, helping in some form is inherent in all professions.

Those who are unmotivated to help others lack something as professionals. Although this type of motivation is usually interpreted in terms of a desire to serve others, it may just as often reflect a desire to serve oneself. This latter process is inherent in the concept of 'helping power' (McClelland, 1975) whereby an individual satisfies certain types of power motives by assuming a role where clients are dependent on him or her for assistance.

Value-based identification with the profession matches with the exhibiting professional commitment role requirement. Professional careers are intended to be of a life-long nature. There is a substantial investment in training and this is expedient only if the individual is to utilize this training over many years. Thus there must be a strong emotional tie to the profession that keeps members in it. This is achieved through value-based identification. This professional commitment also serves to keep members responsive to the profession's ethical norms. Without such an identification, individuals may leave the profession in search of greater opportunities prior to the time the training investment is recovered, and they may also act in 'unprofessional' ways, perhaps to the point of being expelled from the profession. Professional identification or commitment is a crucial ingredient in the profession's survival.

Task roles and motivations

Figure 1.3 outlines the task role motivation theory, applying it specifically to entrepreneurship. This focus on the entrepreneurial organization permits the inclusion of relationships to non-entrepreneurs. In contrast a real estate agent on straight commission would have few if any non-entrepreneurs to deal with. Other than this feature Figure 1.3 is intended to apply to any task system. Task motivation as the term is used here refers to a specific set of motivational patterns that match a particular type of task, that of the entrepreneur or one similar to it. The term is not used in the more general sense of overall work motivation that is often encountered in the literature.

One of the most promising theories dealing with the psychodynamics of entrepreneurship is McClelland's (1961; 1962) theory of achievement motivation. This theory has consistently emphasized the close tie between entrepreneurship and the achievement motive. The primary empirical work on this tie is the McClelland and Winter (1969) volume, which provides evidence indicating a causal impact of achievement motivation on firm growth. McClelland's theory identifies an achievement situation in which achievement motivation is aroused and which people with a strong achievement motive prefer. Task role motivation theory takes its cue from McClelland's theory. In fact the original objective was simply to recast the theory in role motivation format, on the assumption that 'reinventing the wheel' in this area was pointless. In its final form, however, task theory places

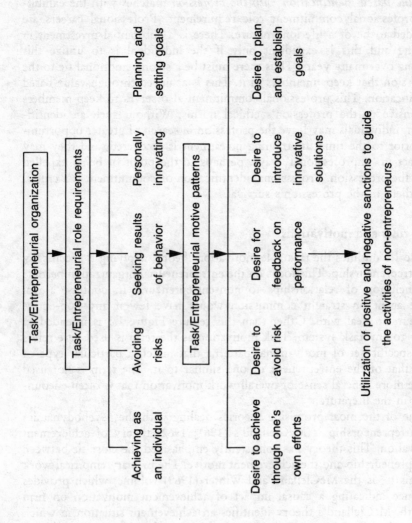

Figure 1.3 Outline of the task role motivation theory applied to entrepreneurial organization

somewhat greater emphasis on the concept of role, and specifies five separate motive patterns rather than the single achievement motive. These motive patterns are modeled after the five aspects of the achievement situation McClelland noted, although in at least one instance a significant departure was introduced.

Desire to achieve through one's own efforts matches with the achieving as an individual role requirement. The key consideration here is being able to attribute success, or failure, to personal causation, the concept of individual responsibility. Entrepreneurs must be pulled into the task situation continually so that they do not simply avoid pressures and anxieties involved by escaping from the work context. The major source of this pull is an intrinsic desire to achieve through one's own efforts and ability, and to experience the enhanced self-esteem that such achievement permits – to be able to say 'I did it myself.' Good team members who are highly cooperative and prefer to share the credit for accomplishments tend to lack this intense desire to achieve through one's own efforts and accordingly lack the drive that makes a task system dynamic and growing.

Desire to avoid risk matches with the avoiding risks role requirement. This represents a departure from the McClelland view, and indeed from the first formulation of task theory as well (Miner, 1980). McClelland emphasized a moderate degree of risk-taking on the theory that a sense of self-achievement would be maximized when the task was neither too difficult (risky) nor too easy (devoid of risk). In the first instance success would be unlikely; in the second instance it would be devoid of challenge. Raynor has the following to say, however:

> ... decisions of success-oriented individuals should not consist of a series of immediate risks in which there is a 50–50 chance of failure, but rather should reflect a much lower degree of risk ... since immediate failure has the consequence of failure to achieve the career goal (operating a successful company) through loss of the opportunity to continue its pursuit.
>
> (Raynor, 1974: 146)

In this view, subsequently endorsed by Atkinson (1977), entrepreneurs are much more risk avoiders than McClelland envisioned. In addition research such as that reported by Brockhaus (1980) clearly fails to support a risk-taking role for entrepreneurs. Certain early research conducted in connection with the development of an instrument to measure the variables of task theory (to be discussed in Chapter 3) reinforced the significance of risk avoidance.

On the basis of all these considerations the theory was changed at an early point to substitute a risk avoidance role for the initial risk-taking role (Smith and Miner, 1984). Consequently, the motivational requirement became a desire to avoid risks of any and all kinds. In contrast, risk-taking may result in the entrepreneur being forced out of the entrepreneurial situation because of business failure. To avoid this, and continue to experience a sense of self-achievement, the entrepreneur attempts to minimize risk. There is ample evidence that a major reason for small company failure is the adoption of a strategic stance which places the entire company at high risk, frequently in connection with some large-scale new venture that puts the company as currently constituted on the line (Richards, 1973). The argument that effective entrepreneurs must avoid risks does not mean that they do not take what others perceive as risks, however. Uncertainty exists in the eyes of the beholder; to be successful, entrepreneurs must avoid it to the degree possible, wherever they see it. Yet the ideal situation for an entrepreneur is one where others perceive that a high degree of risk exists, and thus high rewards are warranted, and the entrepreneur with his or her knowledge sees practically no risk at all.

Desire for feedback on performance matches with the seeking results of behavior role requirement. True entrepreneurs desire some clear index of the level of their performance. They do not enjoy being unsure whether they have performed well or not. Feedback on the level and results of one's performance is necessary in order to attribute any degree of success (or failure) to one's efforts. It is crucial to know whether one has succeeded or failed, and feedback is the means to that end. An individual who is lacking in the desire for performance feedback is inevitably less concerned about achievement as well. An entrepreneur must be motivated to actively seek out results-oriented feedback in terms of measures such as profitability, productive output, wastage, course grades and the like if a sense of self achievement is to be attained.

Desire to introduce innovative solutions matches with the personally innovating role requirement. For entrepreneurs the pull of individual achievement operates only to the extent the individual can attribute personal causation. Original, or novel, or creative, or innovative approaches have a distinctive quality that makes it easier to identify them as one's own, and thus to take personal credit for them. Those who wish to forego innovation give up this opportunity for attaining a sense of self achievement. Thus a desire to introduce innovation is consistent with the concept of achieving through one's own efforts, and experiencing approval for doing so.

Desire to plan and establish goals matches with the planning and setting goals role requirement. Effective entrepreneurship requires a desire to think about the future and anticipate future possibilities. Entrepreneurs must be pulled by the prospect of anticipated future rewards (expectancies), and therefore must approach their work with a strong future orientation. There needs to be a desire to plan, to set personal goals that will signify personal achievement, and to plot paths to goal achievement. This implies a minimal expectation, or fear, of future failure. Without this type of future orientation the gleam in the entrepreneur's eyes tends to dull, and the motivational incentive of striving for a future goal is lost. The entrepreneurial organization loses power.

Group roles and motivations

Figure 1.4 outlines the group role motivation theory. There are five role requirements and matching group member motive patterns. This theory was strongly influenced by the participative and humanistic views emanating from the University of Michigan and the Tavistock organization in England, plus the sensitivity or T-group training movement (Likert, 1961; 1967; Trist, 1969; Emery, 1959; Argyris, 1962). The actual role requirements and motive patterns owe a debt to certain formulations of the organization development process as well (French and Bell, 1973; Golembiewski, 1972; Schmidt, 1970). The theory in this more specific form was first stated in Miner (1980).

Desire to interact socially and affiliate with others matches with the interacting with peers effectively role requirement. Group members are required to spend considerable time interacting with others in order to make, and obtain implementation of, decisions. It thus becomes necessary that they enjoy affiliative relationships and the use of social skills to exert influence and minimize nonproductive conflict. In essence this is the need for affiliation that McClelland and Burnham (1976) discuss. In the more clinical terminology group members need to be sociophilic; to the extent they are sociophobic group interaction will be damaged (Tomkins and Miner, 1957).

Desire for continuing belongingness in a group matches with the gaining group acceptance role requirement. It is necessary that group members maintain identification with the group both to facilitate participation in group processes and to make them responsive to group administered sanctions, including the threat of expulsion. Accordingly a desire not merely for social interaction, but for acceptance and a sense of belongingness in the group is required. Without this, members may simply leave the group when things do not go their way, and they are less likely to support the group's decisions because rejection for not doing so is of little concern.

Favorable attitudes toward peers match with the positive relations with peers role requirement. Just as in hierarchic systems favorable attitudes upward are required to facilitate hierarchic communication, in group systems favorable attitudes toward group members, or potential group members, are required to facilitate the essential communications with peers. These positive attitudes should take such forms as belief in others, trust, consideration, and mutual respect. Where favorable attitudes toward peers are lacking because of other reference groups, strong status-consciousness, or for whatever other reason necessary communications may fail to occur.

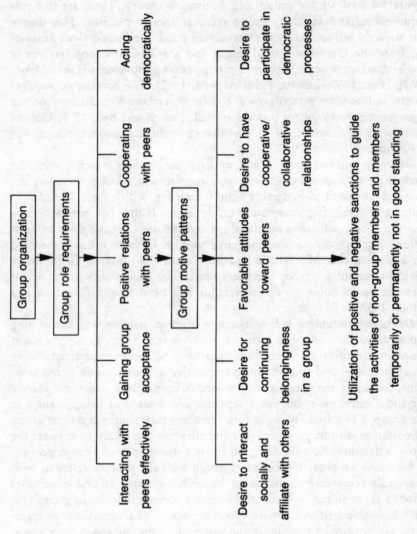

Figure 1.4 Outline of the group role motivation theory

Desire to have cooperative/collaborative relationships matches with the cooperating with peers role requirement. Group systems require that members work together closely. Competition can disrupt communications and lead to withholding of needed information – even to group disintegration. As a result, group members must eschew competition in favor of cooperative, collaborative relations and gain satisfaction from doing so. The case for collaboration in organizations, and against competition, has been argued strongly by Kraus (1980). The key consideration is what type of organization one is dealing with – hierarchic or group.

Desire to participate in democratic processes matches with the acting democratically role requirement. In group systems the primary method of getting things done is some variant of the power equalized, democratic process including open expression of ideas and views, and the use of democratic procedures such as the vote to reach decisions. For these processes to function effectively members must be favorably disposed toward them and desire to contribute to their effective operation. Strong authoritarian views, impatience with lengthy debate, and the like may operate to thwart the democratic process in groups.

The nature of motive patterns

The motive patterns described – six for the hierarchic theory and five each for the other three theories – do not represent all possible patterns for each theory. No doubt more patterns could be identified in all four instances. They are, however, intended to represent very important motive patterns within each theoretical domain. In most multiple-predictor research, adding variables beyond five or six has not increased the explained variance in the criterion to any meaningful degree. Thus, there seems little reason to extend the theories beyond their present scopes, assuming of course that the motive patterns noted do in fact account for substantial criterion variance.

Because of the way they are derived, the motive patterns of role motivation theory cannot be assumed to represent unitary needs or values (Locke and Henne, 1986). The role motivation theories are not need theories in the sense of Maslow's (1954) need hierarchy theory and McClelland's (1961) achievement motivation theory. The reason this is true is that the motive patterns derive from role requirements specified by organizational forms. Anything of a motivational nature that fits or matches the role requirement is included in the pattern. The result is that the motive patterns typically contain a constellation of motives; different people meet the same role requirement in different ways, and it may even be that the same person does so in different ways at different points in time.

Thus, the favorable attitudes to authority of the hierarchic theory may be part of a wider positive feeling toward all people, a manifestation of unresolved positive transference in the sense envisioned by psychoanalytic theory, a consequence of strong heterosexual or homosexual drives depending on the gender mix of superior and subordinate, and so on. Similarly, the desire to learn and acquire knowledge of the professional theory may be broad, extending to practically all knowledge, or narrowly specific to a particular professional specialty, or anything in between. The desire may stem from a pervasive curiosity, the symbolic significance of the particular knowledge constellation for the individual, a need to prove oneself strong by being omniscient, or some other motive. The key factor to be emphasized is that role requirements may be met in multiple ways, and for purposes of role motivation theory it does not matter exactly how. The relevant consideration for theory is the *degree* of role requirement–motive pattern match only.

Another consequence of the derivation of motive patterns from role requirements is that just as the role requirements of a theory can overlap one another, so too can their motive patterns. A given type of motive can, under appropriate circumstances, contribute to satisfying more than one role requirement, thus introducing some degree of positive correlation between the respective motive patterns. For example, in the task theory a strong need to avoid ambiguity (McCaskey, 1982) may lead people to desire feedback on performance, so that they can be sure exactly how well they are doing, thus avoiding the ambiguity of not knowing. At the same time the need to avoid ambiguity may cause a person to want to plan and establish goals so that the ambiguity inherent in facing an unknown future may be reduced also. Numerous other instances of this kind could be noted. One could hope for distinct role prescriptions and motive patterns, in the nature of pure factors derived from factor analysis. But the role requirements that are actually produced by various organizational forms do not appear to come that way, and the motive patterns must match the role requirements. Some degree of overlap or non-independence can thus be anticipated.

A final point related to motive patterns is that they, and the role requirements that determine them, need not be conscious. Sometimes people are fully aware of the motives under consideration, but that cannot be assumed to be the case. For various reasons the types of motives discussed may be held out of consciousness. The motives operate and they serve to predict events, but the person cannot tell you much about them; not infrequently the existence of the motives is completely denied. A manager, for instance, may possess the strong desire to exercise power posited by hierarchic role motivation theory, while at the same time being concerned about viewing himself and being viewed by others as dictatorial and obsessed with power. One way of dealing with the dilemma thus created is to continue to seek gratification of the power motive while making its presence entirely unconscious. If asked, such a person will deny any interest in exercising power over others.

To take an example from group role motivation theory, a man may have very favorable attitudes toward his male peers, based upon a prevailing homosexual identification. Yet this same individual may view homosexuality *per se* with reprehension and loathing. If he acknowledges the basis of his feelings toward his peers, he runs the risk of experiencing continuing self-loathing. One way out is to repress his homosexual tendencies. He is positively disposed to his male peers, but he does not admit it, or if he does, his attitude is justified on grounds far removed from the true motive involved. In short, the underlying need becomes unconscious, but continues to be manifest in behavior.

HYPOTHESIZED CRITERION RELATIONSHIPS

Implicit in the preceding discussion is the idea that greater degrees of match between role requirements and their specific motive patterns, and thus higher levels of domain-appropriate motives, are associated with higher levels of performance on success criteria. The discussion here attempts to make this generalized statement more specific.

Domain specific hypotheses

A useful way of approaching the matter of hypothesized criterion relationships is to begin with a quotation from a prior article dealing with the topic of leadership.

> If one studies leadership in each type of system, a particular motivational constellation should be elevated among the 'leaders,' and that constellation should be more prevalent among the good (valued, high performing) leaders than among the poor leaders. More specifically the hypotheses are:
> **Hypothesis 1.** In hierarchic systems, managerial motivation should be at a high level in top management, and it should be positively correlated with other managerial success indexes; managerial motivation should not differentiate in these ways within other types of systems.
> **Hypothesis 2.** In professional systems, professional motivation should be at a high level among senior professionals, and it should be positively correlated with other professional success indexes; professional motivation should not differentiate in these ways within other types of systems.
> **Hypothesis 3.** In task systems, task (achievement) motivation should be at a high level among task performers (entrepreneurs, for example),

and it should be positively correlated with task success indexes; task motivation should not differentiate in these ways within other types of systems.

Hypothesis 4. In group systems, group motivation should be at a high level among emergent leaders, and it should be positively correlated with other group-determined success indexes; group motivation should not differentiate in these ways within other types of systems.

(Miner, 1982: 298)

These hypotheses are domain specific. They indicate that the motive patterns of a given role motivation theory should predict success criteria within the domain of that theory, i.e. in the appropriate organizational system. They should not predict within other domains. Thus the six motive patterns of hierarchic theory should all predict managerial success in a hierarchic organization. They should not predict non-managerial success in a hierarchic system; nor should they predict success in professional, task, or group systems.

Secondly, the causal arrow is hypothesized to run from motivation to criterion behavior. The relationships may be depicted as follows:

managerial motivation -------------------- > managerial success
professional motivation ------------------- > professional success
task motivation -------------------------- > task success
group motivation ----------------------- > group success

The requisite motivational constellation precedes both the choice of a given occupation or career and performance in it. In both instances these motives exert an impact on subsequent behavior. Thus high managerial motivation causes people to seek out a managerial career and low managerial motivation causes them not to. Furthermore, among those who arrive in management for whatever reason, high managerial motivation contributes to better performance and greater success; low managerial motivation contributes the opposite. The same holds for the other three motive constellations. This is not meant to imply a pure motivational determinism, however. It is apparent that other factors including intellectual ability, relevant knowledge, and alignment with the specific culture of the organization also contribute to the level of achievement on success criteria. The role motivation theories simply are not concerned with these factors. They do assume that motivational variables are some of the most important in both individual and organizational performance, and that appropriately matched to organizational forms they will account for a substantial amount of criterion variance. Yet adding in predictors of a different kind will increase the amount of variance accounted for.

Because the four hypotheses were presented in a leadership context, they focus on such individuals as top managers, senior professionals, entrepreneurs, and emergent leaders. There is no intent to imply that the theories are applicable only to these individuals. As discussed earlier in this chapter, role motivation theories apply to the key performers of each of the four theoretical domains. Thus, for instance, all group members in good standing would be expected to be influenced in their performance by group motivation levels, not just emergent leaders. However, emergent leaders would be expected to show particularly high levels of group motivation; theory would not predict any particular need for managerial motivation within this group domain.

Types of criteria

What behaviors can role motivation theories be expected to predict? For one thing they should predict best using criteria developed and applied within the specific organizations under study. Promotion and demotion decisions, involuntary separations, appraisal ratings, merit-based salary decisions, and the like have a common tie to the actual operation of a business. Such criteria can incorporate the role requirements from role motivation theories and measure the degree to which behavior matches them. Rarely if ever is this done explicitly; rather these factors are folded into an ongoing evaluation process and used, without the evaluators being aware of what is involved. The task theory is somewhat different from the others in that organizational level criteria such as company survival, growth in number of employees, or dollar volume of business can be used directly as criteria of individual effectiveness. With the other theories organizational level criteria are predictable only when the relevant motives of a number of key performers are combined into some composite index.

What is important is that there needs to be an ongoing organizational context within which performance-related judgments can be made. Criteria generated out of highly artificial contexts, such as some laboratory settings, or introduced for research purposes alone without reference to what matters or is valued in an organization, would not be expected to yield the hypothesized results.

Another consideration in criterion selection has to do with the way the motive patterns of the theories are combined. Each motive pattern is expected to predict individually; yet it is also possible to deal with the full constellation of motive patterns as a whole. This is what is meant by managerial motivation (or motivation to manage), professional motivation, task motivation, and group motivation. These latter, total, indexes are obtained by combining the relevant motive patterns additively. This means that a lack of motivation or avoidance motivation in one area may be offset completely by high levels of motivation in another area.

The rationale behind using an additive combination rule is that people making judgments and decisions about performance in organizations appear to operate this way. A subtle averaging process tends to prevail so that a person is seen overall as good or bad, or mediocre, or satisfactory. The high and low points are rounded off in the overall judgment. There is something of the halo process in all this, but many treatments of halo appear to represent an oversimplification of what is involved. The important consideration, however, is that motive patterns are combined additively because overall decisions are made this way. People are promoted, demoted, fired, given pay increases, and so on as a whole, not just part of them. The same thing is true of overall performance ratings. Given the additive component thus built into role motivation theories, these theories are best evaluated against criteria of a judgmental nature, where the same additive combination rule is free to operate. Accordingly, role motivation theory has a preference, at least where an overall measure of relevant motivation in the domain is used, for decision-based or judgmental criteria. Fortunately many criteria including performance-based compensation, position level, turnover, and performance ratings are of this nature.

It should be recognized, nevertheless, that sound research evidence supports the view that actual (real) performance can be a major determinant of such judgments. Ratings typically are related to true performance and error is not inevitably rampant (Bernardin and Beatty, 1984; DeNisi and Stevens, 1981). Thus less judgmental criteria such as sales figures, professional practice income, and group scrap rates should also be predictable from the theories, although probably not at as high a level.

Finally there is the question of job satisfaction, an outcome to which industrial/organizational psychology has devoted much attention. The theories would hypothesize that an appropriate mesh of motivational patterns and role prescriptions should lead to greater satisfaction. However, there is no necessary reason to believe that this satisfaction should generalize beyond the specific intrinsic motives and activities involved to the broad range of extrinsic factors usually measured in job satisfaction questionnaires (benefits, compensation, supervision, and the like). This could happen, but it need not. In essence this represents moving to the fringe areas of the theories. The same logic would appear to apply to correlates of job satisfaction and overall organizational commitment such as absenteeism and tardiness (Mowday, Porter, and Steers, 1982). They could be predicted in certain instances, but the predictive trail is tenuous at best. What can be anticipated is that high motivation to manage managers will enjoy managing, high professional motivation professionals will be highly satisfied with professional work, high task motivation entrepreneurs will find pleasure in operating their own businesses, and high group motivation group members will respond positively to working in a group context.

PORTRAITS OF THE IDEAL

The portraits which follow provide examples of how three of the four role motivation theories work in practice. They are deliberately selected to demonstrate a good motivational match, and this should be of aid in understanding the theories. Because measurement and validation research related to group role motivation theory is only in its early stages, no example is provided in this area. These are real people, although the descriptions have been altered slightly to disguise identities. The cases come from professional practice. The actual test results on which they are based will be discussed in Chapter 3 after we have had a chance to consider the measures of theoretical variables.

R & D Vice President – Andrew Solero

Andy Solero is in charge of the research laboratory of a large oil company. He has a PhD in chemistry and an MBA. His career has involved a mixture of research and managing throughout. On the research side he has established a sound reputation in the industry with a number of patents and several very well-regarded publications. At present, however, his managerial duties require most of his time. Managing scientists is not an easy job, but Andy has proved good at it and has moved up rapidly in the company.

The organizational context that Andy finds himself in as a vice president is a mixture of hierarchic and professional, but with the hierarchic component clearly predominating. Task organization is not really a significant feature and group organization is practically nonexistent. Consistent with the hierarchic emphasis, and his managerial success, Andy has strong managerial motivation. Most pronounced are his desire to compete, his desire to be distinct and different, and his desire to perform routine duties responsibly. His competitive drive is largely restricted to work-related matters and rarely extends into other aspects of his life. He has generally favorable attitudes to superiors, but very little desire to exercise power. This latter motive pattern is unusual relative to other managers at his level.

Andy also has very high professional motivation – approximately the equal of his motivation to manage. Here the most pronounced components are a desire to learn and acquire knowledge, a desire to acquire status, and a value-based identification with his scientific profession. Desire to exhibit independence and the desire to help others are not strong components of his make-up. In contrast to the hierarchic and professional constellations, Andy's task motivation is not at all out of the ordinary. None of the motive patterns in this latter domain are particularly high, and the desire for feedback on performance is in fact rather low.

I/O Psychology Consultant – Beth Ann Doyle

Beth Doyle has a doctorate in industrial/organizational psychology which included considerable clinical coursework. Her children were born during the period after she got her degree, and for a number of years she did not work. Gradually she began to develop a consulting practice which came to involve continuing relationships with several large corporations. Much of her practice involves teaching management development programs and counseling. Although most of the time she works alone, she occasionally combines forces with several other independent consultants on larger jobs. Over the years the practice has grown so that at the present time Beth often has to turn down work, even though she charges above-average rates. Her clients think very highly of her.

As an independent professional practitioner, Beth is clearly involved in a professional organizational context. However, she also sees the work as entrepreneurial in nature. There is, in addition, the group organization that occurs when she works with other consultants. What her work world clearly is not is hierarchic. Beth has very strong professional motivation as might be expected. Most of all she has a strong desire to acquire status. However, all the motive patterns of the professional theory are at a high level. If there is one that stands out besides a desire to acquire status, it is the desire to help others.

Given the nature of her organizational environment, Beth's work does not require hierarchic motivation, and she does not have it. Of the component motive patterns in that area, only the desire to exercise power is at a high level. She is not very competitive and has no real desire to assert herself. She has rather unfavorable attitudes to authority, and little desire to perform routine duties responsibly. Her desire to be distinct and different is within normal bounds. Her task motivation is considerably higher than her hierarchic, but nowhere near the level of her professional motivation. Beth is devoid of any real desire to achieve through her own efforts, but she does want to avoid risks and to introduce innovative solutions. Other than that, there is nothing distinctive about her task motivation.

Business Founder – Abraham Pollack

Abe Pollack has founded several businesses, and sold them. His usual pattern is to get the business up to about three million in sales before looking for a buyer. In a typical case the business manufactures a product that he has either invented or upgraded in some manner. He is an engineer by training. Generally he has been able to grow his businesses quite rapidly. Once he sells out he leaves and takes a vacation. Personally he has been quite successful, but often the purchasers of his businesses have had difficulty maintaining profitability.

Abe works predominantly in a task context. However, there is a degree of professional organization as well. Hierarchy and group systems are at a minimum in his work environment. Abe has a high level of task motivation. In particular he desires to achieve through his own efforts. In this respect he is quite unusual. He also has a strong desire to avoid risks and to a somewhat lesser degree to obtain feedback on performance and to introduce innovative solutions. These strong entrepreneurial assets are offset to some extent by a distinct lack of any desire to plan and establish long-term goals.

Consonant with the lack of hierarchy in his work environment, Abe lacks overall motivation to manage. The only motive pattern in this area that is high is the desire to compete, but even in that instance the motive manifests itself primarily outside the work context. Attitudes to superiors are clearly on the unfavorable side, desire to be distinct and different is at a minimum, and there is little desire to perform routine duties responsibly. Even the desires to exercise power and to assert oneself are not really very high. Much the same pattern is evident with regard to professional motivation. Overall this type of motivation is very low. There is substantial desire to exhibit independence. However, the desire to learn and acquire knowledge is very low, and so too are the desire to help others and value-based identification with a profession. Desire to acquire status is in the middle range.

CHAPTER SUMMARY AND OVERVIEW OF THE BOOK

Role motivation theories deal with four organizational types – hierarchic, professional, task, and group. Within these types the theories focus on key performers – managers, professionals, task performers such as entrepreneurs, and group members. A set of inherent role requirements is identified for each type of key performer. Then, matching motivational patterns are indicated for each role requirement. The specific components of the four theories are identified in Figures 1.1, 1.2, 1.3, and 1.4. When organization types, roles, and motives fit closely together, success at both individual and organizational levels is hypothesized. Thus the role motivation theories are fit or congruence theories in the sense originally set forth by Chandler (1962), and subsequently developed by a number of other theorists including Galbraith and Kazanjian (1986), Nadler and Tushman (1988), and Mackenzie (1991).

Against this background the following chapters deal with a wide range of conceptual and empirical issues raised by the theories. Chapter 2 considers the limited domain approach to theorizing generally and positions the role motivation theories in this context. Chapter 3 describes the measures of role motivation theory constructs that have been developed and the evidence for their reliability. Chapter 4 presents the extensive evidence for the validity of the hierarchic role motivation theory. Chapters 5 and 6 cover the somewhat smaller amounts of evidence for the validities of the professional and task theories respectively. Chapter 7 deals with the use of training interventions to change role-related motivational patterns, and particularly with managerial role motivation training. Chapter 8 presents the evidence for a major decline in managerial motivation during the 1960s and early 1970s, and discusses the implication of this phenomenon. Chapter 9 surveys the rather large body of international research involving the hierarchic role motivation theory and relates it to the concerns expressed in Chapter 8. Chapter 10 treats the existing evidence dealing with age, race, and gender differences across the various role motivation theories. Chapter 11 looks back at some of the criticisms that have been levelled at role motivation theories, and then looks ahead at the prospects for integrating the four theories and the usefulness of the theories in practice.

Chapter 2

Role motivation theory in the wider theoretical context

Chapter 1 described and illustrated the various role motivation theories. These four theories were developed because they deal with organization types that are found frequently in the modern world, and thus have considerable importance. This view appears to be shared by a number of organizational typologies (Wilderom, Miner, and Pastor, 1991). The need now is to put this approach in perspective by relating it to other theories and to other approaches used to construct theories.

THE LIMITED DOMAIN APPROACH

The following quote from Dubin provides an explanation of what is involved when a theory's domain is restricted.

> There is an inverse relationship between the number of boundary-determining criteria employed in a model and the size of the domain covered by the model. . . . I define the domain of a model as being the territory over which we can make truth statements about the model and, therefore, about the values of the units composing the model. The most universal model that can be constructed is one that has only a single boundary-determining criterion. As each additional boundary-determining criterion is added to a model, either a unit is dropped from the model or a greater restriction is placed on the number or character of the laws of interaction remaining in the model.
>
> (Dubin, 1969: 137–8)

When theoretical domains are restricted, the theories are more homogeneous and they generalize less widely. The hierarchic, professional, task, and group theories are limited domain in nature.

Contingency theories

Contingency theories such as the contingency theory of leadership (Fiedler and Chemers, 1974; Fiedler and Garcia, 1987) and the contingency theory of organization (Lawrence and Lorsch, 1967) have certain features in common with limited domain theories. However, they are by no means the same, and the differences provide a useful way of understanding the limited domain approach.

Within contingency theory of leadership, octants are formed based on the state of leader–member relations, task structure, and leader position power as contingency variables. In this form the theory is in fact quite broad. It would be possible, however, to focus only on the octant specified by good leader–member relations, high task structure, and strong leader position power, and to explore this territory in considerable detail. This would be done without reference to, and without concern for the existence of, the other seven octants. The theory might seek to determine key aspects and causes of the three variable states and how they in turn interact with leader behavior and influence leader success. Such a 'theory of octant 1' would have a substantially restricted domain. Similarly, contingency theory of organization in its current form ostensibly applies to all organizations. It specifies environmental uncertainty as a contingency variable and indicates what should be done under various states of this variable. But it would be possible to focus on the very low end of the contingency variable and write a theory for organizations functioning under conditions of high certainty – or for placid clustered environments to draw upon the terminology of sociotechnical systems theory (Emery and Trist, 1965). This more specialized theory would operate in a limited domain.

Why restrict the domain of a theory in this manner? Why not use the more comprehensive contingency approach? The main virtue of limited domain theories is that they simplify the theoretical task to a point where it is amenable to precise conceptualization and intensive research investigation. The field of endeavor is made sufficiently small that human intelligence is capable of coping with it effectively. Key variables delimiting the domain, which might later, with more knowledge, be converted to true contingency variables, can be clearly identified. Over time as various domains are explored, the matrix of possible domains is gradually filled in. Eventually, using this strategy, it may well be possible to develop a comprehensive, and no doubt very complex, contingency (or systems) theory. Ideally the domains explored initially will be those in which the prospect of establishing valid theories is greatest and where the most important practical contribution can be made. One definition of the latter is a domain in which the greatest number of organizations fall for the longest periods of time (Steiner and Miner, 1986). The role motivation theory approach represents an attempt to maximize practical usefulness in this manner. It does not consider anachronistic or infrequently observed organizational forms.

Middle range theories

Much has been written in the sociological and organizational science literature advocating theories of the middle range (see, for example, Pinder and
Moore 1980). This is a concept developed by Merton (1949) in reaction
against prevailing global or grand theories of social behavior with few
boundary-determining criteria. Middle range theories are described as
having neither too few nor too many boundary-determining criteria. They
are, therefore, restricted in the territory to which they apply.

Are limited domain theories part of the middle range variety? Certainly
to the extent multiple boundary-determining criteria are involved, the two
have much in common. However, limited domain theories can be even
more restricted than middle range theories. This raises the real possibility
that they might become trivial, and generate trivial research. This is why
it is so important in constructing these theories to select domains where
practical usefulness is at a maximum – where the greatest number of
organizations fall for the longest periods of time, for example.

The paradigm development strategy

Another perspective from which the role motivation theories may be
viewed is the paradigm development approach to theorizing and research.
This approach consists of fitting data into a theoretical framework with
general laws to explain the data, deducing hypotheses from the general
laws, and subjecting these hypotheses to empirical test. Mackenzie and
House (1978: 18–19) cite the early work with hierarchic role motivation
theory as an example of the paradigm development strategy. Their statements are quoted at length here because the author's original thinking did
not in fact follow this track in all respects, although perhaps it should
have. They make the whole process sound much more logical and rational
than it really was. In doing so, however, they make the case for a paradigm
development strategy much more cogently than the author ever could.

> Based on his observation of the role requirements of managers in a
> large bureaucratic organization, plus his prior training in psychology,
> Miner postulated that individuals whose motivations correspond to the
> requirements of the roles they fill will be more successful in those roles.
> He hypothesized that there are 'certain components (motives) which
> contribute to what amounts to a common variant . . . , which operates
> across a great many managerial positions . . . ' This constituted Miner's
> explanandum sentence. An auxiliary hypothesis was ' . . . are presumed
> to occur with relative high frequency, and across a considerable range
> of positions and organizations'. The specific role requirements which
> were identified theoretically were presumed to be among those which

occur with high frequency in business firms organized in accordance with the Scalar principle. Miner (1965: 42) stated that:

> It is entirely possible that the theory is applicable to managerial, or administrative jobs in educational, governmental, medical, military and other types of organizations, but it was not devised with these positions in mind. The initial tests, at least, should be carried out within the particular segment of society for which it was originally constructed.

Here we see Miner's first transformation of the theory, selection of the test sample for the purpose of specifically testing the theory in question. Observation of role and behavior in an hierarchical organization led Miner to conclude that managerial roles in hierarchical organizations demand their incumbents to have a generally positive orientation towards the use of power as a means of attaining success.

To test the theory a special sentence completion test was constructed. The test was assumed to be a measure of the degree to which the respondent desires to compete for and exercise power over people. Several hypotheses were postulated: (a) that the measure of power motivation, the Miner Sentence Completion Scale (MSCS), should yield both concurrent and predictive validity when compared against such success indexes as organizational level, promotion rate, ratings of effectiveness in managerial work, and rated potential for promotion; (b) that if motivational changes are induced by management education, such changes will be enforced by the role requirements and the reward system of the organization and will thus be sustained; (c) that management education efforts should be differentially effective depending on the personality characteristics of the participant in the education effort; and (d) that different occupational groupings tend to attract individuals having different levels of interest in the exercise of power and that these differences will be reflected in the MSCS scores.

These hypotheses represent the test implications of the theory. Miner's research progressed through a series of stages. He began with a test of the concurrent validity of the MSCS scale and tested the hypothesis that there would be a significant association between the MSCS and various criteria of success: job grade level, performance rating, and potential rating. Having established significant correlations between the scale and the criteria, he raised the possibility that success may serve to precipitate motivational changes and that these in turn contribute to the concurrent validity which had been found, or conceivably some external factor might be responsible for both the motivation and the success. He called for evidence that those who possess the various motives measured tend subsequently to perform particularly well on the various organizational criteria. Miner (1965: 60) stated that:

certainly, if a positive association between motivational variables and behavior in the managerial role cannot be demonstrated under these conditions, the theory is deficient.

Here he stated a criterion for refutation of the theory.

A test of the predictive validity of the MSCS revealed significant correlations between the MSCS and subsequent criteria of managerial success. Miner then tested the possibility that in a somewhat different type of business organization the relationships might not appear. Shifting from the initial sample of managers in an organization producing heavy equipment, he tested the concurrent validity of his scale with a population of male and female managers in a large department store. Results revealed that three subscales of the MSCS held up across samples. Miner (1965: 90) then raised a series of questions concerning the MSCS scale.

Does the MSCS really measure the motivational variables that it is devised to measure? Is it really motivation of this particular kind, motivation that is congruent with managerial role requirements that produces the success? Or is it possible that the MSCS yields the results it does due to the influence of component variables which are not those the test was constructed to measure. Or perhaps some external factor, highly correlated with the MSCS accounts for the findings which have been obtained.

A variety of analyses were conducted in a number of different samples. Correlations between the MSCS and age, intelligence, concept mastery, attitudes toward various stimuli, grades in undergraduate school, and education achievement were computed.

From a strong inference viewpoint, these tests can be considered attempts to rule out competing hypotheses concerning interpretation of the scale. Miner reported several additional tests of the theory. He measured the degree to which a course developed to increase attitudes measured by the MSCS scale, did indeed effect a change in responses to the scale in the predicted dimension as compared with the control group of subjects who did not participate in the educational program. He then tested whether the change produced by the experimental treatment was retained long enough for managerial performance to be affected materially.

Following these validation studies, which can be considered tests of the adequacy of the theory to predict within the specified domain of the theory, several additional studies were conducted to answer descriptive research questions. These concern the effects of motivational education among college students and the retention of change resulting from such education, the degree to which female students respond as well, the relationship between change and the climate in the organization, a search for organizational and personality predictors of change, and a test of the hypothesis that occupations tend to attract individuals having different levels of power motivation. Since the original publication of the research described above, additional studies have been conducted to identify the boundary conditions of the theory. These results generally confirm the proposition that power motivations significantly predict success in hierarchical situations and fail to predict success in nonhierarchical situations in experimental laboratories, consulting firms and non-bureaucratic schools.

The MSCS and the research conducted with it will be the subject of discussion in subsequent chapters. The points to be made here are first that the role motivation theory approach, whatever its author may have thought originally, is distinctly in the paradigm development tradition and second, that the type of research endorsed by that strategy, is practically impossible in the absence of limited domain theorizing. As Merton (1949) recognized, using research in this manner to check and cross check competing hypotheses is out of the question when theories become very broad, if the theories are to be comprehensively tested.

Close to the action

Locke and Henne (1986: 2) set forth the model of Figure 2.1 to explain motivation. In this model goals and intentions are closest to action, and this fact is

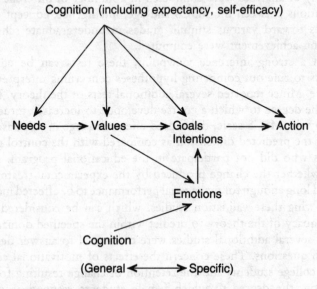

Figure 2.1 Locke and Henne's (1986) model of motivation

used to explain the considerable effectiveness goal setting theory has exhibited in predicting behavior and performance. Certainly goal setting theory has proven valid in the prediction of performance with great consistency and across a wide range of circumstances (Locke and Latham, 1984; 1990).

Within the Locke and Henne model role motivation theory is viewed as a value theory (thus more removed from action than goal setting theory). However, within that classification it is said to have special advantages because it possesses a clearly defined domain, a carefully developed and consistently used measuring device with standardized scoring, and includes multiple values or motives.

The Locke and Henne (1986) argument that goal setting theory works as well as it does because it is close to the action is convincing. However, it is also a limited domain theory which has been researched using a paradigm development strategy. It seems reasonable to view role motivation theory as having much in common with goal setting theory. Contrary to the Locke and Henne view, role motivation theory, with its direct derivation from performance roles, appears to be just as close to action as goal setting theory. Certainly the factors Locke and Henne note as contributing to role motivation theory's effectiveness are important, but in addition this is a particular type of limited domain theory which because of its specific association with roles is very close to action. This would argue that the power of goal setting theory and of role motivation theory derive from essentially the same factors.

It is important to emphasize that limited domain theories are not necessarily close to the action in this manner. Validity seems more likely to be assured if this is the case, and close to action theories must of necessity be limited domain in nature. But it is possible to have limited domain theories that deal with territories much further back in the causal chain. Role motivation theories, however, do not appear to be thus removed.

The context of motivation theory

The issue of how role motivation theory fits within the context of motivation theories generally has been a source of some misunderstanding (see, for example, Mahoney, 1980 and Miner, 1980a). An early statement in this regard is in fact an appeal for a particular limited domain approach to studying motivation in organizations. Miner and Dachler writing in the *Annual Review of Psychology* have this to say:

> One solution to the problem of understanding the significance of different motives for behavior is the integration of the content and process approaches as Lawler (1971) and Ryan (1970) have attempted to do. An alternative approach would be to shift the research emphasis away from the specific needs and motives of most content theories to the

motivational requirements of tasks and to informal and formal job role requirements. Thus the major concern would be with the sum total of motivational inputs needed to satisfy job requirements. Theories of occupation-related motives have made progress along these lines insofar as the entrepreneurial role and the role of manager in a bureaucracy are concerned. If this approach can be extended further to cover a whole network of key jobs in varying organizational contexts, the possibility exists that a base for meaningful organizational change can be developed long before the total complexity of specific human motives is understood. What might well emerge is a highly parsimonious but comprehensive theory which takes job requirements rather than human motives as its starting point.

(Miner and Dachler, 1973: 396–7)

The point is that organizational psychology need not be concerned with all of human motivation, but only with the special case of the relationship between motivation and various job requirements. This permits short-circuiting, much of which has been the subject matter of motivation study and theory in psychology. This is what the role motivation approach does. It is not concerned with the specific motives or needs or values involved, but with the motivational patterns that fit the role requirements. Such a theory can be much less complex and general than a total theory of psychological motivation. It does not need to concern itself with the development of motives within the individual, for instance.

Past theoretical efforts in the field often have applied motivational approaches from general psychology such as drive theory, expectancy theory, balance or homeostatic theories, and behaviorism to industrial/ organizational problems. In a number of instances these efforts have achieved a degree of success. Nevertheless it does appear that this is the long way around. Useful results for industrial/organizational psychology right now are more likely to emerge from applying short cuts that get at practical questions directly (Miner, 1974). That is what limited domain approaches such as the role motivation theories attempt to do. They do not carry the excess baggage of grander motivation theories with them into the theoretical arena. They get directly at a specific practical problem.

THE VALUE OF PARALLEL THEORIZING

Because they are small in scope, limited domain theories lend themselves to parallel theorizing – setting up a number of theories with common types of conceptualizations and measures. The four role motivation theories – hierarchic, professional, task, and group – are parallel in this sense. They all deal with key positions, with role requirements, with motive patterns, with motivation-criterion relationships of the same type, and they are operationalized using the same approach to measurement.

Synergy

One advantage of parallel theorizing with limited domain entries is that a certain amount of what is learned about one theory rubs off on the others. There is no question that what was learned from 20 years of research on the hierarchic theory informed the other three. To some extent research on one theory can be generalized to other, parallel theories. This is particularly true of research on measuring instruments, but it also applies to such things as causal relationships between motive patterns and criteria, and relationships among motive patterns. There is inherent in the parallel theory approach a degree of parsimony that is otherwise difficult to obtain. Examples of synergy effects will emerge at numerous points as the research on the role motivation theories is considered in subsequent chapters.

It should be recognized, however, that similar synergies can be attained in very much the same manner within contingency theories. Measures of contingency variables are utilized under a variety of conditions and other measures may also be extended to multiple contexts. Thus Fiedler and Chemers' (1974) LPC is utilized in some manner in all octants of the theory, and Hackman and Oldham's (1980) job characteristics theory applies the same measures of job aspects and contingency variables throughout all of the theory's variants. Clearly other approaches to theorizing can capitalize on a potential for synergy within a broader purview. Parallel limited domain theories such as the role motivation theories simply serve to facilitate this type of 'value added.'

Preventing the 'wash out' of true variance

Another advantage of using these parallel theories is that, if they are constructed appropriately, they can serve to identify phenomena that simply disappear amidst the more all-encompassing analyses of broader theories. To explain what is involved here, let us take as an example a literature review conducted by Dalton, Todor, Spendolini, Fielding, and Porter (1980). In selecting this particular review there is no intent to criticize this particular analysis as such. There are many similar efforts that suffer from the same problems. However, the topic of this review is very much germane for present purposes.

Dalton *et al.* surveyed studies relating aspects of organizational structure – size, span of control, length of hierarchy, administrative intensity, specialization, formalization, and centralization – to performance. They concluded as follows:

> The literature on structure–performance relationships is among the most vexing and ambiguous in the field of management and organizational behavior. Evaluations and generalizations concerning the nature and directions of these relationships are tenuous. Our review has

underscored the relative lack of generalizability of research in the area and the need for sound research.

(Dalton *et al*. 1980: 60)

One likely reason for this lack of results is that hierarchic, professional, group, and perhaps task organizational systems were all grouped together in the analyses. No attempt was made, accordingly, to fit structural features to differentiated organization types. One would expect for instance that administrative intensity would be most likely to influence performance positively in hierarchic systems; it would seem to be irrelevant or even a negative factor in professional, task, and group systems. Putting such a diverse array of organizational types together in the same box, almost guarantees that any predictive capabilities operating for one type of organization will wash out when other types are added; there is a continuous cancelling out of effects. Yet the studies cited contained in addition to managers, a wide range of professionals including scientists, teachers at all levels, engineers, and health care personnel; numerous work group and voluntary organization members; and certain sales people who may well have been operating in task systems.

An advantage of parallel theories such as those of the role motivation type is that the very existence of the different theories makes one think twice before lumping data from different domains together in composite analyses. Accordingly the probability of wash out, where results in one domain cancel those from another, is drastically reduced. As a consequence the null hypothesis is not confirmed when it should not be.

ROLE MOTIVATION THEORIES AND SUBSTITUTES FOR LEADERSHIP

Leadership substitutes are characteristics – task, organizational, or subordinate – that make leadership impossible and unnecessary. A closely related concept is that of a leadership neutralizer – something that makes it impossible for leadership to make a difference (Howell, Dorfman, and Kerr 1986). In actual practice these two are not typically differentiated, and the term 'substitutes for leadership' is applied to both.

Some leadership substitutes reside in the individual subordinate or follower. The subordinate's knowledge, experience, skill, or professional training may make it unnecessary for a leader to lead. Similarly, certain types of work are structured with relatively little room for leadership. Activities often carried out by leaders are unnecessary when very routine tasks are machine paced (as on an assembly line), or when tasks are structured so as to provide automatic feedback on output (as with an automatic counter), or when work provides its own rewards (when it is intrinsically satisfying).

In addition, work groups themselves may take over activities normally allocated to supervision. This is particularly apparent in sociotechnical, autonomous, or leaderless work groups. Organizational systems and procedures – such as rules, policies, standard operating procedures, and reward systems – may take decisions out of the hands of the leader. Sometimes a strong union has the same effect, if it has a contract that severely constrains management rights.

From its beginnings the idea of multiple role motivation theories was associated with the substitutes for leadership concept (Miner, 1975). In this formulation leadership is equated with the role of the hierarchic manager. Professional, task, and group influences thus represent substitutes for this hierarchic influence (see Kerr, 1977). There are other substitutes beyond those covered by the role motivation theories, such as a strong and militant union, but the professional, task, and group categories appear to encompass much of what is meant by substitutes for leadership.

Profession, task, and group as substitutes

Professional motives, commitments, norms, knowledge and training make hierarchic supervision largely unnecessary. Similarly commission sales people, such as real estate agents, can operate with little or no supervision because the level of their earnings tells them whether or not they are performing adequately; the substitute for leadership is built directly into the task. In group systems, co-workers take over much of the leadership function by training one another, exerting pressure to perform, even allocating compensation. There is little left for a leader to do. Clearly the three theories fit neatly into the substitutes for leadership framework.

Relative effectiveness of organization types

Viewing role motivation theories from the substitutes for leadership context does present one problem, however. It seems to imply that hierarchic management is somehow primary, preferable, or even more effective. The role motivation theories do not say that. In fact within professional, task, and group systems managing does not fit at all; only in hierarchic systems is managing to be preferred. Furthermore, there is no statement as to the normative superiority of one theoretical framework over another. As far as the theories are concerned, and existing knowledge as well, one theory can produce as effective an organization as another, provided there is an adequate supply of the types of motivations that the role prescriptions require. In this view, then, nothing really substitutes for anything else; all the theories are equal.

There is one sense, nevertheless, in which the hierarchic theory does occupy a special position. Professional, task, and group systems by their nature require extensive face-to-face communication to operate. This means that when they get very large they can face major difficulties, especially if they are operating under stress or crisis conditions of a kind that require extensive communication to cope. Hierarchic systems on the other hand are capable of handling large size and remaining effective. They break communications down by hierarchic level and as Weber (1968) noted, they can operate well using written communications and files of paperwork (or computer memories). This capacity for handling size is why one often finds a number of professional departments, venture teams, or autonomous work groups *beneath* a hierarchic overlay.

VALIDITY OF LIMITED DOMAIN THEORIES

Given what has been said, it should prove helpful to actually look at some theories of industrial/organizational psychology and organizational science. Do theories of the kind we have been discussing – limited domain and parallel theorizing – fare particularly well on one or more dimensions of concern to scientists and practitioners? To answer this question, an analysis of 32 theories was carried out. These theories were as follows:

- Contingency theory of organization (Lawrence and Lorsch, 1967)
- Expectancy theories (Vroom, 1964; Porter and Lawler, 1968)
- Contingency theory of leadership (Fiedler, 1967; Fiedler and Chemers, 1974)
- Decision making concepts and constructs (Simon, 1947; March and Simon, 1958; Cyert and March, 1963)
- Need hierarchy theory (Maslow, 1954; 1962)
- Psychological open systems theory (Katz and Kahn, 1966; 1978)
- Technological determinism (Woodward, 1965; 1970)
- Job characteristics theory (Hackman and Oldham, 1980)
- Behavior modification and operant learning (Skinner, 1953; 1971; 1974)
- Path–goal theory (House, 1971; Evans, 1970; 1974)
- Sociological open systems theory (Thompson, 1967)
- Equity theory (Adams, 1963; 1965)
- Theory of system 4 and 4T (Likert, 1961; 1967; Likert and Likert, 1976)
- Motivation–hygiene theory (Herzberg, Mausner, and Snyderman, 1959; Herzberg, 1966; 1976)
- Technology in a comparative framework (Perrow, 1967)
- Goal congruence theory (Argyris, 1957; 1964; 1973)
- Goal setting theory (Locke, 1968; 1970; Locke, Cartledge, and Knerr, 1970)
- Achievement motivation theory (McClelland, 1961; 1975)
- Sociotechnical systems theory (Trist, Higgin, Murray, and Pollock, 1963; Emery and Trist, 1973)

Mechanistic and organic systems theory (Burns and Stalker, 1961)
Theory X and theory Y (McGregor, 1960; 1967)
Decision tree theory of participative leadership (Vroom and Yetton, 1973)
Theory of bureaucracy (Weber, 1968)
Theory of bureaucratic demise (Bennis, 1966; Bennis and Slater, 1968)
Classical management theory (Fayol, 1949)
Control theory (Tannenbaum, 1968)
Theory of strategy and structure (Chandler, 1962; 1977)
Role motivation theories (Miner, 1965; 1980)
Vertical dyad linkage theory (Graen and Cashman, 1975; Dansereau, Graen, and Haga, 1975)
Group-focused systems theory (Stogdill, 1959)
Influence–power continuum theory (Heller, 1971; Heller and Wilpert, 1981)
Leadership pattern choice theory (Tannenbaum and Schmidt, 1958)

A description of how these theories were evaluated will help to explain how they were selected as well.

The nomination analysis

One hundred knowledgeable scholars were contacted in early 1977 (Miner, 1984). These were the 40 current members of the editorial and review boards of the *Academy of Management Review*, the 30 such members for the *Academy of Management Journal*, and 30 former editors, review board members, and presidents of the Academy of Management selected by going backward in time until a total sample of 100 was created. Of the 100, 47 responded in some fashion and 35 provided usable responses in the form of a list of theories. The response rates were almost identical for all of the three sources from which names were derived. No apparent differences between respondents and nonrespondents as to disciplinary origins, geographical location, and the like were evident. The focus on the Academy of Management occurred because the author was an officer of that association at the time, and it was anticipated that a higher response rate might be obtained because of that fact.

Each respondent was asked to nominate theories considered to be important. The theory concept was defined broadly to include definitional systems, analytical schemata, and powerful constructs. The stated criteria for a theory to be important were:

1. It should have proved useful in understanding, explaining, and predicting the functioning of organizations or the behavior of people in them – thus it should have proved to be good or valid to some degree.
2. It should have clear implications for practice and applications in some area of management or organizational functioning – thus it should have practical value or usefulness.

3. It should have generated significant research – thus it should have been in existence long enough to have been tested and have an opportunity to become established.

Respondents were asked to nominate as many theories as they desired by theory title and by the name(s) of the people most clearly associated with the theory. Space was provided for listing up to 30 theories. At least 110 distinct theories were nominated, and the names of over 350 theorists were provided. Using a criterion of 10 or more nominations (out of the possible 35), 24 theories were selected as established. These 24 theories are noted first in Table 2.1, along with their frequencies of nomination. The cut off at 10 was dictated by the need to place some reasonable limit on sample size and the presence of a discontinuity in the frequency distribution just below this point.

Table 2.1 also contains an additional eight theories from among those less frequently nominated. The objective in including these eight was to obtain a full range of nomination frequencies without having a dispro- portionate number in the lower part of the range. The particular theories thus added were selected because the author had considerable knowledge of them.

Using frequency of nomination as an index of how good the theories are provides little support for the limited domain theory hypothesis. In Table 2.1, of the ten most frequently nominated theories only one, job characteristics theory, clearly has a restricted domain. Several others such as expectancy theory appear, based on the research evidence, to have restricted domains, but this is not specified in the theory (Miner, 1980b). In fact one problem with many organizational science theories is that they lack domain statements of any kind. In any event it is apparent that these 35 scholars, although they did not agree to any substantial degree among themselves, viewed some of the broader theories as better, when they did agree.

The validity analysis

A second approach used was to study the 32 theories thus identified, and the research on them, intensively and make a direct judgment of their validity. This rating was made by the author. A 3–point scale was used. A *high* rating was given if substantial segments of the theory had been supported by subsequent research. A *mixed* rating was given if the research evidence was conflicting. A *low* rating was given if the research evidence was primarily nonsupportive, or if the theory had not generated the necessary research in spite of the elapse of sufficient time to permit studies to be conducted. In cases of the latter type, highly abstract or imprecise definitions often made appropriate testing difficult if not impossible. These

Table 2.1 Evaluations of 32 scientific theories

Theory Title	Frequency of nomination – 1977	Rated scientific validity – 1981	Rated humanistic orientation – 1988
Contingency–organization	24	Low	High
Expectancy	24	High	Low
Contingency–leadership	20	Mixed	Medium
Decision making	17	High	Low
Need hierarchy	16	Low	High
Open systems–psychological	16	Mixed	Medium
Technological determinism	15	Low	Low
Job characteristics	15	High	Medium
Behavior modification	15	Mixed	Low
Path–goal	15	Mixed	Low
Open systems–sociological	14	Mixed	Low
Equity	14	High	Low
System 4 and 4T	14	Low	High
Motivation–hygiene	14	Low	High
Technology–comparative	12	Low	Low
Goal congruence	12	Mixed	High
Goal setting	12	High	Low
Achievement motivation	11	High	Low
Sociotechnical systems	11	Mixed	High
Mechanistic and organic systems	10	Low	Medium
Theory X and theory Y	10	Low	High
Decision tree	10	High	Medium
Bureaucracy	10	High	Low
Bureaucratic demise	10	Low	High
Classical management	7	Low	Low
Control	5	High	Medium
Strategy and structure	4	Mixed	Low
Role motivation	4	High	Low
Vertical dyad linkage	4	High	Medium
Group-focused systems	3	Mixed	Medium
Influence–power continuum	2	Mixed	Medium
Leadership pattern choice	2	Low	Medium

ratings were based on almost four years of study of the individual theories and related research, and they were made in early 1981.

Extensive reviews of the specific research studies on which the validity estimates were based are contained in three books (Miner, 1980b; 1981; 1982a). A series of book reviews by Behling (1983), Grimes (1983), Guzzo (1981), London (1981) and Mitchel (1983) provide evaluations of these research reviews with regard to their thoroughness and competence.

Obviously there is a risk of subjective bias in this procedure. However, there are data which suggest bias was at a minimum. Locke and Henne

(1986) rated theories of motivation for validity. The ratings were based on information accumulated preparatory to writing an article on the subject in the *International Review of Industrial and Organizational Psychology*. The correlation between their rank ordering and that from Table 2.1 for the eight theories that overlap was 0.94. Lee and Earley (1988) surveyed 127 scholars asking them to evaluate 15 theories of motivation and leadership in terms of their validity. Unlike the other analyses this one did not involve judges who had been reviewing the literature in connection with a writing project. Nevertheless, for the 13 theories on both lists the correlation was 0.75. Agreement between Locke and Henne (1986) and Lee and Earley (1988) was 0.87. Obviously good agreement can be obtained. Furthermore, independent evaluations by others do corroborate the author's validity judgments.

In Table 2.1 there are 11 theories rated as high in validity. Among them are most of the theories whose domains are more limited – role motivation theory and job characteristics theory, plus the goal setting, achievement motivation, decision tree, bureaucracy, and vertical dyad linkage theories. In addition both equity and control theory are clearly more restricted in domain than many of the theories rated low and mixed on validity. Overall the idea that limited domain theories are able to achieve higher validity receives considerable support from this analysis. It should be noted also that there is no relationship between the frequency of nomination and rated scientific validity data ($\chi^2=1.44$, df=4, p < .90).

In addition to the validity analysis just described, a similar usefulness analysis was also carried out to get at the practical value of the theories. This latter analysis has been described elsewhere (Miner, 1983; 1984; 1990), and since it generally proved less fruitful than the validity analysis, it is not recapitulated here. However, it can be noted that only four theories emerged as high on both validity and usefulness – job characteristics, goal setting, achievement motivation, and role motivation. All are limited domain in nature. All are motivation theories formulated by psychologists. Three of the four utilize parallel theorizing in some form.

In addition to the role motivation theories, achievement motivation theory is clearly of the parallel type. It is really a theory of three motives – achievement, power, and affiliation. However, only the first two have been fully developed in relation to a domain-entrepreneurship and management respectively. Job characteristics theory is contingent in nature, and in fact in more recent versions has several contingency variables. Hackman and Oldham (1980) note knowledge and skill, growth need strength, and context satisfactions. What emerges is a theory of job enrichment responders when these three are high and a theory of non-responders, for whom more routine jobs are appropriate, when they are low; there are two parallel theories. Only goal setting among the four high–high theories does not utilize parallel theorizing.

The role of values – rationale and measurement

These analyses provide strong support for the limited domain approach to theory construction and for parallel theorizing. Yet the nominations are unrelated to validity and usefulness, and point to a very different conclusion. Why should this be? One possibility is that the nominations were in some way influenced by the values of the nominators. In this connection it is important to note that unlike the Lee and Earley (1988) procedure, where a set list of theories for evaluation was specified, the nomination process was open-ended. Nominators were thus free to promote theories that were consonant with their values.

If one looks at the list of 32 theories in Table 2.1, and especially the 24 that were nominated more frequently, it is apparent that a number deal with participative management, power equalization, workplace democracy, and the like. Not at all infrequently these theories espouse a humanistic ethic. They exhibit a marked concern for human welfare, values, and dignity. They indicate that it is good to emphasize the welfare of the individual person even if productivity should suffer. They state that in the workplace employee satisfaction, well-being, and development should be the primary concerns. This type of prevailing humanistic value orientation is clearly exemplified by Tannenbaum, Margulies, and Massarik in their introduction to the book *Human Systems Development*:

> We unashamedly label our own personal value bias as humanistic. We have been and are personally committed to research and practice that help individuals to reach as nearly as possible their basic potential. This commitment also extends to the enhancement of the quality of interpersonal and intergroup relations and to the design, management, and functioning of organizations in ways supportive of the growth potentials of their members. It is also important to us that organizations be entities in the service of people rather than the other way around.
>
> (Tannenbaum, Margulies, and Massarik, 1985: 6)

It seems entirely possible that the nominations may have been influenced by the humanistic values of certain nominators so that scientific validity and usefulness became secondary to humanistic orientation as a criterion for defining theoretical goodness (Miner, 1990). Concern over the conflict between humanistic and scientific values, and how to deal with it, has been expressed on numerous occasions (see, for example, Krell, 1982 and Lawler, Mohrman, Mohrman, Ledford, and Cummings, 1985). Accordingly it seems likely that a journey into the realm of humanistic values might help explain the contradictions inherent in the data of Table 2.1.

To this end two additional analytic variables were developed. The first was the rating of the 32 theories on humanistic orientation noted in Table 2.1. This was done by the author using three categories. *High* humanistic theories are those that clearly promote humanism – a commitment to human welfare, dignity, and growth to full potential above and beyond more organizational concerns. These theories may also contain an alternative form or approach, but this alternative either is largely ignored or it is handled as a straw man. The *medium* humanistic theories tend to contain humanistic and non-humanistic alternatives, but the various contingent components or moderated relationships are taken more seriously. As a result the theory does contain a full-blown non-humanistic component. Finally, *low* humanistic theories do not contain a humanistic alternative as a major aspect, and do not serve to promote humanism. In most cases they are simply concerned with other matters. Although such a theory could be intendedly anti-humanistic, this is not typically the case.

A few examples may make these classifications more meaningful. Contingency theory of organization contains a humanistic alternative in the high differentiation–high integration condition and a non-humanistic alternative in the low differentiation–low integration condition, but when implementations are considered only those relevant to the former alternative, and thus a high uncertainty environment, are given more than passing attention. What needs to be done is discussed only in the sense of increasing differentiation and integration. Contingency theory of leadership on the other hand deals with octants, some of which are consistent with humanitarian values (where leader–member relations are good, task structure is low, and leader position power is weak, for instance) and some of which are not (leader–member relations poor, task structure high, and leader position power strong). Yet all octants are given equal billing in terms of the theory and its implication for action. At the low humanistic end of the continuum, expectancy theory presents a calculus that does not explicitly relate to humanistic concerns at all. Expectancies, valences, outcomes, and instrumentalities could combine to favor humanistic procedures, but there is nothing in the theory that predetermines this result.

To test the hypothesis it also was necessary to determine the degree to which the 35 nominators, those whose reports established the goodness of the theories, possessed humanistic values. The method of choice for this purpose is to administer a standardized instrument. However, this was not feasible. Several of the nominators are deceased, and the likelihood of obtaining a sufficient number of replies was not good. Furthermore, what was needed was a reflection of values in 1977 when the nominations were made. The best way to accomplish this appeared to be to again utilize the judgment of the author. Obviously there is again a potential for bias in this approach. On the plus side, however, it should be said that the author was quite conscious of this potential and made every effort to be objective. It should be noted also that the author was familiar with a substantial portion of the writings of each of the 35 nominators in the period before 1977. These writings were frequently revealing on the subject of value orientation. In addition the author knew 31 of the 35 personally prior to 1977; in most cases he had known these individuals for a number of years. The value categorizations were by no means uninformed guesses. Each nominator was assigned to *strong*, *moderate*, or *weak* categories based on the judged level of humanistic values. The intention was to divide the value continuum into three approximately equal segments. It was not possible to check on these ratings by obtaining independent assessments from other individuals because of prior commitments of anonymity made to the 35 nominators.

Clearly the value measurement process employed is not ideal. Approaches of a similar kind have a long history in the clinical assessment of personality (Hitschmann, 1956), but they have not achieved the same standing in industrial/organizational psychology. Nevertheless, the validity ratings used in the validity analysis were also somewhat suspect at the time that research was done. Yet subsequent independent analyses have given substantial credibility to the author's ratings. Hopefully future research will provide similar support for the values analysis.

Results of the values analysis

Table 2.2 takes the type of theory (high, medium, or low humanistic orientation) as a starting point and then asks how frequently scholars with varying levels of humanistic values nominate each type. High humanistic theories are much more likely to be nominated by scholars with strong humanistic values. Those with weak humanistic values are unlikely to nominate many humanistic theories. The results are highly significant and they remain essentially the same if the data are collapsed at the medians to obtain df=1 with larger expected cell frequencies. No such finding is obtained for the medium humanistic theories, however. The scholars with strong humanistic values do not nominate these more fully contingent theories any more than do those with a lesser preference for humanism. Furthermore, low humanistic theories are not nominated more frequently by those with weak humanistic values.

Table 2.3, in contrast to Table 2.2, takes the level of the scholar's humanistic values as a starting point and then asks how frequently each type of theory is nominated. The data at the top of Table 2.3 border on statistical significance, but this is entirely because scholars with strong humanistic values tend not to nominate medium humanistic theories. What appears to be happening is that these strong humanists tend to favor high humanistic theories and the low humanistic too, but they are much less favorably disposed to theories that consider humanism while still not fully endorsing it. When we move to the scholars with moderate humanistic values something of the same tendency is present, but it has dissipated to a point where nothing approaching statistical significance remains. Among

Table 2.2 Frequency of nomination for high humanistic orientation theories, medium humanistic orientation theories, and low humanistic orientation theories by scholars with varying levels of humanistic values

Level of humanistic values	High humanistic orientation theories (N=8) Frequency of nomination		
	Low (0–1)	Medium (2–4)	High (5–7)
Strong (N=11)	0	4	7
Moderate (N=12)	2	6	4
Weak (N=12)	7	5	0

χ^2=15.58, df=4, p <.01

	Medium humanistic orientation theories (N=10) Frequency of nomination		
	Low (0–1)	Medium (2–3)	High (4–6)
Strong	2	7	2
Moderate	4	3	5
Weak	5	3	4

χ^2=4.71, df=4, p <.50

	Low humanistic orientation theories (N=14) Frequency of nomination		
	Low (0–3)	Medium (4–6)	High (7–10)
Strong	4	4	3
Moderate	2	6	4
Weak	5	3	4

χ^2=2.52, df=4, p <.70

those with relatively weak humanistic values there is a distinct tendency to nominate low humanistic theories, and not to nominate high humanistic theories. Collapsing these data at the medians to produce a 2x2 matrix yields the same statistically significant result. No matter how one views the data, the picture of very few nominations of high humanistic theories by scholars with weak humanistic values emerges.

As noted previously, there is no evidence of a relationship between the validity of a theory and the number of times it is nominated, when all 35 nominators are employed. But what if we look at the nominations made by scholars with different levels of humanistic values separately? The expectation is that a positive relationship should appear at least among those with weak humanistic values. The data are given at the bottom of Table 2.4. They are not significant, but there is a marked change from the distribution for all 35 nominators. A clear trend exists among these non-

Table 2.3 Frequency with which scholars with strong, moderate, and weak humanistic values nominate high humanistic orientation, medium humanistic orientation, and low humanistic orientation theories

Orientation of theories	Scholars with strong humanistic values (N=11) Frequency of nomination		
	Low (0–3)	Medium (4–5)	High (6–10)
High humanistic	3	3	5
Medium humanistic	9	2	0
Low humanistic	4	3	4

$\chi^2=8.90$, df=4, p <.10

Orientation of theories	Scholars with moderate humanistic values (N=12) Frequency of nomination		
	Low (0–2)	Medium (3–4)	High (5–10)
High humanistic	5	3	4
Medium humanistic	5	5	2
Low humanistic	2	3	7

$\chi^2=5.16$, df=4, p <.30

Orientation of theories	Scholars with weak humanistic values (N=12) Frequency of nomination		
	Low (0–1)	Medium (2–3)	High (4–9)
High humanistic	7	5	0
Medium humanistic	5	3	4
Low humanistic	1	4	7

$\chi^2=11.49$, df=4, p <.05

humanists to nominate more valid theories more often and less valid theories less often. Furthermore when the data are collapsed at the medians, significance is obtained ($\chi^2=4.68$, df=1, p <.05).

Among the nominators with moderate humanistic values the picture is much like that for all 35, and no evidence of a relationship is discernible. Among the scholars with strong humanistic values, a trend toward a negative relationship appears. Quite evidently the more valid theories are nominated less, and the less valid (humanistic) theories more. This is only a trend in Table 2.4, but collapsing the data at the medians produces a significant result ($\chi^2=4.40$, df=1, p <.05). This finding is consistent with the view that values may cloud the evaluation process so that scientific validity no longer operates as the major determinant of perceptions of

Table 2.4 Estimated scientific validity and frequency of nomination for 32 theories for scholars with varying levels of humanistic values

Estimated scientific validity	Scholars with strong humanistic values (N=11) Frequency of nomination		
	Low (0–2)	Medium (3–5)	High (6–10)
High	5	4	2
Mixed	3	5	2
Low	1	4	6

$\chi^2=5.65$, df=4, p <.30

	Scholars with moderate humanistic values (N=12) Frequency of nomination		
	Low (0–2)	Medium (3–5)	High (6–9)
High	4	3	4
Mixed	3	2	5
Low	3	5	3

$\chi^2=2.07$, df=4, p <.80

	Scholars with weak humanistic values (N=12) Frequency of nomination		
	Low (0–1)	Medium (2–4)	High (5–7)
High	1	5	5
Mixed	3	3	4
Low	6	4	1

$\chi^2=6.95$, df=4, p <.20

goodness. In fact, if validity gets directly in the way of values, a negative relationship between validity and the goodness of a theory will appear, as it does here.

The values analysis provides considerable insight into the lack of relationship between frequency of nomination and rated scientific validity. If one views the nominators with weak humanistic values separately, most of the broader theories decline in frequency of nomination. This, of course, is quite pronounced for the highly humanistic broad theories, but it also applies to a number of the less humanistic broad theories as well. On the other hand certain limited domain theories are nominated proportionately more frequently by those with weak humanistic values. Among these are job characteristics theory, goal setting theory, achievement motivation theory, and theory of bureaucracy. All in all when the effects of humanistic values are removed from the nomination analysis, it begins to look much more like the validity analysis. It certainly does not move all the way to the point of identity, but it moves a good way nevertheless. In the process it provides increasing support for the use of a limited domain approach to theory construction.

CHAPTER SUMMARY

The limited domain approach in theorizing, as exemplified by role motivation theories, is discussed in relation to the contingency theory approach, middle range theorizing, the paradigm development strategy, Locke's concept of a theory that is close to action, and motivation theory in psychology generally. It is found that a limited domain approach is less constraining than contingency theory and on the restricted side among middle range theories. It certainly fits well with a paradigm development strategy, even if it is not a direct product. It has the advantage of being close to action. It bypasses much of the complexity that has characterized motivation theory in psychology.

The four role motivation theories are parallel theories and enjoy the advantages of the synergies thus created. A clear differentiation of the four organizational types is useful in disentangling the muddied state of current organization theory. When the types are combined we find little that is useful, but this may well be due to the 'wash out' of true variance across types of organizations. Treating each type separately should produce a much clearer picture.

If one considers the hierarchic theory as reflecting true leadership, then the professional, task, and group theories may be considered as dealing with substitutes for leadership. In one sense this is a distortion of theory in that all four organization types, appropriately staffed, are considered equally effective. Yet it is also true that hierarchic systems, among those considered, are most suited to deal with organizations of substantial size.

Finally, evidence is presented to support the view that among theories currently in vogue, those of a limited domain nature, and those utilizing parallel theorizing, are more valid. Initial impressions based on nominations of theories do not entirely vindicate this view. However, when corrections are made for humanistic value preferences, the evidence does appear consistently to support expectations regarding the importance of limited domain theorizing.

The discussion to this point has dealt with theorizing and much of it has been at the conceptual level. But theories need to be tested, and if this is to occur measures of theoretical variables must be created. Without sufficient operationalization theories can be uncritically accepted based on prevailing value premises, as occurred with Maslow's (1954; 1962) need hierarchy theory. They can be uncritically rejected as well, as occurred with many aspects of psychoanalytic theory. In the next chapter we consider the operationalization of role motivation theory constructs. In this instance, theory formulation and measurement were usually closely aligned.

Chapter 3

Operationalizing role motivation theory variables

The role motivation theories explicitly incorporate role requirements and motive patterns that are not available to a person's consciousness. Certainly they do not preclude conscious information, but this is presumed to be only the tip of the iceberg. Within psychology a major way of getting at and measuring unconscious material has been to use projective techniques of some kind. Role motivation theory has in large part adopted this approach. How and why this occurred is the subject of the first part of this chapter.

HISTORICAL DEVELOPMENT OF THE MINER SENTENCE COMPLETION SCALES

Projective techniques have not always enjoyed a good press within industrial/organizational psychology, although the reviews appear to be more mixed than consistently negative. Often clear distinctions between the various types of projective techniques have not been made in summarizing the literature in this area (Kinslinger, 1966; Reilly and Chao, 1982). When such distinctions are made, certain specific projective approaches have in fact elicited quite positive evaluations (Guion and Gottier, 1965; Korman, 1968; Cornelius, 1983). Yet very few psychologists whose primary education has been in the industrial/organizational field have made major contributions in the area of projective measurement. It seems likely that perceptions developed during the course of graduate training, fostered by major professors, have essentially blocked work of this kind by I/O psychology trained scholars. Doing research on projective techniques was not viewed as the best way to advance one's career.

In contrast, psychologists who originally were educated in the clinical area and personality theory, and later moved into the industrial/organizational field, did not face a similar constraint on their thinking. Thus it was much easier for them to work with projective techniques; they understood them better and valued them more (Lowman, 1991). In the author's opinion, this type of cross-fertilization within psychology is important to its development. Increasing standardization of careers, it is hoped, will not serve to prevent it in the future.

Prior experience with projective techniques

The author was one of those educated in clinical psychology and personality theory who learned industrial/organizational psychology in large part 'on the job,' while doing personnel research within a corporate industrial relations setting. In fact, at Clark and Princeton Universities, where he did his graduate work in the early 1950s, there was no course work in the industrial area at all.

Exposure to projective techniques on any meaningful scale first came in connection with an undergraduate thesis, while working with Silvan Tomkins on a study of alcoholics using the Thematic Apperception Test (TAT) (Miner, 1950). Subsequent research with Thelma Alper, culminating in a Master's thesis, utilized the Rorschach, TAT, and Tomkins–Horn Picture Arrangement Test (PAT) to study factors associated with the illusory (or empathic) motion phenomenon as produced through tachistoscopic presentations (Miner, 1952; 1956).

The author's experience with projectives beyond the Master's level concentrated heavily on the PAT – first in collaborating on the basic standardization research for that instrument (Tomkins and Miner, 1957; 1959) and then in a series of studies of various occupational groups. Among the latter were top-level executives and college professors (Miner and Culver, 1955; Miner, 1962), tabulating machine operators (Miner, 1960a; 1961), dealer–salesmen in the oil business (Miner, 1962a), and, considerably later, management consultants (Miner, 1971; 1973a).

Impressions from previous experience

These experiences left certain impressions that accumulated to yield a strong preference for sentence completion measures. The Rorschach produces varying numbers of responses (items) from different people. Where the response rate is low, many of the test's measures tend to become unreliable for those individuals. Toward the top of the management hierarchy, protocols usually become very rich – as Piotrowski and Rock (1963) demonstrated at an early point – but in other contexts they can be equally barren, and reliable measurement is hard to obtain. Furthermore, it is difficult, if not impossible, to structure the highly abstract inkblots to focus on specific topics of theoretical and practical concern. Individual administration is time-consuming and cumbersome, thus making the Rorschach less attractive for I/O psychology purposes. Although group procedures are available, they tend to thwart the use of an inquiry, thus reducing both the number of responses and the reliability of scoring.

The TAT can be structured to focus on particular topics, as McClelland, Atkinson, Clark, and Lowell (1976) have done in studying achievement motivation, and it can be group-administered, although the advantages of prompting are thereby lost. The major problem, however, is instrument unreliability, presumably caused, at least in part, by a limited number of cards (items) and, thus, stories (Miner, 1980b). This difficulty can be overcome by reverting to the original 20-card test, but then the TAT becomes excessively cumbersome for many purposes.

The Tomkins–Horn PAT was created specifically to cope with many of these problems. It is structured to focus primarily on the work setting, contains 25 items, and is capable of group administration. In addition, the arrangements can be scored in a standardized manner so as to eliminate problems of scorer reliability. In actual use, however, many of the measures contain few items, and instrument reliability therefore remains a problem. Accordingly, higher validities have often been obtained in research using measures that draw upon the verbal responses to the pictures. But if this is to be the primary approach used with the PAT, why not use verbal rather than picture stimuli, thus obtaining more responses (items) for the same investment of time?

Origins of the MSCS – Form H at the Atlantic Refining Company

Form H (for hierarchic) is the original measure for the hierarchic role motivation theory. This Miner Sentence Completion Scale (MSCS) has not changed in any way since its original publication in 1961. The scorable items have not changed since the inception of the instrument in 1957. There have been pressures to adapt the items to changing times and culture patterns, and changes have been made on occasion for the purposes of specific studies. However, the basic, published instrument remains the same. To make changes would undermine the cumulative nature of the data and research findings. For many years this instrument was known simply as the Miner Sentence Completion Scale. The designation Form H was added at the time other forms were developed to measure the variables of the other role motivation theories.

The MSCS came about because, shortly after joining the personnel research division at the Atlantic Refining Company (now ARCO), the author was asked to teach a management development program in-house for research and development managers at the Philadelphia refinery. R and D management had emerged from a round of appraisals with a less than satisfactory record, largely because too many individuals were more committed to their engineering and scientific specialties than to the managerial work expected of them. The training need was to create or develop an interest in managing, something that later came to be labeled 'motivation to manage,' in people whose preferences were for other types of activities.

Table 3.1 Correlations between Kuder Preference Record Scales and
management appraisal ratings (N = 420 managers)

Kuder Scale	Rated current job performance	Rated potential for advancement
Supervisory	0.14**	0.24**
Outdoor	0.02	−0.12*
Mechanical	−0.01	−0.01
Computational	0.05	0.04
Scientific	−0.15**	−0.08
Persuasive	0.09	0.20**
Artistic	−0.05	−0.12*
Literary	0.04	0.11*
Musical	0.04	−0.01
Social Service	0.02	0.02
Clerical	−0.03	−0.10*

* p <.05
**p <.01
Source: Miner, 1960b

In order to determine whether the course that was designed to deal with
this need had achieved its ends, some measure of managerial motivation
was required. An extensive literature search at that time yielded nothing
of value.

Initial efforts to deal with this problem focused on the development of
a special supervisory interest scale for the existing Kuder Preference
Record. To a degree these efforts were successful as indicated in Table
3.1. The new scale produced validity coefficients better than those obtained
from the regular Kuder scales. However, these coefficients, though significant, were still low. Furthermore, because the Kuder items are of a self-
report nature, there was a lingering concern over the extent to which
scores might be biased by self-interest. The ratings used as criteria in this
research were made by a panel of managers, primarily superiors, convened
specifically to evaluate the individual.

Ultimately a decision was made to develop a sentence completion measure. A projective instrument seemed the most appropriate way to eliminate or at least reduce self-interest bias and to get at unconscious motives.
These factors were considered particularly important in this instance
because hierarchic managing is an activity about which our democratic
society as a whole is decidedly ambivalent and which is by no means
always viewed as socially desirable. With such an instrument it would be
possible to focus on a limited set of variables and obtain responses to a
sizable number of items, thus, it was hoped, obtaining sufficient reliability.

For purposes of item selection, 60 items, largely based on the author's
personal impressions of managerial values in the company involved, were
written. The items utilized structured stems of a kind that subsequently

have been found to be particularly productive in research on sentence completion measurement (Turnbow and Dana, 1981). The underlying model at this point was that of a generalized managerial interest or motive along the lines of the construct embodied in the Kuder measure. Although components of the model were in mind, they were not articulated to the point of specific subscale components. At this early stage the theory is best described as one of managing in the Atlantic Refining Company in the late 1950s, as experienced by a young psychologist with a strong psychoanalytic orientation.

The 60 items were administered to 21 members of the company's corporate human resource department who were housed on the same floor as the author. Given the fact that the hierarchic levels and general perceptions of performance for these individuals were known, it was possible to conduct a rough item analysis against the external criterion of managerial success. The best items were those that elicited a range of responses both positive and negative, were clearly understood by respondents (while operating within the intended construct domain), and discriminated so that successful and less successful managers responded as hypothesized.

In analyzing items along these lines there were two basic sources of variation: the item or stem itself and the particular scoring system applied to it. In traditional item analysis with multiple-choice alternatives, only the items themselves can vary. With projective measures of this kind, a given response to an item can be designated positive, neutral, or negative, depending on the scoring system in use. One attempts to end with a set of items and a standardized scoring procedure for them that provide a range of responses (large standard deviations), adequate construct measurements, and maximal discriminations against external criteria, but the ultimate test of the adequacy of these judgments comes only from subsequent validation research.

In the case of Form H, the first pass yielded 40 items that seemed to meet the criteria and a scoring system for them. These items were constituted as a single measure of managerial interest or motivation, and were used in a pre-post design with experimental and control groups to evaluate the training program. The results were positive for the program, and indirectly for the instrument (Miner, 1960; 1965).

Differentiating subscales within Form H

In working with the MSCS it became increasingly apparent that the different constructs included could be differentiated in terms of subscales. This was done entirely on a conceptual, not a statistical, basis. Items that appeared to relate to different aspects of the managerial role were grouped together. There was one set dealing with authority figures that related to upward hierarchic communications, another set dealt with horizontal relationships in the form of competition, and a third focused on the exercise of power downward to subordinates. Because there were a number of competition items, a decision was made to separate those concerned with games and sports, and treat them as a distinct subscale. The results of these initial differentiations were the Authority Figures, Competitive Games, Competitive Situations, and Imposing Wishes subscales.

Another set of items seemed to relate to the masculinity–femininity variable widely included in psychological measures at that time. Initially this was labeled Masculine Role; later the name was changed to Assertive Role, but the items remained the same. Findings from the University of Michigan leadership research that effective managers behave in ways that clearly differentiate them from their subordinates (Kahn and Katz, 1953) provided guidance for the creation of another subscale, Standing out from Group. A number of items dealing with basic communication and decision-making tasks in managerial work constituted the Routine Administrative Functions subscale.

Each of the seven subscales contained five items. An additional five items did not fit meaningfully in any subscale category. These were treated as fillers and not scored. When the MSCS was published in 1961, they were replaced with new items intended to hide the purpose of measurement even further and to provide bases for clinical insights. They remain unscored. The number of items per subscale was held to five so that pattern scoring for rares could be carried out along the lines initially proposed by Tomkins (Tomkins and Miner, 1957). In an era when computers were not in widespread use, the prospect of developing norms for scoring through hand tabulations of item combinations numbering more than five was singularly unattractive.

In this early period, instrument development and theory development were very closely related. Clearly there was an implicit theory that guided the writing of the initial 60 items, but it did not become articulated until the subscales were differentiated. The subscales were titled as they were to avoid any implication that unitary motives were involved. From a very early point the guiding conception was one of informal roles and matching motive patterns. It was quite evident for instance that high Authority Figures scores could result either from a positive orientation to people in general or toward those in positions of authority only. For the purposes at hand it did not matter.

At the time the MSCS was developed and the subscales were identified, the author had very little knowledge of bureaucratic theory. The basic stimulus in choosing items came from the Atlantic Refining Company as the author experienced it, a clearly very hierarchic organization. That this company turned out to have much in common with other bureaucratic systems was in fact fortuitous, although those with a broader comprehension of the (particularly sociological) literature would certainly have predicted it. In any event the MSCS – Form H has turned out to be a measure of at least some of the motivational forces that propel managerial work in bureaucratic systems.

This final instrument contains seven subscales of five items each. Each item is scored +, ?(O), or −. Thus subscale scores may vary from +5 to −5 and total scores vary from +35 to −35. In actual practice subscale scores at the extremes (+5 or −5) occur only rarely. It is quite unusual to obtain a total score beyond + or −20. Among corporate managers (N = 695) the mean total score is 4.22 with a standard deviation of 5.51 (Miner, 1989).

Development of the multiple-choice version of Form H

For a number of years the author recorded each new response to an item on one of a number of large sheets divided so as to separate the lists of positive (+), neutral or noncommittal (O), and negative (−) responses obtained. Under increasing pressure from a publisher who had a test in print, but no possible way of responding to requests for information on what to do with it, the sheets finally were used to create a scoring guide (Miner, 1964).

Although the author remained firmly committed to the traditional free-response sentence completion format, others became somewhat impatient with it. Learning to score according to the guide took some time, and some people never seemed to become very good at it. Even with substantial experience a record usually took about ten minutes to score. All in all, the free response approach seemed excessively cumbersome, especially when it would be so easy to develop multiple-choice answer alternatives.

This line of reasoning led a group at Rensselaer Polytechnic Institute to construct a forced-choice form of the MSCS (Steger, Kelley, Chouiniere, and Goldenbaum, 1975). Three alternative answers were provided, in most cases 'like,' 'indifferent,' and 'dislike.' Also, 8 of the 35 stems were altered to varying degrees, to make them more student-oriented. This instrument yielded a total score correlation with the original MSCS of 0.68. Subscale correlations ranged from 0.33 to 0.74, with a median of 0.40. Not surprisingly, the loss of the projective element inherent in the new format produced a sizable inflation of scores on all of the subscales that totaled an increase of almost ten points overall. When alternatives were so clearly presented, respondents no longer selected negative answers with the same frequency. These findings obtained with a group of 50 RPI students are given in Table 3.2. The administrations were separated by an interval of 17 weeks. No items were altered in terms of content in the Authority Figures, Competitive Situations, and Imposing Wishes subscales; in these three instances the changes are entirely attributable to the shift to multiple-choice responses.

Table 3.2 Correlations between the standard MSCS and an altered multiple-choice MSCS, and means for both measures (N = 50)

MSCS measure	Correlations between standard and altered MSCS	Means Free response	Means Multiple-choice
Total score	0.68**	3.18	13.06
Authority figures	0.35*	0.24	2.02
Competitive games	0.40**	1.40	2.68
Competitive situations	0.33*	−0.76	0.46
Assertive role	0.59**	−0.10	1.10
Imposing wishes	0.74**	0.82	2.78
Standing out from group	0.64**	1.24	2.30
Routine administrative functions	0.36**	0.34	1.72

* p <.05
**p <.01
Source: Steger, Kelley, Chouiniere, and Goldenbaum, 1975

Prodded by these results, the author began work on a multiple-choice MSCS of his own. In an attempt to hold down score inflation, actual responses of a positive, neutral, and negative nature taken from previously obtained records were used, rather than the like–indifferent–dislike format. There were two responses of each type, making a total of six for each stem. The six were randomized. No changes in the MSCS, other than the addition of the six alternatives to each stem, were made.

Subsequent findings indicate that score inflation remains a problem with this multiple-choice version of the MSCS, but not nearly to the extent found in the RPI study. The amount of inflation varies in different groups, ranging from something over +1 to over +6 (Miner, 1977; Perham, 1989; Quigley, 1979). Total score correlations between the two versions of up to 0.68 have been obtained (see Table 3.3). Subscale correlations have varied from sample to sample, but the research to date provides no basis for concluding that the Imposing Wishes and Routine Administrative Functions subscales of the multiple-choice MSCS measure the same thing as subscales in the parent measure (Butler, Lardent, and Miner, 1983). For the remaining five subscales, correlations approximating the test–retest reliabilities over the same time span have been obtained. In general, this attempt to construct a multiple-choice measure from sentence completion origins appears to have produced much the same type of results as have other similar efforts (Shouval, Duek, and Ginton, 1975). A supplement to the original MSCS scoring guide has been developed to provide information on scoring the multiple-choice version (Miner, 1977a).

Table 3.3 Correlations between free response MSCS and multiple-choice version in a sample of 64 General Motors Company managers – mean interval between administrations: three months

MSCS measure	Free response vs. multiple-choice correlations
Total score	0.68**
Authority figures	0.48**
Competitive games	0.63**
Competitive situations	0.48**
Assertive role	0.54**
Imposing wishes	−0.02
Standing out from group	0.29**
Routine administrative functions	0.07

Development of the MSCS – Form P

In the case of Form P (for professional), comprehensive theory definitely did precede instrument development. Roles and matching motive patterns were defined; then 12 items were written as candidates for each of five subscales. The resulting 60-item measure was completed by 20 faculty members and advanced doctoral students in the management department at Georgia State University. As in the human resource department at Atlantic, the author had information on success indexes such as academic rank, publications, professional reputation, and the like for these individuals. Thus the data needed to carry out item analyses were present. When these analyses were done, it proved possible to construct subscales containing eight items each that appeared to discriminate between more and less successful professionals. These items were randomized to produce the 40-item Form P. No filler items were included in this instrument.

Subsequent research on a much larger group of management professors provided evidence that the initial item selection process had worked as anticipated (Miner, 1980c). The scoring guide for Form P was constructed by using responses obtained from the faculty samples (Miner, 1981a). As yet no multiple-choice version of Form P has been developed.

Scores on all five Form P subscales may vary from +8 to −8. As with Form H, each item is scored +, ?, or −. Total scores can range from +40 to −40. In actual practice scores at the extremes of + or −7 or 8 on the subscales occur infrequently. Total scores outside the −15 to +25 range are also unusual. In various professional samples the mean total score has ranged from +5.6 to +10.7.

Rare scores of the kind developed for Form H are not calculated for Form P. The experience with Form H was that more often than not the validity coefficients obtained with rare scores exceed those for a simple total score as long as the rare scores are calculated using essentially the same sample as the validation sample. In other words when the sample is normed on itself, rare scores are worth developing; using standardized norms from outside the group under study to determine what combinations of responses are rare, however, appears to add nothing to the total item scores. Users of Form P certainly can create their own rare scoring procedure following the approach detailed in the Form H scoring guide (Miner, 1964) and also in the 1977 supplement (Miner, 1977a). This is feasible, however, only when a large sample is available for normative purposes – at least 150 cases. With computers, determining rare combinations within the eight-item sets presents no problem.

Development of the MSCS – Form T

Since earlier research had demonstrated that Form H was not applicable to entrepreneurs in that the scores obtained were unexpectedly low, the need for a different measure was apparent (Smith and Miner, 1983). There had been some prior efforts to apply sentence completion measures in the study of achievement motivation, with rather mixed results (Singh, 1979). However, in no case had an instrument focused on the full spectrum of the achievement situation in the manner envisaged by the task theory. Thus it seemed appropriate to continue using the same type of measurement strategy that had proved successful in the hierarchic and professional domains. Form T (for task) was the result.

While Forms H and P emerged out of extended organizational experiences of the author, this type of experiential background was available only to a very limited degree for the development of Form T. Feeling somewhat less certain in constructing possible items for Form T, the author started out with more of them, as a hedge against the possibility that many might prove rather poor. The preliminary measure contained 75 items, 15 for each subscale.

This instrument was completed by 17 entrepreneurs, most of whom had survived and prospered in that role. Because the group as a whole was quite successful, it was not possible to carry out any kind of item analyses within this group. Accordingly, comparisons were made with a group of 20 students in entrepreneurship and business policy classes who were known to be currently employed in positions that clearly did not fit in the task domain. This comparison sample averaged 28 years of age, much younger than the entrepreneurs, and this fact may have introduced some confounding. Nevertheless, the less successful people in prior analyses to develop Forms H and P were also younger. In any event, five subscales of eight items each were constructed. As the following data indicate, discriminations appear to be very good for Self Achievement, Avoiding Risks, Feedback of Results, and Personal Innovation; they are somewhat less good for Planning for the Future:

	Mean score for entrepreneurs	Mean score for non-entrepreneurs	Difference
Self achievement	3.94	0.30	3.64
Avoiding risks	2.71	−1.40	4.11
Feedback of results	2.71	−1.00	3.71
Personal innovation	4.59	1.15	3.44
Planning for the future	1.59	0.00	1.59
Totals	15.54	−0.95	16.49

It should be noted that the largest difference was obtained on the subscale measuring the *avoidance* of risk. This is the finding noted in Chapter 1 that contributed to the decision to modify the theory to emphasize risk avoidance rather than moderate risk-*taking*.

As with Form P, Form T subscale scores can vary from +8 to −8, and the total score from +40 to −40. Again each item is scored +, ?, or −. Subscale scores of + or −7 or 8 are not common, although they do occur. Total scores outside the +25 to −15 range are unusual. In a group of 135 entrepreneurs the mean total score was 6.8. However, entrepreneurs heading growing firms, not mom and pop operations or professional practices, tend to score much higher, with a mean of something over 12 (Miner, 1990a).

There is as yet no multiple-choice version of Form T. A detailed scoring guide is available containing scoring examples from a large group of entrepreneurs (Miner, 1986). For the reasons noted with regard to Form P, a rare score has not been developed for Form T.

Form T, like Form P and Form H before it, was developed using external criteria for purposes of item selection. However, in all three instances the criterion samples were rather small, and the requirements of the situation were to select both the test items and a standardized scoring system to use with them. Some concern about rigor is certainly justified at this point. It is hoped that the reader will hold judgment in abeyance for the moment. The crucial question is whether what was done worked. The remainder of this book deals with that question.

Thoughts on Form G

As yet no empirical work has been done toward the development of Form G (for group). However, there are some data from Form H suggesting certain pitfalls to avoid. These have to do with the defining of group domains as applied to sociotechnical, or autonomous, or leaderless work groups.

A study by Beldt (1978) in which the multiple-choice Form H was administered to all managers in two sociotechnically organized and two traditional bureaucratically organized plants in the same company reveals

Table 3.4 MSCS – Form H multiple-choice version scores for managers in sociotechnical and traditional plants within the same company

MSCS measures	Mean score for the 9 managers in sociotechnical plants	Mean score for the 26 managers in traditional plants	Z
Total score	9.00	3.04	2.40*
Authority figures	1.44	0.04	1.96*
Competitive games	2.33	1.31	1.79*
Competitive situations	1.44	0.77	1.04
Assertive role	1.00	0.04	1.16
Imposing wishes	0.33	0.12	0.80
Standing out from group	1.56	0.81	0.90
Routine administrative functions	0.89	0.12	1.23

* p <.05

some unexpected results. There was evidence that the sociotechnical plants were more effective and that they had fewer managers, as the underlying theory would anticipate, but, as shown in Table 3.4, they also had managers with higher Form H scores. Thus the hierarchic superstructure above the autonomous work groups was characterized by stronger motivation to manage in those plants that in an overall sense were characterized by less bureaucracy. A number of hypotheses can be advanced to explain this finding, but at the moment we do not know with any certainty why it occurred.

However, this same study yielded some additional unexpected conclusions regarding the values of autonomous work group members using the Personal Values Questionnaire (England, 1975; England, Olsen, and Agarwal, 1971). In these groups, company owners and stockholders were valued less than in the traditional plants, but blue-collar workers and labor unions were also valued less. Not surprisingly, where multi-skilling is in effect, skill was valued more in the sociotechnical context, but compassion and tolerance were valued less – contrary to most organization development values. Individuality and risk were valued less in the group context, but success was valued more. These findings suggest a complex set of dynamics in group-based work systems. It will be important to be very careful in writing sentence completion items for such a system. Items incorporating many organization development values may not work. Furthermore, group systems should be defined narrowly so as not to include others, such as managers, outside the group itself.

THE OLIVER ORGANIZATION DESCRIPTION QUESTIONNAIRE (OODQ)

The OODQ provided the information used in describing organizational types in Chapter 1. It is a method of determining the extent to which a particular organizational situation is characterized by each of the four types of structures – hierarchic, professional, task, and group. The need for such a measure became apparent early in role motivation theory research, but was skirted by using job titles to determine what organization type the person worked in and what theoretical domain was applicable. A study by Quigley (1979) brought home to us the need for something more precise.

Table 3.5 presents data from this study. The total sample contains individuals designated as managers in district offices throughout the state of Georgia who were involved in delivering health care to the citizens of the state. Although part of the state bureaucracy, these district offices often operated with considerable autonomy. In the total sample the validity coefficients are quite low. However, a number of those included were clearly operating primarily as professionals – physicians, dentists, nurses, or dieticians. Based on job titles, 27 such individuals were removed to leave an administrative component of 47. Now the validity coefficients became more respectable. Without question a number of people in the total sample were experiencing a predominantly professional system and Form H was not a relevant measure. But we had no precise way of defining who these people were. Were certain offices totally professional

Table 3.5 Validation of the MSCS – Form H multiple-choice version in the Georgia Department of Human Resources – total and administrative samples

MSCS measures	Correlation with superior performance ratings	
	Total sample (N = 74)	Administrative component (N = 47)
Total score	0.22*	0.34**
Authority figures	−0.08	−0.21
Competitive games	0.17	0.25*
Competitive situations	0.09	0.19
Assertive role	0.15	0.17
Imposing wishes	0.06	0.37**
Standing out from group	0.09	0.09
Routine administrative functions	0.20*	0.30*

* $p < .05$
** $p < .01$
Source: Quigley, 1979

in nature or only certain individuals within them? A way of answering this kind of question was clearly needed.

Development of the OODQ

The approach to solving this problem developed by Oliver (1981; 1982) involved first creating some 100 items of a forced choice nature which used the following format:

In my work, duties are determined by

a) management	(hierarchic)
b) my profession or occupation	(professional)
c) my work group	(group)
d) me, based on the goal I am trying to accomplish	(task)

Respondents were to make a selection in each instance among multiple-choice alternatives reflecting each of the four organization types. These items were administered to criterion groups of at least 100 subjects drawn from each of the four domains as follows:

Hierarchic: production workers, prison guards and working prisoners, company keypunch operators, U.S. civil service personnel, U.S. Army personnel, company clerical workers.

Professional: members of ministerial associations, college professors, independent professionals (physicians, veterinarians, lawyers, CPAs, etc.)

Task: entrepreneurs, real estate associates, commissioned sales personnel, undergraduate finance students.

Group: personnel from sociotechnically designed plants who were included in self-directing work groups.

Each of the four criterion groups was divided into two approximately equal groups – one for item selection and one to be used as a hold out for cross validation. Each item was then analyzed using a matrix indicating the percent of each item-selection group that gave each response. An example, where (a) is hypothesized to be a professional response is as follows:

Response alternatives	Item selection groups (%)			
	Hierarchic	Professional	Task	Group
(a)	38	85	51	24
(b)	11	0	4	24
(c)	16	6	31	22
(d)	35	9	14	30

Vertical analysis indicates 85 percent of the professionals gave response (a). This is analogous to Berkshire's (1958) applicability index. The horizontal analysis shows that significantly lower percentages from the other groups selected response (a). Items showing at least a 51 percent applicability index and strong horizontal discrimination as well were retained in the final instrument. Following Nunnally (1978), unit weights of one were given to the responses selected.

The resulting instrument contained 43 items. There were 15 responses per domain so that scores could vary from 0 to 15. The four scores were labeled H score, P score, T score, and G score. With 43 items, and thus 172 response alternatives, it is apparent that many alternatives (112 to be exact) are not scored because they do not discriminate.

The effectiveness of the measure thus developed was assessed by first performing a fold-back classification in the item-selection groups using highest score as the classification criterion. This process produced a 72 percent correct classification. Cross validation was then carried out by applying the same procedure to the hold out groups. This analysis yielded a 71 percent correct classification, indicating practically no shrinkage. A chi-square test for goodness of fit indicated no significant score variations between item-selection and hold out groups.

As shown in Table 3.6, the OODQ does discriminate in the manner intended. Multivariate analysis of variance using a repeated measures model (Winer, 1971) applied to these data indicates that the within domain scores are significantly higher than the outside domain scores at $p < .001$. In the great majority of cases they are over twice as large. H scores and P scores of 6 or higher are considered to indicate a significant degree of hierarchy and professionalization respectively. T scores and G scores of 5 or higher reflect significant task structure and group organization (Oliver, 1981).

Table 3.6 Mean OODQ scores in theory relevant samples

Domain of sample	N	H score	P score	T score	G score
Hierarchic	107	9.6	4.3	2.4	2.5
Professional	105	3.8	10.2	4.8	2.6
Task	101	3.8	5.3	9.3	1.6
Group	125	4.9	2.4	2.6	9.1
Total	438	5.8	5.4	4.7	4.2

Source: Oliver, 1982

Table 3.7 Reliability data for OODQ

	H score	P score	T score	G score
Test–retest (30 days)	0.85	0.87	0.84	0.77
Chronbach's alpha	0.86	0.84	0.82	0.88
Spearman–Brown corrected odd–even	0.83	0.81	0.82	0.86

Source: Oliver, 1981

Table 3.7 provides reliability data on the OODQ. All of the reliability coefficients but one are in the 0.80s. The one departure is still very close to the other values. It appears to be a result of restriction of range due to the fact that the test–retest sample of 32 did not contain any members of the self-directing work groups (Oliver, 1982).

As anticipated, the four scores tend to be negatively correlated (in the range −0.17 to −0.43). The one exception is a correlation between the P score and T score of 0.11.

Related instruments

Although there do not appear to be other instruments that measure the same four variables as the OODQ, there are certain measures which seem on their face to tap one or more of the OODQ factors. Likert's (1967) Profile of Organizational Characteristics is oriented to a different theoretical approach, but appears to arrive at features of both hierarchic and group systems. Gulowsen's (1972) Group Autonomy Scale deals with group systems, and a set of questions devised by Hall (1977) provides an index of professionalization, as does another set of questions developed by Kerr and Jermier (1978). Aspects of the Job Diagnostic Survey (Hackman and Oldham, 1975) and other similar instruments would seem to get at components of task systems. Price (1972) describes various measures that may be used in identifying and assessing hierarchic systems. The Aston scales (Pugh and Hickson, 1976) are examples. Baker, Etzioni, Hansen, and Sontag (1973) and Gordon (1970) have devised instruments that measure tolerance for bureaucratic structure, thus providing indexes of hierarchy.

This listing is not meant to be comprehensive. It does indicate, however, that there are other measures that might be expected to yield results similar to the OODQ scores. Whether they actually do is an empirical question that still needs to be answered.

Research with the OODQ

The primary purpose in administering the OODQ is to define domains for validating and using the various MSCS measures. It was the lack of such information on Georgia Department of Human Resources personnel that made interpretation of Quigley's (1979) data difficult.

Several such applications have been carried out. Among a group of entrepreneurs participating in the programs of the Center for Entrepreneurial Leadership at the State University of New York at Buffalo, OODQ scores were as follows:

H score 3.1
P score 5.0
T score 8.4
G score 2.3

Only the T score is significantly elevated. H and G scores are low as expected. The P score is somewhat higher, largely due to the inclusion of several professionals who have started their own professional firms. The data clearly support the use of the MSCS – Form T with this group, although it would be appropriate to exclude the professionals.

In a study of labor arbitrators, over 60 percent of whom held law degrees, the following results were obtained:

H   score   1.4
P   score   10.8
T   score   6.1
G   score   1.2

The P score is high as anticipated. It is the highest of the four scores by a substantial margin and it is above the average for professionals indicated in Table 3.6. In contrast the H and G scores are very low. However, the T score is up. A number of the arbitrators, over 25 percent, describe their organizational context as both professional and task. The data definitely call for the use of the MSCS – Form P in the sample overall, but one would expect somewhat higher validities when the analysis is restricted to arbitrators having only the P score elevated (and not the T score). This in fact turns out to be the case (Miner, Crane, and Vandenberg, 1992).

Another application unearthed a more complex problem. The group studied was composed of members of the Program for Exceptional Children staff in a large metropolitan school district (Pilgrim, 1986). Most were special education teachers with some graduate training. The OODQ scores were as follows:

H   score   7.3
P   score   8.9
T   score   4.1
G   score   2.0

The H and P scores are significantly elevated; the T and G scores are not. Yet neither the H nor P score really stands out, as the P score does among the labor arbitrators. The school district as it applies to its special education personnel is a mixture of hierarchic and professional systems and many describe it as just that, with somewhat elevated scores on both the H and P scales. The professionalization appears not to be sufficiently strong to achieve a dominant position. Accordingly the MSCS – Form P should not be used with this group unless a high P score subgroup is first identified. Many members, and there are a number in administrative positions, fall most appropriately in the domain of Form H.

Factor analysis of the OODQ carried out by Oliver and Fredenberger (1987) using data from 1,256 individuals in 113 different samples, produced strong support for the typology of role motivation theory. A three-factor solution proved optimal. The rotated factor matrix showed all 15 items of

the task scale having a highest positive loading on one factor, all items of
the group scale with a highest positive loading on another factor, and all
items of the professional scale with a highest positive loading on the third
factor. The items of the hierarchic scale were distinguished by the fact
that they loaded negatively or zero on all three of these factors.

These results are consistent with the view that the professional, task,
and group organizational forms are alternatives to hierarchy (Herbst,
1976). They also fit well with the substitutes for leadership formulations
discussed in Chapter 2. The factor analytic results indicate that hierarchy
is in many respects antithetical to professional, task, and group forms.
The implication is that mixing modes, as hierarchy was mixed with the
professional in the special education unit studied by Pilgrim (1986), can
lead to incongruent and conflicting structures and processes. The result
may very well be a less effective organization. However, empirical data
on this point are currently lacking.

Another result of using the OODQ has been to elicit responses not in
terms of the realities of the present but in terms of an ideal world. The
entrepreneurs participating in the Center for Entrepreneurial Leadership
program at SUNY-Buffalo completed the OODQ with the standard
instructions to describe their current work situation, how their job is, and
with the following instructions:

> Please complete this second copy of the Oliver Organization Descrip-
> tion Questionnaire in the same way as you did before. However, this
> time you should answer, not by selecting the response which best
> describes your present work situation, but by selecting the response
> which *best describes your ideal work situation.* What would the organiz-
> ation be like if you were free to choose exactly what characteristics you
> wanted in the work situation. Responding in this way could conceivably
> produce a result much the same as for your present work situation.
> However, for most of us there are real differences between the world
> in which we do work and the one in which we would like to work –
> under ideal circumstances.

To date the ideal responses have on the average patterned themselves
in very much the same manner as the actual. Interestingly, however, there
is some reduction in the T score and some increase in the G score. It is
on the latter two scores that the greatest change occurs. There are several
individuals who would ideally like much more of a task structure, but
they are matched by others who would like less. The same is true of the
group form. These discrepancies are often very revealing regarding the
individuals involved. It appears that they may predict job changes.

A final use to which the OODQ has been put involves the identification
of types of organizations falling in the various domains. In one such
study Wilderom and Miner (1991) investigated voluntary organizations to

determine if they were indeed group systems as originally hypothesized. The OODQ was completed by volunteer workers in a number of organizations providing community services of various kinds. As anticipated, the mean G score was higher than the other three scores. However, this result proved to be a consequence of the data from volunteers working in voluntary groups without paid staff only. There the dominance of group organization was clearly evident. But in the voluntary organizations with paid staff there was no predominant organizational form in evidence. None of the scores achieved the levels designated by Oliver (1981) as indicating a significant presence, and no statistically significant differences were found. Again the issue of the consequences for organizational effectiveness begs for an answer.

RELIABILITY OF THE MINER SENTENCE COMPLETION SCALES

There are three aspects of the reliability question that need to be considered: scorer reliability, test–retest, and internal consistency. Since with projective techniques each of these indexes raises a different set of issues, each is considered separately.

Scorer reliability: same scorer

The author has carried out repeat scoring on an independent basis with all three free response MSCS measures at substantial intervals, sufficient to eliminate memory effects:

   With Form H, 20 records were rescored at a four month interval; there was 95.4 percent agreement on individual items and only an average variation of 1.6 points in total score (Miner, 1965).
   With Form P, 20 records were rescored at an interval of more than two years; agreement on individual item scoring was again at the 95 percent level with the total score mean 10.7 on the first scoring and 9.8 on the second (Miner, 1981a).
   With Form T, 20 records were rescored after an interval of more than three years; the agreement level on individual items was again 95 percent, and the mean total score was 12.1 initially and 10.8 subsequently (Miner, 1986).

Overstreet (1980) also presents evidence on Form H rescoring at a three-month interval by the same scorer. He reports a correlation of 0.94 for the total score and values ranging from 0.81 to 0.98 for the subscales.

Overall it appears that scorers are quite consistent within themselves in scoring the various MSCS instruments. This is true of the total score and of the individual subscales, although some fluctuations in individual subscale scoring both up and down have been identified.

Scorer reliability: different scorers

Table 3.8 presents a large number of scorer reliability correlations. Most are for Form H, but the Form P and Form T data are comparable. Typically the correlations relate the author's scoring to that of some other person. However, there are instances, such as the Dayani (1980) and Overstreet (1980) studies, where both scorers were unknown to the author.

In most, but not all cases involving the author the other scorer received training in scoring the MSCS prior to the scoring reported in Table 3.8. Training normally emphasized feedback on results and discussion of the rationales for scoring difficult items. In some instances the training was given face-to-face, and in other instances there was a written exchange. Both appear to work equally well.

In Table 3.8 the total score correlations range from 0.84 to 0.98. The two values in the 0.80s in the Miner (1978) study involve the same individual. It is apparent that some people find it easier to reach and maintain accurate scoring levels than others. On the subscales the coefficients range down to 0.64, but the great majority are in the 0.90s. For some reason the Imposing Wishes subscale of Form H appears to be more difficult to score reliably. Both of the values in the 0.60s occur on that subscale, but there are four correlations in the 0.90s also. Clearly Imposing Wishes is capable of being scored reliably.

Based on the data, it appears that scorers can, and should, obtain agreement levels in the 0.90s. This conclusion is consistent with findings with other sentence completion instruments (Fuller, Parmelee, and Carroll, 1982; Lah, 1989; Rootes, Moras, and Gordon, 1980; Waugh, 1981). Although in formal studies with the MSCS instruments this has been accomplished most frequently with some training beyond study of the scoring guides; the author's experience is that some individuals can achieve similar levels simply by intensive study of the rationales and examples provided. In fact, several of the scorers in Table 3.8 achieved total score correlations in the 0.90s prior to receiving any feedback at all. There is reason to believe, however, that self-teaching does in some cases fall short of expectations, and the experience to date is that training always raises scorer reliabilities. As with other projective techniques, MSCS scoring can clearly benefit from a certain amount of instruction from an already experienced scorer.

Table 3.8 does not contain data from several studies using Form H where experienced scorer instruction was not utilized *and* known scoring deficiencies existed. In the first of these, Brief, Aldag, and Chacko (1977) obtained subscale reliabilities ranging from 0.58 to 0.91 with a median value of 0.71. They do not present total score figures, but extrapolating from Table 3.8 where the median subscale value is 0.91 and the total score value 0.95, one would project a value of about 0.75. These scorer reliability

Table 3.8 MSCS scorer reliability data

MSCS – Form H

Source	N	Total score	Authority figures	Competitive games	Competitive situations	Assertive role	Imposing wishes	Standing out from group	Routine administrative functions
Miner, 1976	15	0.91	0.84	0.86	0.96	0.94	0.81	0.79	0.87
Miner, 1978 a)	12	0.95	0.92	0.98	0.89	0.86	0.83	0.94	0.96
b)	12	0.91	0.98	0.95	0.95	0.91	0.66	0.90	0.97
c)	10	0.88	0.76	0.88	0.91	0.82	0.84	0.82	0.88
d)	10	0.97	0.96	0.94	0.91	0.97	0.78	0.97	0.97
e)	10	0.86	0.86	0.95	0.89	0.91	0.85	0.90	0.90
Quigley, 1979	10	0.97	0.96	0.92	0.98	0.98	0.81	0.90	0.97
Butler, Lardent, and Miner, 1983	20	0.94	0.89	0.86	0.90	0.88	0.91	0.73	0.81
Singleton, 1976	12	0.95	0.92	0.98	0.89	0.86	0.83	0.94	0.96
Berman and Miner, 1985	140	0.94	0.83	0.93	0.87	0.90	0.82	0.91	0.90
Ebrahimi, 1984	15	0.92	0.95	0.86	0.92	0.92	0.91	0.96	0.89
Wachtel, 1986 a)	14	0.97	0.76	0.93	0.89	0.91	0.64	0.92	0.92
b)	16	0.98	0.98	0.99	0.98	0.94	0.91	0.89	0.94
Dayani, 1980	20	0.95	0.91	0.96	0.94	0.96	0.88	0.98	0.78
Overstreet, 1980 a)	15	0.97	0.98	0.98	0.91	0.88	0.95	0.94	0.89
b)	20	0.84	0.88	0.73	0.83	0.75	0.77	0.83	0.71
Median r		0.95	0.92	0.94	0.91	0.91	0.83	0.91	0.90

MSCS – FORM P

Source	N	Total score	Acquiring knowledge	Independent action	Accepting status	Providing help	Professional commitment
Pilgrim, 1986	10	0.98	0.90	0.89	1.00	0.91	0.98

MSCS – Form T

Source	N	Total score	Self achievement	Avoiding risks	Feedback of results	Personal innovation	Planning for the future
Jourdan, 1987	10	0.95	0.96	0.94	0.94	0.93	0.91

coefficients are well below those consistently reported not only for the MSCSs, but for other sentence completion measures as well. Moreover, additional evidence of scoring deficiencies is present. When the mean scores of the three scorers were compared, over 80 percent of the differences were significant at the $p < .05$ level. One scorer was consistently above the other two to the point where the sum of the subscale scores (total score) was 3.75 points higher than the average of the others (Miner, 1978).

A second analysis not included in Table 3.8 also involved three scorers (Bartol, Anderson, and Schneier, 1980; 1981). Again total score reliabilities were not reported, but the subscale coefficients ranged from 0.61 to 0.91 with an average of 0.83; only one correlation was below 0.75. One would anticipate an item score value approximating 0.87 (extrapolating from Table 3.8 as before). Subsequently a subset of these records was rescored by the author. The total score correlation between the author's data and the average for the previous scorer was 0.80 (Miner, Smith, and Ebrahimi, 1985). The rescoring by the author produced a mean total score 2.35 points below that previously reported, significant at $p < .01$.

In both the Brief, Aldag, and Chacko (1977) and Bartol, Anderson, and Scheier (1980; 1981) studies, the scoring was done by graduate students, presumably as part of their research assistant duties; these scorers had no previous experience with the MSCS. In both instances there was evidence suggesting score inflation. This particular pattern is in fact rather common among scorers just beginning to work with the MSCS. The scores of inexperienced scorers tend to be higher (more positive) than those of experienced scorers (Butler, Lardent, and Miner, 1983; Miner, 1978).

Insight into this phenomenon derives from a study by Perham (1989). Responses from the multiple-choice version, where correct scores are known, were put in a computer along with the Form H Scoring Guide (Miner, 1964). Undergraduate students without scoring experience then scored the protocols. There was significant and consistent evidence of score inflation. These novice scorers, like many studied previously, gave more positive scores than the multiple-choice designations would warrant. Furthermore, the more the scorers consulted the scoring guide as they carried out their task, the fewer their errors and the less the positive score inflation. Also the presence of incentives to score accurately operated to minimize errors in the same manner.

Based on his data, Perham (1989) supports the conclusion that past studies where score inflation produced reduced scorer reliabilities were in all likelihood influenced by the fact that: 'certain individuals check less with the scoring guide and come to introduce a positive bias into their scoring. In essence the scorer does what the multiple-choice approach often does: he or she introduces a certain amount of score inflation. Negative scorings are not given as often as they should be.' (Miner, 1985:

166). Furthermore, the data suggest that using graduate students, who are paid without regard to their performance levels and who will not be credited as authors for their work in any event, to do the scoring produces a low-incentive situation which in turn fosters a failure to check the scoring guide when appropriate and consequently errors.

Test–retest reliability

Given the evidence that good scorer reliabilities can be obtained, it is reasonable to anticipate good test–retest figures as well. Certainly the MSCS total scores are based on a sufficient number of items to support good reliability.

Many of the data sets on test–retest reliability derive from control groups employed in studies carried out to evaluate training programs intended to raise levels of motivation to manage (Miner, 1965). For this reason the intervals between administrations are longer than might otherwise be desired for a reliability study, approximately ten weeks. In different samples the total score reliability coefficients range from 0.68 to 0.84, with a median of 0.83. Subscale coefficients range from 0.44 to 0.63, with a median of 0.48. Data from these studies, all of which employed Form H, are given in Table 3.9.

In contrast, the test–retest correlations obtained among experimental subjects (whose mean scores were raised by the training) were consistently lower, often significantly so. This same type of finding has emerged from work with Fiedler's (1967) Least Preferred Co-worker measure (Rice, 1978). On the evidence it now appears that reliability is not adequately determined when certain kinds of training experiences intervene between

Table 3.9 Test–retest reliabilities over 10 plus weeks for the MSCS – Form H in a mixed sample of business managers, undergraduate business students, and undergraduate education students (N = 112)

MSCS – Form H measures	r
Total score	0.83**
Authority figures	0.55**
Competitive games	0.63**
Competitive situations	0.48**
Assertive role	0.59**
Imposing wishes	0.46**
Standing out from group	0.44**
Routine administrative functions	0.45**

**p <.01
Source: Miner, 1965

testings; pretest–post-test correlations in experimental groups tend to be 0.20 points or so below those obtained from control groups (Miner, 1965).

Table 3.10 gives Form H test–retest data obtained over an interval of one to two weeks in a sample of MBA students at SUNY-Buffalo. The correlations are consistently higher than those of Table 3.9. With the exception of one subscale, no changes in mean scores occur.

While the analyses of Tables 3.9 and 3.10 utilized the free response Form H, with all records scored by the author, a study by Stahl (1986) using Clemson University students employed the Multiple-Choice Form H, thus eliminating the scorer reliability issue. In this instance the retest occurred at a three-week interval. As indicated in Table 3.11, correlations with the Crowne–Marlow Social Desirability Index (1960) are negligible. Thus the test–retest coefficients do not reflect a pervasive social desirability bias in the MSCS scores that might serve to homogenize results across testings and inflate correlations.

Pilgrim (1986) reports test–retest data for a control group of primarily female special educators using Form P. The repeat testing was done at an interval of two months or more. The total score correlation obtained was 0.70 with subscale values ranging from 0.37 to 0.72. These coefficients are clearly on the low side; they are the only ones available for Form P. However, it is unlikely that this reflects a unique problem with Form P. Test–retest total score reliabilities as low as 0.68 have been obtained with Form H. Strangely, this value also came from the education field (a group of female education students at the University of Oregon).

Table 3.12 contains data from a repeat administration of Form T to MBA students at SUNY-Buffalo over a one- to two-week interval. All scoring was done by the author. It is apparent that test–retest coefficients do decline as the interval between testings increases, presumably because real changes contaminate the reliability estimates. The total score correlations for the MSCS measures range from 0.68 to 0.96, but most of the lower values involve control groups measured over intervals of two months or more.

In any event the test–retest reliability of the MSCS measures as a whole appears to be entirely satisfactory, consistent with the scorer reliability data and the number of items used. In contrast, the subscales appear most suitable for group analyses. Without supporting data from other sources, the subscale reliabilities generally are not sufficient to justify comparative interpretations of anything but large score differences. Following the rare score rationale (Tomkins and Miner, 1957), interpretation would appear to be entirely justified when the subscale score is extreme (+ or −).

Table 3.10 Test–retest reliability data for the MSCS – Form H in a sample of 40 SUNY-Buffalo MBA students

MSCS – Form H measures	r	Means		t
		Test	Retest	
Total score	0.88**	0.50	0.35	0.41
Authority figures	0.67**	0.25	0.13	0.93
Competitive games	0.79**	0.33	0.20	0.80
Competitive situations	0.76**	−0.50	−0.65	0.80
Assertive role	0.86**	−0.33	−0.28	0.50
Imposing wishes	0.75**	0.85	0.68	0.94
Standing out from group	0.85**	0.38	0.33	0.39
Routine administrative functions	0.86**	−0.48	−0.05	2.89**

**p <.01

Table 3.11 Test–retest reliability data for the MSCS – Form H multiple-choice version and correlations with the Crowne–Marlow Social Desirability Index (1960) in a sample of 111 Clemson University undergraduate business students

MSCS – Form H measures	Test–retest r	Crowne–Marlow r
Total score	0.78**	0.04
Authority figures	0.45**	0.08
Competitive games	0.69**	−0.03
Competitive situations	0.63**	0.15
Assertive role	0.67**	0.13
Imposing wishes	0.61**	0.00
Standing out from group	0.41**	0.16
Routine administrative functions	0.63**	0.14

**p <.01
Source: Stahl, 1986

Table 3.12 Test–retest reliability data for the MSCS – Form T in a sample of 39 SUNY-Buffalo MBA students

MSCS – Form T measures	r	Means		t
		Test	Retest	
Total score	0.96**	3.13	3.46	1.17
Self achievement	0.91**	0.97	0.95	0.14
Avoiding risks	0.86**	−0.49	−0.33	0.72
Feedback of results	0.66**	−0.64	−0.21	1.51
Personal innovation	0.76**	2.15	2.31	0.67
Planning for the future	0.78**	1.13	0.74	1.55

**p <.01

Internal consistency

Cornelius (1983), in discussing sentence completion measures, notes that good internal consistency reliability can be, and often is, obtained. For example, Waugh (1981), using a sentence completion index of ego development, found corrected split-half coefficients of 0.91 and 0.79 in two different clinical samples. Yet it appears certain that internal consistency of this kind is not characteristic of the MSCS measures.

Data on this point are given in Table 3.13. There is evidence of internal consistency for the total scores, although at a minimally acceptable level. The subscales demonstrate no stable internal consistency at all. There is no reason to believe that further study with other samples would yield substantially higher correlations. One reason is that the item selection process has concentrated on discrimination between external criterion groups, rather than between high-scoring and low-scoring groups on the internal measures themselves. In short, the measures have been constructed with reference to external validity but not internal consistency. It is not surprising that the overall outcome reflects this same distribution of foci. It is important to keep in mind that the MSCS measures deal with motivational patterns composed of whatever works to predict role behaviors. The subscales thus are intendedly a motivational hodgepodge combining a range of motives, and in fact different motives for different people.

Traditional psychometric considerations lead to the conclusion that internal consistency reliability is a necessary condition for validity. However, there is an increasing body of evidence and theory indicating that this is not the case (Atkinson, 1977; 1982; Brody, 1980; Cornelius, 1983). At least for projective techniques, there are good reasons to believe that internal consistency reliability is not an essential condition for construct validity. In fact, it could inhibit validity by reducing the number of facets of a construct that are tapped.

Perhaps most convincing of all is the fact that MSCS instruments lacking internal consistency reliability have yielded substantial empirical validity with marked consistency. Evidence to this effect will be considered at length in subsequent chapters. However, several examples will serve to make the point. Stahl (1986) contains the data on internal consistency for the multiple-choice version of Form H noted in Table 3.13. This same publication reports on the validity of this instrument, also using Clemson University students. The findings are given in Table 3.14. The student leaders score higher on a majority of the MSCS measures including the total score in spite of the lack of internal consistency. A similar differentiation between student leaders and nonleaders has been obtained several times previously with various versions of Form H (Steger, Kelley, Chouiniere, and Goldenbaum, 1975; Singleton, 1976; 1978).

Table 3.13 also contains internal consistency data for Form P using a

Table 3.13 Internal consistencies for the various MSCS measures

	Total score	Authority figures	Competitive games	Competitive situations	Assertive role	Imposing wishes	Standing out from group	Routine administrative functions
MSCS – Form H Spearman–Brown corrected r (N = 46 SUNY-Buffalo MBA students)	0.56	0.00	0.00	0.08	0.00	0.03	0.00	0.18
Coefficient alpha (N = 301 employed adults in Saudi Arabia) from Al-Kelabi, 1991	0.45	0.26	0.30	0.14	0.01	0.18	0.32	0.25
MSCS – Form H multiple-choice version Coefficient alpha (N = 111 Clemson University undergraduates) from Stahl, 1986	0.57	0.24	0.16	0.33	0.00	0.00	0.00	0.41
Coefficient alpha (N = 271 University of North Dakota undergraduates) from Eberhardt, Yap, and Basuray, 1988	0.58	0.34	0.40	0.24	0.34	0.26	0.29	0.15
Coefficient alpha (N = 232 MBA students)	0.68			Not reported				
(N = 115 MBA students) from Bartol and Martin, 1987	0.66			Not reported				
Coefficient alpha (N = 371 management majors at four universities) from Stevens and Brenner, 1990	0.69			Range 0.64 to 0.68				

Table 3.13 Continued

	Total score	Acquiring knowledge	Independent action	Accepting status	Providing help	Professional commitment
MSCS – Form P Spearman–Brown corrected r (N = 112 professors of management)	0.59	0.31	0.43	0.41	0.02	0.17
Coefficient alpha (N = 301 employed adults in Saudi Arabia) from Al-Kelabi, 1991	0.53	0.27	0.03	0.36	0.27	0.19

	Total score	Self-achievement	Avoiding risks	Feedback of results	Personal innovation	Planning for the future
MSCS – Form T Spearman–Brown corrected r (N = 51 SUNY-Buffalo MBA students)	0.45	0.14	0.34	0.02	0.00	0.06

Table 3.14 Validation of the MSCS – Form H multiple-choice version among Clemson University undergraduates

MSCS measures	Mean Scores		
	Fraternity and sorority presidents (N = 31)	Upper-class engineering students-nonleaders (N = 26)	t
Total score	10.65	4.85	5.63**
Authority figures	0.10	0.12	0.06
Competitive games	3.36	3.04	0.85
Competitive situations	1.29	−0.58	4.59**
Assertive role	0.90	0.19	1.68*
Imposing wishes	0.71	−0.23	3.20**
Standing out from group	1.84	1.38	1.51
Routine administrative functions	2.45	0.92	4.46**

* p <.05
**p <.01
Source: Stahl, 1986

sample of professors of management. In this same sample a validity of 0.66 was obtained for the total score and 0.35, 0.53, 0.39, 0.36, and 0.50 for the successive subscales (Miner, 1980c). In five of the six instances these validities exceed the internal consistency of the measure (not just its square root). On the evidence, it appears time to discard the outmoded concept that internal consistency is a necessary condition for an instrument to be considered psychometrically sound.

In connection with his internal consistency analysis of the MSCS – Form H in its multiple-choice format, Stahl (1986) also carried out a factor analysis of the individual items. He started with the assumption that seven factors should emerge with the items loading on factors in accordance with their subscale categorization. Not surprisingly, he did not find the factor pure subscales he was looking for. Instead he found 14 factors with eigenvalues greater than 1.00; he was unable to interpret his results. In contrast Eberhardt, Yap, and Basury (1988) obtained only three factors with eigenvalues at this level in their factor analysis of student scores. This type of analysis assumes that tests must be factor pure to be valid and useful. This simply is not the case. Tests such as the MSCSs appear to be analogous to the Wechsler measures in the intelligence sphere (see Matarazzo, 1972). They derive from the demands of practical reality, not mathematical analysis. Unlike the Thurstones' (1941) measures, for instance, the Wechsler measures are not factor pure. Yet they have proved reliable, valid, and useful for a variety of purposes over many years.

EXAMPLES OF MSCS AND OODQ SCORES

At the end of Chapter 1, three examples of good theoretical matches were presented in role motivation theory terms. Now that the actual instruments used have been considered, it is possible to operationalize these statements in terms of OODQ and MSCS scores. The following score profiles contain both raw scores and percentile equivalents. The OODQ percentiles are from the broad or balanced sample, containing approximately equal numbers of hierarchic, professional, task, and group subjects (Oliver, 1981). The MSCS – Form H (free response) percentile data derive from a sample of corporate managers only; they do not include managers in the non-profit sector (Miner, 1989). The professional scale norms used are from the scoring guide for that instrument, and the percentile equivalents are calculated from that group (Miner, 1981a). The MSCS – Form T percentiles are based on the sample of entrepreneurs discussed in the scoring guide for that instrument (Miner, 1986).

The reader is encouraged to compare the following test profiles with the portraits of the same individuals provided in Chapter 1.

R & D Vice President – Andrew Solero

It is apparent that Andy Solero operates in what he views as a predominantly hierarchic context, but to a lesser degree a professional one as well. As expected, the total MSCS-H score is high (this is a very successful person). Contributing factors are the high scores on Competitive Situations (93rd percentile), Standing out from Group (92nd percentile), and Routine Administrative Functions (92nd percentile). Imposing Wishes (4th percentile) is at a very low level; perhaps in the unique situation of dealing with professionals this is appropriate. The high MSCS-P total score is also consistent with expectations. Andy has both the motivational patterns his OODQ scores would call for. Within his professional motivation Acquiring Knowledge (94th percentile), Accepting Status (93rd percentile), and Professional Commitment (92nd percentile) are all very high. In contrast there is no evidence of any particular idiosyncracies insofar as the MSCS-T scores are concerned. No motivational pattern stands out there, and based on the OODQ score none would be expected.

I/O Psychology Consultant – Beth Ann Doyle

On the OODQ, Beth Ann exhibits a high P score and a high T score. She views her practice as highly professional, but to an almost equal degree as entrepreneurial as well. Consonant with the high P score on the OODQ, Beth Ann exhibits very high professional motivation overall. The major factor contributing to this result is the Accepting Status score (98th percentile). All the other MSCS-P subscales are on the plus side, but none stand out like Accepting Status. The MSCS-T scores are not particularly elevated, and in fact Self Achievement (9th percentile) is low. This is consistent with the fact that Beth Ann is in actuality a private professional practitioner, not an organization builder. On the MSCS-H the total score is distinctly low (5th percentile); this is a person who does not like working in the management hierarchy of a large corporation, and she does not do so. The only subscale that clearly contributes to this negative result is Competitive Games (0 percentile). However, the low Assertive (Masculine) Role score (12th percentile) is at the borderline insofar as interpretation is concerned.

Business Founder – Abraham Pollack

Abraham Pollack describes his work setting on the OODQ as first and foremost entrepreneurial. His T score is the only one that is elevated. Given his success, it is not surprising that the MSCS-T total score is quite high as well. Within that instrument Self Achievement (98th percentile) is the factor that contributes the most. Abe likes to do it his way and he will work very hard to accomplish his goals. On the other hand, Planning for the Future is low (6th percentile) and this is surprising for a successful entrepreneur. Yet the pattern of rapid growth, and then sale before problems surface, is not a long-term strategy. The MSCS-H scores are low. Abe is not a manager and he sells his firms before they need to be managed. Not only is the total score for motivation to manage low, but Authority Figures (2nd percentile), Standing out from Group (10th percentile), and Routine Administrative Functions (7th percentile) are low as well. Yet there is evidence of strong competitive drives apparent in the Competitive Games score (95th percentile). On the MSCS-P the scores are low; Abe is not a professional, in spite of his engineering background. In particular he is down on Acquiring Knowledge (6th percentile), although Providing Help (12th percentile) is in the borderline area as well. Above everything else, Abe is first and foremost a very hard-driving, individualistic entrepreneur who burns himself out and has to rest for a while as he thinks up his next endeavor.

Test scores
Andrew Solero: R & D Vice President

		Score	Percentile equivalent
OODQ –	H score	10	82nd
	P score	7	68th
	T score	4	53rd
	G score	1	22nd

MSCS – Form H		Score	Percentile
MSCS – Form H	Total score	+10	85th
	Authority figures	+2	71st
	Competitive games	0	24th
	Competitive situations	+2	93rd
	Assertive role	+2	85th
	Imposing wishes	−2	4th
	Standing out from group	+3	92nd
	Routine administrative functions	+3	92nd
MSCS – Form P	Total score	+14	86th
	Acquiring knowledge	+5	94th
	Independent action	0	23rd
	Accepting status	+5	93rd
	Providing help	0	21st
	Professional commitment	+4	92nd
MSCS – Form T	Total score	+5	41st
	Self achievement	+2	52nd
	Avoiding risks	+1	51st
	Feedback of results	−2	22nd
	Personal innovation	+3	50th
	Planning for the future	+1	45th

Test scores
Beth Ann Doyle: I/O Psychology Consultant

		Score	Percentile equivalent
OODQ –	H score	0	7th
	P score	11	88th
	T score	9	86th
	G score	4	62nd
MSCS – Form H	Total score	−5	5th
	Authority figures	0	21st
	Competitive games	−5	0
	Competitive situations	−1	40th
	Assertive role	−2	12th
	Imposing wishes	+2	81st
	Standing out from group	+1	54th
	Routine administrative functions	0	36th
MSCS – Form P	Total score	+15	89th
	Acquiring knowledge	+1	62nd
	Independent action	+3	65th
	Accepting status	+6	98th
	Providing help	+4	84th
	Professional commitment	+1	65th
MSCS – Form T	Total score	+4	37th
	Self achievement	−2	9th
	Avoiding risks	+2	66th
	Feedback of results	−1	35th
	Personal innovation	+4	64th
	Planning for the future	+1	45th

Test scores
Abraham Pollack: Business Founder

		Score	Percentile equivalent
OODQ –	H score	3	35th
	P score	5	52nd
	T score	9	86th
	G score	1	22nd
MSCS –	Total score	−4	7th
Form H	Authority figures	−2	2nd
	Competitive games	+4	95th
	Competitive situations	−2	19th
	Assertive role	−1	25th
	Imposing wishes	0	31st
	Standing out from group	−1	10th
	Routine administrative functions	−2	7th
MSCS –	Total score	−4	11th
Form P	Acquiring knowledge	−4	6th
	Independent action	+3	65th
	Accepting status	+1	43rd
	Providing help	−1	12th
	Professional commitment	−3	14th
MSCS –	Total score	+12	72nd
Form T	Self achievement	+7	98th
	Avoiding risks	+4	87th
	Feedback of results	+1	67th
	Personal innovation	+4	64th
	Planning for the future	−4	6th

CHAPTER SUMMARY

This chapter discusses the measures developed to study role motivation theory variables. The OODQ deals with the four organizational types – hierarchic, professional, task, and group – and provides an index of the extent to which each type is present in a particular situation. The MSCS-H measures motivation to manage and its components; it exists in both free response and multiple-choice versions. The MSCS-P measures professional motivation and its components; there is only the free response version. The MSCS-T measures task or entrepreneurial motivation and its components; the free response version is the only one available. At this time there is no MSCS-G. No direct measures of the role requirements of the role motivation theories, as distinct from organization types and motivational patterns, have been created.

In this chapter information regarding item selection, instrument development, and reliability is provided for each measure. Reliabilities are consistently good insofar as the scoring aspects of the MSCSs are concerned.

The OODQ appears entirely adequate in all its psychometric aspects, including reliability. Test reliability is good for the total scores on the MSCS measures using the test–retest method, but only fair when this method is used with the subscales. Accordingly subscale scores, although quite adequate for group analyses, should be interpreted directly for individuals only at the extremes. Internal consistency approaches to reliability determination do not appear to be applicable to the MSCSs, although minimally satisfactory values have been obtained for the total scores. Largely due to difficulties inherent in the development of psychometrically sound projective measures, the item selection research behind the MSCSs was not as rigorous as might be desired. This is not in itself a problem, but it places a heavy burden on subsequent validation research with the instruments.

This research is considered in the next three chapters. Chapter 4 takes up the very extensive validation evidence for the MSCS-H; the research extends over almost 35 years. Chapter 5 considers the much less extensive validation research with the MSCS-P. Chapter 6 deals with the rapidly expanding body of validation data on the MSCS-T.

Chapter 4

Validation of the hierarchic role motivation theory

The very extensive research conducted to test the validity of the hierarchic theory is considered in this chapter. This research is both concurrent and predictive in nature, and extends to various other investigations of construct validity. Research where managerial motivation is experimentally manipulated using management development techniques will be considered in a later chapter. Studies have been carried out within the theory's domain, where the expectation is that positive relationships between predictor and criterion will prevail, and outside the domain, where nonsignificant results are anticipated. The two meta-analyses that have been conducted will be summarized.

VALIDITY WITHIN THE THEORY'S DOMAIN

Research on the hierarchic theory has characteristically used the MSCS-Form H in some form, and with one exception has been conducted without benefit of the OODQ. Decisions as to whether a particular study was carried out within the appropriate domain are to some degree problematic. Nevertheless, the fact that the studies labeled as in-domain deal with managing in relatively large organizations that give every indication of being hierarchic provides a degree of confidence in the classifications. Results are reported as significant (p <.05, <.01) or nonsignificant following the practice of previous reviews (Miner, 1978a; 1979; 1985). This procedure makes it possible to combine and compare the results of all studies, irrespective of the nature of the analyses and any limitations of reporting.

Concurrent validity

Table 4.1 summarizes 29 studies and 44 predictor–criterion relationships where a concurrent design was used. In 12 instances data are available for a total score measure from the MSCS-H only; in the remaining 32 cases subscale findings are included as well. There are only two total score

Table 4.1 Concurrent validation within the domain of the hierarchic theory

N	Criterion	Total score	Authority figures	Competitive games	Competitive situations	Assertive role	Imposing wishes	Standing out from group	Routine administrative functions
	1. R & D Managers – oil company (Miner, 1965)								
100	Grade level	<.01	NS	NS	<.01	NS	NS	NS	NS
81	Performance rating	<.05	<.01	NS	<.05	NS	<.01	NS	NS
81	Advancement potential rating	<.01	<.05	<.05	<.01	NS	<.05	<.01	NS
	2. Managers – department store (Miner, 1965)								
70	Grade level	<.01	NS	NS	<.05	<.05	<.05	NS	<.05
70	Performance rating	NS							
70	Advancement potential rating	<.05	NS	NS	NS	NS	<.05	NS	<.05
	3. School administrators – large city (Miner, 1967; 1968)								
82	Grade level	<.01	NS	NS	NS	NS	NS	NS	<.01
82	Compensation	<.05	NS	NS	NS	NS	NS	NS	<.01
82	Performance rating	<.01	NS	<.01	<.01	<.01	NS	<.05	NS
82	Advancement potential rating	<.01	NS	NS	<.01	<.05	NS	<.05	NS
	4. Graduate education students – University of Oregon (Miner, 1968)								
85	Career choice – administration vs. some educational specialty	<.01	<.05	<.05	NS	<.05	<.01	NS	<.05
	5. Graduate students in business – University of Oregon (Miner, 1968a)								
106	Career choice – managerial vs. nonmanagerial	<.01	<.01	<.05	<.01	<.01	<.01	<.01	<.01
	6. Undergraduate students in business – University of Oregon (Miner and Smith, 1969)								
108	Career choice – managerial vs. nonmanagerial	<.01	NS	NS	<.01	<.05	NS	NS	NS
	7. Undergraduate students in business – simulated bureaucratic organization at Western Michigan University (Miner, Rizzo, Harlow, and Hill, 1974)								
415	Managers vs. nonmanagers	<.01	NS	<.05	<.01	<.01	NS	<.01	<.01
	8. Female managers – department store (Miner, 1974a)								
44	Grade level	<.05	NS	NS	NS	NS	<.05	<.05	NS
	9.* Undergraduate students – Rensselaer Polytechnic Institute (RPI) (Steger, Kelley, Chouiniere, and Goldenbaum, 1975)								
40	Fraternity president vs. no offices in student organizations	<.01	NS	NS	NS	NS	<.05	NS	<.01

No.	N	Description							
10.		Managers – various companies (Miner, 1976)							
	395	Position level	<.01	<.01	<.01	<.01	NS	NS	<.05
11.		Personnel and industrial relations managers – various companies (Miner, 1976; Miner and Miner, 1976)							
	142	Position level	<.05	<.01	<.05	NS	<.05	NS	NS
	101	Composite measure (managerial level and compensation)	<.01	NS	NS	NS	NS	NS	NS
12.		Undergraduate students – Georgia State University (Singleton, 1976)							
	190	Student officer vs. not student officer	<.01	NS	<.05	NS	<.01	NS	NS
13.		Managers – textile companies (Southern, 1976)							
	50	Grade level	<.05						
	37	Grade level	<.05						
14.		Scientists and engineers – government R & D laboratory (Gantz, Erickson, and Stephenson, 1977)							
	117	Peer rating of managerial potential	<.01						
15.		Graduate students in business – Georgia State University (Miner and Crane, 1977)							
	47	Managers vs. nonmanagers	<.05						
16.*		Administrative component – Georgia Department of Human Resources District Offices (Quigley, 1979) See Table 3.5.							
	47	Performance rating	<.01	<.05	NS	<.01	<.05		
17.		Academic library employees – large libraries (Dayani, 1980)							
	68	Managers vs. nonmanagers	<.01	NS	NS	NS	NS		
18.		Graduate students in business – Georgia State University (Miner and Crane, 1981)							
	56	Degree of managerial orientation in present work	<.01	NS	NS	<.05	<.01		
	56	Degree of planned managerial orientation for future work	<.01	NS	NS	NS	<.01		
19.		Selected employees – manufacturing company (Albert, 1981)							
	72	Managers vs. nonmanagers with creative jobs	<.01	NS	NS	<.01	<.05		
20.		Managers at the top and lower levels – various companies (Berman and Miner, 1985)							
	98	Top level status vs. lower managers (matched groups)	<.01	<.01	<.01	NS	NS		
21.*		Undergraduate students – Clemson University (Stahl, 1986) See Table 3.14							
	57	Fraternity or sorority president vs. no office in student organizations	<.01	NS	<.01	<.01	<.01		

Table 4.1 Continued

N	Criterion	Total score	Authority figures	Competitive games	Competitive situations	Assertive role	Imposing wishes	Standing out from group	Routine administrative functions
22.	Managers – manufacturing firm (Nystrom, 1986)								
47	Line managers vs. techno-structure	<.05							
23.*	Vocational school staff – larger schools in the state of Georgia (Goldner, 1986)								
149	Administrators vs. instructors	<.01							
24.*	Hospital chief executives – various hospitals (Holland, Black, and Miner, 1987)								
668	Compensation	<.01							
668	Hospital size	<.01							
668	Promotion rate	<.01							
668	Composite of the 3 criteria	<.01	<.05	<.05	<.01	NS	<.01	<.05	NS
25.*	Graduate students in business (Bartol and Martin, 1987)								
115	Career goal in management hierarchy	<.01							
115	Expected level in management hierarchy	<.01							
26.	Graduate students in business – State University of New York at Buffalo – tested in 1987								
68	Career choice – managerial vs. nonmanagerial	<.01							
27.	Employees of organizations in the People's Republic of China (Miner, Chen, and Yu, 1991)								
170	Managers vs. nonmanagers	<.01	NS	<.01	NS	<.01	NS	<.01	NS
28.	Employees at all levels of a small manufacturing firm (Porter, 1991)								
92	Job level	<.01	NS	NS	<.01	<.05	<.01	NS	<.01
29.	Employees in three organizations in Saudi Arabia with high OODQ H-score and low OODQ P-score (Al-Kelabi, 1991)								
86	Job satisfaction	<.05	<.05	NS	NS	NS	NS	NS	NS
86	Intention to turnover	<.05	NS	NS	NS	<.01	NS	NS	NS

*Multiple-choice adaptation of MSCS – Form H used.
Note: Significance levels are for correlations or mean score comparisons as appropriate.
Source: Developed using Miner, 1978a, 1979, and 1985

relationships not significant at at least the p <.05 level. The median validity coefficient in those instances where correlations are available is 0.35. Several of the studies contain aspects, such as subjects taken from many different organizations and criteria of questionable reliability, that would be expected to lower the median validity to a certain degree. Total score correlations in the 0.40s can be expected from sound validity studies carried out among managers in a single firm.

Generally in Table 4.1 significance is obtained with a specific subscale less frequently than for the total score and the correlations are somewhat lower when there is a significant subscale finding. Competitive Situations and Imposing Wishes produce the most consistently significant results, and much more often than not this significance is at the p <.01 level. The Assertive Role and Routine Administrative Functions subscales yield the next most consistent concurrent validity and the Authority Figures, Competitive Games, and Standing out from Group measures the least. Yet even in these latter instances significance is obtained 31 percent of the time.

Most of the criteria noted in Table 4.1 are self explanatory. However, this is less true of the career choice indexes utilized in studies 4, 5, 6 and 26, and also in slightly different form in studies 18 and 25. In the first four studies students were simply asked to write down the type of position they were preparing for, and what their occupational goal was. Then these statements were scored depending on whether there was some mention of managing or not. In study 25 the approach was essentially the same except that multiple-choice alternatives were provided. Study 18 derived measures of degree of managerial orientation (i.e. match with hierarchic theory) from career planning documents prepared by MBA students, most of whom were also currently employed. The actual correlational results obtained in this study are given in Table 4.2. The results are typical for this line of research when carried out at the graduate level. The degree of differentiation associated with managerial career goals tends to be less among undergraduates (Miner and Smith, 1969).

A problem that can arise in conducting validation research may be illustrated with reference to the Albert (1981) data – study 19. In this instance a clear differentiation between the managerial and nonmanagerial groups studied was obtained on the total score and two subscales. Not indicated in Table 4.1, however, is the fact that MSCS scores were also studied in relation to a performance rating. This rating was obtained from the president of the company for research purposes only, after it was determined that the existing management appraisal ratings suffered from so much restriction of range as to be unusable, and that bonus allocations intended to be based on merit were in fact severely contaminated. The predictor–criterion correlations obtained with the president's ratings turned out to be often *negative*, and in a few cases significantly so (p <.05). It also became apparent that there was a strong negative correlation

Table 4.2 Correlations between MSCS – Form H measures and the degree of theory-congruent managerial orientation indicated in career planning documents (N=56)

MSCS – Form H measure	Degree of managerial orientation of Present position (1)	Planned position (2)	1 and 2 combined
Total score	0.35**	0.40**	0.48**
Authority figures	0.03	0.15	0.11
Competitive games	0.17	−0.07	0.07
Competitive situations	0.03	0.12	0.09
Assertive role	0.31*	0.19	0.32**
Imposing wishes	0.32**	0.48**	0.50**
Standing out from group	0.10	0.17	0.17
Routine administrative functions	0.12	0.27*	0.24*

* p <.05
**p <.01
Source: Miner and Crane, 1981

between the age of the subjects and their ratings; the president evaluated the younger people much more positively than the older. When this age factor was partialled out, the significant negative correlations disappeared, but still no significant positive validities emerged. Given the strong value placed on youth in the ratings, there was reason to believe that real managerial effectiveness might be less of a factor and accordingly the data were not included in Table 4.1. Earlier experience had indicated that evaluating performance represented a problem for this organization. This is a situation where OODQ results would have been helpful. In any event Albert's (1977; 1981) findings make it clear that positive outcomes cannot be anticipated in every instance.

Study 29 in Table 4.1 is unique in several ways. It is the only research that has used job satisfaction, in this case measured by the Hackman and Oldham (1975) index, as a criterion. It also uses a related index of intention to turnover taken from Seashore, Lawler, Mirvis, and Cammann (1982). As predicted, those scoring higher on the MSCS-H do have greater general job satisfaction and are less inclined to leave their current employer. Secondly, study 29 did utilize the OODQ to identify subjects who were within the appropriate theoretical domain; these represent 29 percent of the subjects included in the study.

Table 4.1 does not contain the results of several concurrent studies where specific line and technostructure managerial groups were compared. The expectation is that higher managerial motivation scores will be found in those occupations and units where there is more opportunity to manage, to influence decisions, and to exert authority. The one comprehensive study across multiple units in a company – the Nystrom (1986) research of study 22 – confirms this expectation. However, there are more occupationally circumscribed studies, such as a comparison of sales managers with research and engineering managers in an oil company (Miner, 1965) and another comparison of personnel and human resource managers with other, predominantly line managers (Miner, 1976; 1979a), that also are indicative of the same result. In the former instance the line sales managers had a significantly higher total score as well as four higher subscale scores. In the latter instance the predominantly line managers were higher than those in personnel on total score and on five subscales.

Predictive validity

Table 4.3 describes the seven predictive studies that have been carried out as tests of the hierarchic theory; there are eight predictor–criterion relationships. In all but one instance subscale results are available, along with those for total score. The period between initial measurement and criterion measurement is typically in the three- to five-year range. Only in the case of the officer candidate school research – study 5 – was this period under one year.

The total score correlations in Table 4.3 range up to 0.69 (study 3), but the median value again is 0.35. The proportion of total score results that are significant is roughly the same in Tables 4.1 and 4.3. On the subscales significant predictive validity occurs with at least as high a frequency as concurrent validity in all instances except Routine Administrative Functions, where it is lower by 30 percent. Given that Competitive Games is *more* frequently valid in the predictive studies by about the same proportion, the most likely conclusion is that these are chance fluctuations. Overall it appears that the concurrent and predictive findings are essentially the same, and that as hypothesized the causal arrow flows from motivation to manage and its various aspects to subsequent behavior.

Study 5 in Table 4.3 requires some additional discussion because it is the only instance in which a criterion measure failed to yield at least one significant result. The results for the graduation versus attrition and performance rating criteria are given in Table 4.4. The picture is much like that obtained from the Albert (1977; 1981) research. Again, there were problems with the ratings (Lardent, 1979). The OCS data came from two classes and the performance ratings were obtained at the time of graduation. This meant that the low performing individuals who did not make it to graduation were not included. Whether because of this factor or for other reasons, the ratings at the end of the first class were severely inflated and there was a marked restriction of range. Accordingly the officer in charge took administrative action to correct this situation with the second class, and the ratings dropped substantially. In the research the ratings from each class were standardized and then combined. It is entirely possible, however, that the administrative intervention merely substituted one

Table 4.3 Predictive validation within the domain of the hierarchic theory

N	Criterion	Total score	Authority figures	Competitive games	Competitive situations	Assertive role	Imposing wishes	Standing out from group	Routine administrative functions
1.	R & D managers – oil company (Miner, 1965)								
49	Change in grade level	<.05	<.01	<.05	NS	NS	NS	NS	NS
2.	Marketing managers – oil company (Miner, 1965)								
81	Change in grade level	<.01	<.01	NS	<.01	NS	<.01	NS	NS
3.	R & D and marketing managers – oil company (Miner, 1965)								
61	Performance rating at separation	<.01	<.01	<.05	<.01	<.01	<.01	NS	NS
4.	Scientists, engineers, and managers – government R & D laboratory (Lacey, 1974)								
95	Promotion into management	<.05	NS	<.05	<.05	<.01	<.01	NS	NS
5.*	Army officer candidates – Fort Benning, Georgia (Butler, Lardent, and Miner, 1983)								
251	Graduation vs. attrition from OCS	<.01	NS	<.05	<.05	<.05	NS	<.05	NS
6.	U.S. military academy cadets (Butler, Lardent, and Miner, 1983)								
222	Performance ratings	NS	NS	NS	NS	<.05	NS	<.05	NS
502	Graduation vs. attrition from West Point	<.05	NS	NS	NS	NS	<.05	NS	NS
7.*	Graduate students in business (Bartol and Martin, 1987)								
97	Compensation after graduation	<.01	NS	NS	NS	<.05	<.05	NS	<.01

*Multiple-choice adaptation of MSCS – Form H used.
Note: Significance levels are for correlations or mean score comparisons as appropriate.
Source: Developed using Miner, 1978a, 1979, and 1985

Table 4.4 Correlations between MSCS – Form H scores at the beginning of army officer candidate school and end-of-course criterion measures

MSCS measures	Graduation/ attrition criterion	Overall performance rating criterion
Total score	0.36**	0.05
Authority figures	0.18	−0.06
Competitive games	0.25*	0.06
Competitive situations	0.26*	0.02
Assertive role	0.23*	0.06
Imposing wishes	0.09	0.05
Standing out from group	0.24*	0.12
Routine administrative functions	0.10	−0.05

* p <.05
**p <.01
Source: Butler, Lardent, and Miner, 1983; and Lardent, 1979

type of rating error for another. Again positive results cannot be expected under all circumstances.

Summary calculations

Given the almost identical patterns of concurrent and predictive findings, it is appropriate to combine Tables 4.1 and 4.3. When this is done, 94 percent of the 52 total score relationships included turn out to be significant. One could argue that certain findings discussed in the text perhaps should have been added to the tables, and that a few findings should not have been included in the first place. The fact is, however, that the result would have changed very little. Significance is obtained most frequently with the Competitive Situations and Imposing Wishes subscales – 56 percent of the time in the first instance and 54 percent in the second. Following in order are Assertive Role (44 percent), Routine Administrative Functions (39 percent), Competitive Games (36 percent), Authority Figures (33 percent), and Standing out from Group (31 percent). If one focuses only on findings at the p <.01 level Competitive Situations and Imposing Wishes remain the front-runners, but they are followed by Routine Administrative Functions (26 percent) and Authority Figures (23 percent). On this evidence the Authority Figures subscale is a somewhat stronger predictor than might otherwise be indicated. None of the subscales can be said to lack validity, although there are differences among them.

Another consideration is the extent to which validity has been retained over time. Does Form H, constructed as it was in the 1950s, work as well in the 1980s as it once did? The data are contained in Table 4.5. The dates used are taken from Tables 4.1 and 4.3. In some instances the actual data

Table 4.5 Percent of predictor–criterion relationships significant (p <.05) in each decade

MSCS measures	1960s (Based on 9 studies and 16 relationships)	1970s (Based on 11 studies and 13 relationships)	1980s (Based on 13 studies and 19 relationships)	1990s (Based on 3 studies and 4 relationships)
Total score	88%	100%	95%	100%
Authority figures	47	33	18	25
Competitive games	33	56	27	25
Competitive situations	67	56	45	50
Assertive role	47	11	55	75
Imposing wishes	53	67	55	25
Standing out from group	33	22	36	25
Routine administrative functions	33	44	36	50

were collected in the previous decade – certain 1960s data in the 1950s, for instance. However, the sequencing over time is the same.

The total score findings are consistent; overall the MSCS-H is working as well now as it ever did. The Competitive Situations, Standing out from Group, and Routine Administrative Functions subscales appear to remain equally valid over time, as well. The role of favorable attitudes to authority in managerial success appears to be declining; it now matters less that one have positive attitudes upward. Competitive Games yielded very frequent validity in the 1970s but has dropped to essentially its original level in the 1980s and 1990s. Assertive Role was valid much less often in the 1970s; however, the 1980s saw a substantial rebirth which has continued. Given the discussion of this variable in Chapter 1, this finding is important. Changing gender roles appear to have had an initial impact on the significance of traditional masculine assertiveness for managerial performance, but more recently this factor has emerged as a major input to managerial effectiveness; the subscale clearly is not outmoded. Imposing Wishes has remained quite stable in its validity until the 1990s; now it is down. However, the 1990s data are too sparse to interpret.

What about the use of a multiple-choice version of the MSCS-H? Does validity go up, or down? There are eight studies in the 1970s and 1980s that use the multiple-choice format, and 13 predictor–criterion relationships result. On the total score measure 92 percent of the validities are significant, all at the p <.01 level. Clearly validity does not suffer in this respect. Among the subscales, there is no instance in which the validities can be said to suffer. This is particularly important because the Imposing Wishes and Routine Administrative Functions subscales have not been shown to be related to their free response counterparts. Yet 67 percent of the Imposing Wishes results are significant, and 50 percent of the Routine Administrative Functions findings. To date it cannot be said that these subscales are any the less valid – quite the contrary.

Finally, there is the issue of whether validity is more frequent when Miner is an author. Studies published in the 1960s and early 1970s were almost entirely of this nature. Projective techniques are not widely taught in industrial/organizational psychology and organizational behavior and accordingly studies not involving the author were slow to emerge. There has been a legitimate concern on this matter; is validity something that only Miner can create? There are now 20 studies involving 34 criterion relationships within the domain in which Miner held a degree of authorship, and 16 studies involving 18 relationships where he did not. Among the former, significant total score validities were obtained with 91 percent of the criterion relationships; among the latter, where Miner was not an author, this figure was 100 percent. There are 10 studies in which Miner had absolutely no involvement of any kind, and in every instance the total score validities were statistically significant. In most instances Miner was not aware these studies were being conducted, and none involved people who were or had been his graduate students.

VALIDITY OUTSIDE THE THEORY'S DOMAIN

The hierarchic role motivation theory not only says something about when validity can be expected, but also about when it cannot be expected. Hierarchic theory should not work within the professional, task, and group domains and this includes positions that are designated as managerial or supervisory if they are within these domains rather than the hierarchic. Furthermore, hierarchic theory applies only to the key participants in hierarchic systems – the managers. It should not predict the success of a salesperson or a secretary. Thus success criteria which have no aspects in common with managerial performance would not be expected to yield significant positive validities. Examples are the grade point averages of college students and the earnings of lawyers.

Concurrent validity

Table 4.6 contains the results obtained from 18 studies of a concurrent nature involving 39 criterion relationships. There are five total score relationships that are significant of the 39, but all are negative – high scoring research scientists and engineers being promoted *less* within their professional context and chief executive entrepreneurs in task systems scoring *lower* than corporate managers at the lower and middle levels. There are six significant positive coefficients scattered across the subscales, but these are matched by 13 significant negative coefficients. If there is any overall trend in Table 4.6 it is one toward negative relationships between the MSCS – Form H and criteria, but no single subscale yields more than a 16 percent significance rate; even the negative relationships are scattered. The data come from a wide range of systems including professional (small school systems, a consulting firm, university faculties, a research laboratory, academic libraries, and the nursing components of hospitals), task (a number of entrepreneurs), and group (small unstructured case study groups at a university). There are also sales personnel in a hierarchic system measured against sales success and several samples of university students measured against academic success. A wider sampling of domains outside that of hierarchic theory might unearth certain consistent positive findings, but no concurrent study has done that as yet.

Predictive validity

Table 4.7 describes the four predictive studies that have been done outside the hierarchic domain; there are 10 predictor–criterion relationships. One

Table 4.6 Concurrent validation outside the domain of the hierarchic theory

N	Criterion	Total score	Authority figures	Competitive games	Competitive situations	Assertive role	Imposing wishes	Standing out from group	Routine administrative functions
1.	Dealer sales personnel – oil company (Miner, 1962)								
65	Sales figures	NS	NS	NS	NS	NS	NS	NS	NS
2.	Undergraduate business students – University of Oregon (Miner, 1965)								
190	Grade point average	NS	--------						
3.	School administrators – medium-sized city (Miner, 1967; 1968)								
57	Grade level	NS	NS	NS	NS	NS	NS	NS	NS
57	Compensation	NS	NS	NS	NS	NS	NS	NS	NS
57	Performance rating	NS	NS	NS	NS	<.05	NS	NS	NS
57	Advancement potential rating	NS	<.05	NS	NS	NS	NS	NS	NS
4.	School administrators – small-sized city (Miner, 1967; 1968)								
44	Grade level	NS	NS	NS	NS	NS	NS	NS	NS
44	Compensation	NS	NS	NS	NS	NS	NS	NS	NS
44	Performance rating	NS	NS	NS	NS	NS	NS	NS	NS
44	Advancement potential rating	NS	NS	NS	NS	NS	NS	NS	NS
5.	School administrators – small consolidated district (Miner, 1967; 1968)								
36	Grade level	NS	NS	NS	NS	NS	NS	NS	NS
36	Compensation	NS	NS	NS	NS	NS	NS	NS	NS
36	Performance rating	NS	NS	NS	NS	NS	NS	NS	NS
36	Advancement potential rating	NS	NS	NS	NS	NS	NS	NS	NS
6.	Management consultants – U.S. office of a large international consulting firm (Miner, 1971)								
24	Performance rating	NS	NS	NS	NS	NS	NS	NS	NS
24	Advancement potential rating	NS	NS	NS	NS	NS	NS	NS	NS
24	Compensation	NS	NS	NS	NS	NS	NS	NS	NS

Table 4.6 Continued

N	Criterion	Total score	Authority figures	Competitive games	Competitive situations	Assertive role	Imposing wishes	Standing out from group	Routine administrative functions
7.	Undergraduate students in business in small, unstructured groups – University of South Florida (Miner, Rizzo, Harlow, and Hill, 1974)								
72	Peer rating of leadership potential	NS	NS	NS	NS	NS	NS	NS	NS
8.	Undergraduate management majors – Georgia State University (Albert, 1977)								
66	Grade point average	NS	NS	NS	NS	NS	NS	NS	NS
9.	Undergraduate humanities majors – Georgia State University (Albert, 1977)								
46	Grade point average	NS	NS	(<.05)	NS	NS	NS	NS	NS
10.	Business school faculty members – various schools (Miner, 1977)								
49	Academic rank	NS	NS	NS	NS	NS	NS	NS	NS
49	Promotion into administration	NS	NS	NS	NS	NS	NS	NS	NS
11.	Scientists and engineers – government R & D laboratory (Gantz, Erickson, and Stephenson, 1977a)								
117	Promotion rate	(<.05)							
12.	Academic library employees – small libraries (Dayani, 1980)								
69	Managers vs. nonmanagers	NS	NS	NS	NS	NS	NS	NS	NS
13.	University professors of management – various universities (Miner, 1980c)								
112	Compensation	NS	NS	NS	NS	NS	NS	NS	<.05
112	Academic rank	NS	NS	NS	NS	NS	NS	NS	NS
112	Publications	NS	NS	<.01	NS	NS	NS	NS	NS
112	Promotion into administration	NS	NS	NS	NS	NS	NS	NS	NS
112	Supervising dissertations	NS	NS	NS	NS	NS	NS	NS	NS
14.	Hospital nursing managers – various hospitals (Holland, 1981)								
34	Promotion in administration	NS	NS	NS	NS	NS	NS	NS	NS

15. Entrepreneurs and lower managers – various companies (Smith and Miner, 1983)

155 Entrepreneurs vs. lower managers	NS	NS	NS	NS	NS	NS	NS
88 Entrepreneurs vs. lower managers	NS	NS	NS	(<.05)	NS	(<.05)	NS
68 Entrepreneurs vs. lower managers	(<.01)	(<.05)	(<.05)	(<.01)	(<.05)	NS	NS

16. Entrepreneurs and middle managers – various companies (Smith and Miner, 1983)

68 Entrepreneurs vs. middle managers	(<.01)	(<.05)	NS	NS	NS	NS	NS
68 Entrepreneurs vs. middle managers	(<.01)	(<.05)	(<.01)	(<.05)	(<.05)	NS	NS
75 Entrepreneurs vs. middle managers	(<.01)	(<.05)	NS	(<.05)	NS	NS	NS

17. Entrepreneurs at the top and lower level managers – various companies (Berman and Miner, 1985)

91 Entrepreneurs vs. lower level managers	NS	NS	NS	NS	<.05	NS	NS

18. Employees in three organizations in Saudi Arabia with Low OODQ H-score and High OODQ P-score (Al-Kelabi, 1991)

36 Job satisfaction	NS	NS	<.01	NS	NS	NS	NS
36 Intention to turnover	NS	NS	NS	NS	NS	NS	NS

Note: Significance levels are for correlations or mean score comparisons as appropriate. Parentheses ( ) indicate negative relationships.
Source: Developed using Miner, 1978a and 1979

Table 4.7 Predictive validation outside the domain of the hierarchic theory

N	Criterion	Total score	Authority figures	Competitive games	Competitive situations	Assertive role	Imposing wishes	Standing out from group	Routine administrative functions
1.	R & D researchers – oil company (Miner, 1965a)								
19	Change in grade level	(<.05)							
2.	Management consultants – U.S. offices of a large international consulting firm (Miner, 1971)								
51	Performance rating	NS	NS	NS	NS	NS	<.05	NS	NS
51	Advancement potential rating	NS	NS	NS	NS	NS	<.05	NS	NS
51	Compensation	NS	NS	NS	NS	NS	<.01	NS	NS
51	Per diem charge to clients	NS	NS	NS	NS	NS	<.01	NS	NS
3.	Management consultants – foreign offices of a large international consulting firm (Miner, 1971)								
30	Performance rating	NS	NS	NS	NS	NS	NS	NS	NS
30	Advancement potential rating	NS	NS	NS	NS	NS	NS	NS	NS
30	Compensation	NS	NS	NS	NS	NS	NS	NS	NS
30	Per diem charge to clients	NS	NS	NS	NS	NS	NS	NS	NS
4.*	Graduate students in business (Bartol and Martin, 1987)								
174	Grade point average	NS							

*Multiple-choice adaptation of MSCS – Form H used.
Note: Significance levels are for correlations. Parentheses ( ) indicate negative relationships.
Source: Developed using Miner, 1978a and 1979

total score relationship achieves significance (negatively) and there are four significant positive relationships involving Imposing Wishes. That is the sum total of all significant results obtained using a predictive design. The four criteria used in study 2 are all intercorrelated at the 0.50 level and above, a factor which clearly contributes to the consistency of the Imposing Wishes finding. All four studies are multi-year in duration, extending up to five years. Except for the student study (number 4), all the predictive research has been conducted in professional contexts. The predictive studies, although small in number, yield essentially the same results (or better, lack of results) as the concurrent. Thus, the two types of studies serve to reinforce one another. Strong motivation to manage does not make one a better performer and more successful person in a general sense.

Summary calculations

Across both Tables 4.6 and 4.7 for total score, 12 percent of the criterion relationships are significant, all of which are negative. Thus there are no significant positive total score relationships outside the domain, as contrasted with the 94 percent figure obtained within the domain. Among the subscales, Imposing Wishes and Assertive Role yield the most frequent significance – 13 percent – but only the former produces any meaningful positive significance (11 percent). Competitive Games also has a significance frequency above 10 percent, but in this case the relationships are practically all negative. Actually, except for Imposing Wishes, no subscale yields a positive significance frequency above 4 percent. Even the Imposing Wishes differential is substantial – 11 percent versus 54 percent within the domain.

There are six studies and 15 criterion relationships dated in the 1960s, eight studies and 17 criterion relationships in the 1970s, seven studies and 15 criterion relationships in the 1980s, and one study and two criterion relationships in the 1990s. Thus, the extra-domain research is well distributed over time. Significant positive and negative relationships occur in each decade (except the 1990s). The only consistent patterning is the rather frequent negative results achieved in concurrent studies 15 and 16 with entrepreneurs in the 1980s. These studies utilize the same group of entrepreneurs in all six instances, but in combination with different groups of managers. Overall, the within-domain and outside-domain differential has remained very stable over time.

Research outside the hierarchic domain has made use of the free response MSCS-H almost entirely. Only predictive study 4 employed the multiple-choice version; no significant results were reported.

Only seven of the 22 studies did not involve Miner as an author, all from the latter half of the 1970s or later. Except for a couple of significant negative relationships and one positive, these studies produced no significant results at all. Taking the 25 criterion relationships involving total score reported by authors writing independently of Miner, 100 percent of the within-domain relationships are positive and significant, and none of the outside-domain relationships are positive and significant.

RELATED LITERATURES

Where might one go to find assessments of this research? Has research on managers conducted by others, with different instruments, identified constructs conceptually similar to those of hierarchic theory? These questions are the concern of this section. The section following will take up actual construct validity research where the MSCS – Form H is related to other instruments and measures.

Reviews and discussions

The author has periodically reviewed research on the hierarchic theory over the years. Although the present volume provides by far the most comprehensive and up to date coverage, other efforts along the same lines should be noted. Various books have dealt with this research in varying degrees of detail. These include *Studies in Management Education* (Miner, 1965), *The School Administrator and Organizational Character* (Miner, 1967), *The Human Constraint: The Coming Shortage of Managerial Talent* (Miner, 1974b), *Motivation to Manage: A Ten-year Update on the 'Studies in Management Education' Research* (Miner, 1977), *Organizational Behavior: Performance and Productivity* (Miner, 1988), and *Industrial-Organizational Psychology* (Miner, 1992).

In addition there have been several review articles. The first appeared in the *Harvard Business Review* (Miner, 1973). Subsequently a much more comprehensive review was published in *Personnel Psychology* (Miner, 1978a). Most recently a paper originally presented at a Virginia Polytechnic Institute and State University symposium on personality assessment has been published as a chapter in a book edited by John Bernardin and David Bownas (Miner, 1985). A reading of these books and articles spanning a period of some 25 years will provide considerable insight into how research on hierarchic role motivation theory has expanded over time.

However, such a reading will not necessarily provide an objective, detached assessment of this research. For that it is necessary to shift to reviews and discussions by others. The first such assessment that the author is aware of appears in a general review of predictors of managerial performance written by Korman (1968). Yukl (1981) included a section dealing with the research on managerial motivation in the first edition of his leadership text. Bass (1981) treats this same research at some length in his revision of Stogdill's *Handbook of Leadership*. Reilly and Chao (1982) consider the MSCS-H and certain research related to it in their review of alternative employee selection procedures. Cornelius (1983) provides an extensive review of the use of projective techniques in personnel selection which includes a lengthy treatment of the motivation to manage research. Schneider and Schmitt (1986) draw upon the Cornelius (1983) review and other sources in discussing research on hierarchic theory in the second edition of their staffing text. Locke and Henne (1986) include a section on 'Miner's role motivation theory' in their review of motivation theories generally, and Yukl (1989) provides a substantially updated literature review in his second edition, as does Bass (1990) in his third. Finally, Slevin (1989) summarizes the research for the purpose of applying it to the practical problems of managers.

These reviewers generally have reacted favorably to the research on hierarchic theory. The only real exception is the Reilly and Chao (1982) article, which turned out to be highly selective in its presentation of the available research in spite of the fact that a much more extensive sampling of studies was provided to the authors. Bass (1981; 1990) gives a generally balanced, yet positive treatment, although he has difficulty reconciling the motivation to manage findings with his perception of the research on participative management. It should be noted also that certain writers have incorporated much more negative interpretations of the hierarchic theory research in presentations of their own research findings. An article by Brief, Aldag, and Chacko (1977) and an article by Stahl, Grigsby, and Gulati (1985), followed later by a book by Stahl (1986), are of this nature. The issues involved in these criticisms will be considered at length in the final chapter.

Meta-analyses

A meta-analysis of certain research published through 1980 was carried out by Nathan and Alexander (1985). The results of this treatment are best presented in the authors' own words:

> Miner's theory rests on the proposition that a person's ability to success-fully function in a hierarchic or bureaucratic organization will vary to the degree that an individual possesses the six 'desires' associated with a willingness or motivation to manage. On the other hand, possession of these six desires will not be associated with job performance in other domains of organizations. Our results were quite consistent with the conclusions reached by Miner in his 1978 review article. Miner concluded that total score and competitive motivation are strongly consist-ent with the managerial role theory, imposing wishes and positive atti-tude toward authority figures are generally consistent with the theory,

but some inconsistency with the theory may exist for the desire to stand out from the group. Using meta-analysis, we found that the desire to compete, to impose wishes, to perform routine administrative functions and to a lesser degree, the desire for positive relations with authority figures, were all unrelated to performance outside their theorized domain and related to performance within their theoretical domain (though the results for Authority Figures were somewhat ambiguous within the theoretical domain). Thus for at least three and possibly four constructs, there was evidence of both convergent validity, i.e., a relationship between the instrument designed to measure the constructs (the *MSCS*) and the nontest indicant of the presence of these constructs (performance), and discriminant validity, i.e., a lack of relationship where none was predicted. Construct validity was not found for two subscales, those measuring the desire to be assertive, and the desire to stand out from the group.

(Nathan and Alexander, 1985: 227)

This analysis was conducted at an early point, used only the free response MSCS and did not include data from student samples. As a result the number of studies included is rather small. Nevertheless the findings are entirely consistent with the results reported for the 1960s and 1970s in Table 4.5. The actual data on which the Nathan and Alexander (1985) conclusions are based are given in Table 4.8.

A second meta-analysis based on a much larger number of studies, but restricted to total scores and research within the domain, was conducted by Carson and Gilliard (1992). This analysis utilized 26 published studies. It does not incorporate data from many of the dissertations and unpublished sources noted in Tables 4.1 and 4.3, nor are some of the very recent studies included. The results are given in Table 4.9. Separate analyses are reported for six types of criteria. In five of the six instances the effect sizes are significant, consistent with role motivation theory predictions. The only departure is that managers were not clearly differentiated from entrepreneurs on the MSCS-H. The effect sizes for performance ratings, line as opposed to staff status, and managerial career plans can be viewed as substantial, given that only minimal correction was made for artifacts that might attenuate the results. Again the meta-analytic findings reinforce the conclusions derived from other approaches.

Conceptually similar research

There are, in addition to the research conducted for the specific purpose of testing hierarchic role motivation theory, a number of studies carried out quite independent of the theory, but utilizing conceptually similar measures, which yield results appearing to be generally consistent with it.

Table 4.8 Results of a meta-analysis using MSCS-H total and subscale scores within and outside the hierarchic domain and combined across both domains

Subscale	Domain	Observed				Bayesian prior distribution			In vs out comparison	
		$\bar{r}$	SD	%$\sigma^2 e^a$	$SD\rho^b$	Lower 90% c.v.[c]	$\hat{\rho}$	Upper 90% c.v.[c]	$\hat{\rho}$ diff	% Overlap
Authority figures	Both	0.13	0.139	69	0.147	0.01	0.26	0.50		
	Within	0.18	0.151	49	0.205	0.01	0.35	0.69	0.24	35
	Outside	0.06	0.217	100	0.080	0.03	0.11	0.19		
Compete (games)	Both	0.08	0.098	100	0.059	0.06	0.15	0.25		
	Within	0.11	0.111	91	0.067	0.11	0.21	0.32	0.13	21
	Outside	0.04	0.056	100	0.034	0.02	0.08	0.13		
Compete (situations)	Both	0.18	0.152	58	0.189	0.04	0.35	0.66		
	Within	0.27	0.077	100	0.046	0.45	0.53	0.60	0.45	0
	Outside	0.04	0.127	100	0.077	−0.05	0.08	0.21		
Assertive motivation	Both	0.09	0.099	100	0.059	0.07	0.16	0.26		
	Within	0.09	0.113	86	0.080	0.03	0.17	0.30	0.01	96
	Outside	0.08	0.074	100	0.044	0.09	0.16	0.23		
Impose wishes	Both	0.08	0.136	70	0.142	0.04	0.15	0.38		
	Within	0.14	0.106	100	0.063	0.18	0.27	0.35	0.29	0
	Outside	−0.01	0.126	100	0.077	−0.15	0.03	0.10		
Stand out from group	Both	0.09	0.093	100	0.056	0.08	0.17	0.26		
	Within	0.08	0.104	100	0.063	0.04	0.14	0.25	−0.06	55
	Outside	0.11	0.069	100	0.042	0.14	0.21	0.28		
Routine tasks	Both	0.06	0.097	100	0.059	0.02	0.12	0.21		
	Within	0.08	0.019	100	0.036	0.10	0.16	0.22	0.09	17
	Outside	0.03	0.055	92	0.033	0.01	0.07	0.12		
MSCS total	Both	0.21	0.130	81	0.092	0.19	0.34	0.49		
	Within	0.28	0.094	100	0.048	0.40	0.46	0.52	0.32	0
	Outside	0.09	0.082	100	0.042	0.07	0.14	0.21		

Note: For subscales, total N across 10 studies = 744.33 (fractional N due to sample size weighted average of multiple criteria). Total N for 5 studies within domain = 466.33, total N for 5 studies outside domain = 298. For MSCS total score, total N for 6 studies within domain = 493.33, for 5 studies outside domain N = 298.
[a] Percentage of observed variance accounted for by statistical artifacts.
[b] Residual SD is computed from the greater of: actual residual variance or 10% of total observed variance.
[c] c.v. = credibility value.
Source: Nathan and Alexander, 1985: 226

Ghiselli (1971) presents findings indicating that of the 13 variables measured by the Self-Description Inventory (SDI), six are strongly related to managerial success; in order of correlation magnitude these are supervisory ability, occupational achievement, intelligence, self-actualization, self-assurance, and decisiveness. Of these six, all but intelligence are concep-

Table 4.9 Results of a meta-analysis using MSCS-H total scores within the hierarchic domain

Variable	Number of studies	Total sample size	Corrected mean effect[a]	Credibility interval	Confidence interval
Performance ratings	14	1145	0.35	0.17, 0.53	0.30, 0.40[c]
Management level	27	2151	0.13	−0.20, 0.45	0.06, 0.20[b]
Salary	5	1123	0.13	−0.01, 0.27	0.05, 0.21[b]
Line/staff	5	185	0.34	0.28, 0.39	0.20, 0.47[c]
Manager/ entrepreneur	7	300	0.09	−0.41, 0.60	−0.11, 0.30[b]
Career plan	5	319	0.37	−[d]	0.27, 0.47[c]

[a] Corrected for MSCS unreliability only.
[b] Confidence interval for heterogeneous effects.
[c] Confidence interval for homogeneous effects.
[d] All variance in effects accounted for by sampling error.
Source: Carson and Gilliard, 1993

tually similar to the variables of role motivation theory. Harrell and Harrell (1973) report good results with the SDI when used to predict the subsequent success of Stanford University MBAs. However, the very sizable correlations among the six SDI variables (Miner, 1978) raise questions about the independent designations and suggest a single factor of managerial talent (or motivation) may be operating within the instrument.

A comprehensive study of 468 managers in 13 firms conducted by Mahoney, Jerdee, and Nash (1960) revealed significant relationships with effectiveness ratings for the dominance score obtained from the California Psychological Inventory and for a number of face valid indexes from the Strong Vocational Interest Blank. Nash (1966) subsequently developed a managerial key for the latter instrument which correlated 0.33 with effectiveness ratings in a cross validation sample. His description of the responses of managers scoring high on this key has considerable conceptual similarity to role motivation theory, as reflected in the desire to 'assume a leadership or dominant role', for instance.

An early report of an extensive program of research on executive selection at Sears, Roebuck (Bentz, 1967) reveals certain measures as consistently predictive of success across a number of studies. The most consistent predictors of a personality or motivational nature were the sociability, general activity, social leadership, dominance, self-confidence, and tolerance scales from the Guilford–Martin Personality Inventories; the economic and political value measures from the Allport–Vernon Study of Values; and the persuasive index from the Kuder Preference Record. This pattern has considerable conceptual similarity with the constructs of role motivation theory. It also has been found to be amazingly stable over many years (Bentz, 1985).

The initial assessment center research at AT&T (American Telephone and Telegraph Company) suggested that managerial success in that company required characteristics similar to those identified at Sears, Roebuck (Bray, Campbell, and Grant, 1974). The best predictors among the 25 variables rated in the assessment center were oral communication skills, human relations skills, need for advancement, resistance to stress, tolerance of uncertainty, organization and planning, and energy (all with correlations with promotion of approximately 0.30). The overall findings are summarized as indicating that successful managers are high on administrative skills (organizes work effectively and makes decisions willingly), high on interpersonal skills (makes a forceful and likable impression, leads others to perform), high on intellectual ability, highly stable in performance (even when faced with uncertainty and stress), high on work motivation, high on career orientation (wants to advance rapidly), and low on dependence on others. At the very least these variables are conceptually similar to the competitiveness, assertiveness, and routine administrative functions components of role motivation theory. As at Sears, Roebuck, these kinds of characteristics have continued to operate to determine success levels at AT&T over a number of years (Howard and Bray, 1988).

A recent re-analysis of some of the data used in earlier years to refute the trait theory of leadership not only produced evidence in support of a trait interpretation, but identified certain specific traits much like those of the hierarchic theory (Lord, DeVader, and Alliger, 1986; Lord and Maher, 1991). Evidence was obtained in support of intelligence, dominance, and masculinity–femininity as predictors. The support for masculinity is of particular interest in view of arguments that hierarchic role motivation theory if anything underestimates the significance of macho characteristics for managing (Suojanen and Suojanen, 1980).

There are also a number of conceptually similar findings that have emerged from studies using projective techniques. Piotrowski and Rock (1963) administered the Rorschach Test to over 100 top managers assessed by Edward N. Hay and Associates. The characteristics identified as predominating among the more successful were the drive for power, foresight and anticipation of challenge, self-confidence, friendly cooperation and competition, integration and spontaneity, mental productivity, and controlled aggressiveness. The emphasis on competitiveness, assertiveness, and power motivation seem particularly relevant to hierarchic theory.

An early study of top executives using the Thematic Apperception Test (TAT) found that successful executives had characteristics much like those of hierarchic theory as well (Henry, 1949). They possessed a strong desire for achievement, a strong desire for social advancement, a liking for their superiors, decisiveness, assertiveness, and practicality.

The TAT also plays an important role in research on McClelland's (1975) theory attributing managerial success to socialized power motivation. In this theory the successful manager is one who inhibits or mutes the expression of strong power needs in order to make them conform to the demands of cooperative endeavor. McClelland and Burnham (1976) and McClelland and Boyatzis (1982) present evidence in support of this view. At a very minimum there is a strong parallel between the Imposing Wishes subscale of the MSCS and McClelland's power need.

This brief review of research on managerial success and effectiveness is far from complete. What it does accomplish, however, is to indicate that the kinds of variables incorporated in hierarchic role motivation theory have been found important by other researchers using instruments other than the MSCS – Form H. In the broader context of research on managers it makes sense that the hierarchic theory works as it does. In this sense the review of conceptually similar research represents a contribution to the external validity of the theory.

CONSTRUCT VALIDATION

Much of what has been said previously in this chapter relates to construct validity. These findings consistently support the interpretation that the hierarchic theory as operationalized with the MSCS – Form H *is* dealing with motivation to manage and *not* with some other type of motivation. Where comparisons have been made between managers, or those desiring to become managers, or those picked as having management potential based on their observed performance in a bureaucratic setting, and other groups, significant differences in the expected direction typically have been obtained.

There is, however, a substantial body of research, extending beyond that discussed previously, which bears on the construct validity issue. These studies typically serve to identify other measures that are related to the MSCS – Form H. If construct validity is present, certain relationships would be expected to appear, and others would not. Empirical analyses of this type will concern us here.

Projective and nonprojective measurement

Projective measures are not intended to measure the same concepts as self-report measures, even though they happen to have the same or similar labels. Therefore, a multitrait-multimethod analysis using projectives and self-report measures as alternative methods for assessing the same construct is conceptually inappropriate.

(Cornelius, 1983: 147)

This view has been stated in various forms for many years. For instance, Hermans (1970) presented evidence on the issue at an early point using measures of achievement motivation. Because they tap unconscious motives and allow the individual to exhibit thought processes that are relatively free of social desirability, conformity pressures, and defensiveness compared with nonprojective tests (such as self-report measures that use a multiple-choice format), projective measures would not be expected to correlate highly with nonprojective measures of the same motives. Yet it is also true that some construct overlap would be expected, simply because the conscious processes that are paramount in self-report procedures are not completely lacking in projective measures. To the degree there is some common variance, projective and nonprojective measures should be correlated. Accordingly significant but low correlations between the MSCS – Form H variables and nonprojective measures dealing with conceptually similar constructs should be anticipated.

One line of research bearing on this issue is the work done to develop a supervisory interest scale for the Kuder Preference Record discussed in Chapter 3. Some correlation between MSCS – Form H total score and this supervisory scale would be expected. Within a sample of 77 Atlantic Refining Company managers, this value was 0.45 (p <.01). In this study all of the MSCS subscales correlated significantly with the Kuder measure except Assertive Role and Routine Administrative Functions; these subscale correlations ranged from 0.19 to 0.32 (Miner, 1965). A second study using a diversified sample of human resource managers obtained a total score correlation of 0.38 (p <.01); significant subscale correlations ranging from 0.21 to 0.34 were obtained for Competitive Games, Competitive Situations, Assertive Role, and Standing out from Group (Miner, 1977).

A second approach to the same question utilized self-report items developed by Ebrahimi (1984) and the MSCS – Form H. As indicated in Table 4.10, there was one self-report item which should relate in an overall sense to the MSCS total score, one relating primarily to Authority Figures, two relating to Competitive Games, one relating to Competitive Situations, one relating to Assertive Role, one relating to Imposing Wishes, one relating to Standing out from Group, and two relating to Routine Administrative Functions – ten in all. This analysis utilized samples drawn from two sources (Miner, Wachtel, and Ebrahimi, 1989). The first sample contained 82 graduate business students from some 15 universities distributed throughout the United States. The second sample contained 100 comparable students in the MBA program at Georgia State University in Atlanta.

These analyses with U.S. business students indicate a moderate relationship between the self-report items and both comparable MSCS scales and MSCS total score. In Table 4.10, where significance is not obtained when it would be expected, more than half of the instances involve the Routine Administrative Functions self-report items; in this latter instance the self-

Table 4.10 Correlations between MSCS – Form H measures and self-report items in two samples of graduate business students

| | Correlations for expected relationships | | | | Median correlation where no relationship is expected | |
| | Same concepts | | MSCS total score | | | |
Self-report items	15 University sample	Ga. State sample	15 University sample	Ga. State sample	15 University sample	Ga. State sample
I like managing and supervising people.	0.35**	0.33**	0.35**	0.33**	0.15	0.18*
I like and respect people with power and authority.	0.24*	0.23**	0.24*	0.29**	0.11	0.14
I enjoy participating in competitive games and sports.	0.55**	0.11	0.32**	0.27**	0.06	0.15
I like American football.	0.45**	0.05	0.42**	0.12	0.16	0.12
I enjoy being involved in jobs requiring competition with others.	0.20	0.30**	0.37**	0.34**	0.19**	0.16
I can tactfully say 'no' to a person when I disagree with him or her.	−0.04	0.27**	0.20*	0.23**	0.13	0.09
I usually talk my friends into doing something I like them to do.	0.31**	0.17*	0.24*	0.35**	0.10	0.16
I enjoy being the center of attention.	0.15	0.31**	0.28**	0.28**	0.10	0.10
I keep a very organized set of files and records.	0.13	0.05	0.18	0.15	0.09	0.06
I enjoy making decisions.	0.16	0.09	0.33**	0.36**	0.20*	0.22*

MSCS – Form H subscales					
Authority figures				0.14	0.15
Competitive games				0.16	0.11
Competitive situations				0.10	0.11
Assertive role				0.14	0.16
Imposing wishes				0.17	0.14
Standing out from group				0.11	0.15
Routine administrative functions				0.08	0.05
Median correlation	0.22*	0.20*	0.30**	0.29**	0.13	0.14
Percent significant correlations (p <.05)	60%	60%	90%	80%	12%	12%

Source: Ebrahimi, 1984 and Wachtel, 1986

report measures appear not to have been appropriately conceptualized. In any event the data overall are consistent with expectations. Hypothesized correlations, supporting construct validity, are higher, and more consistently statistically significant, than relationships with variables non-supportive of construct validity. Furthermore, the findings are very consistent across the two samples.

Similar analyses have been carried out using samples of students studying in the United States from Thailand, Iran, Nigeria, India, and a variety of Pacific rim nations. All of these students responded in English (Ebrahimi, 1984; Ebrahimi and Miner, 1991). In addition, Spanish language versions of the instruments have been applied to graduate business students at the Universidad Nacional Autonoma de Mexico and to business students (both graduate and undergraduate) from Mexico studying at 23 United States universities (Wachtel, 1986). Because of language and cultural factors, these analyses may not be as indicative of basic construct validity as the data of Table 4.10. Nevertheless, they yield much the same results. They will be treated further in Chapter 9 dealing with international comparisons.

The results reported to this point are consistent with the view that there is some overlap between managerial motivation as measured by a projective technique and managerial motivation as measured by self-report indexes. Thus, these results support an assessment that construct validity is present. However, certain results reported by Stahl (1986) seem to be at variance with this interpretation.

Stahl has developed an instrument called the Job Choice Exercise (JCE) that purports to measure the needs for affiliation, power, and achievement as incorporated in McClelland's (1961; 1975) theory. Whether in fact the JCE measures the constructs of McClelland's theory is an open question at present, since studies relating JCE and TAT measures do not exist; as we will see, there are questions in this regard. In any event, Stahl (1986) interprets McClelland to the effect that high need for achievement combined with high need for power produce high managerial motivation. This certainly is not McClelland's most recent position (see, for example, McClelland and Boyatzis, 1982). However, Stahl does put forth his index of combined achievement and power motivation as a measure of managerial motivation. He then tests the hypothesis that his and the author's constructs are the same by correlating the JCE with the multiple-choice version of the MSCS – Form H.

The data provide little evidence of any relationship between the two measures, thus appearing to indicate a problem in construct validity. However, this interpretation can be seriously questioned. The JCE asks the respondent to make conscious choices among affiliation, achievement, and power-related alternatives. It is not only a self-report instrument but, like many instruments rooted in behavioral decision theory, it incorporates a strong cognitive component. The extent to which it represents a measure of *motivation* at all has not been established. Accordingly, the best interpretation available at present appears to be that the JCE represents an extreme case of the situation where conscious processes dominate responses, that it is at the far end of the projective–nonprojective continuum and thus furthest removed from the MSCS – Form H. If this is true, the lack of correlation between the JCE and the MSCS – Form H has little relevance for the latter's construct validity. Clearly, however, there is a need for empirical clarification of the many uncertainties surrounding the McClelland, Miner, and Stahl theories, and the relationships among them.

Relationships with other constructs

Another approach to the construct validity question is to correlate the MSCS – Form H with other tests and instruments which although ostensibly measuring different constructs, may have some overlap with the variables of hierarchic role motivation theory. Probably the most comprehensive research of this kind has involved the Ghiselli Self-Description Inventory (SDI) which is an extensively researched instrument of the adjective checklist variety (Ghiselli, 1971). There has been considerable controversy regarding the relationship between the SDI and MSCS – Form H, and what would and would not be expected (Brief, Aldag, and Chacko, 1977; Miner, 1978; Aldag and Brief, undated; Bowin, 1980). The data of Table 4.11 have been brought together from a variety of sources in the hope of answering the questions that have been raised. The studies utilized relatively large samples of human resource managers, students, military officer candidate trainees, and entrepreneurs; thus, the data derive from diverse sources.

What is immediately evident from Table 4.11 is that substantial relationships between the two predictors of managerial success exist. The SDI measures showing relationships most frequently (in order) are Decisiveness, Self assurance, Initiative, Self actualization, Supervisory ability, Lack of need for security, Lack of need for high financial reward, and Occupational achievement. There is little evidence of relationship for Intelligence, Working-class affinity, Need for power, Maturity, and Masculinity–femininity. Among the MSCS measures, the most frequent relationships (in order) are for Competitive Situations, Total Score, Standing out from Group, Competitive Games, Imposing Wishes, Assertive Role, Authority Figures, and Routine Administrative Functions (which really is not related at all). Where one would expect to find relationships are with the SDI measures that involve managerial talent which Ghiselli (1971: 165) says are Supervisory ability, Occupational achievement, Intelligence, Self actualization, Self assurance, and Decisiveness. All of these measures, except Intelligence, show frequent, significant relationships with the MSCS. Being a cognitive

Table 4.11 Relationships between Miner Sentence Completion Scale – Form H and Ghiselli Self-Description Inventory

Ghiselli Self-Description Inventory	MSCS – H measures							
	Total score	Authority figures	Competitive games	Competitive situations	Assertive role	Imposing wishes	Standing out from group	Routine administrative functions
Supervisory ability	++			+		+	+	
Occupational achievement	+			+			+	
Intelligence			+	+	+		+	
Self actualization	+	+	+	++	+	+++	++	
Self assurance	+	+	+	+	+		++	
Decisiveness				+		+	++	
Need for security	−		−	−			−	
Working-class affinity				−				
Initiative	+	+		+	+	+	++	
Need for high financial reward	−				−	−	−	
Need for power				−		−		
Maturity			−				+	
Masculinity–feminity								
Median r	0.26	0.25	0.20	0.29	0.36	0.23	0.23	0.26

+ = a significant positive correlation (p <.05).
− = a significant negative correlation (p <.05).

Source: Lardent, 1979; Miner, 1976a, previously unpublished data; and Brief, Aldag, and Chacko, 1977

rather than motivational construct, one would not expect consistent relationships involving intelligence, and there are none. In addition, Ghiselli posits negative ties to managerial talent for Need for security and Need for high financial reward, and that is what Table 4.11 demonstrates.

The median correlations noted for those instances where significance is obtained are at much the same level as would be expected when projective and nonprojective measures are involved. Overall the data clearly support construct validity. However, the failure of specific measures from the two instruments to relate to each other and only each other raises questions. That Imposing Wishes and Need for power are unrelated is not surprising, since one is part of managerial talent and the other is not. But why does Competitive Situations produce significant correlations at least twice with seven different SDI measures, and why does Decisiveness do the same thing with four of the eight MSCS – Form H measures? Why does Initiative from the SDI relate this way to exactly the same MSCS indexes that Decisiveness does?

As will be seen shortly, the subscales of the MSCS – Form H are intercorrelated, but at a level well below 0.20. In contrast, Ghiselli (1971: 130) reports correlations among his six managerial talent measures which always exceed 0.20 with a substantial number in the 0.40s and some in the 0.50s. Initiative exhibits similar relationships to the managerial talent measures. Need for financial reward is consistently negatively correlated with all these measures except Intelligence, with a median value of −0.25. The same is true of Need for security where the median correlation is −0.39. In short, the SDI measures are not independent entities; they appear to be part of a general factor of managerial talent. That appears to be why the relationships between SDI and MSCS measures are diffused rather than specific one to another.

Table 4.11 indicates no consistent relationship between intelligence and MSCS – Form H variables. Other research yields the same result using several different intelligence measures (Miner, 1965 and unpublished data).

Certain personality and interest measures have demonstrated relationships, however. In Table 4.12 it is apparent that managerial interests are positively correlated with the MSCS – Form H while professional interests are negatively correlated. Similarly more assertive, forceful, dominant characteristics yield positive relationships and more withdrawing, passive, dependent ones yield negative relationships. There is other evidence in the same vein.

On the Levenson (1974) measure of locus of control, those with high motivation to manage report being less at the mercy of chance forces which control their lives ($r = -0.32$). On the Steers and Braunstein (1976) measure of manifest needs, those with high MSCS – Form H scores have higher need for achievement scores ($r = 0.32$) and also higher need for dominance scores ($r = 0.42$); there is no relationship involving either need

Table 4.12 Correlations between MSCS – Form H total score and the Strong Vocational Interest Blank, Gough Adjective Check List, and Myers–Briggs Type Indicator in a sample of 117 scientists and engineers

Strong Vocational Interest Blank	
Credit manager	0.51
Business education teacher	0.44
Sales manager	0.40
Vocational counselor	0.40
Personnel director	0.39
YMCA secretary	0.39
Mortician	0.39
YMCA physical director	0.38
Army officer	0.37
Interest maturity score	0.36
Physical therapist	0.35
Artist	−0.45
Architect	−0.44
Mathematician	−0.44
Author-journalist	−0.42
Chemist	−0.42
Physicist	−0.42
Dentist	−0.38
Gough Adjective Check List	
Dominance	0.38
Favorable self concept	0.36
Defensiveness	0.34
Achievement	0.33
Self-confidence	0.32
Abasement	−0.39
Counseling readiness	−0.34
Succorance	−0.33
Unfavorable self concept	−0.32
Myers–Briggs Type Indicator	
Introversion	−0.40

Source: Gantz, Erickson, and Stephenson, 1977

for affiliation or need for autonomy (Eberhardt, Yap, and Basuray, 1988). Although the relationship is not strong, there appears to be some negative correlation between creative ability as measured by the Remote Association Test (Mendick, 1962) and the MSCS – Form H (Albert, 1977).

There are also data on the relationship of motivation to manage to authoritarianism as measured by the F-Scale (Adorno, Frenkel-Brunswik, Levinson, and Sanford, 1950). This relationship has been studied both among undergraduate students at the University of Maryland and in a sample of human resource managers (Miner, 1974b; 1976a). In the former instance an MSCS – Form H Total Score correlation of 0.32 was obtained.

Table 4.13 Results of a meta-analysis using MSCS-H total score in relation to certain of the 'big five' personality dimensions

Variable	Number of studies	Total sample size	Corrected mean effect[a]	Credibility interval	Confidence interval
Conscientiousness	7	851	0.20	−0.05, 0.45	0.09, 0.30[b]
Extraversion	5	684	0.24	0.16, 0.33[d]	0.17, 0.32[c]
Openness to experience	4	581	0.02	−0.13, 0.18	−0.08, 0.13[b]

[a]   Corrected for MSCS unreliability only.
[b]   Confidence interval for heterogeneous effects.
[c]   Confidence interval for homogeneous effects.
[d]   All variance in effects accounted for by sampling error.
Source: Carson and Gilliard, 1993

However, no significant relationship was found among the human resource managers. The subscale data clearly indicate that the major factor contributing to a relationship is the degree to which a person has a positive attitude to authority figures. A likely interpretation is that somewhat authoritarian family structures tend to spawn both high motivation to manage and high authoritarianism in children, but that as these individuals move out of the parental family context with adulthood, this relationship begins to break down. It is interesting that the F-Scale items relating to motivation to manage are those dealing with respect for parents by the young, punishment of people who are bad, and to a lesser degree the value of hard work. As people mature they may well develop intrinsic satisfactions in managing that extend well beyond such concerns. Even among college students, however, there is a clear tendency for high MSCS-H scores to go with a *lack* of racial prejudice, thus reversing what might be expected from the F-Scale findings (Tomkiewicz, Brenner, and Esinhart, 1991).

A recent meta-analytic study conducted by Carson and Gilliard (1992) attempted to relate the MSCS-Form H to the so-called 'big five' personality dimensions. In this approach personality is viewed in relation to the dimensions of extraversion, agreeableness, conscientiousness, neuroticism, and openness to experience (Digman, 1990; Barrick and Mount, 1991). Carson and Gilliard (1992) hypothesized that MSCS-H total score should be positively related to independent measures of conscientiousness and extraversion, based on their understanding of the MSCS subscales. They did not expect a relationship to the other three dimensions. The results of this meta-analysis are given in Table 4.13. Insufficient data were available to test the hypothesis of no relationship for agreeableness and neuroticism. However, the hypothesized significant relationships to conscientiousness and extraversion and the lack of a relationship with openness to experience were supported.

Finally, certain instances where a failure to find significant relationships has occurred should be noted. These data do not necessarily have negative implications for construct validity, but they do help to position the construct of hierarchic motivation.

1. Lardent (1979) found very little evidence for any relationship between the MSCS – Form H variables and the Motivation Analysis Test (Cattell, Horn, Sweney, and Radcliff, 1964).
2. Goldner (1986) found no relationship between the MSCS – Form H and Type A behavior as measured by the Jenkins Activity Survey (Jenkins, Zyzanski, and Rosenman, 1979). Subsequent research with a measure of Type A behavior developed by Matteson and Ivancevich (1982) also fails to find a relationship.
3. Muczyk and Schuler (1976) found no relationship between the MSCS – Form H and motivational measures derived from expectancy theory, which like the theory emphasized conscious, rational processes.
4. A hypothesis that the MSCS – Form H might be related to the Least Preferred Co-worker score (LPC) from contingency theory of leadership (Fiedler and Chemers, 1974) has been tested with several different samples and has not received support. Not only has a linear relationship failed to emerge, but there is no evidence in support of the curvilinear relationship suggested by Kennedy's (1982) findings either.

Relationships with nontest variables

The finding that the MSCS – Form H is not related to measures of intelligence suggests that it may not be related either to such indexes as grade point average and educational level attained. Early studies supported this conclusion (Miner, 1965). More recently Bartol and Martin (1987) have also reported a lack of relationship with grade point average.

Another area that has been investigated is the relationship between MSCS – Form H scores and functional area. It is apparent that staff managers tend to score below line managers (Nystrom, 1986). Human resource managers have consistently been found to score relatively low (Miner, 1976; 1979a). Sales and marketing managers score at a higher level than either engineering or research managers (Miner, 1965). Also managers in the private sector score at a higher level than those in nonprofit organizations (Miner, 1989).

Among students there are also clear differentiations. Within the business school context, marketing students tend to obtain the highest scores and accounting students the lowest (Miner, 1965). However, the largest differences have been found when management students and humanities students are compared (Albert, 1977). The humanities majors are substantially lower on Total Score and this difference is independent of the fact that many of the humanities students are females. Subscale differences are in evidence on the Authority Figures scale, both competitive motivation scales, and Assertive Role. Engineering students at the U.S. Military Academy at West Point score very high for students, a not surprising finding considering that they are preparing to become military officers (Butler, Lardent, and Miner, 1983). However, engineering students generally appear to score at at least the level of business students.

Discussion of gender, race, and age differences will be delayed until Chapter 10. These are not so much construct validity issues as matters related to adverse impact. However, there is one additional finding obtained with students that deserves discussion here. Albert and Singleton (undated) constituted homogeneous groups of four students based on their MSCS – Form H Total Scores. There were 19 groups where the average score was greater than 0 and 19 groups where it was 0 or less. The 152 subjects had previously completed a problem-solving exercise individually. Subsequently the homogeneous groups were asked to reach a group consensus. The composite group score was then subtracted from the average individual score for the group members. When the high and low managerial motivation groups were contrasted, it was found that the group problem-solving performance of the high motivation groups was substantially superior to that of the low motivation groups. The implication for organizations would appear to be that staffing decision-making positions (management) with high motivation to manage people will have positive consequences; this is what hierarchic role motivation theory would argue as well. Clearly this line of research needs further exploration, but the Albert and Singleton findings are consistent with the overall thrust of the motivation to manage construct.

Alternative forms of the MSCS – Form H

Another way of studying construct validity is to compare alternative measures. Table 3.3 does this for the free response and multiple-choice versions of the MSCS – Form H. Table 4.10 relates the free response (and thus most projective) version to comparable nonprojective, self-report items. Both of these analyses support construct validity.

In addition, an experimental, situation specific MSCS was created at one point, and the results obtained with it also bear on the construct validity issue. This instrument is designated situation specific because, unlike the standard MSCS – Form H, it focuses directly on the work environment of the first-line supervisor. It is identical with the standard MSCS in all respects except the content of the stems, all of which differ. It seeks to measure the same variables using the same number of items distributed through the measure in the same positions. Free response scoring was done using the same guidelines as for the regular MSCS (Miner, 1964). Both free response and multiple-choice versions were developed.

The items of the Authority Figures subscale are concerned with the immediate superior. The Competitive Games items deal with games that are played or are associated with work, such as company sponsored athletics. The Competitive Situations specified are all instances of work or occupational competition, such as striving for promotion and increased pay. The instances involving an Assertive Role all relate to others in the workplace, whether at a higher, lower, or at the same level. Imposing Wishes consistently focuses on subordinates, and taking or not taking direct supervisory action with regard to them. The Standing out from Group items refer to work group relationships and the degree of willingness to assume a distinctive role relative to other workers. The Routine Administrative Functions considered are clearly those of a first-line supervisor, such as filling out attendance sheets and accident reports.

Table 4.14 presents data on the correlations between regular and situation specific Form H items from a number of different samples. The Total Score relationships are very good and so are a number of the subscale values. Problems arise only with Imposing Wishes and perhaps Routine Administrative Functions; these problems are concentrated where multiple-choice measures are used. Note that these are the same subscales previously found to yield difficulties when free response and multiple-choice versions of the standard MSCS – Form H were compared (see Table 3.3). On the evidence there do appear to be construct validity problems in these two areas, at least when multiple-choice measures are employed.

Some idea of the strength of the findings presented in Table 4.14 may be obtained by comparing them with the intercorrelations among subscales obtained with both standard and situation specific measures (both free response) in the automobile company sample. These represent correlations between dissimilar constructs which are nevertheless still part of motivation to manage. The data of Table 4.15 yield median divergent coefficients for the regular MSCS of 0.15 and for the situation specific MSCS of 0.13. Note that these values are essentially the same as those reported in Table 4.10 for the condition where no relationship is expected (the 5th and 6th columns of figures). In contrast the median convergent coefficient in Table 4.14 for the subscales is twice as large (0.28), and for the Total Score it is 0.52. These results are obtained in spite of the fact that the situation specific measure clearly has lost some of its projective flavor, especially in its multiple-choice version.

CHAPTER SUMMARY

The evidence from a number of directions is that the Miner Sentence Completion Scale – Form H is a valid instrument, and, probably more

Table 4.14 Correlations between the MSCS – Form H and an experimental situation specific version

MSCS measures	MSCS – Form H vs. situation specific version		MSCS – Form H multiple-choice vs. situation specific multiple-choice version	
	103 automobile company managers of varied race and sex	35 automobile company managers – hold-out sample of white males	64 automobile company managers of varied race and sex	251 officer candidate school students
Total score	0.56**	0.81**	0.46**	0.47**
Authority figures	0.38**	0.17	0.34**	0.19**
Competitive games	0.37**	0.42**	0.30**	0.24**
Competitive situations	0.33**	0.36*	0.25*	0.30**
Assertive role	0.40**	0.40**	0.35**	0.09
Imposing wishes	0.14	0.27	−0.35	−0.01
Standing out from group	0.25*	0.20	0.31*	0.13*
Routine administrative functions	0.28**	0.47**	0.06	0.11

* p <.05
** p <.01
Source: Miner, 1977; and Butler, Lardent, and Miner, 1983

Table 4.15 Correlations among MSCS – Form H subscale scores within the standard MSCS – Form H and its situation specific version in a sample of 138 automobile company managers

Subscale	1	2	3	4	5	6	7
1. Authority figures	–	0.07	0.17	−0.01	0.00	0.16	−0.01
2. Competitive games	0.28	–	0.15	0.28	0.04	0.19	0.19
3. Competitive situations	0.34	0.14	–	0.18	0.17	0.10	0.25
4. Assertive role	0.04	0.12	0.27	–	0.10	0.21	0.08
5. Imposing wishes	0.04	0.19	−0.05	0.13	–	0.11	0.24
6. Standing out from group	0.06	0.05	0.13	0.15	0.15	–	0.05
7. Routine functions	0.14	0.17	0.07	−0.04	0.05	0.20	–

Note: Standard MSCS intercorrelations are above the diagonal and situation-specific correlations below it.
Source: Miner, 1977b

important, that the hierarchic role motivation theory is a valid theory. Within the domain of the theory, concurrent and predictive results are positive and at roughly the same level, consistent with the causal expectations of the theory. Outside the domain of the theory, the findings are what would be expected by chance. These conclusions are supported by reviews of the research conducted by the author and others, by meta-analytic investigations, and by the results of conceptually similar research. Additional construct validity evidence comes from a number of sources. The MSCS-H has been related to nonprojective measures of its variables, to other tests that have been found useful in predicting managerial effectiveness, to occupational considerations, and to alternative forms of the basic instrument. With substantial consistency, these analyses support construct validity.

Validation of the hierarchic role motivation theory has benefitted from a continuing flow of research extending back to 1958. In the early years this research was conducted almost entirely by the author. Starting in the 1970s others became increasingly involved, to the point now where contributions by the author alone are the exception. In contrast the professional and task role motivation theories have been investigated with or by others almost from the beginning. Chapter 5 deals with this validation research as it relates to the professional theory.

Validation of the professional role motivation theory

Validation research on the professional role motivation theory is limited by the fact that the test and scoring guide did not become generally available until 1981 (Miner, 1981a). In addition, a check of the literature quickly reveals that research on professionals is much less popular in industrial/organizational psychology than research on managers. The net effect is that independent tests of the professional theory are much fewer in number than of the hierarchic theory. Yet there is a body of evidence to draw upon.

Although validation in the professional domain is important in its own right, it also serves to make the point that viable organizational forms are not limited to those of a bureaucratic nature. Professional forms are one of the most frequently occurring extrabureaucratic structures. Too little attention has been given to the operation of such structures (Wilderom and Miner, 1991). Thus, what is learned from conducting validation research on professional organizations serves broadly to extend the boundaries of our understanding of organizations in general.

VALIDATION WITHIN THE THEORY'S DOMAIN

There are two major studies that attempt to validate professional role motivation theory within its domain – one utilizing members of the Academy of Management and another focusing on labor arbitrators, many of whom are lawyers as well. A third study deals with special education teachers, whose positions in the professional domain are less than clearly established; a fourth deals with certain professionals as well as other types of employees in Saudi Arabia. These studies are considered in this section.

The Academy of Management research

This study utilized both Form P and Form H of the MSCS as well as an extensive questionnaire dealing with various indexes of professional success. The subjects were professors at various colleges and universities who were also members of the Academy of Management. As indicated in Table 5.1, Form P Total Scores were related to a wide range of criterion variables. These include a variety of different compensation measures, academic rank, publications, number of memberships in professional organizations, frequency of attendance at Academy of Management meetings, holding an administrative position (primarily department chairperson), and having supervised doctoral dissertations. Actually the highest correlation obtained in the study (not shown separately in Table 5.1) was 0.66 between Total Score and royalty income from publications (Miner, 1980c).

Among the subscales of the MSCS – Form P, the most consistent producer of significant results and the one with the highest median correlation is Independent Action. This motive pattern appears to be particularly important in generating outside earnings, suggesting it may have particular significance for private professional practice. At the other extreme, Acquiring Knowledge has the weakest relationship to success indexes – half of the correlations do not attain significance. Accepting Status appears to be particularly high among academic administrators.

Some of the criteria in Table 5.1 – particularly university compensation and academic rank – are age related. In most cases removing the age factor has little influence on the validity coefficients because age is unrelated or only weakly related to the MSCS – Form P measures. The one exception is Professional Commitment which correlates 0.45 with age. In this instance partialling out age does reduce the correlations so that a number, but not all, become nonsignificant. A likely cause of the strong age relationship on this variable is that highly professionally committed individuals stay in the profession and grow older in it. The less professionally committed are more likely to drop out over time, and thus tend to be found much more frequently in the younger age groups. It is also possible, however, that professional commitment increases in the individual over time with expanding opportunities to play professional roles. There is some evidence that this happens during professional training (Bucher and Stelling, 1977).

The research also utilized the MSCS – Form H, an application noted as outside the domain of the hierarchic theory in Chapter 4. As indicated in Table 4.6 (study 13), few significant criterion correlations were obtained with Form H. None of the criteria noted in Table 5.1 yielded significant Total Score correlations. There are a few significant correlations on certain subscales – both positive and negative – but even these are in the low 0.20s. The only meaningful finding is a correlation between income from speaking engagements and Standing out from Group of 0.41. This result does appear to bear testimony to the construct validity of this particular subscale.

It is particularly interesting that administrative appointments in the professional context tend to go to those with stronger professional motivation in all of its aspects, not to those with stronger managerial motivation

Table 5.1 Correlations between MSCS – Form P and success measures among Academy of Management members (N=112)

Success measures	MSCS – Form P measures					
	Total score	Acquiring knowledge	Independent action	Accepting status	Providing help	Professional commitment
Total compensation	0.55**	0.28**	0.37**	0.30**	0.35**	0.31**
University compensation	0.57**	0.35**	0.21*	0.39**	0.36**	0.36**
Consulting, royalty, and other non-university compensation	0.41**	0.18	0.37**	0.18	0.26**	0.21*
Academic rank	0.51**	0.17	0.27**	0.30**	0.31**	0.44**
Number of books published	0.53**	0.17	0.45**	0.30**	0.28**	0.34**
Number of journal articles	0.42**	0.27**	0.27**	0.24**	0.23*	0.22*
Number of professional memberships	0.30**	0.18	0.19*	0.19*	0.16	0.17
Attendance at professional meetings	0.35**	0.07	0.29**	0.25**	0.07	0.32**
Holding an administrative position	0.43**	0.26**	0.22*	0.37**	0.21*	0.19*
Supervision of doctoral dissertations	0.35**	0.24*	0.33**	0.16	0.24*	0.08

* $p < .05$
** $p < .01$
Source: Miner, 1980c

(in any of its aspects). It should be noted, however, that these administrators are very close to the professional component – the faculty – in positions where rotation in and out of administration tends to occur frequently. In all likelihood the same results would not be obtained in university central administration where bureaucracy is more prevalent and career administrators are more frequently found.

An additional point relates to the overall level of scores. Theory posits that MSCS – Form P scores should be relatively high and Form H scores low. Using the published norms, the mean Form P Total Score of 5.57 is just under the 50th percentile point (Miner, 1981a). However, these norms are heavily weighted with data from the Academy of Management sample itself. More recent findings suggest that the published norms are rather low; accordingly the value of 5.57 may well be down around the 40th percentile for professionals overall, or even somewhat lower. Within the Academy of Management sample, the administrators are at the 74th percentile and the non-administrators are at the 42nd based on the published norms.

While the data place the non-administrative faculty at a somewhat lower professional motivation level than might have been expected, they are still not at a really low level. In contrast, the Form H scores are consistently very low. The mean Total Score value of −2.31 is at the 12th percentile for corporate managers (Miner, 1989). Other studies in the university context have produced similar results (Miner, 1965; 1977). The Academy of Management sample appears to be lowest on Assertive Role and highest on Standing out from Group, relative to managers in the private sector. Overall, these data tend to match theoretical expectations rather well. Career selection and choice processes do tend to steer higher professional motivation people to professional work and higher managerial motivation people to managerial work.

One way of looking at the results of this study is in terms of their implications for professional associations such as the Academy of Management, or the American Psychological Association, or the American Psychological Society. It seems appropriate to view the major role of these organizations as contributing to the satisfaction of motives that are strong among their members and that are closely related to professional career success. The findings from this research indicate accordingly that to be successful themselves, professional associations should:

1. Foster the development and dissemination of knowledge to members, thus meeting the need to acquire knowledge.
2. Protect the freedom of members to act with professional independence, thus meeting the need for independent action.
3. Foster the prestige and status of the profession and of its individual members, thus meeting the need to accept status.

4. Create opportunities for members to serve clients, thus meeting the need to provide help.
5. Define a fully-fledged profession with appropriate norms and values, thus meeting the need for professional commitment.

If one considers some of the more effective professional organizations currently in existence, it seems clear that the major activities of these organizations do indeed tend to mesh closely with these role prescriptions.

Labor arbitrators and lawyers

Professional role motivation theory deals with the professional domain generally, and thus should be applicable to any fully-fledged professional working in a professional organizational context, whether a free-standing professional organization, a professional component of a larger bureaucratic structure, or a private professional practice. The present study was devised to test the theory more broadly, extending beyond university faculty to labor arbitrators and lawyers, and to consider the matter of varying organizational contexts (Miner, Crane, and Vandenberg, 1992).

Table 5.2, at the top, presents the OODQ analyses. First, it says that the labor arbitrator sample numbering 109 does have a high P Score; these people describe their organizational environments as predominantly professional. The mean score is at the 49th percentile for professionals (Oliver, 1981). The T Score is also elevated significantly, although it still is at only the 11th percentile among entrepreneurs. The H and G Scores are relatively low.

A second conclusion from the OODQ analysis is that the pattern of a substantially elevated P Score, somewhat elevated T Score, and low H and G Scores applies consistently across organizational contexts. The P and T Scores do not vary significantly with organizational context. The H Score is significantly higher for university faculty, who can be assumed to typically operate with a bureaucratic overlay, than for any other context. The G Score is significantly depressed in the two private practice contexts, where of course there is no group.

The MSCS – Form P analysis at the bottom of Table 5.2 reinforces the conclusions from the OODQ. The arbitrators score high on the Total Score measure, at the 68th percentile for professionals using the published norms (Miner, 1981), and they do so consistently across organizational contexts. On the subscales there are no differences by context either. However, the arbitrators appear to have relatively higher professional commitment as a group, at the 76th percentile, and relatively lower needs for independent action, at the 50th percentile. The high level of commitment is consistent with the age of the arbitrators which averages 62 years; the correlation between age and Professional Commitment is 0.22. The

Table 5.2 MSCS-P and OODQ scores of labor arbitrators working from various professional organizational contexts

			Organizational contexts			
	University faculty	Law firm	Government	Private practice	Private practice (retired from university)	F
N	28	27	6	34	14	
OODQ measures						
P score	9.68	11.11	11.00	11.18	11.57	1.90
T score	6.57	6.33	4.83	6.26	5.00	1.17
H score	3.64	0.81	1.00	0.50	0.64	15.14**
G score	2.14	1.74	1.17	0.44	0.43	6.17**
MSCS – P measures						
Total score	11.33	7.58	13.00	8.21	10.50	1.29
Acquiring knowledge	0.71	0.92	0.80	0.64	1.25	0.19
Independent action	2.08	1.23	2.40	2.33	2.58	1.47
Accepting status	2.83	2.27	3.00	1.82	2.00	0.59
Providing help	3.25	1.54	4.00	1.82	2.25	2.31
Professional commitment	2.46	1.62	2.80	1.61	2.42	1.11

**p <.01
Source: Miner, Crane, and Vandenberg, 1992

Table 5.3 Correlations between MSCS – Form P and success measures for labor arbitrator sample (N=100)

MSCS – Form P measures	Success measures			
	Number of professional memberships	Union rating	Management ratings	
			Percent negative	Consensus
Total score	0.29**	0.00	−0.26**	−0.32**
Acquiring knowledge	0.24**	0.03	−0.14	−0.21*
Independent action	0.20*	−0.01	−0.16	−0.07
Accepting status	0.19*	−0.01	−0.10	−0.27**
Providing help	0.29**	−0.13	−0.20*	−0.24*
Professional commitment	0.01	0.12	−0.26**	−0.25**

* p <.05
**p <.01
Source: Miner, Crane, and Vandenberg, 1992

somewhat low Independent Action score is entirely consistent with the arbitrator role, which is to choose from among alternatives generated by the parties, not for the arbitrators to generate independent solutions themselves.

Table 5.3 presents the validity coefficients for the total sample. Number of professional memberships is essentially the same measure as was reported in Table 5.1. The union rating is an evaluation on a 7 point scale made independently by union representatives who had faced the arbitrator. The management ratings come from an independent reporting service that collects information from management representatives after they have faced an arbitrator. The percent negative measure is the proportion of all evaluations submitted on a given arbitrator that are disapproving. The consensus measure is a rating on a 4 point scale made by the reporting service based on all the information available to it. All three rating measures are constructed so that low scores indicate effective arbitrators. Thus positive correlations involving professional memberships and negative correlations involving union and management ratings support the hypothesis. A comprehensive analysis indicates that there is a low negative relationship between union and management ratings generally which runs in the −0.01 to −0.21 range depending on the measures (Crane and Miner, 1988).

An additional success measure was contemplated in the original design of the research, namely total professional compensation as utilized in Table 5.1. In fact data were collected on this point. However, it soon became evident that while age and compensation were positively correlated in the much younger Academy of Management sample (at 0.48), they now were negatively correlated (at −0.32). Many of the older arbitrators had retired from some other activity and/or cut back on their arbitration practices. In fact the age–compensation relationship was significantly curvilinear with eta equal to 0.39. The turning point was at approximately age 50; beyond that point arbitrator professional income declined with age. Given this finding, it did not appear appropriate to interpret compensation as an index of success – the arbitrators were not necessarily attempting to maximize it. Accordingly, the compensation measure was dropped from the analysis.

Except for the union ratings, the correlations in Table 5.3 are not as high as in Table 5.1 but they are highly significant. In all cases except the union ratings, the Total Score correlations are significant and all of the subscales produce at least one significant value. Table 5.4 presents the results of the analysis when the data are limited to those for lawyers, defined separately either as a person with a law degree or a person who designates the law (not just arbitration) as his or her primary occupation. The findings in Table 5.4 are patterned much like those of Table 5.3, but they tend generally to be somewhat stronger. In any event it is clearly apparent that professional motivation does make a difference within the legal profession.

The one discordant note throughout these analyses is the failure to obtain significant results with the union ratings. Yet there is evidence that significant results can be obtained with this measure when the analysis is restricted to arbitrators who have high T Scores relative to the P Score on the OODQ – those who perceive their work as more entrepreneurial, although still not lacking in the professional component. Because of the *ad hoc* nature of this analysis, the small sample size, and the fact that significant correlations with criteria other than the union ratings disappear in this group, it is difficult to evaluate the outcome. However, it does appear that there are certain arbitrators of a more entrepreneurial bent who are evaluated more positively by union representatives, when they have stronger professional motivation.

Special education teachers and specialists in a large school district

This third study is somewhat compromised by the OODQ findings noted in Table 5.5. The P Score places the special educators at only the 26th percentile for professionals generally. Clearly a number of these individuals do not see their work as occurring in a very professional organization. The reason for this appears to be that this is a large and rather bureaucratic school district. The mean H Score, like the P Score, is in the range Oliver (1981) considers elevated, although it is still not up to the 10th percentile for a hierarchic sample. The school district as it relates to these individuals appears to be a mixture of professional and hierarchic systems, with neither dominating to any marked degree. Even the T score is raised to some extent.

In spite of the mixed structure in which they work, however, the special educators bring a reasonably high level of professional motivation to their

Table 5.4 Correlations between MSCS – Form P and success measures for arbitrators with a law degree (N=63) and arbitrators considering law the primary occupation (N=20)

| | Success measures | | | | | | Management ratings | |
| | Number of professional memberships | | Union rating | | Percent negative | | Consensus | |
MSCS – Form P measures	Law degree	Legal occupation	Law degree	Legal occupation	Law degree	Legal occupation	Law degree	Legal occupation
Total score	0.21*	0.24	-0.03	-0.09	-0.35**	-0.42*	-0.38**	-0.43*
Acquiring knowledge	0.23*	0.19	0.05	0.07	-0.12	-0.35	-0.21*	-0.34
Independent action	0.17	0.44*	-0.05	-0.24	-0.24*	-0.39*	-0.07	-0.17
Accepting status	0.11	0.11	0.03	-0.11	-0.23*	-0.20	-0.38**	-0.30
Providing help	0.22*	0.26	-0.13	-0.16	-0.31**	-0.35	-0.26*	-0.30
Professional commitment	-0.08	-0.01	0.02	0.11	-0.24*	-0.45*	-0.31**	-0.68**

* $p < .05$
** $p < .01$

Source: Miner, Crane, and Vandenberg, 1992

Table 5.5 OODQ and MSCS – Form P scores for special educators (N=89)

OODQ measures	Mean
P score	8.9
T score	4.1
H score	7.3
G score	2.0
MSCS – Form P measures	
Total score	8.53
Acquiring knowledge	1.53
Independent action	1.72
Accepting status	0.42
Providing help	2.89
Professional commitment	1.97

Source: Pilgrim, 1986

jobs. The Total Score value is at the 63rd percentile on the published norms for professionals – slightly below the labor arbitrators, but above the Academy of Management professors. There clearly is no lack of professional motivation. This is consistent with the fact that some 65 percent hold a graduate degree and a number of others are engaged in graduate study. A diverse array of certifications are represented. Among the subscales Independent Action and Accepting Status yield scores below the 50th percentile; the other three subscale scores are all high. Given the nature of the profession, this pattern makes intuitive sense.

Since the research was carried out primarily for the purpose of evaluating a professional motivation training program, no direct measures of performance effectiveness were utilized (Pilgrim, 1986). Given the mixed nature of the organizational system in which the special educators worked, it is difficult to predict what results should be expected from such an analysis in any event. Certain analyses were carried out in which professional motivation was correlated with professional association activities and publications. However, since nonparticipation in these behaviors was eliminated from the analyses, there is reason to question whether meaningful results should be expected, and sample sizes were often markedly reduced. Ranges on the criterion measures were very small, making it very unlikely that significant results would be obtained – and, in fact, they rarely were. All in all this study raises more questions than it answers. Probably it deals more with a semi-profession than a fully-fledged profession (Etzioni, 1964). Semi-professions are described as including teachers and often being female dominated (92 percent of the special educators were women). The basic problem is that domain position is not well established for such a group, and thus theoretical predictions are difficult to make (see Chapter 3 for additional discussion on this point).

The research in Saudi Arabia

As noted in Chapter 4, Al-Kelabi (1991) conducted studies in Saudi Arabia using the MSCS-Form H. Form P was also used in this research. The base sample contained 301 people employed by three organizations – a hospital, an office automation company, and a computer services company. Thus, in addition to managers and a diverse array of other occupations, there were a number of professionals. This was particularly true in the hospital where many physicians and nurses were included in the study sample. There were also accountants in all three organizations and a number of engineers in the computer services company. These professionals tended to score high on the P scale of the Oliver Organization Description Questionnaire and also on the Kerr and Jermier (1978) measure of professional orientation. The two indexes of professional organization were correlated 0.45 at the unit level.

Table 5.6 shows that the MSCS-P total score and several subscales exhibited good validity within the professional domain, i.e. among those who described their work as distinctly professional in nature, and not hierarchic. The criteria here are job satisfaction (Hackman and Oldham, 1975) and intention to leave the organization (Seashore, Lawler, Mirvis, and Cammann, 1982), both of which are variables that had not been studied previously.

Table 5.6 Correlations between the MSCS – Form P and criteria within and outside the professional domain in Saudi Arabian samples

MSCS-Form P measures	Within the professional domain (OODQ P score high and H score low) N=36		Within the hierarchic domain (OODQ H score high and P score low) N=86	
	Job satisfaction	Intention to turnover	Job satisfaction	Intention to turnover
Total score	0.38**	−0.36*	0.09	−0.12
Acquiring knowledge	0.22	−0.16	0.04	−0.10
Independent action	0.28*	−0.29*	0.03	0.12
Accepting status	0.03	−0.24	0.08	−0.15
Providing help	0.13	−0.11	−0.03	0.05
Professional commitment	0.49**	−0.25	0.03	−0.19

* p <.05
**p <.01
Source: Al-Kelabi, 1991

VALIDITY OUTSIDE THE DOMAIN AND RELATED LITERATURES

Relatively little research has been done to test the proposition that the professional theory will not work outside its specified domain. An analysis has been carried out with a small sample of entrepreneurs using criteria such as the number of people employed by the company, the annual dollar volume of sales, profitability, and income level. Form P of the MSCS did not yield significant results in this context, which OODQ results indicated was essentially of a task nature (see Chapter 3). In addition, as indicated in Table 5.6, the Saudi Arabian research found no relation between MSCS-P variables and criteria within a hierarchic domain, despite good validity within the professional domain.

There are as yet no reviews of the professional role motivation theory literature or discussions of it, other than treatments by the author (for instance Miner, 1988). The theory itself was developed out of the primarily sociological literature of the 1960s and 1970s. However, the theoretical formulations represent an amalgam from diverse theoretical and empirical origins. There is no distinct source that may be referred to, and to the author's knowledge no set of really conceptually similar studies exist. There is, however, strong support for certain of the theory's roles and thus for certain of the subscales of the MSCS – Form P.

Von Glinow (1988) in her treatment of primarily scientific professionals notes that intrinsic motivational forces play the most important role in professional performance. In this context she identifies expertise, ethics, collegial maintenance of standards, autonomy, commitment to calling, and external referents and identification as professional characteristics. The ensuing discussions suggest that she has in mind processes such as acquiring knowledge, independent action, accepting status, and professional commitment; there is no mention of providing help. Perhaps this is a consequence of the type of high-technology professional she is concerned with. In contrast, discussions of the professional burnout phenomenon tend to focus heavily on the problems associated with helping behavior (Pines and Aronson, 1988). Recently considerable attention has been given to matters of professional commitment. It is apparent that this characteristic is a distinct entity, and that it has major implications for professional behavior (Morrow and Goetz, 1988; Morrow and Wirth, 1989). Although it is not possible to point to the same volume of research in support of professional role motivation theory constructs that exist in the hierarchic area, the professional theory is not devoid of support from this source.

CONSTRUCT VALIDITY

Research already discussed provides considerable evidence in support of construct validity for the professional role motivation theory and the MSCS – Form P. There are, however, other findings that need to be considered.

Relationships with other constructs

Although there is very little published material relating professional motivation to other constructs, some data are available. Using the Vocabulary Test GT (Miner, 1961a; 1973b) as a measure of mental ability, no consistent relationship to MSCS – Form P measures was found across a small group of entrepreneurs and a group of MBA students in entrepreneurship classes. It would be anticipated that professional motivation should be related to success in professional training and studies are under way to test that hypothesis. However, no results are available as yet. There seems no reason to anticipate any relationship between Form P and grade point average generally, outside of specifically professional programs.

Among the entrepreneurs there is a positive correlation between the MSCS – Form P Total Score and Ghiselli's (1971) SDI Initiative measure (0.39); Acquiring Knowledge and Professional Commitment appear to be the primary subscales contributing to these findings. There is also a negative relationship to SDI Need for High Financial Reward (−0.41) with the same two subscales playing a significant role. Overall there are few relationships with SDI measures, an unsurprising finding given that the SDI is oriented to the hierarchic domain. However, it does make sense that those with more intrinsic love of professional work would care less about extrinsic reward, and that individuals with less professional motivation would want money more. Actually the correlation rises to −0.53 when Professional Commitment is involved; highly committed individuals care least about money. The finding with Initiative is less predictable, but still not unexpected.

Another finding is that Independent Action, though not Form P Total Score, is related to locus of control as measured by the Levenson (1974) scale in the MBA student sample. As anticipated, Independent Action is associated positively with internal locus of control (0.39) and negatively with both measures of externality – powerful others control (−0.36) and chance control (−0.45). However, this finding is not replicated among the entrepreneurs.

Relationship to the MSCS – Form H

There is nothing in the theories behind the MSCS – Form P and the MSCS – Form H that says they should be positively or negatively related; the two measures simply apply in different domains. However, high correlations, either positive or negative, would not be expected. There would be little point in differentiating the domains if the motive patterns that mattered in each were highly correlated.

In the Academy of Management sample, the Total Score correlation was 0.33 (p <.01) (Miner, 1980c). Pearson and Bracker (1983) report a value of 0.30 (p <.05) for undergraduate students in a business policy course. Among the MBA students in entrepreneurship courses, a correlation of 0.35 (p <.05) was obtained. The value for the entrepreneurs was a nonsignificant 0.24. In all four cases the correlations are positive, but not particularly high; the median value is 0.32.

If one looks at the total pattern of correlations between the two measures across these four data sets, the results indicate an even lower level of relationship. The median correlation is 0.13. There are numerous correlations reaching statistical significance in one sample or another, although predominantly at the p <.05 level, but there are only three instances of any replication (besides the total score results) across samples. The most stable finding is that there is a relationship between Form P Total Score and Form H Standing out from Group; the median r is 0.28 and there are a number of significant correlations between Standing out from Group and Form P subscales. It appears likely that this finding reflects the fact that teaching and making presentations before groups are inherent in much professional work and in the standing out from group role requirement of managerial work.

The only other relationship that emerges with any consistency is that between Form P Acquiring Knowledge and Form H Total Score (median r = 0.27). There is some suggestion that a desire to learn may be a component of managerial work as well as professional. One is reminded of Weber's (1968) contention that bureaucratic systems dominate through knowledge and that this is how they achieve their rationality. Weber devoted considerable attention to this knowledge requirement in managerial work.

On the evidence available, then, there is reason to believe that standing out from a group may be a significant aspect of professional motivation above and beyond the various motive patterns considered in the professional theory, and that acquiring knowledge may be similarly important for hierarchic motivation. If one removes these two factors, there appears to be only a minimal relationship between Form P and H of the MSCS – something approximating a correlation of 0.15.

Relationships among the aspects of professional motivation

Subscale intercorrelations for the MSCS – Form P are available from a number of sources. The median value from the Academy of Management study was 0.16. Among the labor arbitrators it was higher at 0.26. Among the special educators it was 0.10. In the Pearson and Bracker (1983) analysis of undergraduate student data, the median r was 0.21. Among the MBA students in entrepreneurship courses the median value was 0.18. In the entrepreneur sample it was 0.11. In the Saudi Arabian research it was 0.17. There are no two subscales that consistently yield a substantial relationship. As with the MSCS – Form H subscales, the typical Form P analysis indicates an average subscale intercorrelation below 0.20.

It should be noted that none of the studies with the MSCS – Form P utilize a predictive design. It is hoped that this situation will be corrected shortly. In the meantime it is appropriate to rely on extrapolation from parallel theory. There is evidence of predictive validity from the hierarchic theory utilizing a similar MSCS measure and a similar role motivation theory. There is also evidence from the task theory, as will be shown in Chapter 6.

CHAPTER SUMMARY

Validation research on the professional role motivation theory is not extensive, but enough exists to provide some evaluation. Studies have dealt to varying degrees with university professors, labor arbitrators, lawyers, special education teachers, medical professionals (physicians and nurses), accountants, and engineers. On the average it appears that when the MSCS-Form P is used as a predictor within its own domain, the validity evidence closely parallels that found with Form H in its domain. Again a validity coefficient in the mid to upper 0.30s appears to be the mode, although values in the 0.60s have been obtained. To the limited degree that tests have been carried out, they also appear to support theory in that significant results are not obtained outside the domain of professional role motivation theory. Construct validation generally is supportive of the theory, but again it is far from extensive.

Despite being written about for over ten years, and having a good deal of visibility as well, professional role motivation theory has not evoked an outpouring of research or interest to match that of the hierarchic or task theories. Perhaps, because they are professionals themselves, industrial/organizational psychologists and organizational scientists generally feel they understand professional systems well enough, and thus do not need to study them. Yet there is the possibility that more is to be learned here than is readily apparent. It is even possible that we do not want to subject our own world to the same research scrutiny that we apply to others.

In any event, this short chapter does survey the validity evidence for the professional role motivation theory. The next chapter dealing with the validation of task theory, which has been operationalized for only about half as long as the professional theory, but covers considerably more ground.

Chapter 6

Validation of the task role motivation theory

Task role motivation theory, like the professional theory, moves beyond bureaucracy to deal with a type of organization that has received relatively little attention until recently. This fact, coupled with the only very recent publication of a scoring guide for the MSCS – Form T (Miner, 1986), has meant that research on the task theory is far less than that involving the hierarchic theory. Nevertheless, the burgeoning interest in entrepreneurship has incorporated the task theory in its flow to a point where more now appears to be happening with regard to that theory than any other (see, for instance, Miner, Smith, and Bracker, 1992a). As a result there is more validity information available currently on task theory than on the professional theory, and given current trends, the prospect is that in a few years there will be a great deal more.

Before taking up this research, however, it is important to trace how the task theory and the MSCS – Form T came to be developed. The initial research hypothesis regarding entrepreneurs arose out of discussions with Norman Smith, a professor of marketing and entrepreneurship with a strong sociological bent at the University of Oregon. The idea was to combine the Miner concept of motivation to manage with Smith's formulations regarding types of entrepreneurs and entrepreneurial firms (Smith, 1967). This was at a time when the four role motivation theories were just being developed and when the hierarchic theory was clearly dominant (Smith, McCain, and Miner, 1976).

One hypothesis was that high MSCS – Form H scores would be associated with the opportunistic type of entrepreneur – a person with breadth in education and training, high social awareness and involvement, confidence in his ability to deal with the social environment, and an awareness of, and orientation to, the future (Smith, 1967). Such people were expected to head highly adaptive, growth-oriented firms. Another, related hypothesis was that people with strong managerial motivation would be prompted to found firms and create strategies for their growth in order to have something to manage. The thinking was that for certain people this route to management and top level management responsibilities would be more attractive and more realistic than the route up the corporate ladder. If a person viewed the promotional route as improbable for some reason, the entrepreneurial route would become increasingly attractive. Accordingly entrepreneurial positions should be crowded with high motivation to manage people.

The first test of these hypotheses was carried out using a sample of 38 Oregon entrepreneur-founders (Smith and Miner, 1983). This was a diversified group in terms of industry, firm size, and growth rate. The entrepreneurs were compared with lower and middle level corporate managers from an automobile company, an oil company, a baking company, a wood products company, and a department store.

As it turned out, the managerial motivation of the entrepreneurial sample was the lowest when comparisons were made with the three groups of middle managers studied. These middle managers were considered to be the most appropriate of the comparison groups available at the time. Actually the entrepreneurs were the lowest of all the samples, and four of the comparisons were statistically significant (see Table 4.6, studies 15 and 16). The data gave little support to the hypothesis regarding managerial motivation and entrepreneurship. Furthermore, attempts to relate managerial motivation to the type of entrepreneur (opportunistic) and the type of firm (adaptive, growth-oriented) did not produce encouraging results either.

A second opportunity to study these relationships arose in connection with a study of top level corporate executives (Berman and Miner, 1985). This group contained 59 chief executive or chief operating officers and 16 executive or group vice presidents – a total of 75. The mean size of the companies was just over 5,000 employees; total revenues ranged from $2.4 million to $6 billion. Within the group of 75 there were 18 individuals who were founders and chief executives from the beginning and eight others who were family members with a founder. These 26 constituted the entrepreneurial group for comparisons with the 49 executives who had no role in founding the company or familial relationship to a founder. The two groups each contain a high proportion of chief executives and certainly the 49 non-entrepreneurs provide a useful arena for testing the hierarchic motivation hypothesis (see Table 4.1, study 20).

Yet once again the entrepreneurs had the lower managerial motivation. In total these attempts to use the hierarchic theory with entrepreneurs indicated a level of managerial motivation somewhat below that typically found among first level supervisors in large companies. The results from this phase of the research gave no reason to believe that a desire to have something to manage was attracting large numbers of managerially motivated people into the ranks of entrepreneurs.

It was this experience that prompted us to abandon Form H in our research on entrepreneurs, and focus on the development of Form T.

However, it is worth noting that we never have been very successful in linking the Smith and Miner theories, whether with Form H (Smith and Miner, 1983) or Form T (Smith, Bracker, and Miner, 1987), and even when a highly standardized measure of the Smith constructs was employed (Miner, Smith, and Bracker, 1992).

VALIDATION WITHIN THE THEORY'S DOMAIN

Validation research focused initially on a study of high technology entrepreneurs (defined as business founders) seeking funding from the National Science Foundation. It has since expanded to various comparisons of entrepreneurs and managers, an analysis involving entrepreneurs who filed for bankruptcy, a study of planning orientations among entrepreneurs in the electronics industry, a series of studies involving business administration students, a comparison of different types of entrepreneurs, and an investigation into task motivation levels in a single firm.

High technology entrepreneurs

The first study dealing with task theory was a survey utilizing lists obtained from the National Science Foundation. These lists contained the names of applicants for funding of new technological innovations. Sometimes the applications came from entrepreneurs of a scientific bent who headed newly founded firms formed to foster their inventions or ideas. Less frequently they came from manager-scientists who were simply submitting applications developed within their, frequently larger companies (Smith, Bracker, and Miner, 1987; Smith and Miner, 1984; 1985; Miner, Smith, and Bracker, 1989).

An initial comparison of entrepreneurs who were involved in founding their companies with manager-scientists who were not founders, but had also submitted grant applications from small, high technology companies, revealed that the former had higher MSCS – Form T scores. However, the more significant finding was that the major differences involved high growth entrepreneurs, whose firms had been growing at a rate of 1.5 employees per year or more. As noted in Table 6.1, these high growth entrepreneurs not only had higher MSCS – Form T scores across the board than the non-entrepreneur manager-scientists, as the theory would predict, but they also had higher scores than the low growth entrepreneurs. The latter typically headed very small organizations growing only at an average of one employee every two years. From these data it appears that the realm to which task role motivation theory applies is not that of mom and pop operations, private professional practice, part-time self-employment, and the like. The findings given in Table 6.1 indicate

Table 6.1 Comparison of MSCS – Form T scores for high growth entrepreneurs (N=59), low growth entrepreneurs (N=59), and manager-scientists in small firms (N=41)

MSCS – Form T measures	High growth entrepreneurs	Low growth entrepreneurs	Manager–scientists	F
Total score	10.95	0.92	1.95	44.45**
Self achievement	3.10	0.19	0.61	25.69**
Avoiding risks	1.56	0.03	0.00	7.05**
Feedback of results	0.44	−1.53	−1.63	15.09**
Personal innovation	3.98	1.78	2.37	17.29**
Planning for the future	1.86	0.44	0.61	4.66**

$**p < .01$
Note: High growth entrepreneurs are above the other two groups at $p < .05$ or better in all instances except planning for the future among the manager-scientists.
Source: Smith, Bracker, and Miner, 1987

considerable validity for the theory, but only among high growth entrepreneurs.

A second set of findings from this same study is given in Table 6.2. The data using number of employees, dollar volume of sales, and income level as success criteria consistently support the theory's validity. These criteria correlate in the 0.42 to 0.89 range. Net profit as percent of sales consistently fails to demonstrate significant validity, and it yields low negative or non-significant correlations with the other criteria. The problem appears to be that when earnings are put back into growth or paid out in the form of compensation to the entrepreneur, there is often little profit left. Accordingly profit does not appear to be an appropriate index of either firm growth or success. It is too vulnerable to influence by other factors in privately-held companies of the type studied in the high technology research.

Most recently a follow-up has been conducted with the high technology entrepreneurs to determine predictive validity (Miner, Smith, and Bracker, 1992a). The average time between initial testing and follow-up was five years and seven months. There were 16 instances where it could be clearly established that the entrepreneurs and their original firms had gone separate ways. In the majority of these cases the firm appears to have terminated, but there were a number of other scenarios as well; this is where business problems were most evident. A second group numbering 41 were known to have moved, either with or without their firms, but this is all that is known about them. Presumably there were a number of business failures concentrated in this group, but the extent to which this is true remains uncertain. Finally, some 61 entrepreneurs remained with their firms and the firms continued as independent entities. These three groups of companies did not differ in the level of their success initially.

Table 6.2 Correlations between MSCS – Form T and indexes of company growth and success

MSCS – Form T measures	Growth in number of employees	Mean annual growth in number of employees	Growth in dollar volume of sales	Mean annual growth in dollar volume of sales	Net profit as percent of sales	Yearly income from position
Total score	0.35**	0.49**	0.31**	0.39**	0.05	0.36**
Self achievement	0.36**	0.49**	0.27**	0.35**	0.02	0.30**
Avoiding risks	0.11	0.18*	0.19	0.24*	0.03	0.06
Feedback of results	0.26**	0.28**	0.22*	0.21*	0.04	0.24*
Personal innovation	0.16	0.32**	0.08	0.13	−0.01	0.09
Planning for the future	0.18*	0.24*	0.20*	0.25**	0.02	0.30**

* $p < .05$
** $p < .01$
Source: Miner, Smith, and Bracker, 1992a and Smith, Bracker, and Miner, 1987

As indicated in Table 6.3, success level at follow-up clearly was related to the initial Form T scores, as hypothesized. The Total Score results are strong, and among the subscales Planning for the Future produces a particularly striking relationship. Planning does appear to contribute to firm survival.

Entrepreneurs and managers

An outgrowth of the findings in Table 6.1 was a study which looked at high growth entrepreneurs specifically. This sample was drawn from the author's files, built up over various previous studies. The sample contained all individuals who were known to be founders and chief executives of their firms, and whose firms had grown to include at least ten employees. In most instances this growth had occurred gradually, but there were several instances of quantum growth at a point very close to the inception of the firm. The median number of employees was 28 with the largest firm having 225. The median annual sales figure was $1.6 million; the largest such value was 14.5 million. A comparison sample of managers was taken from the same source as the entrepreneurs, and represented all qualifying individuals. They numbered 71; of these, 12 were chief executives (but not founders) and 24 reported directly to chief executives, primarily as vice presidents. The remainder were roughly equally distributed among middle and lower level managerial positions. Like the entrepreneurs, the managers worked for a diverse array of companies both as to geographical location and industry. However, the managers were employed by larger firms (Miner, 1990a).

The results given in Table 6.4 are much the same as those of Table 6.1, and in fact there is some overlap in the samples. A two-group discriminant analysis applied to the Total Score data of Table 6.4 yields a canonical correlation of 0.66 with 84.56 percent of the cases correctly classified by the discriminant function. The standardized canonical discriminant function coefficients for the subscales are 0.59 for Self Achievement, 0.49 for Avoiding Risks, 0.46 for Personal Innovation, 0.23 for Feedback of Results, and 0.17 for Planning for the Future.

These discriminant results can be compared with those obtained previously with the unselected sample of high technology entrepreneurs (Miner, Smith and Bracker, 1989). In that instance, when non-CEO founders and entrepreneurs with very small firms were included in the analysis, the canonical correlation was 0.25 and only 64.15 percent of the cases were correctly classified as entrepreneur or manager by Form T of the MSCS. The difference between the two correlation values of 0.41 points is highly significant (t = 4.52, p <.01). Thus, the hypothesized increase in discrimination anticipated when the analysis is restricted to chief executive

Table 6.3 MSCS – Form T scores for entrepreneurs who at follow-up were no longer operating their firms (N=16), could not be located (N=41), and still remained with their firms (N=61)

MSCS – Form T measures	Entrepreneurs who are no longer with their firms	Entrepreneurs who cannot be located	Entrepreneurs who remain with their firms	F	P
Total score	1.94[a]	4.83[b]	7.72[ab]	3.95	0.02
Subscale scores					
Self achievement	0.44[c]	2.12[c]	1.64	2.19	0.12
Avoiding risks	0.06[c]	0.41	1.25[c]	2.05	0.13
Feedback of results	−0.31	−0.88	−0.38	0.69	0.50
Personal innovation	1.88[c]	2.78	3.21[c]	2.04	0.13
Planning for the future	−0.13[a]	0.39[b]	2.00[ab]	6.10	<.01

[a] Two means differ at p <.01 or better
[b] Two means differ at p <.01 or better
[c] Two means differ at p <.05 or better
Source: Miner, Smith, and Bracker, 1992a

Table 6.4 Comparison of MSCS – Form T scores of high growth entrepreneurs (N=65) and managers (N=71)

MSCS – Form T measures	High growth entrepreneurs	Managers	t
Total score	12.14	2.66	9.32**
Self achievement	3.54	0.65	7.42**
Avoiding risks	1.68	−0.20	4.48**
Feedback of results	0.98	−0.86	4.39**
Personal innovation	4.00	2.32	4.65**
Planning for the future	1.94	0.75	2.61**

**p <.01
Source: Miner, 1990a

entrepreneurs whose firms have grown larger is in fact obtained. The effect size increases from 0.58 to 1.60.

Another set of comparisons involving entrepreneurs and managers first utilized samples from the United States (Bellu, 1988) and then later comparisons were carried out with samples from the north and south of Italy, Israel, and Sweden (Bellu, Davidsson, and Goldfarb, 1990). The results are given in Table 6.5.

Several features of the United States study should be noted. The entrepreneurial firms tend to be consistently small, with over two-thirds having fewer than 10 employees. Most are in retailing or services; less than 10 percent are in manufacturing in any form. Most of the entrepreneurs are in the chief executive role. The comparison managers are also working in small firms. They average only $32,000 in yearly income, in contrast with $56,000 for the entrepreneur-founders. Some of these comparison managers may indeed have been misclassified for lack of sufficient information. The net effects of these sample variations would be expected to be reduced Form T scores in the entrepreneur samples and increased scores in the managerial samples. Yet there are consistent Total Score differences in favor of the entrepreneurs.

Form T was translated into Italian, Hebrew, and Swedish for the other studies noted in Table 6.5. Back translations were used, and the translations adjusted, until results comparable to the English were obtained. In Italy and Israel the results are much like those obtained in the United States, although the differences are somewhat more pronounced. The Swedish results, however, do not replicate, with one exception on the Self Achievement subscale. Note that this measure yields significant differences in all five comparisons. The failure to obtain consistent results in Sweden may be attributable to a number of factors. The managers are heavily in sales and marketing, and several have had previous entrepreneurial experience; these factors may raise their Form T scores. The entrepreneurs are concentrated in service firms with a number being professionals; this could lower

Table 6.5 MSCS – Form T differences between entrepreneurs and managers in various countries

MSCS – Form T measures	United States		Northern Italy		Southern Italy		Israel		Sweden	
	Entre-preneurs (N=70)	Mana-gers (N=67)	Entre-preneurs (N=31)	Mana-gers (N=33)	Entre-preneurs (N=34)	Mana-gers (N=33)	Entre-preneurs (N=35)	Mana-gers (N=36)	Entre-preneurs (N=31)	Mana-gers (N=26)
Total score	9.20	6.16**	13.61	3.55**	14.40	0.55**	11.49	5.35**	5.80	6.50
Self achievement	2.80	1.58**	4.00	1.45**	3.06	0.15**	2.72	0.48**	1.65	0.30*
Avoiding risks	0.86	0.08**	2.58	0.12**	2.82	−0.48**	1.87	−0.09**	1.12	1.00
Feedback of results	1.00	1.22	1.29	0.21	2.33	0.36**	0.69	0.49	0.55	1.65
Personal innovation	2.56	1.57**	3.84	1.18*	3.82	−0.03**	4.89	2.94**	2.00	2.35
Planning for the future	1.99	1.72	1.90	0.58	2.32	0.54*	1.31	1.52	0.48	1.19

* $p < .05$
** $p < .01$

Source: Bellu, 1988 and Bellu, Davidsson, and Goldfarb, 1990

their scores. It could be that the presence of a socialist economic system exerts an influence. There are a number of possible explanations, and it is not at all clear which applies.

Very recently Bellu (1992) has carried out a comparison of 47 female entrepreneur-founders and 66 female managers. The entrepreneurial firms had survived for at least three years and grown to a minimum of 25 employees. The managers were from large firms (250 or more employees) and at the middle level. Both samples derived from the greater New York City area. The total score mean for the entrepreneurs of 7.74 was significantly above the mean of 4.07 for the managers on Form T ($t=2.26$, p $<.05$). Significant results in the predicted direction were also obtained on two subscales – Self Achievement ($t=2.62$, p $<.01$) and Planning for the Future ($t=1.77$, p $<.05$). Thus, task role motivation theory appears to be just as applicable to females as it is to males. This is an important finding because unlike achievement motivation theory (McClelland, 1961), task role motivation theory is not a theory for males only. In this connection it should be noted that achievement motivation theory has not met with nearly the same degree of research success among females as it has with males either. (Alper, 1974; Horner, 1974; Lesser, 1973; Stein and Bailey, 1973).

Bankruptcy as a measure of entrepreneurial failure

A study by Jourdan (1987) compared the Form T scores of 24 entrepreneurs in bankruptcy with 24 entrepreneurs who had achieved some level of success. No statistically significant differences between these groups were identified. What is striking, however, is that the Form T scores are consistently high. The mean Total Score overall was 9.22. Further investigation indicated that the bankrupts previously had started or bought 3.2 businesses on average and the successful entrepreneurs 5.3. Both groups had had failures and successes in the past. Furthermore, the bankrupts actually studied were those who could still be found at their original places of business, either in (in the American legal system) the Chapter 11 form of bankruptcy or in the same business with a new name. In short, many of the bankrupts appear not to have been true, overall business failures, and the sample studied turned out to be quite unrepresentative of bankrupts generally. These factors appear to account for the overall level of the scores and the lack of differences between bankrupt and successful entrepreneurs. This research is useful primarily in establishing some of the problems inherent in defining entrepreneurial success and failure. As actually conducted, it says little regarding the relationship between the MSCS – Form T and entrepreneurial success.

Planning orientation as an intervening variable

Table 6.6 presents results from a study of owner-managed firms in the electronics industry which had been in business at least five years and had less than 100 employees. The objective of the research was to relate the MSCS – Form T to planning sophistication level defined as follows:

No Structured Planning: No measurable structured planning in the firm; defined as the absence of either structured operational or structured strategic plans.

Structured Operational Plans: Written short-range operation budgets and plans of action for current fiscal period. The typical plan of action would include basic output controls such as production quotas, cost constraints, and personnel requirements.

Structured Strategic Plans: Formalized, written, long-range plans covering the process of determining major outside interests focused on the organization; expectations of dominant inside interests; information about past, current, and future performance; environmental analysis; and determination of strengths and weaknesses of the firm and feedback. Typically 3–15 years in nature.

(Bracker, Keats, and Pearson, 1988; Bracker and Pearson, 1986)

As noted, structured strategic planning behavior tends to occur in association with high MSCS – Form T Total Scores. Not surprisingly, the subscales that contribute most to this result are Feedback of Results and Planning for the Future. Formal strategic planning is not frequent in these small firms, but those who do it have high task motivation. Furthermore evidence is presented that among these entrepreneurs, it is the structured strategic planners whose firms have grown the most rapidly (Bracker, Pearson, Keats, and Miner, 1992).

Table 6.6 also contains information on the MSCS – Form T scores of entrepreneurs heading firms that did and did not survive over a five-year period following the original data collection. The results clearly support the predictive validity of task role motivation theory. In this instance, unlike the follow-up study of high technology entrepreneurs (see Table 6.3), it was possible to obtain definitive data on the subsequent status of all entrepreneurs in the sample.

Research among students

Several validation studies have been conducted with business students, primarily MBAs, at the State University of New York at Buffalo. There is ample evidence that research on students need not yield results comparable to those obtained with entrepreneurs (Robinson and Hunt, 1989).

Table 6.6 MSCS – Form T scores related to level of planning sophistication of the firm and to firm survival in the electronics industry

MSCS – Form T measures	Planning sophistication				Survival history		
	No structured planning (N=20)	Structured operational plans (N=22)	Structured strategic plans (N=9)	F	Firms that did not survive (N=10)	Firms that did survive (N=41)	t
Total score	4.15	6.61	12.68	7.60**	1.80	7.90	3.16**
Self achievement	2.00	1.68	3.78	2.40	0.50	2.58	2.45**
Avoiding risks	0.45	0.63	1.89	1.16	-0.50	1.09*	2.23*
Feedback of results	-0.80	0.63	1.78	4.88*	-0.80	0.53*	1.99*
Personal innovation	2.55	2.81	2.67	0.07	2.30	2.78	0.59
Planning for the future	-0.05	0.86	2.56	3.60*	0.30	0.92	0.69

* p < .05
**p < .01
Note: Where F is significant, the structured strategic planners have higher MSCS – T scores than both of the other groups.
Source: Bracker, Pearson, Keats, and Miner, 1992

However, it was felt that when suitable student-level criteria were introduced, meaningful results could be obtained.

Oliver (1981) included a group of undergraduate business students in his T-score criterion group for the OODQ. The rationale was that grades introduced the same kinds of pushes and pulls for students that firm financial performance did for entrepreneurs. One could flunk out or go bankrupt, and one could graduate with high honors or 'make a million.' In actual fact the students did describe their work context as predominantly of a task nature on the OODQ. This suggested that the MSCS – Form T might be a predictor of grade point average.

MSCS – Form T scores and student performance data were obtained for 65 MBAs who had at least 30 hours of coursework at the time their GPAs were calculated. Actually the GPA was based on all coursework to the completion of the MBA in over two-thirds of the cases. The resulting correlations were not significant in any instance. Clearly the MSCS – Form T is not an all-purpose predictor of academic performance. It should be noted also that the mean Form T Total Score among the students, who came from a wide range of majors, was only 3.12, at the 33rd percentile on the entrepreneur norms and well below the values for practicing entrepreneurs noted in Tables 6.1, 6.3, 6.4, 6.5 and 6.6; MBA students do not look much like entrepreneurs in terms of their MSCS – Form T performance.

This conclusion that MBAs in general are not very entrepreneurial was reinforced in a second study. The students completed the MSCS – Form T and also responded to the following questions – What is your career occupational goal; what position do you hope to reach? What kind of organization will this be in – a university, private business, a company you start, whatever? Only 14 percent of the students in a required organizational behavior course gave any indication of entrepreneurship as a goal. Nevertheless, MSCS – Form T score means were calculated for the entrepreneurial intention and no entrepreneurial intention students as indicated in Table 6.8. This is the same approach used in validating Form H against managerial intentions (see Table 4.1, studies 4, 5, 6, 25, and 26). The Total Score results strongly support the hypothesis, but only one subscale, Personal Innovation, yields significant findings as well. The fact that so few MBA students had an interest in entrepreneurship clearly limited the conclusions that could be reached from this line of research. Accordingly attention shifted to students enrolled in an elective course dealing specifically with entrepreneurship.

As indicated in Table 6.8, two criteria were used with the entrepreneurship students – a measure of entrepreneurial propensity and the course grade. The entrepreneurial propensity questions are given in Table 6.7. Each question was scored 0, 1, or 2 indicating no entrepreneurial response, a partial entrepreneurial response, and a full entrepreneurial response

Table 6.7 Questions used to measure entrepreneurial propensity

Questions	Entrepreneurial response
1. Are you working at present and if so, what are you doing?	Self-employed in a business.
2. What is your immediate career objective after you leave school?	Starting or buying a business.
3. What is your long-range career objective?	Starting or buying a business.
4. Have you ever been involved in founding a business? If so, please describe it.	Founded a business that has not failed.
5. What are your reasons for taking this course?	To learn how to start a business.

respectively; the total possible score was thus 10. The data clearly indicate validity using this entrepreneurial propensity criterion. Table 6.8 also gives the correlations between the MSCS – Form T and the grade received at the end of the course. Since Form T was administered during the first class meeting, this is a predictive finding. The course grade was based on content examinations and a business plan presented first orally and then later in written form. It correlates 0.28 with entrepreneurial propensity. Now, with grading focused specifically on the entrepreneurship area, a relationship emerges which was not present when overall grade point average in business courses was used. The conclusion that emerges is that task motivation pushes people to learn and to do well when studying entrepreneurship, but not otherwise.

A final point regarding the students returns to the matter of their overall level of motivation. In the entrepreneurship course the Form T Total Score was 3.35, approximately at the same level as MBA students generally, and well below the typical entrepreneur. On the subscales the highest score is on Personal Innovation and the lowest on Avoidance of Risk. The students are much greater risk-takers than are most entrepreneurs. The mean entrepreneurial propensity score among the entrepreneurship course students is 2.27 out of a possible 10, low and consistent with the low MSCS – Form T scores. Obviously by any measure these students are not all budding entrepreneurs. Yet the course is consistently filled to capacity. It may be that what attracts the students is the practical relevance of the material more than its entrepreneurial content.

Type of entrepreneurship and MSCS – Form T scores

In addition to the student research, an ongoing research program is also being conducted at the State University of New York at Buffalo using actual entrepreneurs as subjects. These are participants in an entrepreneurship

Table 6.8 Relationships between MSCS – Form T scores and entrepreneurial criteria among business graduate students

MSCS – Form T measures	Students in a required organizational behavior course		Students in an elective entrepreneurship course (N=48)	
	No entrepreneurial intentions (N=38) Mean	Intend to become entrepreneur (N=6) Mean	Amount of entrepreneurial propensity r	Course grade r
Total score	0.63	8.50**	0.65**	0.45**
Self achievement	0.05	1.17	0.58**	0.25*
Avoiding risks	−0.71	1.33	0.12	0.26*
Feedback of results	0.08	0.33	0.48**	0.20
Personal innovation	1.61	4.50**	0.33*	0.20
Planning for the future	−0.39	1.17	0.19	0.24*

* p <.05
** p <.01

development effort conducted by the Center for Entrepreneurial Leadership. As part of the year-long training, a variety of types of information is collected on both the entrepreneurs and their firms. Although a full report on the findings is still several years away, certain preliminary analyses have been carried out (Miner, 1991a). These results may change somewhat as the sample size is increased, but the general pattern insofar as the MSCS-Form T is concerned is already quite evident.

Table 6.9 contains both OODQ and MSCS-T scores broken down by the type of entrepreneur. In past studies we have defined entrepreneurship to include only founders who have been involved in the start-up of their firms. However, the Center for Entrepreneurial Leadership group is more broadly designated. To date it has included five types of entrepreneurs:

1. Independent start-up entrepreneurs – those who started the firm as sole founder.
2. Team start-up entrepreneurs – those who started the firm as part of a team of two or more owners.
3. Corporate entrepreneurs – those who either head a new and distinct venture within an established business or are responsible for taking an established business in new directions; the entrepreneurial effort exists within the boundaries of an existing organization of some size.
4. Family successors – those who either have taken over an existing family small business or are in the process of doing so.
5. Private practitioners – those who started a private sales or professional practice to provide a personal vehicle for pursuing the specialty.

There are few differences among these types insofar as size of firm and entrepreneur characteristics are concerned, except that the private practices have much fewer employees and much lower annual sales volume.

On the OODQ the T scores are consistently high across all groups; by this definition entrepreneurship is not restricted to those engaged in start-ups. No group has a meaningfully high H score, but the small private practices, as one would expect, are practically devoid of hierarchy. Only these same private practices have significantly elevated P scores, and these firms do contain a preponderance of professionals. The G scores are all quite low.

Consistent with the high OODQ T scores, and theoretical expectations, the MSCS-T Total Score is very high overall. However, it is less high among the private practitioners, who are beginning to look more and more like professionals rather than entrepreneurs, and also among the corporate entrepreneurs, who on other evidence have a strong managerial bent. In line with their total scores the private practitioners are generally low on the subscales, except for Avoiding Risks, where they are very high. The most striking subscale finding in Table 6.9, however, involves Personal Innovation. Here the founders, whether sole or team, are indeed distinctive.

Table 6.9 OODQ and MSCS – Form T scores for entrepreneurs of different types

| | Type of entrepreneur | | | | | |
| | Start-up | | | | | |
	Independent (N=12)	Team (N=12)	Corporate (N=9)	Family successor (N=9)	Private practice (N=5)	F
OODQ						
T score	8.50	8.58	7.67	9.33	10.20	0.51
H score	2.00	3.00	3.89	3.89	0.20	3.16*
P score	5.33	4.42	5.22	2.11	7.20	4.31**
G score	3.00	3.50	3.44	1.11	1.60	2.24
MSCS – Form T						
Total score	12.00	12.25	7.44	12.44	5.00	2.94*
Self achievement	3.83	3.42	2.89	4.00	1.80	1.04
Avoiding risks	1.00	2.08	1.22	0.67	3.80	1.66
Feedback of results	2.00	0.67	0.11	1.22	−1.00	2.00
Personal innovation	5.42	5.42	2.89	4.33	1.40	4.92**
Planning for the future	−0.25	0.67	0.33	2.22	−1.00	1.71

* p <.05
**p <.01
Source: Miner, 1991a

It appears that what characterizes founders in particular is their propensity for innovation. In other respects related to task role motivation theory, founders do not differ sharply from entrepreneurs more broadly defined.

Task motivation in a single firm

An issue that is not adequately handled by task theory relates to whether task motivation is characteristic in entrepreneurial firms and particularly among their management ranks, or is restricted to those who function in an ownership capacity. Unsystematic evidence from the author's consulting practice suggests that other managers in entrepreneurial firms headed by an individual with high Form T scores do not necessarily have the same high task motivation. But something more definitive is needed. To this end Porter (1991) undertook a study at all levels in a single firm. The results of this research insofar as the MSCS-Form H is concerned have been reported already in Chapter 4. We now turn to the Form T findings.

The company involved is a manufacturing firm with 180 employees. It has grown and prospered under its present owner who purchased the company some years ago. The owner is a true entrepreneur with a very high Form T score. Yet with sales of $21 million, it may be stretching the term somewhat to call the company an entrepreneurial organization. It has five levels of hierarchy, and in a number of respects has made the transition to a bureaucratic form. Yet with the entrepreneur who expanded the organization still in place, many features of an earlier period are also retained. Although not all employees were tested, the 92 who were include all company personnel except for a substantial proportion of the production workforce. In the analyses reported in Table 6.10, the salespeople are included with management because they are paid on a commission basis and work in a context which appears to be consonant with task theory.

Table 6.10 MSCS – Form T score levels in a single entrepreneurial firm

	Mean scores			
MSCS-T measure	Shop and office employees (N=74)	Management and sales employees (N=18)	t	r with occupational level (N=92)
Total score	3.81	12.28	5.08**	0.47**
Self achievement	1.09	3.39	3.43**	0.34**
Avoiding risks	0.97	0.83	0.22	−0.02
Feedback of results	0.38	2.61	4.10**	0.40**
Personal innovation	1.74	3.06	2.28*	0.23*
Planning for the future	−0.38	2.39	3.90**	0.38**

* $p < .05$
**$p < .01$
Source: Porter, 1991

It is apparent that the management and sales employees have unusually high Form T scores (at almost the 75th percentile for entrepreneurs), while the office and shop employees are not particularly high. The elevation is most pronounced on Self Achievement, Feedback of Results and Planning for the Future among the subscales. The correlational analysis with occupational level yields essentially the same result. What this study shows is that true entrepreneurs *can* surround themselves with highly task motivated people, as well as people who are hierarchically motivated. How often this happens we do not know. The theory is mute on the subject. In future research of this type, however, the OODQ should definitely be utilized; it was not possible to do so in the present study.

VALIDITY OUTSIDE THE DOMAIN AND RELATED LITERATURES

Although validation research outside the domain of task theory has not been extensive, it does support theoretical expectations. Without exception where studies of this kind have been conducted, significant validities have failed to emerge using the MSCS – Form T Total Score.

As part of the study described in the first half of Table 6.8, calculations were made as to the relationship between the MSCS – Form T and a managerial career choice. This approach uses a criterion from the domain of hierarchic theory with the predictor for the task domain. There should be no relationship and there is none. Yet in the same sample Form T does predict the choice of an entrepreneurial career.

Saydjari (1987) conducted a study relating MSCS – Form T scores to areas of major concentration among graduate nursing students. The areas considered were advanced clinical, nurse practitioner, and nursing management. Extrapolating from professional role motivation theory, one might expect the nursing management students to score higher. This did not occur; there were no significant differences among the three groups. The mean MSCS – Form T score among the graduate nursing students overall was 3.68, not a particularly high value.

Mayer (1987) extended this type of analysis to the realm of nursing practice. She compared staff nurses and head nurses in two hospitals on the MSCS – Form T. No difference was found on Total Score. However, there were significant differences in favor of the head nurses on two of the subscales – Self Achievement ($p < .01$) and Personal Innovation ($p < .05$). Given the lack of total score results and the fact that the staff nurses actually scored higher, though not significantly so, on the other three subscales, it is not possible to interpret these results as supporting validity in this professional, or perhaps semi-professional, context. Furthermore the mean Total Score for the two groups combined was 4.14, which is at the 37th percentile on the published norms for entrepreneurs (Miner, 1986).

Other than reviews by the author (such as Miner, 1990a), no treatments of the literature on task role motivation theory itself are as yet available. There is, however, a substantial body of research on achievement motivation theory that clearly supports the tack that task theory takes. The contributions of David McClelland (1961) to the development of the theory are indicated in Chapter 1. A review by Steiner and Miner (1986) of research on the achievement motivation–entrepreneurship connection conducted since the original 1961 publication has this to say:

> A sizable amount of study has been devoted to the question of the relationship between entrepreneurship and the desire to achieve. The data consistently indicate that people who found new businesses where none existed before and make them survive have high levels of achievement motivation (Hines, 1973; Hornaday and Aboud, 1971; Hornaday and Bunker, 1970).
>
> ... This finding, that achievement motivation is related to entrepreneurship, extends not only to those who found businesses but to other managers in whose jobs the entrepreneurial role predominates. Furthermore, entrepreneurs who have high levels of achievement motivation tend to head firms that grow more rapidly in terms of such indexes as sales volume, number of employees, and total investment in the business than do companies headed by entrepreneurs with lesser achievement needs (Hundal, 1971; McClelland and Winter, 1969; Wainer and Rubin, 1969).
>
> It is even true that higher levels of achievement motivation are found in those who obtain financing for a new business from lending agencies as opposed to those who are rejected (Pandey and Tewary, 1979). These links between achievement motivation and entrepreneurship appear to take the following form:
>
> 1. Individuals differ in the degree to which achievement is a major source of satisfaction.
> 2. Highly achievement motivated people have certain characteristics:
>   a) They are more concerned with achieving success than avoiding failure and thus do not concentrate their energies on warding off adversity.
>   b) They tend to give close attention to the realistic probabilities for success associated with different alternatives.
>   c) They much prefer situations in which they themselves can influence and control the outcome rather than having success depend on chance factors.
>   d) They are strongly future-oriented and are willing to wait for rewards.

e) They prefer situations in which there is a clear criterion of whether they are succeeding.

f) They prefer situations involving clear-cut individual responsibility so that if they do succeed that fact can be attributed to their own efforts.

3. These characteristics are inherent in the entrepreneurial job, and thus people with high achievement motivation will be attracted to this type of work and, because they fit its requirement more closely, will be more likely to achieve success (business growth).

(Steiner and Miner, 1986: 268–70)

McClelland's preferred method of measuring achievement motivation consistently has been the Thematic Apperception Test, and he has reported good results in predicting entrepreneurial criteria using that approach. An example is his prediction of the careers followed by Wesleyan University students subsequent to graduation (McClelland, 1965). However, others have used a variety of other measures of achievement motivation, many of them of a nonprojective nature. While not all studies in the latter category have been successful in demonstrating an achievement motivation–entrepreneurship link, many have proven quite successful. Thus, Miller and Droge (1986) obtained supportive results using the Steers and Braunstein (1976) instrument with the chief executives of firms in French Canada, and Davidsson (1989) used a measure he himself developed to successfully predict entrepreneurial activity, including firm growth, among Swedish entrepreneurs. All in all the line of research that McClelland's theory set in motion has produced results entirely consistent with those generated by task role motivation theory. These positive results span a 30-year period.

CONSTRUCT VALIDITY

The concurrent and predictive studies already noted provide considerable evidence in support of the construct validity of the task role motivation theory and the way in which its constructs have been operationalized. Here we move beyond this evidence to a new set of considerations.

Relationships with other constructs and variables

One line of evidence in this regard relates to the sources from which entrepreneurs obtain their capitalization. One might expect that entrepreneurs who were more task motivated would not use their personal savings to fund the business unless they had to. In particular those who were most risk averse would not put their personal savings at risk and those who were most innovative would devote their innovative capabilities to finding other avenues for funding. Similarly, high task motivation entrepreneurs would avoid banks because of the numerous controls banks often impose on their creditors; this would be a special problem for high self-achievement entrepreneurs. On the other hand entrepreneurs who are highly task motivated may tend to be attracted to venture capitalists because they are viewed as kindred spirits. Given that venture capitalists often want realistic plans and systems for evaluating venture success, entrepreneurs who are motivated to provide these things may have the best success with venture capitalists. Accordingly, high Planning for the Future and Feedback of Results scores should go with venture capitalist funding.

Table 6.11 provides results related to the matter of funding sources. The data indicate that there is an association between task motivation and funding source. What they do not say, however, is whether those with high task motivation are more likely to seek out certain funding sources or alternatively, whether these funding sources are more likely to respond positively (or negatively) to people with high task motivation. In any event the findings coincide well with prior expectations, and thus contribute to the case for construct validity.

Another source of information derives from various measures related to entrepreneurial activity which were administered to a group of 33 entrepreneurs and 48 graduate students in entrepreneurship courses, both involved in programs administered by the School of Management at the State University of New York at Buffalo. The data from this source indicate no relationship between intelligence and the MSCS – Form T, as with the other MSCS instruments, but there are relationships with a number of measures that have become associated with entrepreneurship through various studies and reviews (Bird, 1989; Brockhaus and Horwitz, 1986; Begley and Boyd, 1987).

One set of findings involves the construct of locus of control as originally formulated by Rotter (1966) and later operationalized by Levenson (1974). MSCS – Form T Total Scores are consistently positively correlated with internal control and negatively correlated with external control, of both the powerful others and chance control varieties. On the subscales the major findings are that Self Achievement is positively related to internal control and Personal Innovation is negatively related to external control by powerful others. In these instances where significance is attained, the correlations are generally in the 0.30s.

Type A behavior, as measured by the instrument developed by Matteson and Ivancevich (1982), shows a strong positive relation; those with high MSCS – Form T Total Scores are very much Type A people. This is particularly true with regard to the Self Achievement subscale where the correlations reach into the 0.50s.

On the Ghiselli (1971) Self Description Inventory the only finding is

Table 6.11 Differences between entrepreneurs who did and did not use various sources of start-up capital on the MSCS – Form T

MSCS – Form T measures	Used personal savings	Did not use personal savings	Used banks	Did not use banks	Used venture capitalists	Did not use venture capitalists
Total score	5.27	9.00*	1.69	6.46*	10.29	5.35*
Self achievement	1.64	1.67	0.31	1.81*	2.43	1.54
Avoiding risks	0.55	1.95*	-0.92	1.01**	1.21	0.74
Feedback of results	-0.64	-0.10	-1.08	-0.48	0.43	-0.67*
Personal innovation	2.70	3.71*	1.92	3.00	3.64	2.78
Planning for the future	1.02	1.76	1.46	1.11	2.57	0.96*

* Difference significant at p <.05
**Difference significant at p <.01
Note: No MSCS – Form T differences were found for the U.S. Small Business Administration, friends and relations, and other business people as sources of start-up capital.
Source: Miner, Smith, and Bracker, 1989

that the MSCS – Form T is significantly positively related to the Initiative scale; this is true for Total Score, Self Achievement, and Planning for the Future. Given the histories and objectives of the SDI and Form T, one would not expect to obtain many relationships between them. It is intriguing that relationships do appear with Initiative, which would seem to be a characteristic closely related to starting a business.

Data are also available using two measures of cognitive style. The first is the Slocum and Hellriegel (1983) instrument which has its origins in the Jungian typology (Jung, 1923). On this measure entrepreneurs are expected to be intuitive but not sensing, and thinking but not feeling. The correlations with the MSCS – Form T only partially follow this pattern. No relationships involving intuition and sensing emerge. However MSCS – Form T Total Score and the Self Achievement subscale consistently are positively related to the Thinking scale and negatively related to the Feeling scale with correlations in the 0.30s. On the Rowe and Mason (1987) instrument, which also follows the Jungian typology, entrepreneurship is associated with higher scores on the Directive and Conceptual styles and lower scores on the Analytical and Behavioral styles. We do find positive correlations between MSCS – Form T Total Score and the Directive style, although the values are only in the 0.20s. The Analytical and Conceptual measures do not yield much, but negative relationships with the Behavioral style are found.

Overall it appears that those with high Form T scores tend to be thinking (directive) in style, and not to be feeling (behavioral). The other cognitive style expectations are not met, but the original empirical support for these expectations was not strong in any event (Slocum and Hellriegel, 1983; Rowe and Mason, 1987).

One additional finding relates to a single subscale. An adaptation of the Personality–Attitude Schedule (Shure and Meeker, 1967) developed by Harnett and Cummings (1980) provides a 17-item index of Risk Avoidance. This Risk Avoidance measure is not significantly related to MSCS – Form T Total Score or any subscale score except Avoiding Risks. There, significant correlations in the 0.30s are found consistently; the two risk avoidance measures are correlated, although given the projective–nonprojective caveat discussed in Chapter 4, one would not expect the correlations to be high, and they are not.

Relationships to the MSCS – Form H and Form P

Substantive information on the relationship of Form T and Form H is available from several sources – the graduate students in an entrepreneurship course, the entrepreneurs in the SUNY-Buffalo program, and a mixed sample of entrepreneurs and managers (Miner, 1990a). The Total Score correlations in these three samples are 0.24, 0.11, and 0.29. Only the last is significant (p <.05). If one limits the analysis to subscales only, the median value is 0.06. The only relationship between subscales that exhibits any stability across samples is between Feedback of Results (Form T) and Competitive Games (Form H); the median r is 0.35. Since games involve scoring which tells you where you stand, this is not an unexpected finding. In two of the three samples Feedback of Results is significantly (p <.05) correlated with Form H Total Score also. Given that the Competitive Games–Feedback of Results relationship is a major contributor here, it probably would be wise to avoid attributing too much to this finding. There is no Form H subscale that correlates consistently with the Form T Total Score.

This analysis has not been informed by the Porter (1991) study. In that instance both Form T and Form H were positively correlated with occupational level, a result that may or may not be typical, but which could well contribute to an inflated correlation between the two measures. The correlation in fact is 0.46 for Total Score. This finding by its very nature suggests that the relationship is exaggerated to some degree, given the previously noted results. The median inter-subscale correlation rises from the previously noted 0.06 to 0.16. The finding of a relationship between Feedback of Results and Competitive Games is replicated in this sample, and at essentially the same level (r=.34, p <.01). There are numerous other significant relationships. In all likelihood these latter are a consequence of the fact that this is a firm engaged in the transition from entrepreneurship to hierarchy, and perhaps, also, an atypical firm of this nature. Subsequent research will have to answer these questions.

With regard to the Form T versus Form P relationship, there are only the two samples of entrepreneurship students and entrepreneurs to rely on. The median Total Score correlation is 0.11, with correlations of −0.08 and 0.29 in the respective samples, neither of which is significant. The median correlation among subscales is 0.07. In no case does a significant relationship between two variables replicate across both samples, and there are only five significant correlations among the 72, in any event. Overall the relationship between Form T and Form P may be somewhat less than the other MSCS relationships, but the low positive trend remains.

Relationship among the aspects of task motivation

Information on subscale interrelations within the MSCS – Form T is available from a number of sources. In the graduate entrepreneurship course, the median r was 0.00 and among the entrepreneurs 0.14. In more diverse samples of graduate students at SUNY-Buffalo median correlations of 0.12, 0.14, and 0.15 have been obtained. Among the high technology entrepreneurs the figure was 0.18 (Miner, Smith, and Bracker, 1989). Bellu, Davidsson, and Goldfarb (1990) report a median r of 0.24 when all their samples are combined. Bellu (1988) obtained a value of 0.13 for his combined U.S. samples. Porter's (1991) finding is 0.19. The greatest clustering appears to be around a value of 0.14. There are no subscale relationships that hold consistently across multiple samples.

Response bias versus activity drive

As one looks at the various relationships among and between MSCS variables discussed in this chapter, and in Chapters 4 and 5, a very consistent pattern emerges. Subscale intercorrelations concentrate heavily in the range just below 0.15. Subscale correlations across scales tend to be lower, below 0.10, while Total Score correlations between versions of the MSCS average about 0.10 points higher at something like 0.25. Yet all of these values are positive and all are low. It is as if there is a pervasive, although weak, wind blowing through the data which creates a tendency for those who score high on one measure to score high on another – not by much and not always in any one study, but with a large number of samples the trend is clearly identifiable.

One possible explanation is that some type of positive response bias is operating, so that those who complete one stem positively have a tendency to complete others positively as well. They are more prone to positive reactions, while others tend to be more negative. Such an interpretation assumes that the processes involved are introducing a source of error into the measurement process, at least insofar as the intended goals of the measure are concerned.

There are two lines of evidence that raise questions regarding this hypothesis. First, one would think, if it were true, that the positive correlations would be higher where a multiple-choice version is used. We know that multiple-choice tests produce more positive scores in any event and this might be expected to extend to correlations, if the introduction of multiple-choice answers permits greater positive response bias. In a study of police officers by Holland (1980), the median subscale intercorrelation on the MSCS – Form H multiple-choice version was 0.22. Lardent (1979) reports multiple-choice intercorrelations of 0.15 and 0.12 for the regular MSCS – Form H and the situation specific version respectively among Army officer candidates. Steger, Kelley, Chouiniere, and Goldenbaum (1975) indicate a median subscale intercorrelation of 0.19 for their highly nonprojective and somewhat altered MSCS – Form H using a multiple-choice format, as contrasted with a value of 0.14 for the regular free response measure. Overall, there may be a slight increase in correlation size with the multiple-choice format, but it is no more than 0.05, if that. Results at this level of marginality cannot be used to support a claim of positive response bias in the MSCS measures overall, although they certainly do not preclude it.

A second line of evidence derives from the items used in the three

MSCS instruments. Form H utilizes only positively scored items, which provide no opportunity to check on positive response bias. Form P has only one item that is reverse scored (in a manner inconsistent with positive response bias) and that in only some of its aspects. However, Form T has 35 percent of its items reverse scored. If response bias were operating in a major way, Form T should yield correlation results very different from Form H and Form P. It clearly does not. Accordingly, positive response bias appears incapable of explaining the overall positive trend in the correlations. Certainly, more research would be desirable, and it is not possible to rule out some error of this kind, but any such error simply does not appear to be sufficient on the evidence to explain the overall findings.

What then may be operating? A real possibility, given the nature of the variables under consideration, is that some very basic, perhaps even inherited, activity drive may be involved. In all instances we are talking about motives. Perhaps, indeed, these are motive patterns or composites, but all of the ingredients are motivational. It is not beyond reason that some motivational force may permeate all of the measures to produce differences in drive level, and a low positive correlation.

CHAPTER SUMMARY

The validation evidence for the task role motivation theory is strong and convincing. It is both concurrent and predictive in nature. The high technology study has produced positive results over a wide range of analyses. Comparisons of entrepreneurs and managers on Form T have yielded higher scores for the former in the U.S., in a number of foreign countries, and among females. Resort to formal planning is associated with greater task motivation among entrepreneurs. MBA students who are more oriented toward entrepreneurship have been found to score higher on the MSCS-T. Scores have also been shown to be high across a broad range of entrepreneurs, extending well beyond the traditional business founders. The only truly negative finding has been a failure to differentiate between bankruptcy filers and successful entrepreneurs. However, confoundings within the samples make interpretation of these findings suspect, and high Form T scores were obtained across both groups.

Validity outside the domain is minimal, if not nonexistent. Findings for the task role motivation theory closely parallel those for achievement motivation theory, although the former is found to be more applicable where females are concerned. Finally there is evidence of a low, consistent positive correlation both within and between the various MSCS measures. Although response bias could account for this finding, this explanation seems unlikely. A more plausible explanation is that some type of activity drive operates across all three measures.

Traditionally, evidence for theoretical validity has focused on the types

of concurrent, predictive, and construct research considered in this and
the two previous chapters. Yet there is another approach in which the
independent variables of a theory are manipulated and dependent variables
are measured. This is the approach considered in Chapter 7. Most of the
research involves the hierarchic theory.

Chapter 7

Changing role motivation experimentally

Up to this point the discussion has dealt with the more traditional modes of validation, such as concurrent and predictive, criterion-related procedures and construct validity evidence. However, there has been another thrust which does not fit neatly within the traditional framework. This involves introducing an experimental intervention and then determining whether this intervention has the intended motivational effect. In the great majority of studies this intervention has been some variant of managerial role motivation training. This training was originally devised with the specific objective of raising motivation to manage levels in a research and development population, where professional activities often seemed to be preferred to managerial (Miner, 1960; 1965). The theoretical hypotheses are:

1. Approaches such as managerial role motivation training will serve to increase the level of the various motive patterns inherent in the hierarchic role motivation theory, thus contributing to greater managerial success.
2. Other training procedures not focused on influencing hierarchic motivation will not have this effect on motivation to manage.
3. Approaches such as managerial role motivation training will not have an effect on role motivation patterns other than the hierarchic, thus on the motives inherent in the professional, task, and group theories.

MANAGERIAL ROLE MOTIVATION TRAINING

The experimental intervention in the research to be described subsequently is managerial role motivation training. It is important at the outset to understand how this training operates.

The nature of training

The following description deals with the version of the training usually employed (Miner, 1986a). The training consists of 11 modules, and the primary method of instruction is lecture and discussion. The participants are to develop skills in decision making and controlling through the study of methods of diagnosing and correcting the ineffective performance of subordinates. The 11 modules deal with the following topics:

1. The nature of ineffective performance, performance criteria and standards, key factors in performance failure, learning about oneself as a manager, and screening and firing as methods of dealing with unsatisfactory work performance.
2. The verbal ability demand levels of occupations, special mental abilities, identifying intellectual factors in failure, intellectual overplacement, and the use of transfer and training.
3. The nature of emotional problems, the effects of emotions on performance, emotions and effectiveness at different job levels, managerial action in dealing with emotional problems, alcoholism and drug problems.
4. The individual's motivational hierarchy, general and specific work motivation, methods of dealing with motivational problems, and the appropriate use of threat and discipline.
5. Physical illness and job performance, physical disorders of emotional origin, the performance consequences of aging, and the role of the manager in dealing with physical problems.
6. Performance effects of family crises, the nature of separation anxiety reactions, predominance of family over job considerations, and possible managerial actions in instances of family-based failure.
7. Group cohesiveness as a cause of failure, failure by managerial definition, inducing a positive group impact, sources of manager-induced performance problems, and dealing with oneself as a manager.
8. Ineffective performance and top level policies, failures of implementation, inappropriate personnel placement, organizational over-permissiveness, excessive spans of control, and the use of inappropriate performance standards and criteria.
9. Job-value conflicts, alternatives for managerial action in dealing with cultural values, and the prospects for value change.
10. Subjective danger situations, dealing with economic and geographic causes of unsatisfactory performance, accident-proneness, danger in the work, and problems in the work itself.
11. The managerial job, aspects of motivation to manage, the managerial job as a subjective danger situation, avoidance motivation and managerial performance, and the difficulties of managerial self-control.

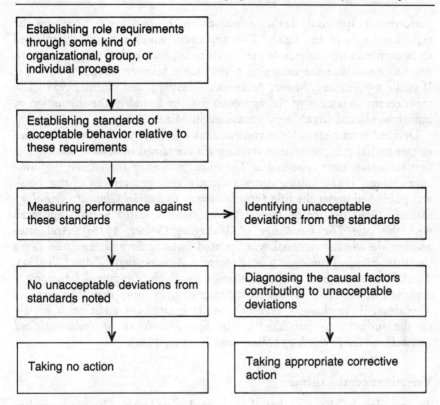

Source: Miner, 1988: 20

Figure 7.1 How the diagnosis and corrective action emphasis in managerial role motivation training relates to other human resource management activities

Frequently the lecture and discussion are supplemented with case analyses. Detailed written cases dealing with instances of ineffective performance are provided to participants and they are to determine what factors combined to cause the performance difficulties, as well as what corrective actions might be taken. Individual participants present their own analyses of the cases orally. Other participants and the trainer then make a critique of these presentations. To encourage individual responsibility, case analyses and presentations are done on an individual rather than a group basis. In addition to this analysis of written cases, participants are also encouraged to discuss specific instances of performance failure from their own experience as the training progresses.

A major thrust of the training is how managers should go about dealing with ineffective performance in subordinates. Figure 7.1 provides an overview of this thrust in relation to procedures such as job analysis and performance appraisal. Training focuses on the two lower boxes on the right-hand side of the figure. This approach, which is variously referred to as performance analysis or performance control, had its origins in work done to determine the causes of performance failures among World War II soldiers (Ginzberg, Miner, Anderson, Ginsburg, and Herma, 1959). The most recent statement of the approach may be found in the discussion of industrial clinical psychology contained in Miner (1992).

Detailed treatments of the content that has been used at various times in managerial role motivation training are contained in several books. The first such statement appeared in *The Management of Ineffective Perform-ance* (Miner, 1963). Subsequently a slightly abridged version of that book was published under the title *Introduction to Industrial Clinical Psychology* (Miner, 1966). A decade later a substantially updated version appeared with the title *The Challenge of Managing* (Miner, 1975a). And after another decade the material was updated once again and rewritten using the title *People Problems: The Executive Answer Book* (Miner, 1985a). The tables of contents of these volumes are given in Figure 7.2 to convey a picture of the changes that have occurred over more than 20 years. As is evident, these changes have been quite limited. In addition, a review on the subject was published in the first *Handbook of Industrial and Organizational Psychology* (Miner and Brewer, 1976).

Variations on the theme

The training has been packaged in a number of ways. The total number of sessions has ranged from 6 to 30, the number of sessions per week from 1 to 6, the length of sessions from 1 to 3 hours, the total duration of training from 3 days to 14 weeks, and the number of participants in the room from 10 to 100. None of these variations has been shown to make a major difference. Even a three-day intensive training effort produces the intended result (Miner, 1988: 169). There does need to be a minimum of some 15 to 20 hours of training. Beyond this the format is largely a matter of convenience.

The extent to which case analysis is included in the training and the way in which the cases are used can vary considerably. The cases are always used as a supplement to the basic lecture and discussion approach, not as the primary instructional approach. They need not be used at all, but they do appear to make the material more vivid and personally mean-ingful. It is desirable to have individuals make case presentations in front of the class (and thus to have them stand out from the group). These presentations may represent personal opinions or the opinions of groups of three to five individuals who work on the analyses together. In any event, the individual is asked to argue for his or her views or against other views (and thus to compete), and to react to views expressed by the

Chapter number	*Miner, 1963, 1966*	*Miner, 1975*	*Miner, 1985*
1	An introduction to performance analysis	Managing as dealing with people (including oneself)	Managing as dealing with people
2	Intelligence and job knowledge	Dealing with problems of intelligence and job knowledge	Dealing with problems of intelligence and job knowledge
3	Emotions and emotional illness	Dealing with emotional problems	Dealing with emotional problems
4	Individual motivation to work	Dealing with motivational problems	Dealing with motivational problems
5	Physical characteristics and disorders	Dealing with physical problems	Dealing with physical problems
6	Family ties	Dealing with family-related problems	Dealing with family-related problems
7	The groups at work	Dealing with problems caused in the work group	Dealing with work-group problems
8	The company	Dealing with problems originating in company policies and higher-level decisions	Dealing with organizational problems
9	Society and its values	Dealing with problems stemming from society and its values	Dealing with society-related problems
10	Situational forces	Dealing with problems growing out of the work context and the work itself	Dealing with problems related to the work situation
11	Special problems in managerial ineffectiveness	Why managers fail and the concept of self-control	Communications skills: Their role in solving employee performance problems
12	Case histories and performance analyses	Case problems in managerial performance	Dealing with problems of managerial subordinates

Figure 7.2 Tables of contents from books presenting managerial role motivation training

instructor (deal with authority). Often written memoranda presenting arguments for various courses of action are solicited from the class (just as they might be if real managerial responsibilities were involved).

Evaluation of these case-related efforts can be in the form of grades, but may also include coaching and evaluative feedback. The evaluations consider the intellectual content of the analyses, but may also go beyond this to deal with the mode of presentation. Is the individual comfortable and effective when cast in the role of manager? If not, why not? And what can be done about it? Often managerial role motivation training involves a certain amount of coaching and counseling with individual participants. In addition, the training is facilitated when the instructor provides a meaningful model of effective managerial behavior.

In addition to cases, films, texts and related readings, role-playing may be incorporated in the training. Singleton (1978) used video-taped scenes dealing with ineffective and effective dispositions of problems role-played by class members, as well as cases written by the participants themselves. In some instances training content has been shifted to give less emphasis to managing ineffective performance and more emphasis to managing other factors. However, the concern with placing participants squarely in the managerial role has been retained. Bowin (in Miner, 1975b: 147–9) has developed an alternative that focuses directly and almost immediately on the various aspects of hierarchic motivation. He utilizes Lewin's (1952) unfreezing–moving–refreezing model quite explicitly to teach the motive patterns of the theory. Readings and cases are added to make his point.

Rationale

The rationale behind the training, irrespective of the variant employed, relies on a distinction between change as reflected in establishing positive motivation and change as reflected in abolishing negative motivation. Where positive motivation evolves, it should be because the course establishes a set of role definitions or role standards for the managerial job; in the psychoanalytic sense, it helps the participants to develop a particular type of ego ideal. They are repeatedly told that as managers or prospective managers they must be responsible for the performance of their subordinates. The job is presented as a complex challenge which can be stimulating, but which is also extremely demanding. Those who undergo training are not only taught *how* to deal with ineffective performance in a subordinate, but they are also taught that they *should* deal with it, and thus maintain satisfactory performance levels within their group. What happens during the course may well be somewhat analogous to the kind of thing Lieberman (1956) found occurring when production workers were promoted into positions as foremen. He was able to demonstrate a reliable increase in pro-management attitudes which developed after the new role was assumed, and which was maintained as long as the person remained a member of management.

The elimination of negative motivation appears on the other hand to derive from a somewhat different type of change process. In this latter case insight into sources of anxiety and distress associated with managerial work should play a more crucial role. The course devotes considerable time to the topic of what is called 'subjective danger,' and to how reactions of this kind may be elicited in the managerial job. To the extent that these discussions are viewed as personally relevant interpretations by the participants, and thus contribute to increased understanding, a reduction in negative motivation should result.

The experimental intervention is thus viewed in ways that derive from psychoanalytic theory in many of their aspects. No doubt other theories now could be mobilized for this purpose, but the fact is that psychoanalytic theory did drive the construction of managerial role motivation training at the time of its inception. To a degree the course was constructed to align itself with certain processes of psychoanalytic therapy.

EFFECTS OF THE EXPERIMENTAL INTERVENTION

What happens when managerial role motivation training in one of its variants is interjected into an ongoing situation? Research on this question goes back to the 1950s and now includes some 15 studies. There are 24 experimental analyses and 11 control group analyses.

Results of training evaluation research

Table 7.1 summarizes the results of these studies in the form of changes from pretest to post-test, or when an after only design is used in the form of comparisons of experimental and control results. When the pretest–post-test type of analysis is employed, it is also useful to consider experimental-control differences at the time of pretest and again at post-test. It is recognized that an approach using analysis of covariance might be more desirable in analyzing the results of this type of research (Arvey and Cole, 1989). In the early years this was not done because the thinking at that time did not call for covariance analysis when pretest differences were not significant; the analyses simply followed common practice. Redoing the analyses now using analysis of covariance procedures is not possible because the data to do so are not available. The problem is compounded by the fact that with one exception all studies carried out since 1970 were conducted by someone other than the author. The one exception is the Miner and Doe (1992) research. In this particular case the analysis reported in Table 7.1 was supplemented with an analysis of covariance to determine if the results would be the same. This proved to be the case, thus giving greater confidence in the overall findings.

Although Table 7.1 contains references to major sources for the various studies, there are several additional sources that report preliminary or partial results (Miner, 1960; 1961b; 1963a). In addition the author has reviewed segments of this research at varying intervals (Miner, 1973; 1974b; 1978a; 1986a).

Table 7.1 Changes attributable to managerial role motivation training

N	Group	Total score	Authority figures	Competitive games	Competitive situations	Assertive role	Imposing wishes	Standing out from group	Routine administrative functions
	1. R & D managers – oil company (Miner, 1965)								
	Pretest–post-test comparison on MSCS – Form H								
56	Experimental	<.01	<.05	NS	NS	NS	<.05	NS	<.01
30	Control	NS	NS	NS	(<.05)	NS	NS	NS	NS
	2. R & D managers – oil company (Miner, 1965)								
	After only comparison on job success indexes								
52	Experimental	p <.01 for difference							
49	Control	between groups							
	3. Undergraduate business students – University of Oregon (Miner, 1965)								
	Pretest–post-test comparison on MSCS – Form H								
59	Experimental – Study 1	<.01							
57	Experimental – Study 2	<.01							
54	Control – Study 2	NS	NS	NS	NS	NS	NS	NS	NS
116	Control – Study 2	NS	NS	NS	NS	NS	NS	NS	NS
89	Experimental – Study 3	<.01							
82	Experimental – Study 4	<.01							
287	Experimental – Studies 1–4	<.01	<.01	<.01	<.01	<.01	<.01	<.05	<.01
	4. Undergraduate business students – University of Oregon (Miner, 1965)								
	Pretest–follow-up comparison on MSCS – Form H								
35	Experimental – Studies 1 & 2	<.01							
46	Experimental – Study 3	<.01							
48	Experimental – Study 4	<.01							
129	Experimental – Studies 1–4	<.01	<.05	<.05	<.05	<.01	<.01	NS	<.01

No.	Study and comparison	n	Group	Significance on MSCS – Form H (total and subscale scores)
5.	Undergraduate business students – University of Oregon (Miner, 1965) — After only comparison on MSCS – Form H at the time of follow-up	82	Experimental	<.01 <.01 NS NS <.01 <.05 NS <.05
		55	Control	
6.	Female undergraduate business students – University of Oregon (Miner, 1965) — Pretest–post-test comparison on MSCS – Form H	41	Experimental	<.01 <.01 NS <.05 NS NS NS NS
	Pretest–follow-up comparison on MSCS – Form H	21	Experimental	<.05 NS NS <.01 NS NS NS NS
7.	Undergraduate business students – San Bernardino State College (Bowin, 1973) — Pretest–post-test comparison on MSCS – Form H	11	Experimental	<.01
		13	Control	NS
8.	Undergraduate business students – University of Oregon – (Korman in Miner, 1977: 172) — Pretest–post-test comparison on MSCS – Form H	18	Experimental	<.01
9.	Undergraduate business students – University of Nevada – (Stoess in Miner, 1977: 173) — Pretest–post-test comparison on MSCS – Form H	62	Experimental	NS
		25	Control	NS
10.	Managers – insurance company central office (Wittreich, 1977) — Pretest–post-test comparison on MSCS – Form H	55	Experimental	<.01 NS NS <.05 <.01 <.05 NS
11.	Student leaders – Georgia State University (Singleton, 1977; 1978) — Pretest–post-test comparison on MSCS – Form H	34	Experimental	<.01 <.05 <.05 <.05 <.01 <.01 <.01 <.01
		20	Control 1	NS NS NS NS NS NS NS NS
		62	Control 2	NS <.05 NS NS NS NS NS NS
12.	Female managers and managerial candidates in a management development program – University of Houston (Singleton and Calvert, 1977) — Pretest–post-test comparison on MSCS – Form H	20	Experimental	<.05

Table 7.1 Continued

N	Group	Total score	Authority figures	Competitive games	Competitive situations	Assertive role	Imposing wishes	Standing out from group	Routine administrative functions
13.	Nursing managers – large metropolitan hospital (Singleton and Calvert, 1978)								
	Pretest–post-test comparison on MSCS – Form H								
43	Experimental	<.01	NS	NS	NS	NS	<.05	<.05	NS
24	Control	(<.01)	NS	NS	NS	NS	NS	NS	NS
14.	Undergraduate business students – Eastern Washington State University (Bowin, 1978)								
	Pretest–post-test comparison on MSCS – Form H								
27	Experimental	<.01							
26	Control	NS							
15.	MBA students – State University of New York at Buffalo (Miner and Doe, 1992)								
	Pretest–post-test comparison on MSCS – Form H								
45	Experimental 1	<.01	<.05	<.05	<.05	NS	<.01	<.05	<.05
45	Experimental 2	<.01	NS	<.01	NS	NS	<.01	NS	<.01

Note: Significance levels are for mean score comparisons. Parentheses ( ) indicate decline in scores.
Source: Developed using Miner, 1978a

Table 7.2 Comparisons of experimental and control subjects at pretest and post-test on MSCS – Form H total score

	Pretest mean score	Post-test mean score	P
Experimental subjects – Managerial role motivation training	2.63	5.95	<.01
Control subjects – Business law course	3.67	3.24	NS
P-experimental vs. control	NS	<.01	
Introductory education course	3.50	3.04	NS
P-experimental vs. control	NS	<.01	

Comparisons between post-test MSCS scores for experimental and control subjects are possible in studies 1, 3, 5, 7, 9, 11, 13, and 14. In studies 1, 3, and 11 the necessary calculations have been reported, and non-significant pretest differences are matched by highly significant post-test differences. The results given in Table 7.2 from study 3 are typical. Here data from two separate control groups are compared with data from an experimental group measured over exactly the same period of time. The effect size of the pretest–post-test change in the experimental group is 0.58. Study 11 is the only one that reports subscale findings. In this instance significant differences in favor of the experimental group were obtained on all subscales except Authority Figures.

Study 5 utilizes an after only design, and thus the results given in Table 7.1 are already those of an experimental-control comparison. Studies 7 and 14 use difference scores for purposes of statistical analysis, and thus an explicit comparison of post-test scores for experimentals and controls is not reported. However, the data do demonstrate significant differences between experimental and control groups in the extent of score changes. Study 13 yields evidence of a significant pretest difference, thus suggesting a need for covariance analysis. Inspection of the findings appears to indicate that such an analysis would have identified a highly significant result in favor of the experimental subjects. Study 9, unlike all the others, yields no evidence of statistically significant change irrespective of how the data are analyzed.

Although several of the studies in Table 7.1 obtained at least part of their post-test data on a delayed basis, rather than immediately subsequent to training, only studies 4, 5, and 6 dealt specifically with the issue of the retention of change. These studies indicate that there is a roughly 25 percent loss in the MSCS – Form H score increase from pretest to post-test that occurs shortly after training is completed. By the time five months have elapsed, however, this delay effect has run its course, and the remaining motivational increase is retained until at least a year and a half after training is completed (Miner, 1965). It may very well be retained much longer, but follow-up testing did not extend beyond this point.

Some idea of the nature of this retention process, and of the changes that occur with training as well, may be gained by looking at certain MSCS – Form H responses obtained from the same subject at three points in time. On the Authority Figures subscale the following pattern of responses to the stem eliciting feelings toward the subject's father is characteristic.

> Pretest: Is a dope. (−)
> Post-test: Is very smart. (+)
> Follow-up: Is a smart man. (+)

An example drawn from the Competitive Games measure deals with yacht racing.

> Pretest: Isn't as exciting as water skiing. (−)
> Post-test: Is very enjoyable. (+)
> Follow-up: Is very enjoyable. (+)

On Competitive Situations one subject responded as follows with regard to the job interview situation. It is noteworthy that the post-test and follow-up statements, although both positive, are in other respects quite different; there is a definite shift from positive emotion to an emphasis on winning out in a competitive situation.

> Pretest: Is a very nervous time, because it is so important for your future. (−)
> Post-test: Is a lot of fun. (+)
> Follow-up: Is a time to look your best. (+)

The Assertive Role subscale item dealing with shooting a rifle elicited this set of completions.

> Pretest: Is exciting, but it can be dangerous. (−)
> Post-test: Is fun. (+)
> Follow-up: Is rather exciting. (+)

Here the reference to danger, which produced the negative scoring initially, disappears, and remains absent.

On Imposing Wishes a subject responded as follows to an item concerned with reactions to a subordinate's request for advice.

> Pretest: I will try to give him the information he wants, but I will let him make the decision. (−)
> Post-test: I will try to give it to the best of my ability. (+)
> Follow-up: I try to give him the best advice I can. (+)

On Standing out from Group another subject produced these statements with reference to operating a business of his own.

> Pretest: The government would probably contrive some method of ruining me. (−)

Post-test: I would feel more secure. (+)
Follow-up: I'd be happier. (+)

And finally, an example from the Routine Administrative Functions subscale deals with making long-distance telephone calls.

Pretest: Is not a thrifty way to communicate. (−)
Post-test: Makes the subject of your call take more notice of what you may offer. (+)
Follow-up: Is perhaps the best way to get immediate attention. (+)

Summary calculations

It is possible to develop summary statistics using the data of Table 7.1, in much the same way as was done in Chapter 4. Among the 24 experimental group analyses 96 percent indicate an overall improvement subsequent to managerial role motivation training. Among the 11 control group analyses none indicate a total score improvement, and in fact there is one instance of significant decline. It is hard to argue with the conclusion that the training does have an impact on motivation.

A number of the studies do not report subscale results, but there are 11 instances involving experimental groups and 6 involving control groups where these results are available. Just over half of these experimental group findings are significant in the expected direction. Only two control group subscale findings are significant – one positive and one negative. The training appears to exert its greatest impact on Imposing Wishes with 82 percent of the analyses demonstrating a significant improvement. Authority Figures, Assertive Role, and Routine Administrative Functions also are influenced frequently – all 64 percent of the time. Competitive Games yields a significant increase in 54 percent of the analyses, Standing out from Group in 45 percent, and Competitive Situations in 36 percent. Apparently the training can have an effect on all aspects of motivation to manage, but it is most likely to increase power motivation and influences competitive drives much less frequently.

A breakdown of these results by time periods is given in Table 7.3. The dates used are those for publication noted in Table 7.1. Clearly some of the 1960s data came from the late 1950s and some of the 1970s studies used data from the 1960s, but the sequencing is stable. The Total Score results indicate no real change in the effectiveness of the training over time. However, there do appear to have been certain subscale shifts. The impact on Imposing Wishes appears to have become even more pronounced in the more recent period, and Standing out from Group which was relatively unaffected in the earlier period has been influenced much more often more recently. On the other hand Authority Figures and Assertive Role appear to have become more resistant to training effects. It is interesting to compare these results with the validity changes noted

Table 7.3 Percent of significant (p <.05) improvements in experimental groups in different time periods

MSCS – Form H measure	1960s (Based on 14 analyses) %	1970s and later (Based on 10 analyses) %
Total score	100	90
Authority figures	83	40
Competitive games	50	60
Competitive situations	34	40
Assertive role	83	40
Imposing wishes	66	100
Standing out from group	17	80
Routine administrative functions	83	60

in Table 4.5. The decline in both the validity and the ability to influence Authority Figures is particularly noteworthy.

A final point relates to authorship. Are training effects found more frequently when Miner is the author? There are eight experimental group analyses in Table 7.1 which were conducted by someone other than Miner. These extend over eight studies and six authors. Only one of these analyses failed to obtain a significant total score result, as contrasted with all of Miner's analyses. What is particularly important about these eight studies is that not only the analysis, but the training itself, was conducted by someone other than Miner. We are not dealing with a phenomenon that is somehow unique to the author.

Effects on success rates

Study 2 in Table 7.1 deserves special consideration because it is the only instance in which subsequent success, not merely motivational change, was used to evaluate the effects of the experimental intervention. The follow-up period in this instance was just over five years. The comparison samples consisted of managers who did and did not experience managerial role motivation training, and who prior to training were at the same managerial grade levels and who were at that time rated as having the same potential for advancement.

Table 7.4 describes what happened in the two groups during the five years subsequent to training. A chi-square analysis on these data defining success as involving either recommendation for rehire or some level of promotion yielded a value of 8.70 (p <.01). The data clearly indicate that those with training outran those without it.

The following examples explain how in specific instances motivational changes linked up with career advances. Clearly these are among the more

Table 7.4 Subsequent success of managers with and without managerial role motivation training

	Participants in managerial role motivation training	Never participated in this type of training
	%	%
Managers who left the company		
Recommended for rehire (if available) at the time of separation – superior rating	69	30
Recommendation against rehiring subsequently at the time of separation – a number were fired	31	70
Total	100	100
Managers still employed		
Promoted 3 or more levels in the 5 years	28	21
Promoted 1 or 2 levels	58	36
No change in level – either promotion or demotion	14	33
Demoted 1 or more levels	0	10
Total	100	100

extreme cases, but they do provide an indication of how the results set forth in Table 7.4 came about.

1. A supervising engineer in research and development received a major promotion a year and a half after training to a position in product development and technical services. Something over three years later he moved up again to become administrative assistant in finance and accounting, and shortly thereafter assistant to the company's executive vice president.

   This young man exhibited a high level of motivation to manage prior to training. Even so there was further improvement after exposure to managerial role motivation training. In particular he developed a more pronounced assertiveness and desire to take charge, as well as a greater interest in standing out so as to assume what amounts to center stage. There is every reason to believe that his newly acquired propensity for visibility accounted for his meteoric rise in the company. In any event his motivation to manage after training achieved an unusually high level, exceeding many top managers.

2. A group leader was promoted several months after training to a full supervisory position within manufacturing's technical services component. Less than a year later he left the company to become assistant technical director in a division of a competing firm. His superior strongly recommended him for rehire should that become feasible. He

was described as having excellent ability and attitude toward his work. He was held in very high regard within the company, and his superiors badly wanted to keep him.

Although initially reasonably high in motivation to manage, this individual still experienced a sizable increase from training. After training he exhibited a strong desire to compete, high assertiveness, an intense need for power, and considerable interest in standing out so as to become the center of attention. These hard driving tendencies no doubt contributed to his seeking, and obtaining, a major career advancement with another firm.

3. A supervising engineer in research and development moved up gradually and something over three years after completing training was appointed assistant to the general manager and vice president of the research and development department.

This individual did not have a particularly high level of motivation to manage prior to training, being somewhat below average in this regard. However, the impact of training was unusually pronounced with major improvements in competitiveness, desire to stand out, and in particular the desire to take on routine administrative functions. These motivational changes appear closely allied with the type of career changes experienced afterward.

There is a possibility that these results reflect a contaminating effect. Those who made the career decisions affecting these individuals could have known who received training and who did not. It is possible that what is involved here is merely a self-fulfilling prophecy. For a number of reasons related to the culture of the organization this is extremely unlikely, but from a scientific viewpoint the possibility needs to be recognized (Miner, 1965). It also should be recognized that this study represents a long-term follow-up. We do not know with certainty that the motivational changes introduced by training were maintained for five years; there was no motivational measurement at the five-year interval. However, the behavior of these individuals appears to indicate that the motivational shifts were maintained, and undergirded the subsequent pattern of success.

Effects of 'teaching the theory'

The following quotes describe an alternative to motivational change that has been proposed to explain the type of results set forth in Table 7.1:

If motivation to manage is a relatively stable personality trait, then it would seem likely that one would encounter extreme difficulty in attempting significantly to alter motivation to manage levels within training programmes of one semester or less in duration. Yet attempts to alter motivation to manage levels through short, specialized training programmes report some success (Bowin, 1973; 1978; Miner, 1977; Singleton, 1977). However, at least some of these programmes apparently included direct exposure of the students to the motivation to manage theory itself (e.g. Bowin, 1973; 1978; Miner, 1975a). Thus, there is a possibility that the students unwittingly may have been trained to complete the post-training motivation to manage measure in line with the theory, particularly since they had already seen the measurement instrument during the pre-test.

(Bartol and Martin, 1987: 3)

Training programmes which incorporate the motivation to manage theory directly run the risk of training students to complete the MSCS in consonance with the theory rather than fundamentally changing motivation to manage.

(Bartol and Martin, 1987: 11)

The original assumption in conducting studies to evaluate managerial role motivation training with the MSCS – Form H was that the projective nature of the instrument prevented respondents from knowing what was being measured. Accordingly training content could not consciously be introduced into the post-test responses to achieve a desired result. This was one of the reasons for developing the MSCS – Form H originally, as an alternative to the supervisory measure created from the Kuder Preference Record (Miner, 1960b). This argument from the projective nature of the measurement process still appears to be valid; respondents in fact do not know what is being measured.

Secondly, the results given in Table 7.4 argue against the 'teaching the theory' hypothesis. Here the evaluation is in terms of judgments and decisions made by others who have observed the training participants' subsequent behavior, not test responses by the participants themselves. There is no opportunity for contamination by virtue of the fact the theory was taught within the course.

In spite of these arguments, there remains a need to test the Bartol and Martin (1987) hypothesis directly. Table 7.5 presents the results of such a test (Miner and Doe, 1992). The data are from two parallel sections of a required MBA course in organizational behavior taught by the author at SUNY-Buffalo. The theory is typically taught in the standard version of managerial role motivation training during the last regular meeting; it is not taught at any earlier point. The thrust of the presentation in the last meeting is that the various role requirements of managerial work can engage motives and emotions which are threatening and highly stressful to an individual, thus making the managerial position a 'subjective danger situation.' Accordingly people may avoid managing and do poorly at it if they try. The six role requirements are discussed in order within this

Table 7.5 Changes in MSCS – Form H scores when the hierarchic theory is and is not taught within managerial role motivation training

MSCS – Form H measure	Group to whom the theory was taught (N=45)			Group to whom the theory was not taught (N=45)		
	Pretest Mean	Post-test Mean	t	Pretest Mean	Post-test Mean	t
Total score	−0.64	3.13	4.01**	−0.51	2.02	4.19**
Authority figures	0.22	0.58	1.70*	0.27	0.44	0.70
Competitive games	0.18	0.91	2.26*	0.38	0.93	2.53**
Competitive situations	−1.16	−0.69	1.68*	−0.89	−0.71	0.62
Assertive role	−0.56	−0.18	1.17	−0.87	−0.56	1.24
Imposing wishes	0.51	1.42	3.15**	0.24	0.93	2.93**
Standing out from group	0.56	0.96	1.83*	0.67	0.40	1.27
Routine administrative functions	−0.40	0.13	1.71*	−0.31	0.58	3.70**

* p <.05
**p <.01
Source: Miner and Doe, 1992

framework – positive attitudes to authority as a source of sexual (possibly homosexual) arousal, competitive needs as a source of cut-throat aggression, and so on. This component was retained in the course for the group to whom the theory was taught. It was omitted in the other group. All other aspects of the training were the same in both groups; the same notes were used for teaching purposes.

As indicated in Table 7.5, both courses appear to have increased motivation to manage (see study 15 in Table 7.1). There is some variation in the particular subscales affected, but even in this respect the results are remarkably similar. Given the nature of the hypothesis under investigation and the fact that control analyses in the past have consistently failed to produce evidence of change (see Table 7.1), a third control group did not seem necessary. Comparisons of the pretest scores on all eight MSCS – Form H measures indicate no instance in which the two groups even approximate a significant difference. Comparisons of the two groups at post-test yield the same results; there are no significant differences. As noted previously, analysis of covariance produced identical findings. The results consistently support the view that 'teaching the theory' is not an adequate explanation of the great majority of the findings contained in Table 7.1. Given the arguments from projective measurement and the results when the post-test analyses utilized success measures rather than the MSCS, it seems appropriate now to reject the 'teaching the theory' explanation.

Effects on correlation coefficients

There is some evidence that managerial role motivation training not only increases mean MSCS – Form H scores, but also reduces the correlation between scores. Across the period of training the correlations between pretest and post-test total score measures in control groups run in the low 0.80s (see, for example, Table 3.9). As indicated in Chapter 3 these same correlations across experimental groups run some 0.20 points lower – at approximately 0.60 (Miner, 1965). Data are not available for most of the studies conducted since the early period, but they are available for the two experimental groups of study 15. Again the median total score correlation is in the vicinity of 0.60. What appears to happen is that the training produces a general reshuffling of scores, above and beyond the overall upward movement. It seems to have a distinctly disturbing effect on the participants' motivational hierarchies.

This is not a new finding. The same results emerged from the early International Harvester studies (Fleishman, Harris, and Burtt, 1955; Harris and Fleishman, 1955). Similarly comparisons of LPC (Least Preferred Co-worker) scores obtained across significant training interventions indicated substantially reduced correlations (Miner, 1980b; Rice, 1978).

Predicting change effects

Such factors as age, job grade level, performance ratings, advancement potential ratings, intelligence, college grade point average, and grades based on managerial role motivation training performance appear to have no capacity to predict increases in MSCS – Form H scores over the period of training (Miner, 1965). Yet there are personality characteristics that can predict this result. These derive from the Tomkins–Horn Picture Arrangement Test (Tomkins and Miner, 1957; 1959).

Table 7.6 presents the results obtained using both the standard scoring keys and verbal measures, after an extensive search for possible predictors across multiple measures from the Picture Arrangement Test; this search included cross validation. The subjects were undergraduate business students at the University of Oregon and the Picture Arrangement Test was administered just prior to managerial role motivation training.

The data appear to indicate that active and independent people are particularly sensitive, and thus responsive, to attempts to alter their motives so as to improve performance in the managerial role. Conversely more passive and dependent people tend to resist this type of influence. These findings possess a certain intuitive logic. One might expect that physically active individuals would be particularly prone to seek out new environments and experiences, and that accordingly the complex demands of the managerial role would appeal to them. After all, managers are

Table 7.6 Mean amount of change from pretest to post-test across managerial role motivation training for individuals with different personality characteristics

MSCS – Form H measure	Mean change among active subjects (N=47)	Mean change among passive subjects (N=110)	Mean change among independent subjects (N=106)	Mean change among dependent subjects (N=51)
Total score	+3.83	+1.72**	+3.25	+0.51**
Authority figures	+0.47	+0.19	+0.42	−0.04*
Competitive games	+0.47	+0.16	+0.35	+0.06
Competitive situations	+0.68	+0.26	+0.52	+0.12
Assertive role	+0.74	+0.42	+0.59	+0.35
Imposing wishes	+0.79	+0.48	+0.77	+0.16*
Standing out from group	+0.23	−0.03	+0.13	−0.12
Routine administrative functions	+0.45	+0.24	+0.45	−0.02

* p <.05
** p <.01
Source: Miner, 1965

generally conceived to be doers much more than thinkers. In addition, the particular measures involved may well reflect not only a tendency to engage in physical activity but a degree of active mastery, such that the individual feels capable of exerting a real influence on the world around him or her. This is exactly the type of person who should be responsive to a course which deals with methods for modifying the behavior of other individuals, in this particular case the behavior of ineffective subordinates. The lack of impact on passive people is not surprising.

There is, in fact, a surprisingly close parallel between the results obtained using the PAT as a predictor of change and the findings reported by Papaloizos (1962) for the Maudsley Personality Inventory. Papaloizos separated his subjects into Neurotic Introverted, Neurotic Extroverted, Normal Introverted and Normal Extroverted groups on the basis of the test results, and then measured the amount of attitude change which occurred with training in each of these groups. Just as on the Picture Arrangement Test where it was the active, 'doing' subjects who changed, so on the Maudsley Personality Inventory it was the Normal Extroverted group. None of the other three groups experienced any modification of their attitudes at all.

The findings with regard to dependency are also generally consistent with what is otherwise known about such people. Again it seems unlikely that dependent people are necessarily resistant to change in all spheres, any more than active individuals would be expected to be especially sensitized to all influence attempts, irrespective of the content. Rather it appears probable that something about the specific kind of change which the experimental course attempted to produce served to arouse resistance in these subjects. The type of dependence measured involves a desire to lean on others for support in the form of praise, assistance, or instruction. The experimental course, on the other hand, tended to portray managerial work as requiring considerable independence, and a capacity to make decisions and act on one's own. It is not surprising that dependent people would reject this type of situation, and fail to develop strong positive motivation appropriate to managerial role requirements.

It should be noted in Table 7.6 that even though the difference in MSCS Total Score between active and passive subjects, and independent and dependent, is substantial, there are few significant subscale differences. What is present is a consistent tendency for those who are more active and more independent to experience change and those who are more passive and dependent to experience little if any change at all.

EFFECTS OUTSIDE THE DOMAIN

There are a number of studies which in various ways are placed outside the domain of the hierarchic theory as it relates to management development.

These studies by definition should not produce significant results; as we shall see they do not.

The same intervention but different motives

As a follow-on to study 15 in Table 7.1, the study undertaken to evaluate the 'teaching the theory' hypothesis, managerial role motivation theory was subsequently evaluated using the MSCS – Form T, not Form H. Would the training yield an impact on motives completely outside its domain? It should not, but would it? The subjects were 34 students in a required MBA course in organizational behavior who completed the MSCS – Form T at the very beginning and at the end of the course. The intervention was the standard version of managerial role motivation training including the 'teaching the theory' segment.

The pretest–post-test comparison produces a slight decline in MSCS – Form T total score from 1.97 to 1.53 (t = 0.49, NS). On the subscales there are no significant changes either positive or negative except for a decline on Feedback of Results (p <.05). This is apparently the factor that accounts for the small total score decrease. In any event the pattern of results obtained with Form T does not in any way approximate those for Form H (see Table 7.5); there are no increases in means with Form T.

Yet there is one finding that parallels the earlier results. The pretest–post-test score correlation is 0.48 for Total Score and the median subscale value is 0.55. Clearly the depression evident across other administrations of managerial role motivation training is still in evidence, even though the measure now is Form T, not Form H. These results should be compared with the test–retest reliability data for Form T where the Total Score correlation is 0.96 and the median subscale correlation 0.78 (see Table 3.12). It appears that although the training does not raise entrepreneurial motivation in the way that it raises managerial, it does reshuffle motivational hierarchies in the same manner.

Different interventions but the same motives

There are several instances where the MSCS – Form H has been administered pre- and post across a principles of management course. Such courses typically deal with the content of the field of management rather than with how to manage effectively, and thus with actually managing something. They do not cast the student in the managerial role, and thus there should be no increase in motivation to manage. If managerial skills are taught at all in these courses, they are given very low priority.

Singleton (1976) compared the MSCS – Form H scores of 74 students in an undergraduate principles of management course at Georgia State University at pretest and at post-test. The overall trend of the data was negative suggesting some decline in scores. However, none of the changes were significant. The findings are entirely consistent with expectations. They are also consistent with the findings from study 5 in Table 7.1 where the experimental subjects who experienced managerial role motivation training had consistently higher post-test scores than the control subjects, most of whom had completed the required organizational behavior course, but in some form that was content rather than skill oriented (Miner, 1965).

A somewhat different type of test of the same hypothesis was carried out by White (1974; 1975). The subjects were supervisors in clinical, hospital, or public health laboratories who underwent training in the form of a concentrated management development course dealing with management subject matter. Topics covered were management and the role of the supervisor, motivation and leadership, use of weights and relative values in planning and control, use of weights and relative values in cost accounting, preventive maintenance, recruitment and orientation, handling personnel problems, performance evaluation, and management for results.

On a specially designed test of content knowledge the supervisors, all of whom were also medical technologists, exhibited a substantial gain from pretest to post-test. However, there was no significant change in MSCS – Form H Total Score. Subscale score results are not reported. Again a basic course in management focused primarily on cognitive rather than motivational objectives failed to produce an increase in motivation to manage.

A management development program studied by Camealy (1968) provided an opportunity to investigate the influence of human relations training on motivation to manage. The program concentrated heavily on case analysis and dealt with such topics as conference leadership, administrative skills, role conflicts experienced by foremen, managerial climates, the managerial grid, need hierarchies, resistance to change, communications problems, and participative management. Readings sampled various approaches to participative management and managerial humanism (Katz, 1955; Roethlisberger, 1945; McGregor, 1960; Blake and Mouton, 1964; Maslow, 1954; Rogers and Roethlisberger, 1952; Meyer, Kay, and French, 1965; Tannenbaum and Schmidt, 1958). The course is variously described as oriented toward human relations according to the Harvard school and toward Likert's (1961) group pattern of leadership. Overall it appears to be rather typical of the human relations courses that were popular from the late 1940s until quite recently.

Evidence of the course's orientation derives from the fact that it appears to have produced a substantial decline on the Initiating Structure measure from the Leader Opinion Questionnaire (Fleishman, 1960). The Consideration measure increased across training, but not as markedly as Initiating Structure declined. Clearly this is not the type of training that would be expected to increase motivation to manage, quite the contrary. The evidence supports this expectation. There was no change in MSCS – Form H Total Score across 30 hours of training administered in ten weekly sessions. There was also no change in the control group. There was, however, a decrease in experimental group scores on one of the MSCS – Form H subscales – Imposing Wishes. This is not surprising given the essentially power-sharing orientation of the training. To this extent the human relations training appears likely to have had a detrimental effect on managerial performance.

A final instance which involves training that derives from a theoretical base other than that of managerial role motivation theory and still uses the MSCS – Form H actually is an application of two different approaches (Myerchin, 1980). The study utilized three conditions, two experimental and one control. The subjects were senior level army officers and civilian officials working for the army. The two experimental courses are described as follows:

Motivation to manage development course (five days)	Personnel management for executives development course (eight days)
Theoretical basis This course is both cognitive and experientially based. It is directly related to the research and writings of David McClelland.	*Theoretical basis* This course is eclectic and is developed from a variety of management theories and individuals. It is primarily cognitive in nature and does not include any experientially based course work.
Practice Five days (40 hours) The course includes selected readings, survey questionnaires, simulations, games, role playing, films, and case discussions. Students are given feedback on their own motives, attitudes, and an inventory of their interpersonal skills. They are taught how to set goals and to integrate the constructs of job requirements, organizational climate, personal qualifications, and managerial style.	*Practice* Eight days (64 hours) This course includes case discussions, lectures, films, conferences, work group discussions, readings, and individual research. The basic design includes case discussion leaders and, minimally, eight guest speakers from universities, industry, and government who provide the stimulus for learning through analysis of case studies and speaker presentations.

Comparison of pretest and post-test measures on several different variables including the MSCS – Form H indicated that no changes occurred in the control group or across the Personnel Management for Executives

Table 7.7 Changes across the motivation to manage development course

	Pretest Scores	Post-test Scores
MSCS – Form H total score	4.27	9.73*
Test of knowledge of management concepts	23.92	29.38*
Thematic Apperception Test (TAT) measures of –		
Achievement motivation	6.50	18.38**
Affiliation motivation	4.15	7.27*
Power motivation	2.08	9.23**

* p <.05
**p <.01
Source: Myerchin, 1980

Development Course. This latter was clearly a content course; the lack of change is consistent with the previously noted findings of Singleton (1976) and White (1974) regarding this type of training.

The Motivation to Manage Development Course, in spite of its name, was not a variant of managerial role motivation training. It was modeled on McClelland and Winter's (1969) achievement motivation training, but went beyond that to deal with affiliation and power motivation as well. As noted in Table 7.7, this course produced a number of changes. It did yield an increase in knowledge of management concepts even though the Personnel Management for Executives Development Course did not. It increased achievement motivation substantially, consistent with the orientation of the course, but it also increased affiliation and power motivation. The power motivation increase would be expected to contribute to managerial effectiveness, but the affiliation motivation increase would not (McClelland, 1975; McClelland and Burnham, 1976; McClelland and Boyatzis, 1982). In fact in most managerial jobs the greater affiliation motivation would represent a detriment.

Given the nature of the course and the changes noted, it is not appropriate to hypothesize that the Motivation to Manage Development Course should increase motivation to manage. The achievement motivation aspect should be irrelevant, the affiliation motivation aspect a negative force, and the power motivation aspect a positive force for that purpose. Yet the MSCS – Form H score did increase (p <.05). Unfortunately subscale data are not available. The findings beg for clarification, but the necessary information is not available.

Change across MBA programs

Two studies have been conducted to evaluate changes across a total masters level program in business administration. The first was conducted at the Advanced Management Institute at Lake Forest College in Illinois in conjunction with Norris Love and Albert Furbay of the Institute. The students are primarily in their 30s and hold full-time positions in their companies. The program is intentionally practical in orientation. The MSCS – Form H was administered to 98 entering students and 55 students who were about to graduate. No significant differences were found on any MSCS measure.

The second study was conducted pre- and post on the same 115 MBA students across the total program at a large Eastern state university (Bartol and Martin, 1987). The MSCS – Form H multiple-choice version was used. The students did not obtain significantly higher Total Scores at graduation than they had obtained before starting the program; subscale results were not reported.

These results are consistent with expectations. Like principles of management courses, MBA programs are primarily content oriented. They prepare students to work in the functional areas of business and they impart the knowledge to do this. There is little that has to do with developing specific managerial skills, or attitudes, or values, or motives. Furthermore those who do the teaching are not managerially motivated; they are basically professionals (Miner, 1977; 1980c). Perhaps there are MBA programs at some universities that do stimulate motivation to manage, but it seems unlikely that many such programs exist.

RELATED LITERATURES

Over the years a number of literature reviews have been published that deal with managerial role motivation training as one of the approaches considered. In the early years there was a marked tendency to contrast the role motivation approach with human relations and sensitivity training (Wohlking, 1971; Campbell, Dunnette, Lawler, and Weick, 1970). The lack of a humanistic bent has been of concern to some, but not to others (see Giegold, 1982). Textbook coverages of the approach within the training literature include discussions by Wexley and Latham (1981) and Goldstein (1986). Latham (1988) considers the extent to which motivation to manage might be involved in management development techniques other than managerial role motivation training. Overall the reaction appears to be that the managerial role motivation approach is somewhat at variance with the major trends that have characterized the training and development field over the past 35 years, but that it is soundly grounded in research, and does produce substantial change.

Courses dealing with ineffective performance

A reading of the management development literature and discussions with practitioners in the area suggest that there are a number of courses being taught which focus on the theme of managing ineffective performance. To what extent these efforts owe a debt to managerial role motivation training is an open question. There have been several books published which deal with the matter of handling the poorly performing employee (see, for example, Steinmetz, 1969; Roseman, 1982; Stewart and Stewart, 1982). No doubt these books have also contributed to the outpouring of management development programs on the subject. In any event it is clear that most of these programs have not been evaluated using the MSCS – Form H. It is interesting to speculate what impact they may have on motivation to manage.

One such program which has been evaluated, although not with explicitly motivation-to-manage-based measures, does offer some insight in this regard. Belasco and Trice (1969) conducted a training program which like managerial role motivation training admittedly had roots in the psychotherapeutic process. The program dealt with methods of handling poor performance in employees. Although the effects of training were not pronounced, they indicated an increasing identification with management and a somewhat decreased tendency to empathize with employee problems. In short, the participants become more fully managerial in their orientation and viewed ineffective employees as managerial problems to be solved rather than individuals to be sympathized with. The overall thrust of these results is consistent with an increase in motivation to manage. Other programs devoted to the management of ineffective performance may well achieve the same result.

Making management education managerial

A recent in-depth analysis of business school education concluded that there was a need for major change (Porter and McKibbin, 1988). Among the points made was that business education should become more relevant, and by implication more managerial. Yet there was little explicit discussion of how this goal might be achieved. The following quotes provide an indication of the nature of this managerial need:

> Managers are not taught in formal education programs what they most need to know to build successful careers in management . . . Professor Lewis B. Ward of the Harvard Business School has found that the median salaries of graduates of that institution's MBA program plateau approximately 15 years after they enter business and, on the average, do not increase significantly thereafter . . . men who attend Harvard's Advanced Management Program after having had approximately 15

years of business experience, but who – for the most part – have had no formal education in management, earn almost a third more than men who hold MBA degrees from Harvard and other leading business schools. Thus the arrested career progress of MBA degree holders strongly suggests that men who get to the top in management have developed skills that are not taught in formal management education programs.

(Livingston, 1971: 79–80)

What student of management is taught how to develop liaison contacts, handle the disturbances that inevitably arise, negotiate with other organizations, innovate in his organization? Some notions of leadership are usually taught, but the fact is that in general we know very little about teaching the managerial roles. Our schools of administration and management have designed their curricula to do other things . . . the management school has been more effective at training technocrats to deal with structured problems than managers to deal with unstructured ones. . . . Although the management school gives students M.B.A. and M.P.A. degrees, it does not in fact teach them how to manage. Hence, these degrees can hardly be considered prerequisites for managing and the world is full of highly competent managers who never spent one day in a management course. The management school will significantly influence management practice only when it becomes capable of teaching a specific set of skills associated with the job of managing.

(Mintzberg, 1973: 187–8)

In only a handful of collegiate schools of business or administration does the faculty systematically, overtly, and deliberately attempt to *train* students to become managers, or, as the modern euphemism puts it, 'to prepare them for a career in management.' Unlike many faculty members in medicine, nursing, dentistry, or law, the contemporary management professor often finds the vocational connotations of 'training' or 'career preparation' to be distasteful to his academic value system. . . . It is their objective to teach *about* management, just as a professor of history would teach his subject with little expectation that his students would all want to become professional historians.

(McGuire, 1974: 3–4)

The important distinction is between (on the one hand) imparting and mastering something called knowledge of business operations and techniques, even the literature of management; and (on the other) developing the socialization, the self-concept, the outlook, the confidence, the sense of responsibility, the commitment and the capacity organizationally and personally to function effectively in a variety of managerial roles.

(Gordon, 1976: 61)

In recent years we have almost forgotten about these issues as the business schools have achieved increasing levels of success. Yet the Porter and McKibbin (1988) report has revived the same concern. Not discussed in that report, however, is the possibility that managerial role motivation training might serve as a basis for structuring business programs that are more managerial in nature (Miner, 1977c). This is a potentially very important outgrowth of the work dealing with the hierarchic theory and particularly the type of experimental intervention considered in this chapter. A business school experience in actually managing, not just understanding what we know about management, could be moulded out of the managerial role motivation training concept. Guidelines for doing this are given in the 1977 article.

Achievement motivation training as task role motivation training

No attempt has been made to develop a task role motivation training program comparable to managerial role motivation training. However, achievement motivation training is oriented to essentially the same objectives and appears to produce the same results that one would hope to achieve with a task role motivation training effort. We have already touched on the subject of achievement motivation training in connection with the discussion of Myerchin's (1980) research. A more extended treatment is given here. Much of the research on achievement motivation training has dealt with programs to stimulate economic growth in developing countries through increased entrepreneurship, and to promote minority enterprises in this country, also through increased entrepreneurship (McClelland and Winter, 1969; Miron and McClelland, 1979).

Figure 7.3 provides an outline for a typical achievement motivation course for prospective or present minority entrepreneurs. A particular course may be longer, or somewhat shorter, and it may be spread out in time rather than concentrated in a single period. However, the content tends to remain the same. The objective is to induce 12 conditions hypothesized as conducive to motivational change:

1. When the person has numerous reasons to believe that he or she can, will, or should develop the motive.
2. When developing the motive appears to be rational in the light of career and life situation considerations.
3. When the individual understands the meaning and various aspects of the motive.
4. When this understanding of the motive is linked to actions and behavior.
5. When the understanding is closely tied to everyday events.

	Day 1	**Day 2**	**Day 3**
Morning			
Session I		Review and critique	Review and critique
Session II		Goal setting	Scoring own TATs for achievement needs
Session III		Discussion of self-perceptions and expectations	Goal setting
Afternoon			
Session I		Origin-pawn game	Goal setting: action team discussion
Session II		Lecture on achievement thinking and business success	General discussion of goal setting
Session III		Analyzing TATs for achievement thinking	Business game
Evening			
Session I	Introduction	Case discussions	Discussion
Session II	Complete TAT	Lecture on business and entrepreneurial leadership	Review and critique
Session III	The ring toss game as an index of risk taking	Review and critique	
Session IV	Organize action teams		

	Day 4	**Day 5**	**Day 6**
Morning			
Session I	Review and critique	Review and critique	Review and critique
Session II	Film on organizational climates	Business development case	Contest in achievement thinking
Session III	Personal managerial style: action team discussion	New enterprise case	Discussion of helping each other to achieve goals
Afternoon			
Session I	General discussion of personal managerial style	Goal setting	Discussion of helping each other to achieve goals
Session II	Goal setting	Goal setting: action team discussion	Development of follow-up plans
Session III	Goal setting: action team discussion	Individual planning	Course summary
Evening			
Session I	Disarmament game	The inner city investment game	
Session II	Review and critique	Review and critique	

Source: Timmons, 1971

Figure 7.3 Outline of an achievement motivation training program

6. When the motive is viewed positively as contributing to an improved self-image.
7. When the motive is viewed as consistent with prevailing cultural values.
8. When the individual commits to achieving concrete goals that are related to the motive.
9. When the individual maintains progress toward attaining these goals.
10. When the environment in which change occurs is one in which the person feels supported and respected as an individual who can guide his or her own future.
11. When the environment dramatizes the importance of self-study and makes it an important value of the group involved in the change effort.
12. When the motive is viewed as an indication of membership in a new reference group (McClelland, 1965a).

There is considerable evidence now that such achievement motivation training does increase the target motive, and that given appropriate external circumstances, this increased motivation will yield expanded entrepreneurial behavior (Durand, 1975; Timmons, 1971). Training of this kind has been provided quite widely in urban areas, often with federal government support. An example is the Metropolitan Economic Development Association program, located in the Minneapolis-St. Paul area of Minnesota, which was funded by the local business community and the Office of Minority Business Enterprise of the U.S. Department of Commerce. One weekend a month – from noon Friday to noon Sunday over a four-month period – MEDA has conducted a program of achievement–motivation training under the title 'Business Leadership Training.' The participants are small-business owners and potential entrepreneurs – most of them members of minority groups.

The training enables participants to develop achievement-motivated behavior patterns – problem-solving, goal-setting, business planning, and risk-taking – through specially designed business games. Participants experience both the anxieties and satisfactions of setting and achieving personal and business goals; and the experiences are conceptualized to real-life situations through practice. Considerable emphasis is placed on examining and testing goals for specificity, realism, challenge, time-phasing, and personal commitment. Any obstacle that may hinder attaining a goal is closely evaluated.

Topics discussed during training include state-created opportunities for small businesses owned by the socially or economically disadvantaged. Participants also complete the Thematic Apperception Test and learn to interpret it so as to understand their own motives.

An evaluation of the program revealed that after training the participants clearly felt they had changed. Follow-up data over a one- to two-year period seemed to indicate they were right:

Participants, especially business owners, showed personal income increases well above the national average.

Among business owners, gross sales increased at a rate well above the national average.

Over half the business owners expanded their business by adding a new product or service or by opening a new business.

Twelve percent of those participants who had not previously owned a business started one after training.

(Metropolitan Economic Development Association, 1977)

Table 7.8 provides information on the effectiveness of an achievement–motivation program conducted in India to foster entrepreneurship there. The comparisons of the trained group with a similar group that was not trained indicate that the training did stimulate desired behavior, especially among individuals who were in charge of their own businesses and thus in the best position to foster business growth (McClelland and Winter, 1969). In this study the training was specifically designed to include the 12 conditions hypothesized to make it work, with the intent of subtracting various conditions in subsequent studies to determine which conditions

Table 7.8 Results of achievement motivation training in India

	Two years before course	Two years after course
Percent active in business development		
Trained group (N=76)	18	51
Untrained controls (N=73)	22	25
Percent increasing hours worked		
Trained group (N=61)	7	20
Untrained controls (N=44)	11	7
Percent starting new businesses		
Trained group (N=76)	4	22
Untrained group (N=73)	7	8
Percent making specific fixed capital Investment (in charge of a firm only)		
Trained group (N=47)	32	74
Untrained controls (N=45)	29	40
Percent increasing number of employees (in charge of a firm only)		
Trained group (N=44)	35	59
Untrained controls (N=46)	31	33

Source: McClelland and Winter, 1969

were crucial. However, it was not possible to carry through on this subtractive design, so we are unable to evaluate the separate hypotheses.

Much of the training that has been conducted in this country and abroad has utilized the McClelland format, following generally the outline of Figure 7.3; it is this approach that has been studied most widely and that has received the strongest research support. However, a number of related, derivative techniques have also been developed, often under names such as personal causation training, self-esteem training, and the like. In some cases these, too, have been found to increase achievement motivation (Jackson and Shea, 1972).

Professional role motivation training

In contrast to the hierarchic and task theories where a substantial body of research exists related to motivation development, there is only one such study within the domain of the professional theory. This study evaluated the effects of a training program designed to increase professional motivation which had its theoretical roots neither in psychoanalysis and psychotherapy as did managerial role motivation training, nor in the 12 conditions McClelland (1965a) set forth as a basis for achievement–motivation training.

The training involved five sessions of two hours each. The participants, as well as the control group members, were all special education teachers or specialists in a single school district (Pilgrim, 1986). Activities included in the training were role-playing, group discussion, self-assessment, lectures, brainstorming, and written responses. The various roles and motive patterns of the professional theory were explicitly addressed during all sessions. Thus, there was considerable repetition in this respect. The activities used to teach each of the five roles were:

Acquiring knowledge – exposure to the training and to the professional literatures.

Independent action – recognition of personal strengths and weaknesses, resolution of problems, decision making and goal-setting.

Accepting status – recognition of status and its symbols, learning how to influence others, and understanding power.

Providing help – learning how to communicate with the clientele served – students, parents, families, colleagues.

Professional commitment – enhancing awareness of the dimensions of commitment and examining the professional ethics and standards of the field.

Extrinsic rewards were provided at various points in the training for completing the various activities. Clearly the theory was taught. The orientation was very much that of learning theory (Skinner, 1938; 1963; Marshak, 1983; Scherer, 1984; Lippitt, 1983). The idea was to make the motive patterns of the professional theory conscious so that learning could occur.

The results were far from striking. In fact one of the most interesting findings was that even when one teaches the theory of the measuring instrument in the most blatant manner, pretest–post-test change need not occur. The only significant finding appears to have been an increase in Accepting Status score with training. The MSCS – Form P Total Score did not change. Inspection of the training materials suggests that what the participants learned was to view their profession as more professional, respectable, and even prestigious than they had previously. Consequently they were more comfortable in the profession and with themselves; accepting status became more attractive. Clearly there is a need for more research on various approaches to professional role motivation training. It seems likely also that the training should be somewhat longer in duration.

CHAPTER SUMMARY

Managerial role motivation training is an intervention intended to increase motivation to manage and thus improve managerial performance. It teaches participants how to diagnose the causes of ineffective performance in subordinates and to use this information to correct performance failures. The individual is cast in the role of a responsible manager attempting to be proactive in dealing with a problem to be managed.

Training of this kind has been studied extensively over a number of years. It clearly has a motivational impact and it appears to improve performance. The positive results obtained by the author have been duplicated by many others. The changes induced are retained over substantial periods. These effects are not produced in everyone; more passive–dependent people appear to be largely unresponsive. Claims that the results obtained are simply an artifact of 'teaching the theory' do not appear to be justified.

Studies indicate that managerial role motivation training does not influence other motives in the same way that it does motivation to manage. Typical management principles courses have no impact on managerial motivation, nor do MBA programs as a whole. Evidence from research on achievement–motivation training indicates that task motivation may be subject to influence in essentially the same manner as hierarchic motivation. An attempt to develop a procedure for increasing professional motivation yielded only very limited results, but deficiencies in training design probably account for the results.

This chapter has considered one type of motivational change – primarily the change in managerial motivation that is produced by management development. In Chapter 8 we turn to another type of change. In this instance the change agent is somewhat more problematic, since no clear experimental intervention is involved. Yet it is evident that major motivational changes did occur, and something must have caused them.

Chapter 8

Changes in managerial talent supplies over time

During the years 1964 to 1966, the author collected MSCS data from graduate students in a required organizational behavior course at the University of Oregon. These data subsequently were used in a career choice study summarized in Table 4.1 (study 5). The students averaged 26.6 years of age and their MSCS – Form H total scores averaged 3.56 – at essentially the same level found among undergraduate business students at the University of Oregon in 1960–1. In actual fact these graduate students, some five years older and five years later, were from the same age cohort.

A reviewer, after reading the manuscript in which study 5 from Table 4.1 was described (Miner, 1968a), suggested that it might be of interest to conduct the same type of career choice study with undergraduates. To accomplish this, data were collected, again at the University of Oregon but now in a required undergraduate business course. This was done in the period 1967–8 entirely for the purpose of replicating the earlier study in the undergraduate context. The results are also given in Table 4.1 (study 6) (Miner and Smith, 1969).

As the second study progressed, however, it became evident that we were dealing with a brand of student very different from the undergraduates of 1960–1 and the graduate students of 1964–6. Now the scores on the MSCS were consistently and substantially lower. The Total Score difference was approximately three full points, more than half a standard deviation. With this happenstance finding a series of studies among university business administration students began, which has now extended over some 30 years. Publications dealing with the topic have appeared in several scholarly books and journals (Miner, 1971a; 1974c; Miner and Crane, 1977; Miner and Smith, 1982; Miner, Smith, and Ebrahimi, 1985). However, at least as much has been written for the purpose of bringing the talent supply question to the attention of practicing managers (Miner, 1973; 1973c; 1974b; 1979b; Miner and Smith, 1981). Research into managerial talent supplies has attracted much more attention in the media than any other line of inquiry related to role motivation theory.

EVIDENCE OF DECLINE FROM THE MSCS – FORM H

The University of Oregon trend data

Table 8.1 presents the initial comparison between what happened in 1960–1 and in 1967–8, the comparison that instigated this line of research. The data for 1960–1 might be considered outliers, because no similar data are available for that period, were it not for the 1964–6 graduate data which led to an identical conclusion (Miner, 1968a). All four samples in Table 8.1 came from required undergraduate courses, which by their nature could be assumed to produce representative samples of students in the program; in all cases the average age was in the early 20s.

Notice that in the ensuing five years after 1967–8 the rate of decline remained almost identical. For at least a period of 13 years motivation to manage declined at a substantial and steady rate at the University of Oregon. The decline may have started earlier, in the 1950s, but we have no evidence in that regard. Furthermore, at no point in the 13-year period do either the Imposing Wishes or Standing out from Group subscales show a significant decline. All other subscales did decline over the period.

Yet in the period from 1972–3 to 1980 there was no evidence of change at all. This was a period of stabilization at the University of Oregon, but the stabilization occurred at a very low level of motivation to manage. Furthermore, it occurred in the face of increasing proportions of female students – from 14% to 12% to 20% to 43%. In the very early period females earned significantly lower total scores, but they were few in number; later this score differential decreased to the point where in 1980 it was totally gone; yet in 1980 there were three times as many females as in 1960–1. A likely explanation is that increasingly females who had majored in education (1961 Total Score at the University of Oregon = 3.59) majored instead in business administration over the ensuing years as the relative opportunities in the two fields changed. Scores decreased in both groups, but less rapidly for the females.

The model set forth in Table 8.1 has been used for the analysis of data from other sources. Although it started as an extrapolation from happenstance data, the decline hypothesis – and the stabilization hypothesis which followed – have received considerable support, beyond the confines of the University of Oregon.

Trend data from other universities

One source of backing for the University of Oregon comparisons given in Table 8.1 is the use of similar comparison data over shorter time spans from other universities. At the University of Maryland trend data are available from 1969 to 1972 for samples of undergraduate business students

Table 8.1 Changes in MSCS – Form H scores among University of Oregon undergraduate business students

MSCS – Form H measures	1960–1 (N=287)	Change/ year	1967–8 (N=129)	Change/ year	1972–3 (N=86)	Change/ year	1980 (N=124)
Total score	3.33	−0.40**	0.52	−0.47**	−1.84	0.00	−1.86
Authority figures	1.17	−0.10**	0.47	−0.06	0.15	0.00	0.14
Competitive games	1.18	−0.07**	0.71	−0.06	0.40	0.00	0.39
Competitive situations	−0.55	−0.07**	−1.04	−0.11**	−1.60	0.05	−1.23
Assertive role	0.32	−0.05*	0.00	−0.15**	−0.77	−0.03	−0.99
Imposing wishes	0.37	−0.01	0.33	−0.04	0.15	−0.01	0.11
Standing out from group	0.38	−0.02	0.26	−0.01	0.22	0.01	0.27
Routine administrative functions	0.45	−0.09**	−0.20	−0.04	−0.38	−0.02	−0.55

* p <.05
** p <.01
Note: Change/year values refer to the difference between the two adjacent mean scores; significance for these values was determined using t tests.
Source: Miner and Smith, 1982.

Table 8.2 Changes in MSCS – Form H scores among University of Maryland undergraduate business students

MSCS – Form H measures	1969 (N=122)	Change/ year	1972 (N=73)
Total score	0.80	−0.59*	−0.96
Authority figures	0.46	−0.18*	−0.08
Competitive games	1.09	−0.27**	0.27
Competitive situations	−1.26	0.04	−1.15
Assertive role	−0.11	−0.30**	−1.00
Imposing wishes	0.66	−0.12	0.30
Standing out from group	0.23	0.11	0.56
Routine administrative functions	−0.26	0.13	0.14

* $p < .05$
**$p < .01$
Note: Change/year values refer to the difference between the two adjacent mean scores; significance for these values was determined using t tests.
Source: Miner and Smith, 1982

in their early twenties. There should be a decline, and there is. Significant results are obtained for Total Score, Authority Figures, Competitive Games, and Assertive Role. Imposing Wishes and Standing out from Group continue to exhibit no change (see Table 8.2).

There are data from the University of Maryland in 1977 which suggest a substantial upswing in scores at that point, although only for Total Score comparisons, not at the subscale level (Bartol, Anderson, and Schneier, 1980; 1981). A subsequent rescoring of a sample of MSCS – Form H records from this data set suggests that the usual initial positive scoring bias operated in this case to produce the reported results (Miner, Smith, and Ebrahimi, 1985; Perham, 1989). Accordingly these 1977 results must be discredited; when corrected for scoring bias the Bartol, Anderson, and Schneier (1980; 1981) data show no change in Total Score from 1972 to 1977.

Table 8.3 deals with changes obtained at Georgia State University in the period from 1975 to 1979. This should be a period of quiescence and stability. The data suggest that it was. There is in fact an increase in Total Score, but not a significant one. The increase is almost fully accounted for by a significant increase on the Imposing Wishes subscale. This is probably a chance fluctuation; in any event it does not occur on a subscale influenced in accordance with the basic model (see Table 8.1). In short, if this is a real phenomenon, it is a new one – not part of the process of managerial talent supply decline.

The final source of trend data is Portland State University in Oregon. The measurement was made over a rather short period, 1966–7 to 1970. However, from the University of Oregon data it appears to have been a period of sharp decline, and thus significant changes are to be expected.

Table 8.3 Changes in MSCS – Form H scores among Georgia State University undergraduate business students

MSCS – Form H measure	1975 (N=74)	Change/ year	1979 (N=51)
Total score	−0.51	0.14	0.04
Authority figures	0.66	0.00	0.67
Competitive games	0.62	−0.14	0.06
Competitive situations	−1.28	0.04	−1.14
Assertive role	−0.31	−0.10	−0.71
Imposing wishes	−0.23	0.22*	0.65
Standing out from group	0.15	0.09	0.49
Routine administrative functions	−0.12	0.03	0.02

*p <.05
Note: Change/year values refer to the difference between the two adjacent mean scores; significance for these values was determined using t tests.
Source: Miner and Smith, 1982

The 1966–7 data are for students in their early twenties in a required management course – the basic pattern. The 1970 sample, however, although from the same course, included a large proportion of older students over 30 years of age. Actually 26 percent of the students fell in this category, and their mean age was 36.8. On the average these students were in their early twenties around 1955, when motivation to manage presumably was at a much higher level.

In order to make the comparison in Table 8.4 meaningful, these older students had to be deleted. The data for 1970 at Portland State are accordingly for the 48 younger students in the sample, and do not include the 17 older students. The change per year rate in Table 8.4 on the Total Score is essentially the same as at the University of Oregon over the same period, and it is significant. Subscale declines do not perfectly match those at the University of Oregon, but three are significant and again these do not include Imposing Wishes and Standing out from Group. All in all what trend data are available from other universities do match the pattern established by the University of Oregon findings set forth in Table 8.1.

Sources of older and younger students

As noted in the discussion of the 1970 Portland State sample, problems can arise in making comparisons involving differing numbers of older students. A large number of older students can be expected to mean higher scores simply because these people are from age cohorts that never experienced the decline, or experienced it at less than its full intensity. If a person was younger than say 21 in 1970, one can be reasonably certain that the full decline has operated. But the older a person was in 1970, the less that is true. A person in the early thirties in 1970 in fact would be

Table 8.4 Changes in MSCS – Form H scores among Portland State University undergraduate business students

MSCS – Form H measure	1966–7 (N=117)	Change year	1970 (N=48)
Total score	−0.03	−0.45*	−1.81
Authority figures	0.57	−0.21**	−0.25
Competitive games	0.78	0.05	0.96
Competitive situations	−1.22	−0.03	−1.34
Assertive role	−0.05	−0.15*	−0.65
Imposing wishes	0.40	−0.05	0.19
Standing out from group	−0.17	0.08	0.16
Routine administrative functions	−0.34	−0.14*	−0.88

* p <.05
**p <.01
Note: Change/year values refer to the difference between the two adjacent mean scores; significance for these values was determined using t tests.
Source: Miner, 1974c

expected to score like the students of 1960. By 1980 a student in the early thirties still could experience some slight effect of this kind, but one would have to be over 40 to be like the 1960s students; in 1990 that same effect requires a person over 50.

Table 8.5 illustrates what an impact these sample differences can have. The scores for the older 1970 Portland State students are listed first; these may be compared with the scores for the younger segment of the same sample given in Table 8.4. On Total Score, Authority Figures, and Competitive Situations there are significant differences between the two groups, always with the higher mean score occurring among the older students.

Table 8.5 also contains data for the older segment of a Georgia State sample. In this instance the younger segment (30 or less in 1975) had a Total Score mean of −2.19 – significantly different at p <.01. There are other significant differences on Authority Figures, Competitive Situations, Assertive Role, Standing out from Group, and Routine Administrative Functions, and again the higher scores always go to the older students (Miner and Crane, 1977). It is very clear that if comparisons are to be made across time periods, samples either must be matched on age or statistical adjustments are required.

Study results from varied universities during the 1970s

In addition to the trend data from the University of Oregon, the University of Maryland, Georgia State University, and Portland State University, there are a number of samples from various universities collected during the 1970s. Five of these samples contain students with an average age in the early twenties, and thus are comparable to the previous samples taken

Table 8.5 Mean MSCS – Form H scores for older students who completed the MSCS during the 1970s

	Older students in an undergraduate management course at Portland State University (N=17)	Older students in a graduate management course at Georgia State University (N=21)
Year	1970	1975
Mean age	36.8	36.8
MSCS – Form H measures		
Total score	1.59	3.67
Authority figures	1.06	1.00
Competitive games	1.41	0.57
Competitive situations	−0.59	−0.57
Assertive role	−0.35	0.29
Imposing wishes	0.65	1.00
Standing out from group	−0.24	1.24
Routine administrative functions	−0.35	0.14

Source: Miner, 1974c; Miner and Crane, 1977

in this time period. These samples would be expected to have low scores; as noted in Table 8.6, they do. The mean Total Score for the five studies is −1.67. The mean Total Score for this period using the data from Tables 8.1 to 8.4 is −1.16. The difference is accounted for by the extremely low scores obtained at Eastern Washington State College. If this sample is treated as an outlier and deleted, the results are practically identical from the two sources. The data from the first part of Table 8.6, where comparison is appropriate, clearly reinforce the previous findings. The median Total Score for these samples through the 1970s is −0.96. This compares with a value of 3.45 for the early 1960s and 0.52 for the late 1960s.

This latter figure is based on studies discussed to date. There is one study from the 1966–7 period that should be added. In a sample of 202 University of Nevada undergraduate business students, a mean Total Score of 3.02 was obtained. There is reason to believe that the decline set in somewhat later at the University of Nevada. There had not yet been any student unrest there by 1967, although there was later, while the West Coast universities had been experiencing protests for several years. The data seem to suggest that decline came later in the Rocky Mountain and Plains States, and in the South, but that by the early 1970s it was every-where. In any event the Nevada data need to be entered in the calculations for the late 1960s. When this is done the median Total Score becomes 0.66; the mean is 1.08.

Probably Total Score figures of 3.5 for the early 1960s, 1.0 for the late

Table 8.6 MSCS – Form H total scores obtained in student samples during the 1970s

Sample	Reference	N	Date	Mean age	MSCS – Form H total score
Samples containing predominantly younger students					
Undergraduate business students at Western Michigan University	Miner, Rizzo, Harlow, and Hill, 1974	349	1971	21	−0.81
Undergraduate business students at the University of South Florida	Miner, Rizzo, Harlow, and Hill, 1974	72	1972	Early 20s	−0.91
Undergraduate business students at Eastern Washington State University	Bowin, 1978	53	1974	Early 20s	−3.83
Undergraduate business students at a large southern university	Brief, Aldag, and Chacko, 1977	103	1975	Early 20s	−0.82
Undergraduate business students at Cleveland State University	Muczyk and Schuler, 1978	183	1974–1976	Early 20s	−1.96
Samples containing substantial proportions of older students					
Junior college business students in northwest Georgia	Southern, 1976	54	1974	26	1.54
Junior college business students in northwest Georgia	Southern, 1976	59	1974	28	−0.24
Advanced Management Institute MBA students		98	1975	33	2.07
Undergraduate business students at Georgia State University	Albert, 1977	69	1976	27	−0.12
Advanced Management Institute MBA students		153	1977	34	2.28
Florida State University MBA students	Overstreet, 1980	78	1979	28	0.32

1960s and −1.0 for the 1970s would be about right for the country as a whole, given the data available.

These calculations do not utilize the six samples noted in the second part of Table 8.6. These samples contain students with an average age of 26 years or more and thus the means should be influenced by a number of individuals who are old enough to predate the decline, or at least part of it. The scores should be higher than those of the younger students during the 1970s, and they are. The mean Total Score is 0.98. Unfortunately age data are not available for these samples in a form suitable to permit correcting for this sort of bias. However, the results are generally what one would expect. The Advanced Management Institute samples contain by far the oldest students and they score highest. No doubt these latter results are also influenced by the fact that a high proportion of these individuals are already managers and were selected for attendance in the program by their companies because they had done well as managers.

The only data in the second half of Table 8.6 that appear to be out of line with expectations in any way are those from the first junior college in northwest Georgia. These are the youngest students and yet the scores are relatively high. No explanation for this finding is available.

There are certain other findings for the 1970s that require discussion. Along with the 1977 University of Maryland sample noted previously, Bartol, Anderson, and Schneier (1980) also report on a 1977 sample of business students from Syracuse University and on a 1977 sample of business students from a predominantly black university (1981). As with the University of Maryland sample there is certain evidence of an upswing in these two samples, and the data are interpreted to that effect. As previously indicated, however, these studies suffered from serious problems in the scoring of the MSCS – problems that have since been studied and found to represent a natural outgrowth of using inexperienced and unmotivated scorers (Perham, 1989). An attempt to correct the original scores for scoring error yielded results which on the average were much like those reported for other studies conducted in the 1970s (Miner, Smith, and Ebrahimi, 1985).

Two other studies produced higher scores than has been the pattern. In 1972, 502 cadets at the U.S. Military Academy at West Point had an average MSCS Total Score of 2.95. This translates to some four points higher than the scores reported previously for students at that time and of a similar age. In all probability this result is a reflection of the particular nature and mission of this institution. The students are there to be trained to become officers in the military and presumably that is what they want to do. In 1972 such a person was hardly one of the vast college student majority (Butler, Lardent, and Miner, 1983). It seems safe to assume this was an atypical finding.

The second sample with unexpectedly high scores came from Rensselaer

Polytechnic Institute (Steger, Kelley, Chouiniere, and Goldenbaum, 1975) sometime in the early 1970s. The age of the 50 students is not given, but would appear to be around 20. Testing was done in a management course, but the students had a variety of majors. From information provided it appears that at least one-third were engineers and it is possible that well over half were. That the mean Total Score was 3.18 may be associated with this fact. The Military Academy cadets also are awarded degrees in engineering. Thus, a likely hypothesis is that technical schools generally and engineering students in particular did not experience the decline in motivation to manage that hit most universities – or these students may have had extremely high scores back in the 1950s before the process began. In any event there is reason to believe that something different may have happened in the technical, engineering context during the 1960s and 1970s than happened elsewhere.

Managerial talent supplies in the 1980s

Published data on changes in managerial talent supplies cut off for all practical purposes with the 1980 University of Oregon sample (Miner and Smith, 1982), although certain information on the subject for the early 1980s has been presented in a somewhat different context (Miner, Wachtel, and Ebrahimi, 1989). The objective here is to update this line of inquiry for the 1980s as a whole using both published and unpublished data. The starting point is the Total Score value of -1.86 obtained at the University of Oregon in 1980, although this figure is probably a little lower than the national average at that time.

The remaining data for the 1980s are given in Table 8.7. These are all graduate student groups. The 1982–3 and 1985 samples have been considered previously (see Table 4.8). All of the samples except for the one from the entrepreneurship course are diverse in terms of major and makeup, and would appear to be representative for the period. Given the ages of the students and the dates of measurement, the difficulty of including students who predate the full decline is less acute in this set of samples than previously. Thus, the fact that the ages here are not unlike those noted in the second half of Table 8.6 does not represent a major problem; it is 10 years later. The only exception would appear to be the 1982–3 sample which does contain a number of older students and also has a higher mean Total Score than the 1985, 1987, and 1988 samples. The difference in this latter respect is not large, but removing the older students, say all those over 35, from this sample might very well eliminate it completely.

The 1988–90 results from the entrepreneurship course cannot be explained away so easily, however. Inclusion of pre-decline students is simply not a factor now. Also the highest scores were obtained by the

Table 8.7 MSCS – Form H scores for graduate business student samples in the 1980s

MSCS – Form H measures	1982–3 15 different universities across the U.S. (N=82)	1985 Georgia State University – varied courses (N=100)	1987 SUNY-Buffalo – required course (N=102)	1988 SUNY-Buffalo – required course (N=46)	1988–90 SUNY-Buffalo Entrepreneurship course (N=72)
Total score	0.24	−0.79	−0.55	−0.66	0.69
Authority figures	0.49	0.20	0.23	0.16	−0.08
Competitive games	0.42	0.13	0.27	0.74	0.74
Competitive situations	−1.17	−1.04	−1.02	−1.29	−0.90
Assertive role	−0.95	−0.69	−0.72	−0.96	−0.38
Imposing wishes	0.52	0.56	0.35	0.74	0.72
Standing out from group	1.39	0.48	0.63	0.66	1.15
Routine administrative functions	−0.45	−0.43	−0.31	−0.70	−0.56
Mean age	29.0	27.8	25.4	29.2	28.4

Source: In part from Miner, Wachtel, and Ebrahimi, 1989

roughly one-third of these students measured in 1990. Could it be that the long-heralded reversal is finally underway (Gould and Werbel, 1983; Howard and Wilson, 1982; Driver, 1988)?

There is no final answer on that point, but several considerations give pause. It is possible that dramatic changes have occurred in the SUNY-Buffalo student population during the very recent past, but nothing else gives any indication to that effect. The higher scores in the 1990 entrepreneurship group are entirely accounted for by the fact that almost 50 percent of these students held managerial positions while no students in the 1988 and 1989 entrepreneurship groups were managers. Take these managers out and the 1990 differential disappears completely. Furthermore, there is no reason to believe the entrepreneurship students are representative of the graduate student body. The course is an elective one and tends to attract students with a special interest in the subject matter.

If one compares the 1988–90 entrepreneurship students with the 1987–8 students in a required course, who do represent a cross-section, the most pronounced subscale differences occur on first, Standing out from Group and second, Assertive Role. It so happens that the entrepreneurship course requires an individual oral presentation and defense of a new business plan and the students were made aware of this before registering for the course. Such a presentation requirement would not be expected in the required course. It is entirely possible that being entirely voluntary, the entrepreneurship course attracted students for whom the oral presentation was not much of a problem – those who liked to stand out and assert themselves more. If one were to correct for this possible selective bias, and take out the managers in the entrepreneurship course as well, the mean Total Score in the last column of Table 8.7 would drop to −0.50. This may not be an entirely appropriate procedure, but it does illustrate how fragile any assumption of reversal based on these findings is.

Overall the data of Table 8.7 seem to say that a slight rise in student motivation to manage, say from −1.0 to −0.6 or −0.7, may have occurred during the 1980s, but that in any event the rise was inconsequential, and it may not have occurred at all. It would be premature to conclude that we are 'out of the woods' yet, especially when faced with a low motivation to manage age cohort extending over some 20 years now which is advancing across the period of potential managerial employment at a very steady rate.

RELATED LITERATURES

It is obvious that the changes in motivation to manage which occurred during the 1960s and early 1970s did not occur in isolation. There is no question that there were also changes in such areas as student activism, drug use, dress, and sexual behavior. Some evidence is available regarding changes in values, attitudes, and motives other than motivation to manage during the period of decline. Also relevant are surveys of students taken during and after the decline, and of company experience with the so-called 'new breed.'

Research on trust, control, and authoritarianism

Rotter (1971) began administering his measure of trust in others to students at the University of Connecticut in 1964. Each year there was a sizable decrease in scores continuing through the 1960s. A similar finding was obtained with a somewhat different measure of trust among students at Vanderbilt University, in a study extending back to 1954. Thus, the decline does not appear to have been specific to either one measurement process or one university. The tendency for students to be increasingly distrustful was most pronounced with regard to people in positions of authority in society and in organizations. There was relatively little change with regard to ordinary people with whom the students had direct contact, such as parents, repairmen, or salesmen.

A second, and related, research program was undertaken by Rotter (1971a) in the area of perceived sources of control. This research indicated that a sense of being powerless and at the mercy of one's environment was on the increase. In tandem with the decline in trust there was a decline in the feeling of being personally able to influence the distrusted external world – a decline not in the desire for power, but in the expectation of being able to exercise it. The studies went back to 1962 and indicated a similar pattern across the country, although Midwest campuses appeared to have been affected somewhat less than those on either coast. Thus during the 1960s there was a sharp shift from internal toward external perceptions of the locus of control. In Chapter 4 it was noted that motivation to manage tends to be associated with an internal locus of control.

Ondrack (1971) compiled a number of studies of authoritarianism extending from the middle 1950s through the 1960s. He found a regular decline in scores among college students over this period. Similarly Freedman and Kanzer (1970) reported the same pattern of decline in scores based on studies conducted on various campuses over the same time period. Their scales measure not only authoritarianism, but also what they call rebellious independence and impulse expression. The sharp decline in authoritarianism was matched by a similar rise in rebelliousness and uncontrolled expression of emotional impulses.

The parallel decline in motivation to manage and in authoritarianism reflects the presence of a relationship between the two in the college student population. As noted in Chapter 4, this relationship is certainly not great enough to justify interpreting motivation to manage as synonymous with authoritarianism; there is a great deal more to it than that. But the relationship is of sufficient magnitude to be considered meaningful.

Changes in values

There were a number of studies based on measures of values, which revealed certain dimensions of the change that occurred on college campuses. These studies serve to expand on the scope of the change; they also indicate the particular and continuing importance of authority relationships.

Lehman and Hill (1969) conducted surveys of the values of incoming freshmen at Michigan State University throughout the 1960s. Among other things, they note a decreasing concern about the future and a shift to moral values relative to the situation and group involved, thus indicating a decline in adherence to moral absolutes. An increasing degree of questioning of university authority also was in evidence.

A more extensive and lengthy inquiry was carried out by Morris and Small (1971) at a wide range of different colleges. Students were surveyed in 1970 and the results compared with those obtained using the same measure in the early 1950s. The more recent students placed less value on social restraint, self-control, and progress through action and more on withdrawal, self-sufficiency, social concern, and self-indulgence. The data indicated that these values were particularly characteristic of the roughly 50 percent of students who felt that society as it exists today does not permit them sufficient opportunity to develop their abilities and express their wishes. This appears to be the same sense of powerlessness and being at the mercy of external forces described by Rotter.

Work done by Ondrack (1973) with students at the University of Toronto and at the University of Michigan emphasized the increasing desire for independence that others have noted. His studies also pointed to a greater desire for relationships within one's own age and peer group as contrasted with status and authority relationships, and an increased social concern. In general, Ondrack concluded that college students shifted their values away from those characteristic of business executives and in the direction of those of university professors – from those of managers to those of professionals.

Evidence from the 1970s clearly indicates that these new values were not left in the university setting as these students moved on to the world of work (Inglehart, 1981; 1990). The values are distinctly in evidence in this age cohort up to the present.

The Harvard Business School research

As part of a comprehensive study of student expectations of corporate life, Ward and Athos (1972) administered a questionnaire measuring individuals' perceptions of themselves to students in 1962 and in 1970. The 1962 students came from 33 different universities, and all were headed for positions in business. Within this group, the Harvard Business School students proved to be very little different from those in other universities in the characteristics measured. For this reason, and to save effort and expense, the 1970 students were all drawn from the Harvard Business School. The measure used required the students to choose among pairs of adjectives (some pairs favorable and some pairs unfavorable) to provide descriptions of themselves.

The changes noted over the eight-year period seemed to point up certain findings from studies already discussed. The themes emphasized were *love* (self and other), *down with the establishment* (less emphasis on respectability and dignified style), *power to the people* (don't just passively accept or withdraw), *let go* (don't hold back in fear), *do it* (don't just be dissatisfied), *get in the action* (operate, don't administrate).

The study tended to confirm the change to greater social concern, more negative attitudes toward established authority, and more uncontrolled emotional expression that others have noted, and it did so among students at a business school which has won worldwide renown as a source of top-level executive talent.

This research also provided insight into the kind of company the students wanted to work in. Information on this point was obtained in both 1962 and 1970 and, as might be expected, there were some drastic changes. The most pronounced increases were in the number of students who preferred small companies and in the wish to have the company actively involved in community needs (social concern).

On the other hand, there are a number of company characteristics for which the student preferences showed decreases. The 1970 students appear to have shifted sharply in the direction of wanting more from the company and giving it less. They were no longer willing to forego fringe benefits, and they wanted a top management that was not too concerned with profits or costs, for example – presumably a top management that would share with them their concern for social action. They did not want to do routine administrative work, such as writing reports, and there was a strong desire to get away from restraints, rules, and pressures that might limit their freedom. Finally, they did not want to have to be nice to anyone in order to get ahead.

Survey data

It is evident that a number of trend studies lend support to the MSCS –
Form H findings. To these can be added the findings from several studies
utilizing opinion survey procedures.

A survey reported by Yankelovich (1969) covered a variety of topics
and included respondents of college age who had not continued their
education, as well as those who had. It is of greatest interest, however,
for the insights it provides into the attitudes toward authority of the
college students sampled. In order to study the generation gap, the students
were asked to indicate whether certain attitudes were more typical of them
or their parents. In terms of those factors which most sharply differentiate
the two groups, the parents are depicted as more compromising, more
respectful of authority, less tolerant, less interested in people, less prin-
cipled, less open, less interested in beauty, and less self-centered. In general
the students are quite critical of their parents, especially when their
responses are viewed in terms of what is known about their own values.
The students view themselves as particularly tolerant and open and strikingly devoid of respect for authority. However, when the students say
they are tolerant they are thinking of their attitudes toward peers and age-
mates, rather than their attitudes toward parents and those in positions of
authority.

Furthermore, the students indicated a considerable unwillingness to
accept the restraints of authority, whether reflected in society's laws or in
the form of constraint by an employing organization. Close to a half
found it difficult to accept the power and authority of a boss at work.
Draft resistance and civil disobedience were as likely to be considered
justified as they were to be rejected.

A second survey by Hadden (1969) occurred at roughly the same time,
in 1969, and also involved many students from many campuses. The
questions, however, were somewhat different in form and content than
those used in the previous survey. As a result, the anti-authority theme
is somewhat less in evidence and the independence and freedom-of-
expression themes are more pronounced. Yet the overall conclusion is the
same: 'Their predominant mood is the rejection of authority and the desire
to follow their own modes of conduct.' To the question of whether
universities should try to control student life outside the classroom, 79 percent answered in the negative. And 82 percent felt that they would not
sacrifice their private lives, even if this should mean making less money.

In the Yankelovich (1969) survey, business was viewed by the student
respondents as competitive, making a major contribution, a key element
for the future, and a major factor in society; but also as requiring conformity, being large and overwhelming, not having very high ethics, and not
allowing for individuality. Roughly one-third of the college students made

it clear that they definitely did not want to become involved in business, and only one-quarter gave a business career a solid yes vote. Data presented by Benham (1972) from Opinion Research Corporation, based on that organization's surveys over the years, make it clear that these attitudes toward business reflected a distinct negative shift since the early 1950s.

There is good reason to believe that the college experience itself typically had a negative impact on attitudes toward business. Studies conducted by Dawson (1969) at Michigan State University revealed that the attitudes of students in their junior and senior years were much more unfavorable than those of freshmen and sophomores. This negative shift was most pronounced in the liberal arts group; it did not occur among business administration students.

A study conducted by Barnett and Tagiuri (1973) utilized data obtained through the readers of the *Harvard Business Review* from young people ranging in age from 9 to 17. A high proportion had managers as parents, and the group as a whole proved to be unexpectedly well informed about managerial work. Yet interest in a managerial career was far from overwhelming. When asked what they would most like to do when they grew up, 40 percent of the males and 20 percent of the females mentioned either management or business. But 50 percent of both the males and the females indicated that management was what they would *least* like to go into.

Much the same conclusion emerged from a study conducted by Braunstein and Haines (1971) among high school students. The career of business executive was about intermediate in preference among those studied, with a value of −1 on a scale from +100 to −100. However, it was clearly viewed less favorably than that of research scientist or of lawyer. Furthermore, this scale value dropped to −7 among the students who intended to go on to college. It was −15 among the females.

Business organizations also rated as intermediate as a place of employment, being less desired than the Federal Government or a college faculty. However, the large corporations were viewed more favorably than small businesses, and their scale value of +5 placed them well above an executive career in rated preference. Braunstein and Haines (1971) suggest that there may be a significant difference between a career as a business executive and a career in a business organization. They indicate that many students would find work in a business organization satisfying if it involved a nonmanagement career such as law or research. The implication appears to be that managing in business is viewed more negatively than holding a number of other nonmanagerial jobs in the same context.

These and other studies seem to add up to the conclusion that negative sentiments toward business careers were on the increase in the 1960s, and that it was managing in particular that was being rejected. A study by DeSalvia and Gemmill (1971) indicates as one of the major problems that students grossly misperceived the values of managers. They saw managers as being more 'organization men' than they really were.

Company experience

The evidence available indicates that in general the attitudes, values, and motives identified on campus have carried over into the business world. There is substantial anecdotal testimony to this effect extending back to about 1970 (Miner, 1974b). However, there are empirical data as well. Many of the latter came to light in the early 1970s, either before the decline was complete or very shortly after it had ended. The field of human resource management clearly found itself faced with a new and rather difficult type of recruit.

An American Management Association survey, conducted by Tarnowieski (1973) indicated considerable dissatisfaction among younger managers. In particular there was concern about opportunities for personal growth and development, and about the arbitrariness of promotion decisions by superiors. A *Fortune* study conducted by Gooding (1971) repeatedly noted the same characteristics among managers under 30 that had been identified among college students. A survey of the members of the American Society for Personnel Administration conducted by Prentice-Hall (1971) indicates marked concern among human resource managers over the problem of adapting company practices to the demands of the younger generation. Many of the same problems were evidenced in a similar survey conducted by The Bureau of National Affairs (1969).

More recently a series of attitude surveys conducted by Opinion Research Corporation (1980) indicated similar problems. The managers surveyed manifested much the same attitudes, values and motives that characterized the students of the late 1960s and early 1970s. What is clearly evident from these data is that entry into the corporate world had very little impact on these individuals. They stayed much the same type of people they were in college.

The most convincing evidence on this point comes from the AT&T research that grew out of the development of assessment centers. Although this research itself derives from what was originally only one company, almost identical results have been obtained in 10 other organizations (Howard and Bray, 1988). The research compared AT&T managers who entered the company in the late 1950s (and were re-assessed 8 and 20 years afterwards) with a cross-section of managers who entered the company in the late 1970s and early 1980s. The late 1950s data are ideally timed to antedate the decline. The 1977–82 data derive from a period well after the decline had ended.

Comparison of the pre- and post decline managers on a wide range of assessment center instruments produced the following results:

The post decline group –

1. Were more negative about their future managerial careers; many conditions in the work situation were simply less acceptable to them.
2. Had a great deal less drive to advance to higher levels in the organization.
3. Considered positions of leadership much less attractive.
4. Were less interested in bettering themselves, setting high goals, and striving to extend themselves.
5. Were less inclined to defer to those in positions of authority.
6. Had a greater desire to nurture others, and also a greater desire to be nurtured by others.
7. Gave evidence of a lessening of certain aspects of masculinity.
8. Communicated less effectively in making oral presentations.
9. Were both more independent and more nonconforming.

Although there is more here than what the MSCS – Form H measures, these findings clearly reinforce the conclusions reached using the Authority Figures, Competitive Situations, Assertive Role, and Routine Administrative Functions subscales.

In summarizing their results with regard to the MCS (Management Continuity Study) managers – the post decline group – Howard and Bray have this to say:

A few characteristics defined the MCS group as a generation apart from its predecessors, regardless of when the predecessors were measured. The MCS group's decline in interest in leading others (lower Edwards Dominance scores) posed a possible threat for organizations searching for strong leaders. Miner and Smith (1982) reported a similar decline in the motivation to manage among a series of college students tested across a number of years with the Miner Sentence Completion Scale. Declines continued through the 1960s and have plateaued at a lower level since the 1970s. The lower Oral Communication Skills, less Identification (with management), and increasing Nonconformity for the MCS group were no doubt related to their greater indifference to the management role. On the positive side, this was a generation more aware of its state of physical health and with an abundance of energy (high G-Z General Activity). But the direction of that energy into the acceptance of responsibilities necessary for the future of organizations might prove to be a particularly difficult challenge for those organizations.

The emphasis on giving and receiving emotional support (higher Edwards Nurturance and Succorance scores) suggests that the younger generation might be more compassionate. Another interpretation comes from the findings of Veroff et al. (1981), who noted that seeking informal support had become the primary coping style of the new generation. In reconciling this finding with the tilt toward greater self-sufficiency, found in their data as well as ours, they noted decreased dependence on specific individuals and greater orientation toward seeking more support from a variety of individuals. This approach is more self-protective in the event of losing any single source of support.

(Howard and Bray, 1988: 406)

In concluding another, interim report on this same research the authors sound an alarm very similar to the one that Ward and Athos (1972) sounded in summarizing their research on Harvard Business School students:

In conclusion, then, our studies of Bell System managers point to a potential crisis brewing as the next generation meets and replaces the last. A generally reassuring continuity in managerial abilities is matched by a disturbing discontinuity in managerial motivation. For the sake of our organizations, our economy, and our country, we hope a solution can be found.

(Howard and Bray, 1981: 28)

Ties to activism

At various points during the previous discussion the close relationship between the decline in motivation to manage and the rise in student activism or protest has been noted. Given the almost perfect temporal contiguity of the two phenomena, it seems imperative to explore the relationship more fully.

The first two years of the 1960s, like the 1950s, were relatively quiescent, but, starting in 1962, with the peace demonstrations in Washington early in the year and the formation of Students for a Democratic Society during the summer, the pace of student activism and militancy began to quicken. By the fall of 1964, the Berkeley campus of the University of California was faced with large-scale demonstrations, which subsequently spread to most of the larger campuses in the country.

As Lipset (1967) pointed out, the particular form this behavior took derives from the civil rights activities which preceded it and in which some students participated. The tactics of confrontation and civil disobedience were highly visible and available at that particular time, and this probably accounts for the fact that student attitudes were transformed into student activism when they were.

There are certainly many other types of behavior, including the avoidance of managerial work, which can well derive from these changing attitudes and motives. It seems very likely that the student protests in question were a manifestation of this change which occurred as the result of a particular combination of external circumstances, among which the civil rights movement, the war in Vietnam, and the rapid growth of

American universities appear to have been most prominent. Accordingly, a decrease in violent protest need not signal a reversal in the process.

What appears to have happened is that more students entering colleges and universities came with attitudes, values, and motives that differed sharply from those of earlier generations. These new attitudes predisposed the individual against authority, large and impersonal organizations, and the Protestant ethic of hard work and individual competition. When such students faced the authority of large and complex universities, they generated leaders who epitomized the attitudes and motives of the majority, and the path to activism was opened.

In large universities with many formal rules and procedures the new attitudes did not need to be as prevalent or as widespread to produce demonstrations, because the bureaucratization was complete, at least from the vantage point of the new student. In less formalized colleges and universities with less complex structures, a greater student attitude base was needed to produce unrest. Different colleges attract students with differing degrees of activism in their attitudes. Smaller schools which were more informal, such as Swarthmore and Antioch, appeared to need a strong attitude base to spawn activism. The very large state universities rapidly produced activism, even though students' attitudes were more widely spread over the entire spectrum.

There is a marked parallel between what is known about the behavior of campus activists and the changes in motivation to manage. The parallel is sufficiently close, in fact, that it would be almost impossible not to in some way implicate the motivational changes in the rise of student protest. The changes appear to have provided an attitude base favorable to the emergence of a certain kind of student leadership.

The most pronounced shift in attitude was in the area of authority relationships. Students became increasingly negative toward people holding positions of authority and toward the idea of hierarchical authority in human groups and organizations. Since demonstrations frequently involved confrontations with authority, and on occasion even physical attacks on authority figures, an obvious parallel does exist between the attitude changes identified and the changed patterns of behavior.

Studies of activist students reported by Block, Haan, and Smith (1968) at the Berkeley campus of the University of California, have consistently provided evidence of their basic rebelliousness and restlessness. The strong emphasis on participatory democracy which permeated the activist movement reflected this view of authority. Leadership was essentially devalued and denied, although it clearly existed to some degree. Meetings typically were open; anyone could come in and express a viewpoint. Decisions were at least ostensibly achieved through consensus, and they were often long in the making.

The decline we have noted in competitive motivation is also consonant with what is known about student activism. There was a strong tendency for activists to be identified politically with the far left and to oppose a competitive economic system. Clearly, opposition to the American business system stemmed from a number of causes, but at least one of these was the fact that it was viewed as highly competitive and acquisitive.

Activists tended to identify with the loser and the underdog, rather than with the winner; there was a strong desire to alleviate the oppression of others and to help the needy. The studies reported by Block, Haan, and Smith (1968) indicated a very limited commitment to the Protestant work ethic, and little concern with achievement and success. There was a marked rejection of competition in the economic sphere, as well as in other areas.

The sharp reduction in assertiveness, traditionally considered a masculine trait, is reflected in the minimal differentiation of sex roles in the activist movement. Activism was closely associated with women's liberation, gay liberation, and other movements which argue for a merging of 'masculine' and 'feminine' roles. It was also associated with the hippie alternative and the drug culture, both of which advocate dropping out and escapism, a passive turning in to one's own personal experience rather than an active coping with one's environment. This is not to say that all aspects of the student protest movement exhibited a lack of assertiveness, but major components of it clearly did.

The decrease in sense of responsibility for administrative tasks merges easily with the overall rejection of the managerial aspects of large, formal organizations. Horowitz and Friedland (1970) described this phenomenon as follows: 'Much of the student movement is rebelling against bureaucratic forms of organization, perfected and extended by the older generation, preferring spontaneous "community" and "happenings," wholeness, and a moral laissez-faire [to rules and plans].'

There is considerable evidence from other sources in support of this antibureaucratic trend, although much of it has not been so interpreted. For example, activists consistently evinced a strong tendency to reject formal religion. The rule-oriented, authority-based nature of much formal religion and the church organizations which perpetuate it appear to be the major culprits.

Similarly, it is the very large and complex universities that experienced the greatest unrest, and it is these universities that made the most extensive use of impersonal rules and procedures in dealing with students. Although faculty organization tends to be participative and 'academic freedom' is stressed, student-university relations were highly bureaucratized. Student protests were directed against much of this, including grading systems, class size, dormitory regulations, required attendance, disciplinary practices, food services, dress rules, faculty promotion and tenure policies, censorship of publications, and housing policies.

Silver (1969) reported that half of all Columbia University students wanted to become professors before entering the university, but only one-sixth indicated the same career choice during the senior year of college. He interpreted this change as reflecting a feeling, with increased exposure in the student role, that large universities are essentially bureaucracies, coupled with a strong desire to avoid that kind of organization in the future.

In addition to university governance, a major set of issues in student demonstrations throughout the country was the Vietnam War and the draft. Although a number of students participated in demonstrations because of pacifist values and revulsion against physical violence, these factors seem insufficient to account for the extent and nature of the participation. A major factor in the anti-war demonstrations appears to have been a rejection of bureaucratic and authoritarian systems as represented by military organizations. This suggests that the draft, rather than the war itself, was the major object of discontent, and that anti-war sentiment represented, for many students, a displacement to a more socially acceptable objective. These students not only did not want to fight in Vietnam, but really preferred not to enter the armed forces at all. This interpretation is reinforced by the fact that student sentiment against the war did not solidify until the 1967–8 academic year. Lubell (1968) attributed this turn against the war on campus to the revised draft law, which eliminated graduate student deferments and accelerated the drafting of seniors upon graduation.

The stability of power motivation and of the desire to stand out and be in a distinctive position represent a striking contrast with the changes in other aspects of managerial motivation discussed. Evidence of strong power motivation within the activist sector, if not the sense of having achieved power, parallels these findings. Activist students consistently demanded a greater voice in university affairs and greater power over decision-making processes. This extended beyond the student–university relationship to matters of building construction, investment policy, and recruiting on campus.

At Columbia University, surveys of student attitudes reported by Barton (1968) indicated widespread support for the view that students should exercise more control over university policymaking. Similar results were obtained at Berkeley and elsewhere. A major source of student unrest throughout the country was the matter of student participation in, if not control over, campus governance. Student power, as opposed to faculty or administrative power, increased steadily as an issue in demonstrations. The demands advanced indicated a desire to exercise power over many aspects of university operations, not just those directly related to student behavior.

The significance of this strong power motivation, coupled with a desire to move to center stage to perpetuate it, is difficult to interpret against a backdrop of increasingly less favorable attitudes toward authority, competitiveness, assertiveness, and responsibility. In large, complex organizations all of these factors move together; on the campus, they did not. When all move together, power motivation is typically muted and channeled so as to be consistent with organizational goals. The more naked power motivation noted among college students is not so restrained and controlled by other attitudes within the individual.

THE DYNAMICS AND ETIOLOGY OF DECLINE

That a massive culture change occurred during the 1960s and early 1970s really cannot be doubted. The decline in motivation to manage was part of an overarching cultural process. What is much less certain is how this change came about. In any final sense we do not know. However, it is useful to speculate, in the hope of gaining some understanding.

The central role of authority relationships

The most consistent and pervasive finding from research on the period of decline is that there was a major disturbance in authority relationships among college students. America's youth became more negative to authority, less accepting of the legitimacy of authority, more rebellious and defiant of authority, less tolerant of authority, less accepting of the moral values held by established authority, and more opposed to organizations viewed as authoritarian, and its behavior was frequently in opposition to existing authority. The decline in motivation to manage can be viewed as reflecting a rejection of the authority role in organizations. Youth's strong ties to peer and age groups appeared frequently to be associated with a pulling together or coalescing against authority. There was an increase in the freedom with which feelings and impulses were expressed, and a greater self-indulgence; here, too, there was a sense of breaking away from controls, and often the uncontrolled expression was in defiance of, or in opposition to, authority.

There are some apparent contradictions in this constellation of authority-related factors, but on further consideration it appears that these can be reconciled. The fact that those who are angry at or hate authority may not trust it is not too surprising. Those in authority may well retaliate, and therefore it is important to be on guard against the prospect of a counter-attack. This would seem to be the essence of distrust. One expects to be 'hurt' back; or sometimes the sequence gets confused and authority is viewed *a priori* as oppressive and inhuman, which then becomes justification for open attacks on authority.

It also is true that individuals who harbor strong feelings of anger and resentment against authority rarely desire to hold positions of authority themselves. To do so would mean assuming the role of being hated. In part these individuals anticipate that those over whom authority is exercised will resent it, just as they resented the same authority in others. In part there is a hatred of themselves in the new and uncomfortable role of authority figure, which is what is commonly meant by feeling guilty. Often people with low motivation to manage are plagued with strong feelings of guilt about performing certain types of managerial tasks. There is thus good reason why members of the college generation involved who had strong negative feelings toward authority did not want to manage or exercise authority either.

Authority, guilt, and social concern

This formulation, based on the assumption of a widespread disturbance in authority relationships, serves to explain a number of the changes in student attitudes unearthed through research. It does not yet explain the changes in social concern; nor does it explain the increased sense of being controlled by external events described by Rotter (1971a). These additional changes are best understood as reflecting the feeling of guilt which often accompanies rebellion against authority.

It has long been recognized that there is a close association between anger against authority figures and feelings of guilt. Although the two are certainly not inseparable, they do travel together quite often. Thoughts and behavior viewed as representing attacks on appropriate, legitimate authority elicit a feeling of being bad and deserving of punishment. This guilt is often extremely unpleasant, and people develop a variety of techniques for avoiding it.

One approach, of course, is to contend that the authority is not legitimate; that it is oppressive, unfair, hypocritical, criminal, or anything else which would shift the blame and alleviate the individual's guilt. Another approach is to contend one is really not responsible for one's own behavior. If a person is completely at the mercy of external forces, then how can that person be blamed for defiance of authority? It seems not at all surprising that a generation which was increasingly in rebellion against authority should increasingly describe itself as not responsible for its behavior. To present a picture of oneself as powerless in the grip of external forces is a very effective method of pleading 'not guilty.'

Another approach to avoiding guilt is to lose oneself in a crowd, on the assumption that if so many people are involved in the attack on authority it cannot be wrong. The working of this defense against guilt can be observed frequently in mass demonstrations, and accounts for the frequently observed fact that individuals will do things with a crowd that they will not do alone. The approach was clearly evident in campus protest activities, and would seem to account for the increasing sense of togetherness among participants. If a whole generation is in this together, then how can it be wrong?

Finally, one can deny guilt, by presenting oneself as a basically good person – tolerant, loving, helpful to the less fortunate, considerate of others. This is the approach that appears to have generated the increasing social concern. In this context it is important to re-emphasize that this reaching out to others did not include those in positions of established authority. It was directed either to 'mankind' in the abstract or to the less fortunate. It seemed to say, 'How can a person, a group, a generation that is so good and concerned for others have done anything that is really bad?' This approach can, of course, easily evolve into an actual identification with the oppressed and the underdog, in an effort to expiate sins and atone for the wrong that has been done. This latter process would have to be considered a more extreme reaction to the guilt aroused by increasing opposition to authority.

It is important to recognize that struggles of the kind described, with their seemingly inevitable circularity of anger and guilt, are not necessarily pathological. They are part of all human experience to some degree. It is unfortunate that our youth appear to have become entangled in this particular emotional web, however. The possibility that the social concern, and the social work, of these people may stem from underlying psychological processes which appear more self-serving than altruistic need not make them any less praiseworthy. A business person who contributes an important product or service to society is not less deserving of credit for his contribution because it is made out of a desire for personal profit.

Disturbed authority relationships and managing

How might these problems of authority, anger, and guilt relate to managing and managerial talent shortages? What can be expected of a generation that seems to be struggling with such problems to a much greater extent than have previous generations?

For one thing, assuming a managerial position can mean self-hatred and the anticipation of hatred from others in a person who typically experiences strong anti-authority feelings. Among those who have learned to associate such unpleasantness with managerial work, the answer may well be the choice of some other career, perhaps one of the professions where such problems are less likely.

However, there are many who no doubt will end up managing for some period of time. They may not be aware of the difficulties their attitudes toward authority will create for them, or there may be strong forces, such as family pressures, which at least temporarily override any anticipated unpleasantness. From what is known about the ways people attempt to cope with guilt, one can piece together a picture of some of the problems they may experience in managing, and the approaches they may take to resolve them.

One approach would be to deny the legitimacy of one's own authority, thus essentially abdicating while continuing officially to hold the position. Such a manager is often described as using a *laissez-faire* style. Managers of this kind have not been found to be very effective (Bass, 1981; Brightman, 1975).

Another approach would be to portray oneself as being at the mercy of overwhelming forces, such as higher authority or governmental constraints. Because they must ward off guilt by maintaining the image of external control, such managers are unable to initiate anything on their own. They certainly will contribute little to growth and change in their company.

Finally, there is an approach that involves convincing oneself and others that one is really a good person in spite of one's authority, or perhaps attempting to atone for the 'sin' of managing by identifying with the less fortunate. Such a manager may become extensively involved in community action, and these activities may assume much greater importance than profits, so that company resources in sizable quantities are devoted to them. In the ultimate, management may literally give the company away.

It seems likely that these approaches – *laissez-faire*, paralysis of initiative, excessive participation, and social action at the expense of profit – will be among the major problems for management in the future. This seems almost inevitable as the guilt that is a product of hating authority travels from the college campus to the shop floor, sales territory, and office landscape, and ultimately into the boardroom itself.

The break in value transmission

Clearly some break in the value and motive transmission process in American society began to occur during and after World War II, so that parents did not teach their children what they had in the past. There are several factors that may well have been involved at that time.

One factor that is related to affluence is the advent of technology and mechanization in the home. A high proportion of families have simply not had to teach work-related values at home, because the total amount of work to be done there has decreased to the point where heavy involvement of children is not necessary. A major exception, however, appears to be those families that conduct a family enterprise to which the children must contribute their share of time and effort. The largest remaining societal sector of this type is the farm population. Not surprisingly, the children of farm parents have been least likely, by a sizable margin, to participate in demonstrations on campus. Also faculty support for student activism was lowest in schools of agriculture (Lipset and Ladd, 1970). But it is also true that the number of farm families has been declining for many years.

One consequence of this removal of work from the home environment appears to be a reduction in the extent to which children are exposed to, and thus learn to cope with, the demands of adult authority. This, of course, is particularly true of authority in the work sphere.

A second factor is the increasing number of working mothers who spend less time at home, and thus have less time to spend transmitting values. The trend toward increased labor force participation by women has occurred at the same time that many fathers (and mothers too) are engaged in increasing amounts of travel and thus are away from home for longer and longer periods of time. It is not at all unlikely that babysitters, day care centers, and other parent-substitutes can play much the same role in contributing to a break in value transmission as slavery did in societies of the past. The parent-substitutes may well lack either the desire or the ability to teach parental values.

In all probability, neither mechanization of the home nor the departure of parents has been as instrumental for change as a third factor, the widespread embracing of a highly permissive approach to rearing children, particularly in the more affluent and intellectual sectors of society. Permissiveness, with its failure to use punishment and discipline, can mean that attitudes, values, and motives are developed quite independent of parental influence. Society's values are thus transmitted less forcefully because parents often stop consciously transmitting values at all, and may, in fact, make a determined effort *not* to transmit values, on the theory that children should develop their own. In this vacuum other influences may take over and a new value system may emerge, thus yielding major social change.

That one result of this process is a disturbance in authority relations seems highly predictable. Because they grow up having little experience with authority, children have no opportunity to learn how to cope with it. Some may have no meaningful conception of what formal, appropriate authority really is. Later on, when they come into contact with the authority systems of large organizations, they are frustrated, confused, and end by forming strong negative attitudes, with results like those considered earlier in this chapter. Keniston (1970) noted that ' . . . most entering Freshmen have extremely high hopes regarding the freedom of speech and action they will be able to exercise during college. Most of them . . . graduate thoroughly disabused of their illusions.'

In many cases this process may be supplemented with another in which rebellion against authority becomes manifest at an earlier age. Angered by the failure of their permissive parents to provide some structure for their lives and to help them with the problems they face, children can develop strong negative feelings toward their parents, feelings which are subsequently transferred to other authority figures and in fact to everything that is viewed as reflecting authority.

One might expect that under conditions where parents are highly permissive, guilt would not develop in relation to anti-authority attitudes and behavior, and thus that in later life the coupling of anger and guilt would not appear. However, when children become angry at permissive parents (and all children become angry at their parents sometimes), they tend to experience more guilt than they would if the parents were highly punitive. Permissive parents typically present themselves to their children as very concerned about the child's welfare and development, and thus as altruistic and unselfish. Such parents are likely to be perceived by the children as basically good people, incapable of doing wrong. The full weight of guilt, therefore, falls on the child. In contrast, more punitive parents are likely to be viewed as indulging in excesses, and, accordingly, as bad. The child, although frequently angry, may well be saved from feelings of guilt because it is so clear that the blame belongs elsewhere.

It is important to recognize that the philosophy of permissiveness came primarily from educators, and is, therefore, certainly no less prevalent in the schools than among parents. It dates back at least to the progressive education theories advocated by John Dewey (1916) in writings around the time of World War I and for many years thereafter. Dewey's influence on developing conceptions of the educational process was tremendous. Somewhat later Benjamin Spock (1946) and a number of child psychologists were to have a similar influence when they presented the doctrine of permissiveness to parents. Because of this dual impact, in both home and school, deficiencies in learning to deal with authority appear to have achieved an unusual pervasiveness. Children did not learn about authority when they left home and went to school, since the situation was much the same there, particularly in the lower grades.

There may well be other factors that have contributed to the break in the value-transmission process, but the coalescing of just these three – less work to be performed at home, less time at home for both mothers and fathers, and a more permissive attitude on the part of both parents and teachers – seems adequate to account for major social change. All three appear to have started slowly, probably during World War II, and to have grown thereafter, although at somewhat differing rates.

The family backgrounds of activist leaders

It is interesting to note that the dynamics we have been considering do not appear to have operated in all instances. There is another pattern that has emerged from studies of activist leaders.

Apparently, many of the very early activists on the Berkeley campus of the University of California were in chronic rebellion against their parents and most other sources of authority. However, data marshalled by Flacks (1970) make it evident that this was not the subsequent pattern.

Most leaders came from relatively high-income families, and their parents were college graduates. The parents tended to be employed in occupations of an intellectual or professional nature, but rarely in business. The mothers often worked. In political ideology the parents were typically quite liberal. A not inconsequential minority were on the extreme left of the political spectrum – radicals or socialists. Yet, overall, the parents were not as radical as their activist children.

Although the parents did adopt many permissive practices in rearing their children, this was not true in all respects. When it came to intellectual and social values, the parents made a conscious effort to influence their children. In general they were in complete sympathy with the subsequent activist activities of their children, holding similar attitudes themselves toward business organizations and institutionalized authority. The homes are described as ' . . . democratic, egalitarian, and anti-authoritarian' in atmosphere. 'The traditional domination of the father is likely to be totally absent.'

Taken as a whole, the research seems to indicate that among those at the forefront of campus protest, anti-authority attitudes and various manifestations of humanism may well have been actively taught in the home, and that relationships with parents as authority figures were likely to be quite serene. Here there was no break in the value-transmission process, relationships with parents were supportive, and guilt may well have been less. On the other hand, the values transmitted clearly were not those of the dominant American culture. In all likelihood the capacity to exhibit overt activist behavior and to lead others in such behavior reflects the security inherent in this knowledge of parental support.

CHAPTER SUMMARY

In one sense this chapter represents a side excursion. It reports on a program of research into changes in managerial motivation that have occurred since 1960. It was largely happenstance that these changes were first noted among undergraduate business students at the University of Oregon. Theory did not predict them. Yet in following the trail of change through numerous samples of university students across the country, and comparing the results obtained with what others were finding using different measures, considerable evidence for the construct validity of the MSCS – Form H and its theory have been accumulated.

The evidence indicates that the MSCS-H Total Scores of business students declined from roughly 3.50 in the early 1960s to around 1.00 in the late 1960s, and then further to the vicinity of −1.00 by the mid-1970s. The estimated effect size for the overall decline would be 0.82. At the

University of Oregon where data are available extending over a 20-year period, this effect size is 0.91. It appears that by the mid-1970s the decline had stopped, and a period of stabilization (although at a quite low level) set in. Extensive evidence from other sources supporting the existence of this social phenomenon is reviewed. In many instances this evidence amplifies on the MSCS-H findings, but at the same time it solidifies confidence that a decline really did occur. The result has been a substantial and continuing diminution in managerial talent supplies in this country.

In the following chapter the scene changes to the international arena. Shifts in the managerial talent base in the United States are of particular interest in relation to the international competition. There is a compelling parallel between the decline in motivation to manage in U.S. universities in the 1960s and the decline in competitive advantage suffered by the U.S. economy in the 1980s. Evidence bearing on this issue is considered in Chapter 9.

Chapter 9

International comparisons

The findings considered in Chapter 8 raise a question as to whether the decline in motivation to manage may have put the United States at a relative economic disadvantage now that, more than 25 years after the decline began, substantial numbers of lower motivation to manage individuals have come of managerial age. For this to happen the decline would have had to have been either a distinctly U.S. phenomenon or it would have had to have been more pronounced in this country.

The slowing pattern of productivity growth in the United States, variously referred to as the 'productivity problem' or the decline in 'competitiveness,' is consistent with a view that this country has experienced a loss in managerial talent that certain other countries have not. This theme has been given particular attention in the *Harvard Business Review*, which has published a number of articles on the subject.

Probably the best known of these publications are those by Hayes and Abernathy (1980) and Abernathy, Clark, and Kantrow (1981). Scott (1987) summarized these articles placing their themes in three categories:

1. The United States suffers from the British disease.
2. Management must shape up.
3. Painful adjustments, possible remedies.

More recently the same author has reiterated his concerns in another *Harvard Business Review* article (Scott, 1989). Michael Porter of the Harvard Business School has also added his voice to the chorus (Porter, 1990; 1990a). A survey of nearly 4,000 *Harvard Business Review* readers produced the following results:

o 92% believed that U.S. competitiveness is deteriorating.
o 87% believed that the problem predated the overvalued dollar of the 1980s.
o 95% thought that diminished competitiveness would hurt America's economic performance for the foreseeable future.

o 89% believed that the problem represented a threat to the country's standard of living and economic power.
o Almost 90% placed the burden on the shoulders of U.S. managers.

According to HBR's editors (1987: 8), the survey's results indicated a belief that 'America's competitiveness is declining – largely because of the performance of U.S. managers – and it is up to them to respond to the challenge.'

Two years later a similar survey indicated a perception that the competitiveness problem still existed, and that it indeed was getting worse.

The United States has a serious competitiveness problem with Japan and other Far Eastern nations. The problem is getting worse, and U.S. managers shoulder much of the blame. . . . Today, as two years ago, HBR readers are still overwhelmingly concerned about the performance of U.S. companies in world markets and are equally clear about the primary cause of the problem: American managers.'

(Ehrenfeld, 1989: 222)

The theme of managerial deficiency and competitive failure appeared in many other publications during the 1980s. Examples from the popular media may be found in *U.S. News and World Report* (Karmin, 1987; Baer, 1988), *Fortune* (Kiechel, 1981), and *Management Review* (Kearns, 1981). Examples from the more scholarly literature are a book by Levitan and Werneke (1984) and a survey conducted by McInnes (1984) on differing perceptions of the productivity problem among managers in different countries.

This review is by no means exhaustive, but it is sufficient to warrant the hypothesis that motivation to manage may well be at a low level in the United States relative to what exists in many other countries of the world. This hypothesis has been investigated, and will provide the theme around which this presentation of the international research generated by role motivation theories is organized.

THAILAND, IRAN, NIGERIA, INDIA, AND VARIED PACIFIC NATIONS VERSUS THE UNITED STATES

The first set of comparisons focused on certain more rapidly developing nations in Asia, Africa, and the Pacific rim. The strategy was to compare students from the various nations who were studying in the United States with U.S. students. The MSCS – Form H was administered in English. The students came from 32 different universities among which the major contributors were: North Texas State University; University of California, Berkeley; Georgia State University; American Graduate School of International Management; Texas Woman's University; Oklahoma State

University; University of Pennsylvania; Mercer University, and the University of Dallas. There was no significant relationship between the university attended and the MSCS score (Ebrahimi, 1983; 1984; Ebrahimi and Miner, 1991; Miner, Wachtel, and Ebrahimi, 1989).

In addition to the U.S. sample which has already been described (see Chapters 4 and 8), samples were obtained from Thailand, Iran, Nigeria, and India. The varied Pacific nations sample was constituted as an alternative to the originally intended Japanese sample, which proved impossible to obtain in sufficient size. Within this sample over 70% of the students came from Japan, Korea, and Taiwan – all nations that have experienced rapid economic growth relative to the U.S. There were also students from Hong Kong, the Philippines, Malaysia, and mainland China.

The students were concentrated in their late twenties (mean ages in the various samples ranged from 25.7 to 29.3) and were largely males. In the United States almost all were graduate business students. This tended to be characteristic in the other samples as well, but both undergraduates and non-business majors were more frequent outside the U.S. Overall, 77 percent of the students were majoring in some aspect of business administration; the rest were spread over a wide range of majors.

Comparisons with the United States

Although differences in age composition, the proportion of females, the number of business majors, the percent seeking graduate degrees, and the extent of employment exist, as they do between the U.S. students and the other samples, analyses indicate that these differences cannot account for the results obtained (Miner, Wachtel, and Ebrahimi, 1989). These results are given in Table 9.1.

What emerges is that on the MSCS total score measure, the United States has the lowest mean and is significantly below both Nigeria and the varied Pacific nations. The F-value for the overall analysis stands at 0.07, not quite significant at the 0.05 level, but sufficiently close so that the results cannot be rejected summarily. If one goes on to analyze the subscale means, the pattern becomes much more understandable. Two subscales, Competitive Situations and Assertive Role, are clearly significant; at the same time, they make the major contribution to the total score findings. On Competitive Situations, the United States mean is the lowest. It is significantly below all other sample means except that for the varied Pacific nations. On Assertive Role the pattern is the same except that in this instance the mean score for India is the one that does not differ significantly from the United States.

A significant F-value is also obtained on the Routine Administrative Functions subscale. However, in this instance the United States mean holds a more intermediate position. It is significantly below the mean for

Table 9.1 Comparison of MSCS – Form H scores for United States students and students from Thailand, Iran, Nigeria, India, and varied Pacific nations

MSCS – Form H measures	United States (N=82)	Thailand (N=52)	Iran (N=47)	Nigeria (N=32)	India (N=34)	Varied Pacific (N=64)	Non-U.S. combined (N=229)
Total score	0.24	1.85	1.70	3.38*	0.97	2.66*	2.13*
Authority figures	0.49	0.73	0.38	0.78	0.94	0.72	0.69
Competitive games	0.42	0.17	0.13	0.56	0.09	0.59	0.32
Competitive situations	−1.17	−0.29*	−0.30*	−0.09*	−0.35*	−0.84	−0.43*
Assertive role	−0.95	0.54*	0.30*	−0.16*	−0.65	0.00*	0.05*
Imposing wishes	0.52	0.08	−0.06	0.56	0.21	0.26	0.19
Standing out from group	1.39	1.02	1.45	1.66	1.50	1.56	1.42
Routine administrative functions	−0.45	−0.40	−0.19	0.06	−0.76	0.36*	−0.14

*Significantly above the United States sample at p <.05 or better.
Source: Miner, Wachtel, and Ebrahimi, 1989

the varied Pacific nations, as are Thailand and India with India providing the lowest mean value in an absolute sense.

A second way of evaluating the marginally significant total score F for Exhibit 9.1 is to combine the five country samples from outside the United States and then replicate the prior analysis. When this is done the picture becomes much clearer, primarily because the samples being compared are now both of substantial size. The U.S. total score mean is significantly low and the Competitive Situations and Assertive Role subscales account for this difference. There is no longer a significant difference involving the Routine Administrative Functions subscale. Taken as a whole, the data clearly confirm the hypothesis of low managerial motivation in the United States. It is important to note as well that the two subscales on which the U.S. student scores are clearly depressed are also subscales on which substantial declines were indicated in Chapter 8.

Analyses carried out within the varied Pacific sample indicate that students from the particularly rapidly developing countries – Japan, Korea, and Taiwan – contribute disproportionately to the high scores in this sample. There are 45 students from these three countries and 30 of them have MSCS total scores above the average in Table 9.1. Among the remaining 19 students in the sample, nine score at this same level. High managerial motivation in a country does not guarantee rapid economic development. Many factors may intervene to restrict the effects of motivational talent differentials. Nevertheless, the data from Japan, Korea, and Taiwan do appear to indicate that high levels of motivation to manage can manifest themselves in the statistics of macro-economics.

Relationships with Americanization and internationalization

The results in Table 9.1 could be a consequence of differences between the students studying in the U.S. and students remaining in their home country; the students who leave, and whom we studied, may simply not be representative. One way this could come about is that the processes of living in the United States, or away from the home country, and being exposed to new cultural influences may serve to raise the level of MSCS – Form H scores in some manner.

To test this hypothesis, data on degree of Americanization were obtained from the students. Questions were asked about:

1. Fluency in English
2. Number of years in the United States
3. U.S. citizenship
4. Level of friendship with Americans
5. The degree to which others consider the individual Americanized
6. The degree to which the individual feels Americanized

7. The degree to which the individual believes living in the U.S. has exerted an influence on the person
8. Percent of social time spent with Americans

Relationships between these measures and MSCS Total Score were calculated in each of the five non-U.S. samples. Of the 40 relationships four were significant and one of these was negative. The only possible finding in support of the Americanization hypothesis occurs in the Nigerian sample; items 5 and 6 above both yield positive relationships in that sample. The results could as well be a function of chance, however.

Questions were also asked dealing with the individual's overall internationalization –

1. Number of countries visited
2. Number of years outside native country
3. Interest in working for a multinational firm
4. Number of languages known
5. Degree of fluency in non-native languages

Again there is little to support the hypothesis that internationalization may increase motivation to manage. Of the 25 relationships, three are significant – two in a negative direction, and one positive (Miner, Wachtel, and Ebrahimi, 1989).

It may still be that the non-U.S. students are not representative of students from a country overall, but the data do not support the view that exposure to American or other foreign cultures produces the MSCS differentials noted in Table 9.1.

Construct validity outside the United States

Chapter 4 and in particular Table 4.8 present evidence on the relationships between MSCS – Form H measures and self-report items designed to tap similar constructs. Data were given for two samples of U.S. students. The discussion there indicated that because of differences in underlying constructs, such correlations should not be expected to be high. Yet some positive relationships should be found. This in fact did prove to be the case, and the findings were interpreted as further evidence of construct validity.

Analyses of the same kind as those reported in Chapter 4 were carried out using the Thailand, Iran, Nigeria, India, and varied Pacific samples. The question under consideration was whether this particular type of construct validity could be demonstrated across the diverse array of nations studied, many of which are culturally quite distinct from the United States. The results are given in Table 9.2.

Certainly significant correlations are not reported as frequently as for

Table 9.2 Correlations between MSCS – Form H measures and self-report items in samples of students from outside the U.S.

| | Correlations for expected relationships | | | | | | | | | | | |
| | Same concepts | | | | | | MSCS total score | | | | | |
Self-report items	Thailand	Iran	Nigeria	India	Pacific	Median	Thailand	Iran	Nigeria	India	Pacific	Median
I like managing and supervising people.	0.25*	0.03	0.16	0.43**	0.22*	0.22**	0.25*	0.03	0.16	0.43**	0.22*	0.22**
I like and respect people with power and authority.	0.33**	0.20	0.17	0.05	−0.13	0.17**	0.33**	−0.03	0.25	0.01	0.10	0.10
I enjoy participating in competitive games and sports.	0.18	0.28*	0.32*	0.40**	0.25*	0.28**	0.25*	0.16	0.36**	0.28	0.24*	0.25**
I like American football.	0.09	0.03	0.08	0.01	0.27*	0.08	−0.09	0.04	0.13	0.16	0.34**	0.13*
I enjoy being involved in jobs requiring competition with others.	0.15	0.24*	−0.19	0.13	0.13	0.13*	0.28**	0.20	0.14	0.13	0.35**	0.20**
I can tactfully say 'no' to a person when I disagree with him or her.	0.14	0.04	0.25	0.02	−0.07	0.04	0.30**	0.06	0.19	0.13	0.13	0.13*
I usually talk my friends into doing something I like them to do.	0.44**	0.00	0.22	0.59**	0.37**	0.37**	−0.01	−0.05	0.15	0.23	0.33**	0.15*
I enjoy being the center of attention.	0.07	−0.02	−0.11	0.07	0.23*	0.07	0.25*	0.07	0.11	−0.01	0.00	0.07
I keep a very organized set of files and records.	0.15	0.01	0.03	0.29**	0.21*	0.15*	0.22	0.06	0.20	0.22	−0.01	0.20**
I enjoy making decisions.	0.12	−0.02	0.00	0.16	0.25*	0.12*	0.26*	−0.05	−0.03	0.23	0.29**	0.23*
Median correlation	0.15	0.03	0.12	0.15	0.22		0.25*	0.05	0.16	0.19	0.23*	

* p <.05
**p <.01

Source: Ebrahimi, 1984

the U.S. samples in Table 4.8. A factor in this may well be the considerably smaller sample sizes. When median correlations for the various self-report items are used, and thus a larger number of cases, 15 of the 20 expected correlations are significant, and all are positive. Overall the data of Table 9.2 indicate that the MSCS – Form H measures much the same constructs among the students from other countries that it does with U.S. students. The findings for Iran, however, are quite weak.

In Table 4.8 correlations for expected relationships were contrasted with correlations across dissimilar constructs. It is important to do that here as well. The correlations where no relationship is expected provide a baseline for comparison. The median such correlations for the samples of Table 9.2 are as follows:

Thailand	0.12
Iran	0.01
Nigeria	0.04
India	0.09
Varied Pacific	0.10

In all cases the median correlations for samples at the bottom of Table 9.2 exceed those noted above. On the average the expected correlations, although higher, are not elevated to quite the same degree as in the U.S. samples. However, the varied Pacific and Nigeria results are very similar, and Thailand and India do not depart a great deal from the U.S. pattern. Iran continues to represent an anomaly. It appears that language and cultural factors can influence MSCS responses, and exert an influence on what is measured. In most instances, however, such influences are minimal.

MEXICO VERSUS THE UNITED STATES

The Mexican study had two purposes. One was to test the hypothesis of relatively depressed motivation to manage in the United States in a new context. The second was to close a possible loophole in the previous studies. We needed to determine directly whether students from other countries studying in the United States differ from their compatriots back home. The original design called for comparisons among graduate business students with the MSCS-Form H in four samples: Mexicans in Mexico, Mexicans in the United States, U.S. citizens in the United States, and U.S. citizens in Mexico. Extensive efforts to locate a sufficient number of Americans studying in Mexico ended in failure. Consequently, only the first three groups were compared (Miner, Wachtel, and Ebrahimi, 1989; Wachtel, 1986).

Samples and measures

The Mexicans in Mexico sample was obtained at the Universidad Nacional Autonoma de Mexico, Facultad de Contaduria y Administracion, Divesion de Estudios de Posgrado. This is one of the largest business programs in the country. Classes are taught in the evening and many of the students hold full-time jobs. The MSCS – Form H was administered to 96 students in nine different core courses. Administration was done in class by the primary researcher, a U.S. citizen who also spoke Spanish reasonably fluently. All respondents were Mexican citizens.

The Mexicans in the United States sample was collected from 23 universities. However, the great majority of the 101 subjects were obtained from six universities in the southwest – University of Texas at El Paso; University of Texas at Austin; St. Edwards University; University of Houston; University of Arizona; and Texas A & M University. Students were located with the aid of international student advisors. In some cases these advisors contacted the students themselves; in others they provided lists that could be used to make direct contact. Although the original intent was to utilize graduate students only, this did not prove to be feasible. As a result the final sample was composed of more than half undergraduates.

The U.S. sample was obtained at Georgia State University. The university has a large masters' level enrollment in business. The majority of the students take evening courses because they work full-time. As in Mexico, instruments were administered in core courses, with five different courses included. The number of students studying in the various subject matter areas was about the same in Mexico and the United States. One hundred graduate level students were included in the sample. This sample has been previously discussed in both Chapters 4 and 8.

The MSCS was translated and then back-translated with the objective of achieving a culturally equivalent measure (Sekaran, 1983). The MSCS was simultaneously translated into Spanish by one Mexican alone and another two Mexicans working as a pair. All three were bilingual and knowledgeable regarding both U.S. and Mexican cultures. Their translations were compared and then combined into a version which was given to a specialist, who was certified by a university foreign language department, for back translation. This effort proved successful. After further pilot testing, and a few adjustments, the Spanish version of the MSCS was established.

This instrument was then administered in a commercial Spanish class at Georgia State University with half of the class receiving the Spanish and half the English version on day one; two days later the languages were reversed. This approach incorporates both reliability and translation inconsistencies. Comparing the results in Table 9.3 with previous test–retest reliability data (see Table 3.10) indicates very little difference. The corre-

Table 9.3 Comparability analysis of the English and Spanish versions of the MSCS – Form H

MSCS – Form H measures	r
Total score	0.80**
Authority figures	0.80**
Competitive games	0.91**
Competitive situations	0.71*
Assertive role	0.68*
Imposing wishes	0.96**
Standing out from group	0.46
Routine administrative functions	0.80**

* p <.05
**p <.01
Source: Miner, Wachtel, and Ebrahimi, 1989

lations in Table 9.3 fluctuate more widely, presumably due to the small number of cases (nine) but the overall results are very similar. Thus it appears that translation inconsistencies do not represent a meaningful factor. This conclusion is reinforced by the fact that mean scores on the English and Spanish versions do not differ.

Comparisons with the United States

Although differences in age, proportion of females, and employment status exist among the three samples, analyses indicate that these differences cannot account for the results obtained (Miner, Wachtel, and Ebrahimi, 1989). There are no differences in MSCS score associated with the various universities contributing to the Mexicans in the United States sample.

As indicated in Table 9.4, except for a drop on the Authority Figures subscale for the Mexicans in Mexico, the pattern is consistently one of higher scores in the two Mexican samples. The data overall are entirely consistent with the hypotheses. The U.S. scores match well with results obtained previously at Georgia State University, and at other universities in the United States. With the exception of the difference on the Authority Figures measure, the Mexicans studying in the United States do not differ from the students in their home country. This subscale difference is not sufficient to produce any variation in Total Score.

In actual fact, the MSCS scores obtained in both Mexican samples proved to be unexpectedly high. The Mexico City students are attending what many in Mexico consider to be an elite program and a number of these students are also managers in business and government. These factors, perhaps, explain the high scores. Yet the Mexicans in the United States have equally high scores while attending a wide range of U.S.

Table 9.4 Comparison of MSCS – Form H scores for United States students and Mexican students studying in Mexico and in the United States

MSCS – Form H	United States (N=100)	Mexicans in the United States (N=101)	Mexicans in Mexico (N=96)
Total score	−0.79	5.78*	5.77*
Authority figures	0.20	1.16*	0.19
Competitive games	0.13	0.87*	0.94*
Competitive situations	−1.04	0.05*	0.41*
Assertive role	−0.69	0.76*	0.35*
Imposing wishes	0.56	1.06*	1.22*
Standing out from group	0.48	1.15*	1.70*
Routine administrative functions	−0.43	0.73*	0.98*

*Significantly above the United States sample at p <.05 or better.
Source: Miner, Wachtel, and Ebrahimi, 1989

universities and included only a very few managers; a majority are not employed at all. It does not appear that the unique status of the National University students can serve to explain the high scores. It is important to recognize, however, that neither of the studies reported here utilizes a sample of Mexican managers *per se*. It is entirely possible that Mexican managers as a group are less managerially motivated than the student samples.

An analysis carried out within the Mexicans in the United States sample once again indicated that Americanization and internationalization have little if any relation to MSCS – Form H score. The only significant result was that those Mexicans considered by others to be Americanized had *less* motivation to manage. Since this finding was not replicated in any of the earlier samples, it probably should not be given much weight. All in all it now appears that student samples in the U.S. can provide a reasonably good approximation to the scores that would be obtained were testing done in the home country.

Construct validity issues

Table 9.5 provides the same type of construct validity information previously provided in Table 9.2. The correlations for Mexicans in the United States are typically positive, significant, and at a level entirely consistent with prior expectations. However, the findings for Mexicans in Mexico are much weaker.

When the Table 9.5 results are compared with those obtained outside the range of expectations, much the same picture emerges. The median correlation where no relationship is expected for the Mexicans in the U.S. is 0.10. Comparisons with the expected relationships in Table 9.5 provide

Table 9.5 Correlations between MSCS – Form H measures and self-report items in samples of Mexican students

Self-report items	Correlations for expected relationships			
	Same concepts		MSCS total score	
	Mexicans in the United States	Mexicans in Mexico	Mexicans in the United States	Mexicans in Mexico
I like managing and supervising people.	0.28**	0.16	0.28**	0.16
I like and respect people with power and authority.	0.16	0.03	0.15	0.09
I enjoy participating in competitive games and sports.	0.28**	0.13	0.27**	0.15
I like American football.	0.24**	0.35**	0.25**	0.20*
I enjoy being involved in jobs requiring competition with others.	0.26**	-0.03	0.17*	0.08
I can tactfully say 'no' to a person when I disagree with him or her.	-0.03	0.02	0.03	0.09
I usually talk my friends into doing something I like them to do.	0.18*	0.12	0.08	0.16
I enjoy being the center of attention.	0.25**	0.06	0.09	0.07
I keep a very organized set of files and records.	-0.01	0.04	-0.02	0.12
I enjoy making decisions.	-0.05	0.23**	0.15	0.22*
Median correlation	0.21*	0.09	0.15	0.14

* p <.05
**p <.01
Source: Wachtel, 1986

considerable evidence for construct validity, especially insofar as the same concepts are involved. However, the median correlation where no relationship is expected for Mexicans in Mexico is 0.09; the correlations for expected relationships in Table 9.5 improve on this by very little, if at all. On this evidence we have considerable support for construct validity in the Mexicans in the United States sample, but much less in the Mexicans in Mexico sample. This differential cannot be attributed to translation factors, since both groups took the Spanish version of the MSCS – Form H.

A possible explanation for these results may be that conscious defenses reflected in the responses to the self-report items are more widely operative in Mexico. This is the only Mexican sample where the tests were administered in a group context, and by a foreigner as well. Sekeran (1983) reports that in certain cultures characteristics of the person conducting the research can create a difference in responses. This may be one such instance. There were various indications at the time the measures were administered that the students at the National University were very sensitive about filling out questionnaires. The result could well have been that they were less truthful than the respondents in the other samples.

RESEARCH IN THE PEOPLE'S REPUBLIC OF CHINA

Another area of the world where research on motivation to manage began to bloom in the late 1980s was the People's Republic of China. This research presented major difficulties because of substantial differences in language and culture.

Chinese students

The first of these studies utilized 57 students majoring in commercial economics at Yangzhou Teachers College. The mean age was 21.6 years and 40 percent were female. The students responded in Chinese to a Chinese version of the MSCS – Form H; the responses were translated to English and then scored. For comparison purposes a similar sample was obtained at the Chinese University of Hong Kong. These students were obtaining an undergraduate degree in business and averaged 22.6 years of age. The 60 students were roughly half female. The MSCS – Form H was administered in English, since that is the language in which courses at the Chinese University are taught.

In both instances the standard MSCS – Form H was revised to some extent to make it more culturally relevant. Eight of the 35 scorable items were changed. Terms such as 'yacht' were changed to 'boat,' 'car' to 'motorcycle,' and so on. As we will see shortly, this may have had some influence on the results.

Table 9.6 MSCS – Form H (revised) scores of Chinese and Hong Kong students

MSCS – Form H (revised) measure	Chinese students	Hong Kong students
Total score	5.00	4.25
Authority figures	0.72	1.30*
Competitive games	1.46*	0.88
Competitive situations	0.21	−0.32
Assertive role	1.16	1.13
Imposing wishes	−0.05	0.43
Standing out from group	1.37	0.93
Routine administrative functions	0.14	−0.12

*$p < .05$
Source: Singleton, Kelley, Yao, and White, 1987

Table 9.6 contains the scores for both samples. There are few differences between them; the subscale differences tend to cancel each other out. What is really striking about the Table 9.6 results, however, is the high level of the scores relative to U.S. students of the 1980s (see Table 8.7). This differential is not necessarily present on the Imposing Wishes and Standing out from Group subscales, the subscales that did not show a decline, but it is clearly evident on all the other scores. Once again it appears that students from outside the U.S. score higher than U.S. students to a significant and meaningful degree.

The comparability of a culturally adapted MSCS – Form H

There is some reason to believe, however, that the scores in Table 9.6 may have been inflated as a consequence of the culturally based revision. In a study conducted with 40 MBA students at SUNY-Buffalo, a culturally adapted version of the MSCS – Form H very similar to the one used by Singleton, Kelley, Yao, and White (1987) was administered along with the standard form. All eight altered items in the previous version were used in this new version, and in addition two more items were changed – 'golf' was changed to 'table tennis' and 'dictating letters' to 'drafting letter outlines.' Again the objective was to produce a measure more compatible with Chinese culture and the day-to-day experiences of Chinese people. An English language version of this culturally adapted instrument and the standard measure were completed by the SUNY-Buffalo students at a one-week interval with half taking the standard version first and half the Chinese version. In actual fact no order effects were found.

Table 9.7 gives the results. The correlations between the two versions are substantial, as they should be with 25 identical items, but there are significant differences between means. These differences consistently

Table 9.7 Comparison of the MSCS – Form H and the culturally adapted Chinese version

MSCS – Form H measure	Correlation between measures	Means for standard version	Means for Chinese version
Total score	0.86**	−0.40	1.20**
Authority figures	0.71**	0.23	0.10
Competitive games	0.61**	0.78	0.73
Competitive situations	0.58**	−1.23	−0.73*
Assertive role	0.65**	−1.00	0.00**
Imposing wishes	0.68**	0.85	0.68
Standing out from group	0.79**	0.63	0.43
Routine administrative functions	0.73**	−0.65	0.00**

* p <.05
**p <.01
Source: Miner, Chen, and Yu, 1991

indicate higher scores for the Chinese version. Furthermore it is the altered items that produce the effect. On the Imposing Wishes subscale, for instance, where no items were changed the scores are very close to each other. It is not possible to apply the differentials in Table 9.7 to the data of Table 9.6 because the Chinese versions used in the two instances are not identical, but it does appear that the Table 9.6 data are somewhat inflated. Even so a correction could not possibly bring the scores of the Chinese and Hong Kong students down to the level of the U.S. students in Table 8.7. The interpretation that motivation to manage is stronger outside the United States remains valid.

The motivation to manage of Chinese managers

For use in China the culturally adapted MSCS – Form H was translated into Chinese by one bilingual Chinese organizational behavior scholar and then translated back to English by another. Agreement was good, although a few adjustments in the translation to Chinese were made. This instrument was administered to 170 employed individuals at locations in the vicinity of Dalian, China. Of these, 55 were in managerial positions; 131 were males and 39 were females. The largest group worked in enterprises of a profit-making nature. There were 112 such individuals – 94 employed by the Dalian Harbor Administration Bureau, an organization only recently placed on a for-profit basis, and 18 from a diverse array of enterprises who were attending a management training program at the Managerial Cadre College in Dalian. The remaining respondents were employed in the nonprofit sector. The majority worked for the party committee of Dalian's city government – 51 of the 58 nonprofit organization employees. The remaining seven subjects in the nonprofit group were obtained from the management training program at the Managerial Cadre College. For purposes of comparing Chinese and U.S. managers in terms of their motivation to manage, only the 55 managers were used. This group was almost exclusively male. The remaining individuals were used in the validity analyses described in the next section.

Table 9.8 contains comparisons between the Chinese data and normative data for United States managers. The scores for the Chinese managers have been adjusted (downward in most cases) to make them comparable to what would have been expected if the standard MSCS – Form H could have been used. The adjustment factors are the mean differences from Table 9.7.

The normative data from the U.S. used for the comparisons are of two types. The corporation norms are based on 16 different samples and contain a total of 695 managers. Thirteen of the samples are drawn from individual companies and contain managers from a variety of levels within each company. The remaining three samples are made up of managers from a number of different firms. (An example is a management development group containing managers from various companies in a local area.) Over half of the managers in the corporate sample are from *Fortune 500* firms. The second type of normative data is for managers in nonprofit organizations. These scores are significantly below those for the corporate managers on all MSCS – Form H measures except authority figures. The nonprofit norms utilize 383 managers and are based on 10 different samples, of which seven are within-organization in nature and three are multi-organizational. Most of the organizations are governmental; local, state, and federal units are included.

In general the data of Table 9.8 do not indicate unusually high motivation to manage among Chinese managers. Relative to their U.S. corporate counterparts, the Chinese enterprise managers are distinguished only by a somewhat higher competitive motive and a lower predisposition to stand out from the group. The Chinese nonprofit managers are slightly above similar managers in the U.S. overall, but they have a substantially higher competitive motive and assertiveness. They are also less positively disposed to authority. Given that only five of the 16 comparisons, and none of those involving total scores, are outside the ±10 percentiles band, it is not possible to say that these Chinese managers represent a pool of managerial talent superior to that found in the United States.

Given the findings for students in Table 9.6, it is tempting to conclude that there has been a generational change in China just the reverse of the one that occurred in the United States. This may be true. However, within the sample of 170 employed individuals studied, the correlation between age and MSCS Total Score is positive and significant, though low (r=0.16). The most likely conclusion, once appropriate corrections are made, is that there has been little change in China one way or another, that students

Table 9.8 Culturally adapted MSCS – Form H scores adjusted to approximate standard Form H scores and percentile equivalents for U.S. managers

MSCS measure	Total managerial sample mean score (N=55)	Enterprise sample of managers (N=38)		Nonprofit sample of managers (N=17)	
		Mean	US percentile[a]	Mean	US percentile[b]
Total score	3.35	3.82	46th	2.28	58th
Authority figures	0.91	1.21	51st	0.25	28th
Competitive games	1.10	1.31	50th	0.64	50th
Competitive situations	−0.01	−0.03	62nd	0.03	71st
Assertive role	0.15	0.05	46th	0.35	63rd
Imposing wishes	0.33	0.41	42nd	0.17	58th
Standing out from group	0.40	0.20	32nd	0.85	53rd
Routine administrative functions	0.46	0.67	51st	0.00	50th

[a] Utilizing the published norms for managers in medium and large sized corporations in the United States (Miner, 1989).
[b] Utilizing the published norms for managers in nonprofit organizations in the United States (Miner, 1989).

and employed people have much the same level of motivation to manage, and that the decline did not occur there.

Hierarchic theory validation in China

The Miner, Chen, and Yu (1991) research provides evidence on the validity of the adapted MSCS – Form H in China. The findings are in the same vein as the construct validity data reported on previously. They speak to the issue of whether the hierarchic theory continues to operate effectively beyond the borders of the U.S..

Table 9.9 contains the correlations between the motivation to manage measure and a four-point position level scale (party and government leader, middle level cadre, professional, administrative clerk). The total score findings are consistently positive and significant. The enterprise sample correlation is higher than that for the nonprofit sector, but not significantly so. The level of correlation is roughly equal to that obtained in the United States (see Chapter 4). The subscale correlations with two exceptions are positive, and many attain significance; the median value, however, is only 0.19.

Table 9.9 also compares the scores of the 55 managers with those of the 115 non-managers. Managers are those in the two upper position levels. The results closely parallel those of the correlation analysis. Again the findings for the enterprise sample are more pronounced. The total score effect size in favor of the enterprise managers is 0.85; for the nonprofit managers, it is 0.57.

The Table 9.9 data indicate a trend toward higher validity in the enterprise sample. They also appear to indicate higher scores in the enterprise sample. When appropriate significance tests are applied, the enterprise sample scores do indeed turn out to be higher, but only marginally so; certainly not to anywhere near the extent found in the United States (Miner, 1989).

ADDITIONAL FINDINGS FROM BEYOND U.S. BORDERS

There is a scattering of additional studies that are relevant to this discussion. Almost without exception these involve Form H. The only international research utilizing Form T of the MSCS currently available is the Bellu, Davidsson, and Goldfarb (1990) study noted in Table 6.4 and a study by O'del (1990) of Canadian students. Little evidence was obtained in the latter study of any differences from U.S. students. Both the U.S. and Canadian students were enrolled in entrepreneurship courses. Form P has been applied outside the United States in one instance (Al-Kelabi, 1991). This is the research in Saudi Arabia, and both the Form P and Form H findings will be considered shortly.

Table 9.9 Relationship between MSCS – Form H measures and position level in Chinese samples

MSCS – Form H measures	Enterprise sample			Nonprofit sample		
	Correlation with position level	Means		Correlation with position level	Means	
		Managers	Nonmanagers		Managers	Nonmanagers
Total score	0.40**	5.42	1.77**	0.25*	3.88	0.88*
Authority figures	0.18*	1.08	0.59*	-0.11	0.12	0.54
Competitive games	0.18*	1.26	0.55*	-0.08	0.59	0.76
Competitive situations	0.17*	0.47	0.01*	0.22*	0.53	-0.17
Assertive role	0.15	1.05	0.72	0.22*	1.35	0.24*
Imposing wishes	0.25**	0.24	-0.57**	0.22*	0.00	-0.51
Standing out from group	0.01	0.00	0.05	0.22*	0.65	-0.05
Routine administrative functions	0.30**	1.32	0.41**	0.22*	0.65	0.07*

* p <.05
** p <.01
Source: Miner, Chen, and Yu, 1991

South African managers

A diverse sample of 19 South African managers who participated in a management development program at the University of Witwatersrand was tested in 1975 (Miner, 1977). The sample ranged from group leader to top management, and the firms represented were mostly large and located in the Johannesburg area. The average age of the respondents at the time was 38 years.

The mean MSCS – Form H Total Score was 1.16, at about the 28th percentile for U.S. corporate managers. The subscale scores are universally on the low side. Because of the small sample size and questions regarding representativeness, these data cannot be considered in any way conclusive. However, they do not support the possibility of a motivation to manage differential in favor of South Africa at the managerial level in 1975. Actually, arguing from the decline data in Chapter 8, one would not expect such a differential at that time.

Turkish managers and students

The source of the Turkish managerial sample was also a management development program. The managers, who came from 23 of the larger Turkish firms, participated in a program at Bogazici University. They were tested in 1982 and there were 52 of them (Arsan, Hunsicker, and Southern, 1983). The MSCS – Form H was translated into Turkish, and the responses, also in Turkish, were then translated to English before scoring. The managers were predominantly at the middle and top levels, although there also were some at the first level.

The mean Total Score was 6.12, at the 62nd percentile for U.S. corporate managers. The scores tend to be elevated on all subscales except Authority Figures. No doubt one factor in the relatively high scores is the fact that the Turkish sample contained a disproportionately large number of top managers. In fact, the results are not unlike those obtained with top managers in the United States (Berman and Miner, 1985). In any event the results clearly support a view of somewhat higher levels of motivation to manage in Turkey in the early 1980s.

Data are also available for a sample of Turkish business administration students tested in 1982. There were 47 male and 42 female respondents. The MSCS – Form H multiple-choice measure was used and the measurement process was carried out in English, since that is the language used to teach the university's courses (Arsan, Hunsicker, and Southern, 1983a).

Since the multiple-choice measure yields higher scores than the free response version, it is difficult to make direct comparisons with available U.S. data (see Chapter 3). The male Turkish students have a mean Total Score of 3.30, and the females 2.62. These would translate into scores of roughly −1.00 and −0.50 respectively on the free response MSCS – Form H, about the level expected among U.S. business students of the same period. On the subscales the Turkish students appear to be particularly low on Authority Figures (like the Turkish managers) and on Imposing Wishes. Comparing the managerial and student results overall, the pattern clearly fits the decline model. However, the low Imposing Wishes scores among the students do not match expectations derived from U.S. measurements. Perhaps the decline took a somewhat different course in Turkey.

Taiwanese students

A study of Taiwanese business students at Tunghai University in the mid-1980s also used the English language, multiple-choice version of the MSCS - Form H. However, in this instance four items were changed to make them more culturally relevant (Southern and Pih, 1987). The Taiwanese group contained 23 males and 22 females.

The Taiwanese students score well above those from Turkey. The mean Total Scores are 6.09 and 4.09 for the males and females respectively. Applying the same multiple-choice corrections to these figures as were used in Turkey, we get free response equivalents of something like 1.80 and 1.00 for the males and females. These figures are not as high as might have been expected, but they are not out of line with the data of Table 9.1. The scores do seem to be higher than those being obtained among U.S. students of this period (see Table 8.7). Among the subscales the only particularly striking finding is that like the Turkish students, those from Taiwan also have noticeably depressed Imposing Wishes scores. Again it is not evident why this is so.

European students

Table 9.10 presents data for two rather small samples of European students. These data are part of a more comprehensive study that is incomplete at this writing. The Netherlands sample was obtained in late 1988 among economics (business) students at the Free University in Amsterdam. The average age was 20.8 years and 28 percent were female. The Belgian sample was obtained in early 1990 at the Vlekho Business School in Brussels. The average age was 21.0 years and 61 percent were female. In both cases the instruments were completed in English.

The results in Table 9.10 clearly are consistent with the view that the decline in motivation to manage that occurred in the U.S. did not occur in Europe. Comparisons with Table 8.7 indicate that the two European samples not only are substantially higher on the MSCS – Form H Total Score, but they are consistently higher on Authority Figures, Competitive Situations, Assertive Role, and Routine Administrative Functions as well.

Table 9.10 MSCS – Form H results for European students

MSCS – measures	The Netherlands (N=43)	Belgium (N=33)
Total score	3.23	2.34
Authority figures	0.56	0.73
Competitive games	1.16	0.64
Competitive situations	−0.09	−0.24
Assertive role	0.00	−0.06
Imposing wishes	1.26	0.75
Standing out from group	0.56	0.48
Routine administrative functions	−0.21	0.06

These findings fit well with the data for non-U.S. students in Table 9.1, especially the Nigerian and varied Pacific samples. They run lower than those for the two Mexican samples of Table 9.4, but they lead to essentially the same conclusions. The data are also congruent with the general level of economic performance in Europe in recent years.

However, they do not match up with Inglehart's (1990) arguments and data. He finds evidence consistent with the view that the decline did occur in Europe and was still in evidence up to 1988. His measures and constructs differ from the MSCS – Form H, although on the face of it there appear to be substantial similarities. Perhaps the differing results are attributable to the different measures. Perhaps further research with European samples will lead to a revision of the conclusions derived from Table 9.10.

Employees in Saudi Arabia

This study, which has been considered previously in both Chapters 4 and 5, utilized a sample of 301 employees in three Saudi Arabian organizations. Approximately half of these employees were either professional or semi-professional in nature. Many had come to Saudi Arabia from other parts of the world to bring professional expertise to that country (Al-Kelabi, 1991). As Table 9.11 indicates, they had very high professional motivation scores, especially for a group that contained other than professional employees. On the other hand the very fact that many had come to Saudi Arabia to practice their professions may well have introduced an atypical element.

However, for present purposes, the key data in Table 9.11 relate to the MSCS-H scores. Only 13 percent of the sample carry any kind of managerial or supervisory title. Given this fact, the scores in Table 9.11 are rather high. The Total Score is somewhat below the U.S. norm for corporate managers, but above the norm for non-profit managers. The Authority

Table 9.11 Mean MSCS – Form P and Form H scores for employees of three Saudi Arabian organizations (N=301)

MSCS-P		MSCS-H	
Total score	10.77	Total score	2.95
Acquiring knowledge	1.63	Authority figures	1.20
Independent action	1.99	Competitive games	0.40
Accepting status	2.79	Competitive situations	−0.25
Providing help	2.79	Assertive role	0.42
Professional commitment	1.58	Imposing wishes	0.28
		Standing out from group	0.77
		Routine administrative functions	0.13

Source: Al-Kelabi, 1991

Figures, Competitive Situations, and Assertive Role figures are above normal expectations for managers, which these people mostly are not. Overall, the Saudi Arabian data are above, but not strikingly above, what one would expect to find in a comparable group in the United States.

CHAPTER SUMMARY

Is there evidence that the decline in motivation to manage in the United States has placed this country at a competitive disadvantage in the world arena? The answer appears to be Yes. The data that support this conclusion came primarily from student samples. The countries involved are Thailand, Iran, Nigeria, India, Japan, Korea, Taiwan, Mexico, China, Hong Kong, the Netherlands, and Belgium. In these countries either the MSCS-H Total Score or Competitive Situations or more usually both are above the level found in the United States in the same period. The only student comparison that did not indicate a difference comes from Turkey. If one were to aggregate the non-United States data over the 13 countries, the effect revealed would be substantial. Unfortunately, because of different measures and unavailable information, it is not possible actually to do this, but the last column of Table 9.1 provides an approximation. What is particularly striking is that the students from outside the United States are consistently higher on Competitive Situations. There are other subscale differences, but this is the one that appears repeatedly. It also is the one that should stand out if the U.S. has a 'competitiveness problem.'

Studies utilizing older, employed people and managers in particular do not indicate nearly the same differential. In most instances the decline hypothesis would not predict a difference, given the ages of those involved and the timing of the study. Here the data come from China, South Africa, Turkey, and Saudi Arabia. Only in the latter instance is there any evidence of a difference, and that cannot be fully certified because data for managers are not available separately. One problem with the managerial level analyses is that comparisons must be made with United States managers of the past; a large, diversified sample of managers from the 1990s is not available. If it were, the decline hypothesis would anticipate some rather low scores, and some major differences in comparisons with other countries. For the moment, however, it is necessary to rely on the student data, and when that is done it is quite apparent that the United States has, and will have for some time, a real competitiveness problem. This appears to be true not just in an economic sense, but in an underlying motivational sense as well.

Chapter 10 now turns to the research on age, race, and gender differences as related to the role motivation theories. We have touched on these differences at various points in previous chapters, but a more comprehensive treatment is needed.

Age, race, and gender differences

Age, race, and gender are of importance in a program of research for two reasons. One has the goal of finding differences and studying them to increase scientific understanding. This is the role that Eagly and Wood (1990) have emphasized. It is important to identify areas of differences so that insights may be gained into social phenomena. A second perspective has the objective of minimizing differences so that selection procedures do not exert adverse impact and thus are fair to all. This is the role that guided research on the General Aptitude Test Battery, for instance (Hartigan and Wigdor, 1989). The source of this approach is more legal than scientific, but nevertheless it has had a major impact on industrial/ organizational psychology.

This chapter is concerned with age, race, and gender differences from both perspectives, but the primary emphasis is on the former. The major focus is on identifying areas of difference and pursuing them to increase scientific understanding. In this connection it is important to recognize that the development of the hierarchic role motivation theory and of the MSCS – Form H preceded passage of the Civil Rights Act in 1964, and substantially preceded the creation of a consistent body of law that would serve to define what is and is not discriminatory (Miner and Miner, 1979). Nevertheless, attention is given to issues of adverse impact and fairness in testing. In fact the selection of these particular variables for consideration was influenced to a substantial degree by legal enactments.

AGE DIFFERENCES

Hierarchic theory and Form H among the employed

In order to understand the age differences to be discussed, it is necessary to keep in mind the results presented in Chapter 8 related to the decline and stabilization hypotheses. Correlations between age and MSCS-H scores are likely to be strongly influenced by the mix of people who were of college age before the mid-1960s and after the decline started in the sample used. We will see how this factor operates.

Assuming that the decline took a few years to get moving and that college graduates take a few years before they move up to managerial responsibilities in any substantial numbers, one would not expect any meaningful impact of the decline on age correlations among managers until the latter 1970s at the very minimum. Even then the results would depend upon company screening and promotion criteria. If a firm took active steps to promote only the most talented into management, then the impact of the decline should be minimal. Otherwise the decline effects would move on unabated into the ranks of management, and positive age correlations should begin to occur.

In a sample of 160 oil company managers tested in the late 1950s and another sample of 70 department store managers tested in the early 1960s, the MSCS – Form H correlated −0.06 and −0.05 with age (neither significant) (Miner, 1965). In a sample of 42 managers in a large company tested in the late 1960s, no significant age relationships were found. The same result was obtained in another sample of managers from the same company numbering 28. In both instances the mean age was 41 (Camealy, 1968). Albert (1977) reports a non-significant relationship between age and the MSCS – Form H in a sample of 70 managers and non-managers from a manufacturing firm who averaged 40 years of age. Testing was done in the mid-1970s. When the half of this sample holding a managerial position was considered separately, there was still no significant age relationship. In 1977 a sample of 49 top level corporate executives averaging 48 years of age and a sample of 26 entrepreneur-managers averaging 49 years of age were tested (Berman, 1979). MSCS Total Score results were non-significant and so were all subscale results for the entrepreneur-managers. Among the corporate top managers, two significant subscale findings were obtained – $r = 0.38$ for Authority Figures and $r = -0.31$ for Routine Administrative Functions.

In a sample of 109 middle and lower level Florida state government managers tested in the late 1970s and averaging 40 years of age, Overstreet (1980) found only one significant age correlation; that was for the Authority Figures subscale ($r = 0.28$). In a sample of 34 nursing managers tested at about the same time and averaging again around 40 years of age, there was no significant age relationship either for MSCS – Form H Total Score or for any subscale (Holland, 1981). Black (1981) studied over 600 hospital administrators with an average age of 46, again in the late 1970s, and found no meaningful age relationships. This study utilized the multiple-choice version of Form H. Southern (1976) carried out age analyses with two samples of textile and tufted carpet managers (representing two plants) and obtained a nonsignificant correlation in the first group (average age 40) and a marginally significant positive correlation ($r = 0.34$) in the second (average age 49). Both samples were tested in the mid-1970s. The increased range of MSCS scores and ages in the second sample appear to account for the results obtained.

A study of 170 employed individuals in the People's Republic of China in the late 1980s (a third of whom were managers) yielded a significant age correlation of 0.16 for MSCS – Form H Total Score and significant subscale relationships for Authority Figures and Routine Administrative Functions as well. The sample averaged 37 years of age, but there is no basis for concluding that the decline hypothesis applies in this context (Miner, Chen, and Yu, 1991).

An early study of the MSCS – Form H scores of university professors indicated no relationship to age (Miner, 1977). Testing occurred over a period from the mid-1960s to the early 1970s and the average age was 40 years. A later more comprehensive study of 112 management professors yielded no significant age relationship for Total Score, but significant subscale correlations of −0.30 for Competitive Situations and 0.20 for Assertive Role were obtained. This was in 1978 and the average age was 43 years (Miner, 1980c). In a group of 33 entrepreneurs tested during the latter 1980s and averaging 43 years of age, the only significant correlation occurred on Competitive Situations ($r = -0.46$). This group was predominantly in the post-decline category.

A particularly revealing study utilized librarians and managers in academic libraries (Dayani, 1980). Among the managers, who averaged 39 years of age in the late 1970s and where very few subjects were in their twenties, no significant age correlations with MSCS variables were found. Among the librarians, where the average age was 34 years and the standard deviation greater, so that the decline period was more fully engaged, significant correlations in the 0.20s began to emerge ($r = 0.27$ for Authority Figures and 0.28 for Routine Administrative Functions).

Overall, these results indicate that among those who are of an age to be employed there is little relationship between age and MSCS – Form H variables. When significant positive relationships are found it is because substantial numbers of both pre-decline and decline subjects are included. When subscale results are analyzed, and this is far from universal, the overall pattern is generally consistent with chance expectations. There is, however, some tendency for the Authority Figures subscale to yield positive correlations with age more frequently than the other measures.

Hierarchic theory and Form H among students

Student samples, especially among undergraduates, tend to be rather homogeneous as to age, and thus significant age correlations are unlikely in any event. There simply is not enough age variance. Studies by Albert (1977) and Singleton (1976) using various samples of Georgia State University undergraduate students clearly are of this nature; in no case are significant age correlations obtained. Note, however, that when Albert's (1977) 70 managers and employed nonmanagers are added to the undergraduates, so that the sample spans the decline, a significant age correlation does appear (r = 0.28).

Studies conducted among graduate students introduce a wider age variation and thus provide a better test, as do certain undergraduate groups obtained in night classes. Thus in a study of Portland State University students in 1970, where a number of pre-decline age students were included in the sample, a clear positive relationship between age and motivation to manage was evident. This was true not only for Total Score but also for the Authority Figures subscale (Miner, 1974c). The results are contained in Tables 8.4 and 8.5. A similar study with Georgia State University students in 1975, which again spanned the decline, yielded much the same results (Miner and Crane, 1977). The scores for the older students are given in Table 8.5. When these are compared with the scores for the younger group, positive age relationships are found for MSCS – Form H Total Score as well as the Authority Figures and Competitive Situations subscales. However, Overstreet (1980) did not report any significant age relationships in a sample of 86 Florida State University students tested in the late 1970s. The students averaged 28 years of age; it appears that very few students of pre-decline age were included in this sample.

As research has moved into the 1980s, the prospect of engaging the pre-decline period in student samples decreases substantially. One would expect age correlations to be absent, and for the most part they are. Ebrahimi (1984) studied samples of U.S. students as well as students from India, Iran, Nigeria, and Thailand who were studying in the United States. The average ages in different samples varied from 25.7 to 29.3. Only in one instance was a significant age relationship found. That was for the Nigerian students, and the relationship was negative. When all samples were combined the results were nonsignificant. Studies at the State University of New York at Buffalo in the late 1980s have consistently failed to yield significant results. One analysis of 102 graduate students in a required organizational behavior course produced a correlation of −0.07 with MSCS – Form H Total Score and no significant subscale correlations. Another analysis with 45 graduate students in an entrepreneurship course produced a Total Score correlation of 0.23 (non-significant) and only one significant subscale finding – for Routine Administrative Functions (r = 0.32).

A study by Wachtel (1986) involved analyses of a United States student sample from Georgia State University and two Mexican samples – one containing students in Mexico and one students in the U.S. Neither Mexican sample produced any significant age correlations. However, in the

Georgia State University sample Total MSCS – Form H Score was significantly related to age ($r = -0.25$) and so was Competitive Situations ($r = -0.20$). Now the *younger* students score higher. However, given the failure to replicate this finding in any other 1980s sample and the fact that when Wachtel's (1986) three samples are combined no significant findings are obtained, it probably would not be wise to generalize from this result.

Is Form H related to age? The answer clearly depends on the time frame involved. It certainly can be, although the more usual finding appears to be that it is not. Can it serve to discriminate against older individuals, say those over the legally specified age of 40? At present it would seem to *favor* the great majority of these individuals since their pre-decline scores tend to be higher. However, increasing numbers of decline age people are now passing across the age 40 demarcation point and into the status of a protected group. These individuals have lower scores and thus might be viewed under the law as having suffered unfair treatment when a static cutting score is applied to all. This effect would be accentuated should a massive reversal of the decline effects, along the lines detected at Georgia State University by Wachtel (1986), become widespread. Clearly legal formulations and scientific knowledge are not perfectly coordinated in this instance.

Professional theory and Form P

Unlike Form H, Form P has not accumulated a substantial body of research extending over many years. Thus we do not know about any possible decline, or upsurge. Yet there are certain findings regarding age that are important.

Table 10.1 contains the results of five studies. The management professors averaged 43 years of age and were spread over a wide age range (Miner, 1980c). The labor arbitrators were similarly dispersed, but around a mean age of 62 (Miner, Crane, and Vandenberg, 1992). The special educators, all from the same school district, were concentrated in the younger age groups with a mean of 33 (Pilgrim, 1986). The entrepreneurs averaged 43 years of age, the same as the management professors, but they were more concentrated around the mean and the sample included few older individuals beyond the age of 55. The students in the entrepreneurship course at SUNY-Buffalo had a mean age of 26 and were the most concentrated of any sample.

Interpreting these results presents something of an enigma. From the management professor findings it is apparent that in a sample of widely dispersed ages a substantial positive relationship between age and MSCS – Form P scores can occur. However, the other sample results demonstrate that this need not be the case. The restricted range characterizing the entrepreneurship students is not a factor among the labor arbitrators, for

Table 10.1 Correlations between age and MSCS – Form P variables in different samples

MSCS – Form P measures	Management professors (N=112)	Labor arbitrators (N=100)	Special educators (N=89)	Entrepreneurs (N=33)	Entrepreneurial students (N=45)
Total score	0.38**	0.04	-0.08	-0.11	0.09
Acquiring knowledge	0.07	0.07	0.05	-0.34*	0.11
Independent action	0.09	-0.08	0.07	0.03	0.20
Accepting status	0.24*	-0.04	-0.18	-0.20	0.02
Providing help	0.27**	0.00	-0.01	0.16	-0.06
Professional commitment	0.45**	0.22*	-0.12	0.11	-0.01

* p <.05
**p <.01

Source: Miner, 1980c; Miner, Crane, and Vandenberg, 1992; Pilgrim, 1986

instance. In samples that contain a number of older individuals a positive relationship involving Professional Commitment is to be expected simply because more committed professionals stay in the profession, while by mid-career the less committed are likely to have left; in the younger age groups the less committed are much more likely to be still represented. This process seems reasonable, and certainly is a major factor in the high Total Score correlation for the management professors. Except for this relationship involving Professional Commitment, which may be expected under appropriate circumstances, it seems unlikely that age is a consistent factor in MSCS – Form P scores. In the management professor sample Professional Commitment is significantly related to the Accepting Status and Providing Help subscales, but not to the other two subscales. Thus, it appears that it is the pervasive influence of Professional Commitment in this sample that accounts for the disparate results.

Task theory and Form T

Table 10.2 presents available results for the MSCS – Form T. The technologically innovative entrepreneur correlations derive from a study conducted by Miner, Smith, and Bracker (1989) in which the average age for this sample was 47 years. The combined high growth entrepreneur and company manager sample contains roughly equal proportions of each group and averages 43 years of age (Miner, 1990a). The three SUNY-Buffalo samples have mean ages of 26, 28, and 26 respectively. The student samples, unlike the older ones, are highly concentrated agewise.

In general the data of Table 10.2 do not suggest strong age relationships for Form T. The Feedback of Results correlation in the 1989 student sample is only marginally significant and the impact is not sufficient to produce a significant Total Score correlation. However, the Avoiding Risk correlation in the high growth entrepreneur and company manager sample is both more significant and impacts more heavily on the Total Score results. Because of the limited age ranges in the student samples, the probability of obtaining significant correlations there is reduced. What is important, however, is that all student samples studied to date have had low scores on Avoiding Risks, over into the range where the average student, unlike the average entrepreneur, is more of a risk-taker than a risk avoider. It seems very likely that Avoiding Risks is indeed an age related variable. Young people, having little to lose, are more likely to be motivated to take risks. Older people, who are more apt to have much to lose, are more likely to be motivated to avoid suffering losses, and thus risking loss. Thus samples that span the age range are likely to reveal a significant positive age correlation for the Avoiding Risks subscale (and perhaps as a consequence on Total Score as well). No other age relationships involving the MSCS – Form T appear likely.

Table 10.2 Correlations between age and MSCS – Form T variables in different samples

MSCS – Form T measures	Technologically innovative entrepreneurs (N=116)	High growth entrepreneurs and company managers (N=133)	SUNY-Buffalo graduate students		Entrepreneurship course (N=45)
			Organizational behavior course		
			1988 (N=38)	1989 (N=51)	
Total score	−0.09	0.20*	−0.22	0.04	0.03
Self achievement	0.02	0.12	−0.29	−0.10	−0.21
Avoiding risks	−0.03	0.26**	−0.05	−0.17	0.10
Feedback of results	0.05	0.04	0.04	0.28*	0.06
Personal innovation	−0.17	0.16	−0.09	0.05	0.14
Planning for the future	−0.13	0.02	−0.19	0.10	−0.02

* p <.05
**p <.01

RACE DIFFERENCES

Less is known regarding how the races differ in MSCS performance than with regard to the other characteristics considered in this chapter. Numerous studies have included small numbers of individuals from various minority groups, but rarely in sufficient numbers to carry out separate analyses. It appears necessary deliberately to set out to include more minorities if one is to obtain sufficient sample sizes for comparisons. This has been done on a number of occasions with Form H, particularly the multiple-choice version. It has not been done at all with Form P or Form T. Thus, the discussion here is limited to the hierarchic theory. Determining how the professional and task theories relate to race is a task for the future.

Research with the free response Form H

The primary source of information on black–white differences using free response measures is a study conducted among General Motors Company managers (Miner, 1977; 1977b). The original design called for comparisons by both sex and race. However, it proved impossible to obtain enough black females to do this. In fact the final black male sample was rather small (N=23), in comparison with a white male sample of 75. Both the standard MSCS – Form H and a situation specific version were administered at the same time. This latter version has been discussed previously in Chapter 4, and data regarding it are given in Tables 4.14 and 4.15. The two Form H versions are positively correlated and these correlations do not differ as between the black male and white male samples.

The data in Table 10.3 support a hypothesis that motivation to manage may well be higher among black males (Crane, 1971; Fernandez, 1975). The Total Score results are consistent on this point. The subscale differences are scattered, but they suggest that the black males are more competitive, more desirous of exercising power, and more motivated to perform routine managerial activities. These findings could reflect a degree of overqualification, whereby blacks need to bring more to their jobs than whites to achieve the same result. Yet the black managers are neither older nor better educated than the whites.

There are two other studies that should also be noted. Overstreet (1980) compared managers in Florida state government using the standard MSCS – Form H. Both blacks and whites scored low, but there was a tendency toward lower scores among the blacks; this trend achieved significance only on the Standing Out from Group subscale, however. A major problem is that there were only 10 managers in the black sample, as contrasted with 98 in the white. Overall little can be concluded from this study.

The same holds for another study, although for quite different reasons. Bartol, Anderson, and Schneier (1981) administered the standard MSCS – Form H to samples of 108 undergraduate business students each at the

Table 10.3 Comparisons between black and white male managers at General
Motors on various free response versions of the MSCS – Form H

MSCS – Form H measures	Black male managers	White male managers
Total score		
– standard version	5.26	2.81*
– situation specific	5.57	2.31*
Authority figures		
– standard version	0.78	0.61
– situation specific	1.43	0.80
Competitive games		
– standard version	1.30	1.49
– situation specific	0.74	0.05
Competitive situations		
– standard version	−0.48	−1.25*
– situation specific	1.13	1.09
Assertive role		
– standard version	0.65	0.11
– situation specific	0.57	−0.04
Imposing wishes		
– standard version	0.96	0.44
– situation specific	0.91	−0.09**
Standing out from group		
– standard version	0.78	0.84
– situation specific	0.26	0.27
Routine administrative functions		
– standard version	1.26	0.57*
– situation specific	0.52	0.23

* p <.05
**p <.01
Source: Miner, 1977b

University of Maryland and at a predominantly black university; the two
samples were all white and all black respectively. Significant, although in
a practical sense rather small, differences favoring the whites were found
on Total Score, and the subscales of Standing out from Group and
Imposing Wishes. However, the blacks were higher on Assertive Role.
The difficulty is that a rescoring of sample of Bartol, Anderson, and
Schneier (1980; 1981) MSCS protocols produced results that were often
sharply at variance with the results previously published (Miner, Smith,
and Ebrahimi, 1985). It is not entirely clear from the data available exactly
how these scoring problems might have influenced the black–white comparisons; it is clear that they influenced certain gender comparisons.
Accordingly, placing a great deal of faith in the Bartol, Anderson, and
Schneier (1981) results is probably not justified.

Research with the multiple-choice Form H

A study conducted with post-secondary vocational educators in the state of Georgia yields sample sizes for blacks which, although still not ideal are acceptable, at least in the case of the females (Hoffman, 1983). The results are given in Table 10.4. Overall, there appears to be little difference between blacks and whites. There is a problem in that the subscale scores for white males add up to 2.91 (not 2.28), but using the subscale total figure would only further reduce the black–white difference. The two subscale differences that are significant favor the white females, but they do not yield a significant Total Score differential.

Table 10.5 contains the results of a very comprehensive research program into undergraduate student differences. The study was conducted using comparable black and white samples from 25 different colleges. The students were all headed for a business career. An analysis comparing predominantly black colleges with integrated institutions indicated no significant differences (Nellen, 1986). The data show a clear superiority of black over white males; this occurs not only on Total Score, but also on Competitive Games, Competitive Situations, and Imposing Wishes. The Competitive Games finding is the only one replicated among the females. In fact the white females score higher on Routine Administrative Functions.

Stevens and Brenner (1990) have conducted a study very similar to Nellen's (1986), but with students from only four institutions. The sample sizes in the two studies are quite similar, but the results are not. As indicated in Table 10.6, Stevens and Brenner (1990) found no Total Score differences. There is a problem with the black female results in that the subscales add to more than the reported Total Score value, but using the subscale sum would only reduce the difference. On the subscales whites consistently score higher on Assertive Role and Routine Administrative Functions; on Imposing Wishes it is the white males and the black females that score higher. Only one of these findings matches the Nellen results in Table 10.5.

Taking these findings as a whole, there is little to indicate a consistent race difference, except possibly that white females score higher on Routine Administrative Functions. Yet there are additional findings from the General Motors study supplementing those in Table 10.3, which raise some questions. In Table 10.3 the free response results clearly favor the black males. Approximately three months after these results were obtained, a multiple-choice version of both the standard MSCS – Form H and its situation specific adaptation were also administered. As indicated in Table 3.3, these free response and multiple-choice measures correlate reasonably well. Unfortunately it was possible to compare samples of only 16 black males and 21 white males on the multiple-choice tests. The results are

Table 10.4 Comparisons between black and white vocational educators in Georgia on the multiple-choice MSCS – Form H

MSCS – Form H measures	Males		Females	
	Black (N=24)	White (N=98)	Black (N=50)	White (N=154)
Total score	3.92	2.28	2.28	3.27
Authority figures	0.38	−0.07	−0.08	0.20
Competitive games	0.79	0.54	0.40	0.40
Competitive situations	0.54	0.71	0.52	0.43
Assertive role	0.33	−0.38	−0.42	−0.44
Imposing wishes	0.04	−0.07	0.04	−0.21
Standing out from group	1.17	1.19	1.14	1.62*
Routine administrative functions	0.67	0.99	0.68	1.27*

*p <.05
Source: Hoffman, 1983

Table 10.5 Comparisons between black and white undergraduate students from 25 institutions on the multiple-choice MSCS – Form H

MSCS – Form H measures	Males		Females	
	Black (N=140)	White (N=87)	Black (N=113)	White (N=86)
Total score	7.17	3.69**	2.63	3.00
Authority figures	−0.16	−0.20	−0.06	−0.09
Competitive games	2.09	1.31**	0.84	0.28*
Competitive situations	1.54	0.74**	0.68	0.29
Assertive role	0.91	0.43	−0.22	−0.09
Imposing wishes	0.69	−0.14**	0.12	0.23
Standing out from group	1.54	1.24	1.27	1.57
Routine administrative functions	0.56	0.31	0.00	0.81**

* p <.05
**p <.01
Source: Nellen, 1986

given in Table 10.7. None of the black–white comparisons are significant, contrary to the prior findings. What appears to have happened comparing the Table 10.3 and Table 10.7 results, is that the black males remained essentially the same on the standard MSCS with the shift to multiple-choice scoring, but increased their situation specific score (t = 2.56, p <.05). In contrast the white males increased their scores on both the standard multiple-choice version (t = 2.12, p <.05) and on the situation specific multiple-choice version (t = 4.63, p <.01). In short the white males took greater advantage of the opportunity to present themselves positively than the black males did. This suggests a possible bias against blacks inherent in the multiple-choice format.

Yet the results for black males in Tables 10.4, 10.5, and 10.6 taken as

Table 10.6 Comparisons between black and white management majors at 4 institutions on the multiple-choice MSCS-H

MSCS – Form H measures	Males		Females	
	Black (N=78)	White (N=115)	Black (N=97)	White (N=81)
Total score	4.22	5.40	1.66	2.63
Authority figures	−0.06	−0.30	0.14	−0.15
Competitive games	1.43	1.85	0.52	0.73
Competitive situations	0.43	0.35	0.30	−0.06
Assertive role	0.52	0.75*	−0.97	−0.01*
Imposing wishes	−0.03	0.32*	0.39	−0.05*
Standing out from group	1.38	1.25	1.25	1.23
Routine administrative functions	0.55	1.22*	0.45	0.96*

*p <.05 or better
Source: Stevens and Brenner, 1990

Table 10.7 Comparisons between black and white male managers at General Motors on various multiple-choice versions of the MSCS – Form H

MSCS – Form H measures	Black male managers	White male managers
Total score		
– standard version	4.44	5.52
– situation specific	8.69	8.10
Authority figures		
– standard version	0.06	0.33
– situation specific	2.06	1.24
Competitive games		
– standard version	1.31	2.05
– situation specific	0.69	1.05
Competitive situations		
– standard version	0.44	0.43
– situation specific	1.25	0.62
Assertive role		
– standard version	−0.19	0.62
– situation specific	1.31	1.38
Imposing wishes		
– standard version	0.56	0.00
– situation specific	0.19	0.00
Standing out from group		
– standard version	1.13	1.09
– situation specific	1.75	2.00
Routine administrative functions		
– standard version	1.13	1.00
– situation specific	1.44	1.81

a whole do not support this conclusion. There is no consistent evidence that the black males are at a disadvantage. Furthermore, the data of Table 10.7 are based on very small samples. The white male findings are supported by data from another sample where essentially the same Total Score results were obtained, but the black male findings hinge on the responses of only 16 managers. It is not possible, given the overall pattern of results, to say that multiple-choice testing introduces problems for black males. Interpreting this situation is made even more difficult because black females were not included in the General Motors study. Using the data on females that do exist, and assuming that there is a tendency for white females to score somewhat higher on Routine Administrative Functions, there is nothing to indicate any other consistent difference in Tables 10.4, 10.5, and 10.6. Overall, on the MSCS-H racial differences appear minimal; when they are found they favor black males.

GENDER DIFFERENCES

Almost everything there is to say about gender differences relates to the hierarchic theory and the MSCS – Form H. Form P has been utilized almost exclusively in samples that are either almost all male (such as the labor arbitrators) or almost all female (such as the special educators). The only approximation to usable sample sizes occurred among the management professors where there were nine females. The only significant gender difference was on Professional Commitment (favoring the males) and that disappeared completely when the effects of age differences were removed.

With Form T, appropriate sample sizes for females have been attained only with the business administration student samples at the State University of New York at Buffalo, and even then the samples are small (under 20). There is no evidence of any Total Score difference. Marginally significant results in favor of the males have been obtained on two subscales in a single sample each – once on Personal Innovation and once on Planning for the Future.

An analysis of 41 free response Form H comparisons

A substantial data base of Form H comparisons by gender has been accumulated. A total of 61 usable comparisons have been identified, 20 of which involve the multiple-choice Form H. It should be noted that these data do not appear to suffer from the so-called 'file drawer' problem. The majority of the comparisons derive from conference papers, dissertations and theses, and unpublished sources; in only a few instances are the data reported in regular published outlets.

This section considers the 41 comparisons involving the original free response Form H or some variant of it. Because of the concerns noted

Table 10.8 Comparisons between the MSCS – Form H scores of male and female business students at the University of Oregon

MSCS – Form H measures	1960–1 Males (N=246)	1960–1 Females (N=41)	1980 Males (N=71)	1980 Females (N=53)
Total score	3.62	1.59*	−1.93	−1.78
Authority figures	1.18	1.15	0.01	0.30
Competitive games	1.29	0.54*	0.47	0.28
Competitive situations	−0.50	−0.85	−1.27	−1.19
Assertive role	0.40	−0.17*	−0.92	−1.08
Imposing wishes	0.45	−0.12**	0.08	0.15
Standing out from group	0.42	0.15	0.28	0.25
Routine administrative functions	0.37	0.90*	−0.59	−0.49

* $p < .05$
** $p < .01$
Source: Miner and Smith, 1982

previously, the data of Bartol, Anderson, and Schneier (1980; 1981) were not utilized. For whatever reasons (Bartol, Schneier, and Anderson, 1985; Miner, Smith, and Ebrahimi, 1985), the protocols used in these studies do not appear to have been correctly scored.

Analysis of the substantial number of studies involving students is complicated by what appears to be a disappearing gender difference over the years. In the early period, at least among business administration students, the typical finding was that males outscored females (Miner, 1974d). During the 1980s that tendency is much less in evidence. The data of Table 10.8 provide findings from the only instance in which it is possible to make comparisons between the 1960s and 1980s with the institutional context held constant. The males are significantly higher in the early 1960s on Total Score and on three subscales; the females are higher on a single subscale. By 1980 no differences are found. The rather obvious decline in scores for both sexes from 1960–1 to 1980 is discussed in Chapter 8.

The fact of a higher motivation to manage among male business students in the 1960s cannot be doubted. Of the five comparisons available for this period, four favor the males and these include significant Total Score differences from both the University of Oregon and the University of Maryland. The one instance of slightly higher scores among females occurred with education students.

During the 1970s data were obtained on 13 different samples from eight universities. There are no significant Total Score differences, but the majority of the comparisons favor the males (10 of the 13). However, the only two samples from the end of the decade (1978–9) yield higher Total Scores for females. This appears to presage what was to come. For the 1980s there are 11 student comparisons. Four of these are of a multi-university nature (from 7 to 23 universities were included); the remainder derive from five different institutions. In six instances the male Total Score is higher and in five instances the female score is higher. The only significant difference favors the males and occurs in a sample of students from Pacific rim nations studying in the United States. The pattern for students who are U.S. nationals is entirely consistent with that for 1980 noted in Table 10.8. From the latter 1970s on, the students do not exhibit a gender difference by any criterion.

Thus, it is clear that gender differences existed on free response Total Score among business students during the 1960s and are non-existent in the more recent period. What is not entirely clear is the pattern that existed in the intervening years; trend analyses over time do not appear to yield a consistent picture in terms of significance, although the direction of the change is quite evident. Where subscale differences are found they favor males on Competitive Games, Competitive Situations, Assertive Role, and Imposing Wishes; they favor females on Authority Figures and Routine Administrative Functions. Thus, the Total Score findings represent an amalgam of conflicting tendencies insofar as the sexes are concerned. Within the motivation to manage construct there are motive patterns that females are more likely to utilize in attaining high scores and other motive patterns that males are more likely to emphasize. These subscale differences have been in evidence from the early studies (Miner, 1974a; 1974d). They continue on into the present.

The second group that has been studied extensively from the viewpoint of gender differences is managers. There are 10 managerial samples spread over the years on which Form H free response data are available, although in several instances the comparisons are not entirely independent of one another. Females have higher Total Scores in three samples – among Florida state government managers (Overstreet, 1980), among managers in academic libraries (Dayani, 1980), and among General Motors managers (Miner, 1977b). None of these differences are significant. The males score higher in the remaining seven comparisons, but this overstates the case because in two instances black and then white male managers were compared with the same female managers.

There are two instances where male managers score significantly above females. One involves a comparison of black male managers with white female managers (Miner, 1977b). The black males possess rather strong motivation to manage. However, the amount of solid research in this area is limited, and nothing is known about black female managers as indicated in the previous section. The second finding of a significant difference was obtained in a study by Harlan and Weiss whose results are described as follows:

> Results showed no significant differences between men and women in Company 19 on subscale scores or overall score. For Company 6,

however, men had a much higher overall score on the measure of
motivation to manage than did the women, although most of the overall
score difference was accounted for by strong differences between men
and women on the subscale Competitive Games. This subscale, designed
to measure competitive drive and interest in sports and games, appeared
to be the least work-related scale. On all other scales, including the
more general scale of Competitive Situations, the scores of men and
women in Company 6 were not significantly different.

(Harlan and Weiss, 1982: 72)

The authors conclude from this research, which utilized a number of
different measures in addition to Form H, that there is a striking degree
of similarity between male and female managers.

A study conducted in various organizations in the People's Republic of
China (Miner, Chen, and Yu, 1991) compared males and females, about
a third of whom were managers, and found the males scored higher,
although not significantly so. However, there were only three female
managers, out of a total of 55; all three score well above the average for
the males. Also, in the study by Dayani (1980) it was not only the female
managers in academic libraries that scored higher. The same differential
was found among librarians who were not managers.

Taking all of the comparisons involving the free response Form H into
account, there is a small but meaningful tendency for males to score higher
overall. When the data are broken down, however, it appears that this
small difference is attributable to the student samples of the 1960s and on
up through the mid-1970s. In other groups there is no evidence of a Total
Score difference one way or the other.

An analysis of 20 multiple-choice Form H comparisons

The General Motors study discussed at several points previously suggested
that black males do not increase their Form H scores to nearly the extent
that white males do with a shift from free response to multiple-choice
formats. There was some evidence from this same study that this tendency
not to take advantage of the opportunity to present oneself more favorably
was also characteristic of white females (Miner, 1977; 1985). The effect
was less pronounced than that found in the racial comparisons, but there
was reason to believe it was operating. Based on this finding one might
expect that when gender comparisons are made using multiple-choice
measures, males would score consistently higher, simply because of their
tendency to capitalize more on the opportunity presented.

There are 12 comparisons involving students with the multiple-choice
measure, all extending into the 1980s; thus, trends over time cannot be
studied with this index. Five studies were conducted at five different

universities. The remainder were multi-university studies with the number of sites varying from 4 to 15. In all 12 instances the males scored higher. Significant Total Score differences were obtained by Nellen (1986) for black students at both black and integrated colleges, by Bartol and Martin (1987) at the University of Maryland, by Arsan, Hunsicker, and Southern (1983) at West Georgia College, and by Stevens and Brenner (1990) for both black and white college students. The results are strikingly different than those obtained over the same time period with the free response Form H. Some examples of these findings are given in Tables 10.5 and 10.6.

This same pattern extends to the managerial gender comparisons. There are five of these available and all favor the males. The only significant difference, however, was obtained in a sample of chief executive officers of hospitals in Georgia. In addition there are three comparisons that extend to groups other than students and managers. Swisher, DuMont, and Boyer (1985) studied academic librarians and found, as they had with library science students, that the males scored slightly higher. Dayani (1980) found the reverse using the free response Form H; his results were significant. Hoffman (1983) carried out gender comparisons using both black and white samples from the instructional staffs of post-secondary vocational education schools in Georgia. Among the blacks the males' Total Score was higher, while among the whites the females scored higher. This latter is the only instance among the 20 multiple-choice comparisons where a female group had the higher score.

A meta-analysis

The preceding discussion has been based on comparisons of frequencies utilizing 61 data sets. Of these, 51 contained sufficient data and were otherwise suitable for inclusion in a meta-analysis (Eagly, Karau, Miner, and Johnson, 1992). The results of this analysis for all studies are given in Table 10.9. All of the MSCS-H measures yield significant effect sizes. In all but two instances the differences favor the males. Females score higher on the Authority Figures and Routine Administrative Functions subscales. The effect sizes favoring males on Competitive Games and Assertive Role are the largest. As would be expected from the preceding discussion, there is an overall trend with males having the higher scores, but the effect sizes are not large and reversals occur on two subscales.

As indicated in Table 10.10 there is a substantially greater Total Score difference when the multiple-choice MSCS-H is used. Beyond this, interpretations become difficult because of the small numbers of data sets in some of the categories. However, significance is obtained with the free response MSCS-H only among the business students; the findings for other students and the employed groups are not significant. Using the

Table 10.9 Differences between males and females for MSCS – Form H measures

Measure	Total n of studies	All effect sizes			Homogeneity (Q) of effect sizes[b]	Effect sizes excluding outliers			
		M weighted effect size (d+)[a]	95% CI for d+ Lower	Upper		n removed outliers[c]	M weighted effect size (d+)	95% CI for d+ Lower	Upper
Total score	51	0.22	0.16	0.27	103.77*	3(.06)	0.18	0.11	0.24
Subscales									
Authority figures	45	-0.17[a]	-0.24	-0.11	122.76**	7(.16)	-0.24	-0.31	-0.17
Competitive games	46	0.31[d]	0.24	0.37	110.28**	3(.07)	0.30	0.24	0.37
Competitive situations	45	0.15[b]	0.09	0.21	91.48**	5(.11)	0.16	0.09	0.22
Assertive role	45	0.27[cd]	0.21	0.34	105.36***	5(.11)	0.25	0.18	0.32
Imposing wishes	45	0.19[bc]	0.13	0.26	97.98*	5(.11)	0.21	0.14	0.27
Standing out from the group	45	0.12[b]	0.05	0.18	139.94*	7(.16)	0.18	0.11	0.26
Routine administrative functions	45	-0.09[a]	-0.15	-0.03	102.91*	3(.07)	-0.12	-0.19	-0.05

Note: Positive effect sizes indicate that men have higher motivation to manage scores than women, and negative effect sizes indicate that women have higher scores than men. CI = confidence interval.
[a] Effect sizes were weighted by the reciprocal of the variance. Differences between subscale means that do not have a subscript in common are significant (p <.05, post-hoc contrasts).
[b] Significance indicates rejection of the hypothesis of homogeneity.
[c] The proportion appears in parentheses.
* p <.01.
**p <.001
Source: Eagly, Karau, Miner, and Johnson, 1992

Table 10.10 Categorical models for version of the MSCS – Form H and status of subjects

Variable and class	Between-classes effect	n	Mean weighted effect size (d_{i+})	95% CI for d_{i+} Lower	95% CI for d_{i+} Upper	Homogeneity within each class (Q_{wi})[a]
Version of MSCS	7.40**					
Free response		37	0.15	0.08	0.23	46.48
Multiple-choice		14	0.32	0.22	0.42	49.88**
Version of MSCS and status of subjects	35.89**					
Free response						
Business students		24	0.17	0.07	0.27	22.27
Other students		4	0.15	−0.05	0.35	3.06
Business managers		7	0.16	−0.01	0.34	12.54
Other employees		2	−0.08	−0.37	0.22	6.11
Multiple-choice						
Business students		8	0.51	0.38	0.64	18.32*
Other students		2	0.16	−0.14	0.46	0.17
Business managers		1	1.09	0.32	1.85	0.00
Other employees		3	0.01	−0.16	0.18	5.42

Note: Positive effect sizes indicate that men have higher motivation to manage scores than women. CI = confidence interval. The 'other employees' classes include librarians, teachers, managers in academic libraries, managers in government agencies, and non-managerial business employees.

[a] Significance indicates rejection of the hypothesis of homogeneity.

* p < .05

** p < .01

Source: Eagly, Karau, Miner, and Johnson, 1992

multiple-choice version yields significant and rather large differences in favor of males among the business students and managers, not elsewhere. However, the managerial result is based on only a single data set.

Other findings not shown in the tables are that the tendency for men to have higher motivation to manage is particularly large in the five analyses that used samples of blacks, and that effect sizes tended to become significantly smaller in the older, predominantly managerial samples than they were among the younger students. When the relation between the year the data were collected and effect size was computed for the multiple-choice MSCS-H, a significant effect size decrease was found in the most recent years. Overall, this was not true for the free response measure, but it was true within the predominant group of business students. Effect sizes did not vary depending on whether the studies involved the author in some way or were conducted completely independent of him, and whether the research reports were authored by men or women.

Item-level analyses

Questions have been raised about the content of particular items on the MSCS – Form H. Specifically, Bartol and Martin (1987) suggested that some items on the MSCS might produce sex differences because they inquire about activities that are more typical of men than women. These authors noted several such items, specifically those said to utilize the following sentence stems from the MSCS: *athletic contests, shooting a rifle, when one of my men asks me for advice, wearing a necktie, playing golf,* and *getting my shoes shined.* These six stems provide a comprehensive listing of all items that to the authors' knowledge have been questioned on these grounds. As these items illustrate, the sentence stems of the MSCS-H do not necessarily describe activities required by the managerial role. Given that the MSCS is a *projective* instrument that assesses underlying motivation, this indirect approach to the measurement task is entirely reasonable. Nonetheless, women might engage in the activities described in such items less than men do and have less positive reactions to them, not because of a lower level of motivation to manage, but because of gender-specific rules about appropriate behavior. Normative barriers to highly sex-typed activities may cause items that name such activities to be poorer indicants for women of the general construct that the MSCS is intended to measure. Such items might produce distinctively larger sex differences than other items used in the instrument to measure the same constructs. To test this hypothesis, item-level data for several samples of respondents were examined to determine whether certain items on the MSCS produce exaggerated sex differences.

Item-level data were obtained for the free response version of the scale for five samples: 124 U.S. undergraduate business students tested in 1980

(Miner and Smith, 1982); 102 U.S. graduate business students tested in 1987; 76 U.S. undergraduate liberal arts students tested in 1973 (Miner, 1974d); 76 European business students tested in 1988 and 1990; 80 U.S. managers tested in 1974 (Miner, 1977). In addition, item-level data were available for the multiple-choice version of the scale for one sample consisting of 48 U.S. managers (from among the previously noted 80) retested later in 1974 (Miner, 1977). Items were scored as +1 (high motivation to manage), 0 (indeterminate motivation to manage), or −1 (lower motivation to manage). Using a chi-square test, female and male distributions were compared both within samples and with the data pooled across the samples. Support for the hypothesis that certain items yield exaggerated sex differences would be provided if the six items designated by Bartol and Martin (1987) were to yield significant chi-squares favoring males more frequently than the other items in the same subscales not considered to suffer from the same problems.

The necessary comparisons are summarized in Table 10.11. There are three subscales in which the designated items fall, and there are five items in each of these subscales; thus, in the overall, the six items are compared with nine others measuring the same constructs. Focusing first on the sample level analyses, two of the designated items yield no significant sex differences across the six samples (when one of my men asks me for advice; getting my shoes shined). Three more of the items yield only one significant difference across the six samples (athletic contests; shooting a rifle; playing golf). The item stem – wearing a necktie – produces two significant sample results favoring males (out of six), but both are in the overlapping managerial samples where the condition of independence is not met and where the multiple-choice data are derived from a repeat administration. This same item produces significant chi-squares in two additional samples, but the data are curvilinear, and do not favor the males. Within the nine items utilized for comparison purposes significant sample differences favoring males are even less frequent, numbering only two (on two different items), but significant differences are so infrequent on the six designated items that any conclusion that certain items unfairly favor males hardly seems justified based on the sample level analyses.

However, the limited size of the six samples, ranging from 48 to 124 individuals, may camouflage real but small differences in favor of the hypothesis. Accordingly, the data for the first five samples were pooled to yield an N of 458; the sixth sample of managers using the multiple-choice measure could not be included because of a lack of independence. In this expanded sample three significant results were obtained on the six designated items; however, in one of these instances the data were curvilinear and the results did not favor the males. The remaining two items – athletic contests and shooting a rifle – clearly did yield findings in support of the hypothesis. Yet this conclusion is tempered by the fact that two

Table 10.11 Item-level analysis results for MSCS – Form H in six samples

	Number of items	Results significant at p <.05 or better	
		Number of sample findings yielding hypothesized results	Number of pooled findings yielding hypothesized results
Competitive games			
Hypothesized as favoring males	2	2 of 12	1 of 2
Not so hypothesized	3	0 of 18	1 of 3
Assertive role			
Hypothesized as favoring males	3	3 of 18	1 of 3
Not so hypothesized	2	0 of 12	0 of 2
Imposing wishes			
Hypothesized as favoring males	1	0 of 6	0 of 1
Not so hypothesized	4	2 of 24	1 of 4
Total of 3 subscales			
Hypothesized as favoring males	6	5 of 36	2 of 6
Not so hypothesized	9	2 of 54	2 of 9

others, among the comparison items, also yield a significant finding favoring the males (and two more yield significance without a clear directionality); again there is little hard evidence to support the view that females are at a disadvantage. Apparently an activity can be more prevalent among one sex or the other, without that differential translating into a special advantage when test items are scored. This conclusion is based much more on free response data than multiple-choice, but there is nothing in what analyses were carried out to suggest a special problem with the designated items in the multiple-choice format. On only one of the 15 items studied was significance obtained in the multiple-choice sample, and that result perfectly paralleled the free response finding.

Interpretations

The results obtained with the free response Form H suggest that the instrument is highly responsive to changes in cultural norms related to gender. When there were few women in the business schools, males had the higher scores on average. With changing norms, proportionately more women arrived and eventually the differential disappeared. The data are insufficient to consider time trends of this kind at the managerial level, but it appears very likely that the same phenomenon operates there as well. Harlan and Weiss (1982) found a significant MSCS – Form H score difference in favor of males in a company with only six percent female managers, but no difference in a company with 19 percent female managers. It seems tenable that in theory-relevant contexts where females are under-represented, motivation to manage will be relatively low among them as well. By the same token where males are under-represented one might expect their scores to be lower. Given that during the 1980s the United States began to approach equal representation in both the business schools and the ranks of management (although not at the top), parity in Form H scores would be expected, and that is what we find. Thus at the present time there does not appear to be any overall difference. With changing norms and pragmatic realities, however, this situation could change. In the past there clearly have been circumstances where males had the stronger managerial motivation. In a re-emerging Amazonian world the reverse could be true. The legal concept of adverse impact as currently formulated simply does not handle cultural changes of this kind very well.

The subscale data suggest that women may achieve high managerial motivation in somewhat different ways than men. Within the hierarchic construct men tend to be higher on the competitive, assertive (masculine), power-oriented motive patterns. Women have more favorable reactions to authority and find more pleasure in routine managerial duties. These findings are consistent with Eagly and Johnson's (1990) conclusion that women tend to be more collaborative and democratic as they approach the leadership role. This differential could represent a gender-specific imperative. It seems more likely, though, that it too is a consequence of existing cultural norms, and could change with time.

The one set of findings that does not appear to fit snugly into the motivation to manage puzzle involves the multiple-choice Form H. Could it be that these results are the correct ones, and that the free response measure is the one in error? This seems unlikely. There is overwhelming evidence that multiple-choicing removes the projective element and increases scores. Probably somewhere in this process is the answer to why using a multiple-choice format introduces a score differential in favor of males as well. Whether this phenomenon is specific to Form H of the MSCS or more widely present in other sentence completion-type items, or even personality tests generally, is an open question at this point. The question definitely needs more study. In fact, given the extensive use of self-report items in the multiple-choice format in personality testing generally, there would appear to be some urgency in this regard. Yet it is also possible that the problem resides in the specific multiple-choice alternatives incorporated in the multiple-choice version of the MSCS-H.

In any event it is apparent that at the present time the multiple-choice Form H does produce a gender differential with the net effect that women tend to score lower. On the average the effect size favoring males is 0.32 – not large, but meaningful. Furthermore this differential may quite possibly result more from measurement error than from cultural variations. If so, it should be removed. Given an average standard deviation for the multiple choice MSCS – Form H Total Score of 5.85 across the studies reviewed, adding two points to the scores of females would produce parity with males. However, the Civil Rights Act of 1991 gives pause to recommending this approach, thus providing another example of how scientific and legal considerations may move in different directions.

In winding up this discussion, some mention needs to be made of differential validity. There is evidence that with the free response Form H the validity results for males and females are essentially the same (Miner, 1974a) and that the role motivation training intervention operates in essentially the same manner for both sexes (Miner, 1965). Substantial validities have been obtained in samples with a heavy representation of women. Comparable evidence for the multiple-choice version is unavailable. However, considering what is known about the comparability of the two measures (Chapter 3) and the validity of the multiple-choice version in general (Chapter 4), there is no reason to suspect that the introduction of forced choice alternatives produces any particular change in validity – certainly no change that would yield differential consequences for one sex or the other. In actual fact there are eight studies that deal with the validity of the multiple-choice measure – six concurrent and two predictive. In three instances the samples are predominantly male. In the remaining five studies roughly 40 percent are females. The findings show no relation between the proportion of women in the samples and the validity results obtained. There is no evidence that the multiple-choice measure is any less valid for women than for men.

CHAPTER SUMMARY

Age, race, and gender differences on the MSCS measures are important in their own right, but they also carry major legal ramifications. In general Form H has been found to be unrelated to age. However, the decline and stabilization findings noted in Chapter 8 can influence this conclusion. To the extent they are engaged, positive age correlations can be expected. Age does not seem to be related to Form P scores except to the extent that Professional Commitment is involved. In the latter instance a positive correlation can be expected. Form T does not appear to yield meaningful age correlations except in the case of Avoiding Risks, where the relationship tends to be positive; younger people are more disposed to take risks.

Racial differences on Form P and Form T simply have not been investigated. On Form H the results are much more extensive, but they are mixed. Among females there is a tendency for whites to score higher than blacks on Routine Administrative Functions, but this does not enter into the Total Score results. Overall, it appears that racial differences on Form H are not to be expected, but when they do occur it is because black males score higher than white males.

Gender differences have been studied extensively, but only with Form H. The limited data for Form P and Form T suggest no differences. On Form H there are substantial differences between the results obtained with the free response and multiple-choice versions. In the former case there appears to be little by way of a sex difference at the adult level, although these studies have focused heavily on managers. Among business school students, an early difference in favor of males has been narrowing to the point where in most schools it has now disappeared. Thus for all practical purposes males and females, to the extent they have been studied, now seem to score at about the same level on the MSCS-H. The overall differences found are largely a result of an earlier period. On the multiple-choice Form H, however, meaningful differences in favor of males still exist among business school students, although they are narrowing. These appear to be a consequence of measurement factors of one kind or another. Thus, primary consideration should be given to the free response results.

As we move now to the final chapter, there are a number of loose ends to be considered. In part these involve looking back to the criticisms and controversy that have on occasion surrounded the role motivation theories. We also look forward to certain advances in theory and research, and to evolving practical applications.

Chapter 11

Looking back and looking forward

In concluding previous books presenting role motivation theory research, I have attempted to outline areas where I thought research would and should move in the future (Miner, 1965; 1977). It is not my intention to do that here. With the advantage of somewhat more wisdom than I possessed in the past I now feel that predicting which direction future research will take is almost impossible, and specifying what direction it should take is pointless. People will pursue what interests *them* and what *they* consider important.

There are three things, however, that do need to be done. First is the matter of dealing directly with certain criticisms that have been directed not so much at role motivation theory, as at the MSCS – Form H. The subject matter of these criticisms has been considered at various points throughout this book, but they need more explicit attention here. This is the looking back part. Second, the preceding discussion has dealt with four parallel, limited domain theories that have much in common with Merton's (1949) concept of middle range theories. The strategy inherent in building middle range theory is that ultimately, as more and more of these theories are validated, it should be possible to fill in the blanks between them, thus building up to grand theory. We need to take a look at what is involved and what the prospects for success are in attempting to bridge between the four role motivation theories to create an overarching theory of higher sophistication. Third, there is a need to spell out exactly what implications for practice are inherent in role motivation theory and its research. This will be done by considering how productivity might be fostered by putting these ideas to use. Special attention is given to the assessment procedures that role motivation theory has spawned.

CRITICISM AND CONTROVERSY

At least in the social sciences it is safe to assume that any theory that is long standing in nature and that has achieved some scientific stature will come under attack. Whether these attacks will ultimately serve to invalidate the theory or prove unfounded varies from theory to theory. The fact is that they can invariably be anticipated. Role motivation theory is no exception. When such criticisms occur, one strategy has been to ignore them, either in the hope that they will go away or because no countervailing arguments come readily to mind. On the other hand many theorists have chosen to argue their cases at some length, either with or without the support of new evidence, on the grounds that their scientific peers should have the benefit of all available information (see for example Alderfer, 1977; Hofstede, 1981; Lawrence and Lorsch, 1973; Mitroff and Mason, 1981; and Simon, 1973).

In general the approach I have taken with role motivation theory is to present the countervailing arguments, when I have previously unpublished data bearing on the issues raised. I am convinced from my reviews of the theoretical literature (Miner, 1980b; 1982a) that theoretical criticisms typically do not go away, and that often they contain errors or misinterpretations that need to be dealt with. In the end a response may prove ungrounded, but the scientific community deserves the right to judge all the available evidence. It is in this vein that the following is written.

There appear to be four different bodies of criticism directed against role motivation theories, their research evidence, and the measures on which this evidence is based. In all four instances some contrary research evidence is brought to bear in one publication or another. These four criticisms are contained in the following publications:

1. Brief, Aldag, and Chacko (1977), and Aldag and Brief (undated).
2. Bartol, Anderson, and Schneier (1980; 1981), Bartol, Schneier, and Anderson (1985), and Bartol and Martin (1987).
3. Stahl, Grigsby, and Gulati (1985), and Stahl (1986).
4. Eberhardt, Yap, and Basuray (1988).

Anyone reading these criticisms needs to place them in the context of the related literatures reviewed previously. In addition there are two specific replies containing new evidence that should be taken into account.

1. Miner (1978) – a response to the Aldag, Brief, Chacko criticisms.
2. Miner, Smith, and Ebrahimi (1985) – a response to the Anderson, Bartol, Schneier criticisms.

The following discussion treats the criticisms in terms of the various issues raised, rather than dealing with each of the four bodies of criticism separately. Frequent reference is made back to previously presented data and previous discussions.

Construct validity is lacking

This criticism is leveled at the hierarchic theory specifically. Since the constructs of the various role motivation theories differ, any such criticism would have to deal with each theory separately. Two of the four bodies of criticism take this tack – the one by Brief *et al.* and the one by Stahl *et al.* The Eberhardt *et al.* article concludes, based on the authors' own research, that construct validity is *not* a problem.

The Brief *et al.* criticisms relate to a failure to find certain relationships between the MSCS – Form H and Ghiselli's (1971) Self-Description Inventory, as well as England's (1975) Personal Values Questionnaire. Chapter 4, and in particular Table 4.11, deals with the SDI relationships. In view of what has been learned since the original criticisms relating to the SDI were made, it would seem that this is essentially a non-issue at the present time. The PVQ, however, has not been studied in relation to the MSCS – Form H subsequent to the Brief *et al.* research. Thus, the finding of a lack of relationship still stands. Whether this is damaging evidence for the construct validity of the MSCS represents in large part a matter of personal taste. It would have to be the pragmatic values measure from the PVQ that would relate to the MSCS, because that is the PVQ measure that has been found to associate with managerial success. Yet the MSCS is not intended to measure either values, or pragmatism. To this author at least, it is not at all clear why any relationship would be expected.

The Stahl *et al.* criticisms regarding construct validity do not focus on relationships to other test measures. One source is a study comparing the MSCS – Form H scores of student leaders and non-leaders at Clemson University (see Study 21 in Table 4.1 and also Table 3.14). The data indicate a clear differentiation for Total Score and for four of the seven subscales; the leaders do score significantly higher, even though the samples are quite small. Yet Stahl *et al.* interpret this as evidence questioning the construct validity of the MSCS. It is the old question of perceiving the glass as half-full or half-empty. To this author the Stahl *et al.* results do not question the MSCS's validity; they strongly support it. Stahl *et al.* also interpret the results of their factor analysis of the MSCS as evidence against construct validity. The discussion of this research in Chapter 3 rejects the idea that a test must be factor pure to be valid. But beyond this it is not at all clear why Stahl *et al.* invoke the concept of construct validity in this instance at all. Factor purity and internal consistency would appear to be much more relevant for test reliability than for construct validity. Perhaps a clue to the prevailing negativisms of the Stahl *et al.* interpretations is provided by the fact that they seem to be most interested in extolling their own Job Choice Exercise. At times the MSCS – Form H seems to have been cast in the role of strawman in this endeavor.

Reliability is lacking

The most consistent criticism of the MSCS – Form H is that it is a less than reliable instrument. Yet there is no consistency on the basis for this charge. Scorer reliability is challenged in two instances – by Brief *et al.* and by Bartol *et al.* Internal consistency reliability is also questioned twice – by Stahl *et al.* and Eberhardt *et al.* Only Stahl *et al.* attack the test–retest reliability of the MSCS–H.

The discussion in Chapter 3 presents a great deal of evidence on all aspects of the reliability question, much of it obtained since the original criticisms were leveled. Data such as those contained in Table 3.8 clearly indicate that scorer reliability at a high level is readily attainable. On the other hand it is also evident that it is not always obtained. Scorers with little incentive who make only limited reference to the examples in the scoring guide tend to do poorly (Perham, 1989). It is not that standardized scoring of sentence completion measures cannot work; the situation is identical to that faced by numerous content analysis procedures. But the results are not always what might be hoped for, and those who are involved in failing efforts tend to end by attacking the whole process.

Having had a considerable amount of experience in these matters, it may be helpful for the author to offer some insights. One is that training can matter; an experienced scorer can help the less experienced to see where they may go wrong. I believe now that I underestimated this factor because training in using projectives was taken for granted in my own experience. I believe that training with the Rorschach and the TAT and other such instruments is transferable to sentence completion measures such as the MSCSs, and that those who lack such a background are at a disadvantage. On the other hand my work with graduate students convinces me that such deficiencies in those who lack clinical training can be easily overcome. However, it takes hard work. There are, in addition, those to whom this sort of thing comes easily, and who really for all practical purposes do not need training. There are also those to whom the attention to detail, the constant checking against the scoring guide, and the need to re-evaluate initial scorings before coming to a final conclusion come very hard at best. Training tends to build in an ego ideal and a self-imposed standard of proficiency. I am now convinced that, without that, effective scoring is impossible. What is involved here is nothing more than is inherent in clinical diagnostic training generally. I had hoped that with the highly standardized MSCS scoring procedures this step could be circumvented. I am still convinced that it can for some. But not as widely as I had hoped.

A second point relates to the scoring guides themselves. Anyone who compares the three guides – for Form H, Form P, and Form T – will see changes. Each new guide adds in a greater degree of specificity and detail;

each makes it easier to carry out the scoring process, *if it is used religiously*. The Form H guide could be improved if it were rewritten today. Then, why not rewrite it, taking into account what has been learned since 1964? There are two reasons. For one thing the various supplements (Miner, 1977a; 1989) do contribute to this objective, especially in the area of interpretation. Second, I am convinced that the amount of error variance introduced by scoring guide differentials is miniscule in comparison with the error variance associated with variations in individual effort and skill. The real need is to work harder, pay more attention, and maintain higher standards. Training can contribute to these goals; I am not convinced that improved scoring guides will accomplish nearly as much.

An obvious solution is that free response scoring be replaced with multiple-choice testing. Those who criticize the free response approach as unreliable invariably advocate a multiple-choice approach. Yet, as detailed at various points throughout this book, there are problems inherent in the multiple-choice procedures as well. What is important is that the user be able to make a choice based on knowledge of the evidence. That type of situation exists for Form H. It is important that similar choices be developed for Form P and Form T. Developing multiple-choice versions of those two instruments is a high priority for the future.

Internal consistency for the various MSCS measures is not high. The criticisms have been focused on the Form H measures, but they could as well apply to Form P and Form T. The data of Table 3.13 are very consistent on this point. Nor surprisingly these results extend to various factor analytic studies. The factor structures obtained with Form H vary greatly, but none reflect the subscale structure inherent in the hierarchic theory. As argued repeatedly throughout this book, and especially in Chapter 3, all this makes no difference whatsoever. Validity is not limited by internal consistency, and factor purity is not a necessary condition for valid measurement. These are empirical facts. The evidence presented throughout this book is overwhelming on this point. The MSCS measures are not lacking in psychometric soundness because of their failure to demonstrate internal consistency. If this is the position of current psychometric theory, then how can one explain the validity evidence obtained. One cannot attribute it to erroneous scoring, because identical results have been obtained with the multiple-choice MSCS – Form H (see Tables 4.1 and 4.3).

The ultimate test then, when it comes to reliability, is the test–retest procedure. Only Stahl *et al.* offer a challenge on this score. Results from various test–retest studies are given in Tables 3.9, 3.10, 3.11, and 3.12. The median Total Score reliability coefficient reported in those tables is 0.86 and the median subscale value is 0.66. These are low estimates for reliability because in several instances they incorporate real changes (not error) occurring over rather lengthy time periods. The Stahl *et al.* data

(Table 3.11) tend to be on the low side in comparison with the other figures reported, but they are clearly within the range of expected sampling fluctuations. The Total Score coefficients are quite adequate to support MSCS validity. The subscales are intended to indicate which motive patterns contribute the most when Total Score is high or low. The subscale test–retest coefficients appear to be sufficient for this purpose. Certainly it would be desirable to have higher reliabilities, to always obtain results comparable to those reported in Table 3.12, for instance. However, the available data, part of which has been obtained since the Stahl *et al.* criticism was published, do not give reason to reject the MSCS measures as psychometrically unsound due to unreliability.

Role motivation training teaches the theory

The teaching the theory criticism of managerial role motivation training research derives from Bartol and Martin (1987). It is detailed in Chapter 7. Subsequent to the publication of this criticism, a study was designed and conducted to test the teaching the theory hypothesis (Miner and Doe, 1992). The results of this study are given in Table 7.5. They give no support to the view that the changes reported across role motivation training represent an artifact resulting from the interaction of measurement procedures and cognitive course content, rather than a reflection of true motivational change. Based on this research and other consideration discussed in Chapter 7, it is now possible to reject the teaching the theory criticism.

The decline is questionable

Bartol *et al.* have developed two types of criticisms of the concept of a decline in motivation to manage and the research related to it. Initially the argument was that a reversal occurred by 1977 and that accordingly any concept of stabilization after the decline in the late 1960s and early 1970s was in error. Bartol *et al.* report data to support the 1977 reversal and they argue that the decline was a sufficiently transitory phenomenon so that the impact on national managerial talent supplies was minimal. This criticism is really aimed at the stabilization hypothesis, not the decline.

Later, Bartol *et al.* questioned the evidence for the decline itself, arguing that it was anchored in inadequate data:

Acceptance of the shortage of managerial talent thesis requires acceptance of three rather untenable premises:
1. one set of scores from a single school is representative of the score of all business school students in the United States for the 1960–1 time period;

2. these data measured on a single instrument constitute a sufficient base from which to argue that the motivation to manage scores of all business students have subsequently declined and/or stabilized; and

3. these data from a single school and a single instrument are a sufficient base from which to then predict a serious and general shortage of managerial talent in large bureaucratic organizations.

(Bartol, Schneier, and Anderson, 1985: 303)

The hypothesis of a reversal in the late 1970s is by now discredited. As indicated in Chapter 8, serious scoring errors were found in the data from which the reversal hypothesis was derived, and studies carried out subsequently (see Table 8.7) do not indicate a reversal of any meaningful magnitude. Bartol and Martin (1987) argue from multiple-choice Form H data collected in 1979–80 that these findings support the concept of a reversal. However, they present no previous multiple-choice results that would permit direct comparisons, and as we have seen, score inflation makes moving back and forth between free response and multiple-choice findings tenuous at best. In general, the Bartol and Martin (1987) scores appear to be quite consistent with what others have found with the multiple-choice instrument during the 1980s among business students. The problem is that the instrument involved was only published in 1977.

The second criticism, that the whole decline hypothesis hangs on a single set of MSCS – Form H scores from the University of Oregon (in 1960–1), is simply not true. It is hard to understand how others, such as Driver (1988), could have come to accept this interpretation. Even within the Oregon data set forth in Table 8.1, it is quite evident that significant declines occurred not only from the 1960–1 figures, but also from 1967–8 to 1972–3. To this should be added the fact that the 1960–1 sample numbering 287 was in fact a composite of four samples obtained over four successive quarters, all of which scored relatively high, and that supportive findings are available from two other samples in 1961 (Miner, 1965: 115), and from graduate student samples collected in the 1964–6 period (Miner, 1968a). There can be no question about score levels existing at the University of Oregon in the early to mid-1960s.

But as shown in Table 8.2 (University of Maryland) and 8.4 (Portland State University), evidence of decline in Form H scores was not limited to the University of Oregon. Furthermore, comparisons between age cohorts at the same universities are entirely consistent with the decline concept (see Table 8.5).

These are all studies utilizing Form H, but as the section on related literatures in Chapter 8 demonstrates, many other investigators have obtained evidence of a decline using constructs and measures conceptually similar to Form H. The most striking results derive from the Ward and

Athos (1972) research at the Harvard Business School and the Howard and Bray (1988) studies at AT & T, but there are many others. It is hoped that the idea that the decline has not been sufficiently documented can be put to rest. For those who have any lingering doubts on this score, it might prove helpful to read my book, *The Human Constraint* (Miner, 1974b).

Gender effects are widespread

Bartol *et al.* in their various publications repeatedly take the position that Form H favors males over females. They view the difference as small, less than 10 percent, and of limited practical significance, but nevertheless pervasive. In part this position stems from their findings in their own studies that males do outscore females. In part it appears to be a function of their reading of the MSCS items themselves. On the latter point they have this to say:

> Female scores on motivation to manage also may have been negatively affected by the nature of the MSCS. A few sentence stems (e.g. athletic contests . . . wearing a necktie . . . playing golf . . . and getting my shoes shined . . .) appear more likely to engender a positive response from males than from females. Thus the possibility of some bias in the MSCS warrants inquiry.
>
> (Bartol, Anderson, and Schneier, 1980: 30)

With regard to the fact that Bartol *et al.* repeatedly found higher scores among males than females, there are two types of explanation. The findings reported in Bartol, Anderson, and Schneier (1980; 1981) for the free response Form H appear to be attributable to scoring errors as noted previously (see Miner, Smith, and Ebrahimi, 1985: 293–5). The findings reported in Bartol and Martin (1987) are consistent with other results obtained with the multiple-choice version as noted in Chapter 10, and appear to be associated with certain specific features of that instrument.

The issue of the wording of specific MSCS items in terms of their potential for bias is a complex one. In the early years of research with the MSCS, this issue was never raised, to the author's knowledge. But sometime during the 1970s one began to hear questions along these lines. They were not frequent, but Bartol *et al.* are not alone in raising these questions and they persist to the present. It is necessary to know whether certain items actually yield differential scoring for males and females as a function of their specific wording. This is an empirical question. The research dealing with item-level analyses described in Chapter 10 goes a long way toward providing an answer. This research is also discussed in an article by Eagly, Karau, Miner, and Johnson (1992).

The item-level analyses, as summarized in Table 10.11, give no support to the thesis set forth by Bartol and Martin (1987) that six specific items in the MSCS-H are worded so as to yield a bias in favor of males. At least insofar as the free response version of the MSCS – Form H is concerned, the hypothesis is not confirmed. What data are available suggest a similar conclusion for the multiple-choice version, but further study appears necessary in that regard. Furthermore, others may well advance a different list of potentially biased items in the future. The Bartol and Martin (1987) list is the most comprehensive available to date, and that is why it served to guide the conduct of the item-level analyses described in Chapter 10. However, others may have different views.

A question remains, given the findings noted in Chapter 10, as to whether the multiple-choice instrument should continue to be made available. This is an interesting quandary. Two of the major critics of role motivation theory and Form H (Brief et al. and Bartol et al.) have strongly recommended forced choice measurement over the more projective free response approach. The remaining two critics (Stahl et al. and Eberhardt et al.) have chosen to use the multiple-choice version rather than the free response one in their own research. Yet there are those (among them an anonymous reviewer) who seem to believe the test should be removed from the market. The problem is that any action which served to reduce the use of the multiple-choice measure in research would make it less likely that solutions would be found to the problems unearthed originally through its use. Furthermore, the instrument is a valid predictor of managerial success, and not too many of those exist. The old 'throwing the baby out with the bath water' analogy comes to mind. It does not yet seem time to shut the door on the multiple-choice version of Form H, or to cease all efforts to develop multiple-choice versions of Forms P and T. There are too many uncertainties out there that such instruments can help unravel.

TOWARD A SINGLE INTEGRATED THEORY: FILLING IN THE GAPS

Moving now to the second issue noted at the beginning of this chapter, let us consider what would be involved in filling in the gaps between the four parallel role motivation theories and thus creating a more comprehensive integrated theory. One effort to move in this direction involves the ground between the task theory and the hierarchic theory. It should prove instructive to consider this effort, and see what might be learned from it that could be generalized to integrated theory construction overall.

There are two primary situations where the domain of managers, the hierarchic organization, and the domain of entrepreneurs, the task organization, come in close proximity. The first involves a growing entrepreneurial firm which at some point reaches a stage in its life cycle where managers tend to displace the entrepreneur in the strategic leadership role (Miner, 1990a). The second situation arises when an established hierarchic organization moves to acquire or create new ventures which are to operate at least initially in an entrepreneurial mode. Both of these situations present major problems of a theoretical and research nature; both also represent areas in which practice is groping for solutions. Given the state to which hierarchic and task theory have now progressed, it seems possible that these theories might be combined in some manner to help solve these problems.

Life cycle shifts from task to hierarchic domains

The idea of an organizational life cycle owes a primary debt to Chandler (1962), although Chandler did not probe deeply into the early stages of the companies he studied. Subsequently a number of life cycle concepts appeared with differentiations into a variety of stages. Among these are the formulations of Thain (1969), Steinmetz (1969), Greiner (1972), Scott (1973), Tuason (1973), and James (1973). In this period the major concern was with adding stages to those proposed by Chandler, particularly in the later, more mature period of a firm's existence. Where the earlier, more entrepreneurial, phases of firm development were considered in these theories, treatment was limited to a statement that the entrepreneur would have to shift to a more managerial style or actually relinquish strategic leadership to a manager.

A decade later there was another burst of activity in the life cycle area, but again the emphasis was primarily on specifications regarding the states to be achieved at the mature end of the cycle (Galbraith and Nathanson, 1978; Leontiades, 1980; Kimberly and Miles, 1980).

More recently there has been a shift to concentration on the entrepreneurial end of the life cycle. Typical formulations are those of Galbraith (1982), Churchill and Lewis (1983), and Mintzberg (1984). In these views the distinction between the early entrepreneurial stage and the later managerial one is clearly specified. For example:

The task changes from – Invent and make it, to . . . Make it profitable.
The people change from – Jacks of all trades, to . . . Business people, planners.
The rewards change from – Equity, nonbureaucratic climate, make a mark, to . . . Career, salary.
The processes change from – Informal, face-to-face contact, personal control, to . . . Formal control, planning and budget, information systems.
The structure changes from – Informal, little needed, to . . . Functional with overlays, division of labor, decentralize.

The leadership changes from – Quarterback, to . . . Manager.

(Galbraith, 1982: 74)

Using hierarchic and task theory and assuming that motivation-organization fit is the key to effective pursuit of goals, the following propositions may be set forth:

1. Many entrepreneurs will prefer the founder role and following the corridor principle (Ronstadt, 1988) will undertake a variety of new ventures. In such cases they are likely to turn over control of previous ventures to managers to ensure growth. When this is done the managers must have high managerial motivation and be able to create a hierarchic system to work in if the firm is to prosper. In the early stages of each enterprise the desired fit is that of a high task motivation entrepreneur and a task system.

2. Other entrepreneurs will prefer to found a company and steer it through major growth. For this to be possible one of two scenarios must exist.

   a) The entrepreneur must maintain a task system at the top of the organization, while gradually adding or getting others to add layers of hierarchy below as the company grows. These layers below should be staffed with high motivation to manage people and run as a bureaucracy. The resulting composite system can even survive a transition from one entrepreneur to another, if the composite state is established and stable, and the new leader has high task motivation. Usually these transitions will involve a relative.

   b) The entrepreneur must convert the system from a task to a hierarchic form as growth proceeds. At the same time the entrepreneur must shift from satisfying primarily task motives at work to satisfying hierarchic motives. Accordingly the entrepreneur needs to be high on *both* task and hierarchic motivation.

3. Inherent in these propositions is the view that small organizations need task motivation in the chief executive to grow, and a task system to match, but that at some point size becomes such that the entrepreneur cannot control the system. When exactly this point occurs depends on the capabilities of the entrepreneur and the degree of stress on the system. In any event, when the pure task system has been extended to its breaking point, hierarchy needs to be introduced in some form or the firm will either shrink or fail.

4. Many, in fact most, small firms are founded by entrepreneurs who lack the task motivation necessary to engineer growth. A task system exists, but there is insufficient energy to drive it. These firms are vulnerable to environmental stress, but may survive for long periods; they are unlikely to grow unless new strategic leadership, and with it higher task motivation, is introduced.

Corporate new venturing and the task–hierarchy interface

New venturing by large corporations may take a number of forms; among these are an informal task force, a formal venture management department with its own budget, and a separate venture management company sponsored by the larger corporation (Rind, 1981; Burgelman, 1984). The distinguishing characteristic is that a new line of business is started where none existed before; thus a form of entrepreneurship is involved.

There is now ample evidence that corporate new venturing of this kind faces major obstacles (Fast, 1977; Dunn, 1977; Biggadike, 1979; Weiss, 1981; Sykes, 1986). The ventures tend to be slow in reaching profitability, yield relatively low profit figures, and frequently are terminated by corporate management short of the planned start-up period. They fall far short of what is typically attained by independent entrepreneurial start-ups. In addition there is frequent conflict at the interface between the corporate hierarchy and new venture management. Quinn (1979: 23) attributes the problems to:

1. Corporate time horizons not being long enough to play the probability game and wait for results.
2. Staffing venture teams with professional managers balanced as to their marketing, financial, and technical skills, rather than infused with the deep-seated expertise and personal commitment a real entrepreneur needs.
3. Full costing of ventures (including all overheads) making those ventures difficult to justify in financial terms and excellent targets for cutbacks during short-term economic or organizational crunches.

There is some evidence that new ventures can yield successful results under certain circumstances (Hobson and Morrison, 1983; Kanter, 1985; Miller and Camp, 1985; Macmillan, Block, and Narasimha, 1986). Unfortunately, however, the data currently available yield somewhat conflicting conclusions regarding what the necessary circumstances are. In the hope of circumventing the high uncertainty levels surrounding the corporate-new venture interface, some firms have resorted to acquisitions of entrepreneurial firms. Thus, Cox (1982: 104–5) describes the acquisition program at General Mills in the course of which many small unrelated businesses were brought into the company. The strategy initially was to have the entrepreneurs continue to head their firms and to give them considerable autonomy. Ultimately this strategy came to be viewed as unsatisfactory, and the autonomy of the entrepreneurs was reduced through the imposition of a number of controls. The result was a substantial increase in resistance and conflict across the corporate–new venture interface.

Clearly we have not yet learned how to manage this interface, and we do not have the theory or research data to say how it might best be managed. Again there is the possibility that hierarchic and task theory can be used to gain new insights. It is to this end that the following propositions are set forth:

1. A common scenario is that new ventures are staffed with a team of managers who have shown promise during their rise in the parent corporation and who are characterized primarily by strong hierarchic motivation. However, the entrepreneurial nature of the job to be done fosters elements of a task system and the resulting lack of motivation-organization fit would be expected to work to the disadvantage of the new venture. In many situations of this type the new venture is, in fact, guided strategically by existing corporate executives, and not by the new venture managers at all; this merely accentuates the lack of fit, and the likelihood of failure.

2. Another scenario, often present when ventures are obtained by acquisition, involves high levels of task motivation in an intrepreneur or entrepreneur, but the imposition of extensive controls by the corporation. As a result a sizable bureaucratic element intrudes into the venture's operation, a lack of fit occurs, and the venture is put at a disadvantage.

3. There clearly is a need for high task motivation in an intrepreneur for a venture to succeed. This virtually precludes achieving success when a management team structure is imposed on the venture by the parent corporation. Beyond this, however, there appear to be two ways that a new venture headed by a task motivated entrepreneur can achieve success.

   a) The new venture is given substantial autonomy so that the intrepreneur can operate as an entrepreneur would. There should be an opportunity to succeed and obtain major rewards, or fail and lose one's job. Funding by the corporation in the manner of a bank or venture capital firm is consistent with this approach. The difficulty is that few high managerial motivation corporate executives can pass up an opportunity to manage in this manner; over time the venture's autonomy may well be eroded.

   b) Accordingly it should be best to staff new ventures with intrepreneurs who are high on both task and hierarchic motivation. Such people can gain satisfactions from operating in both types of systems and thus are more likely to be comfortable with the imposition of certain hierarchic controls. By the nature of the task, bureaucratic interventions should be minimized in the early survival and growth period, when a task system is essential, however. Furthermore, under this strategy close attention needs to be given to the selection of the intrepreneur. An appropriate motivational balance is essential.

Implications for constructing an integrated theory

If we are to follow the type of path taken with the life cycle and business venturing problems in future theorizing, the process of filling in the gaps is likely to be a lengthy one. What is involved is identifying an important problem in the space between two or more role motivation theories, studying that problem to understand what variables may be operating and how, constructing hypotheses making as extensive use of variables from existing role motivation theories as possible, and attempting to be as parsimonious as possible in the introduction of new variables. If a large number of new variables are introduced, one may well end not by building on existing, validated role motivation theories, and the knowledge thus made available, but merely by creating new theory. There is nothing wrong with this except that it wastes the foundation already laid; it is not filling in the gaps.

Yet it is also evident that the introduction of new variables cannot be avoided entirely. Examples in the preceding instances are environmental stress in the life cycle theorizing and degree of venture autonomy in the corporate venturing theorizing. The key appears to be to use the variables of the existing theories to the absolute maximum and only when they simply will not stretch any further introduce something new.

As indicated, this approach to the development of integrated theory is likely to be time consuming. Each problem in the space between theories has to be identified, studied, evaluated as to its importance, and then bound into the theoretical web. There may well be hundreds of problems that emerge as sufficiently important to warrant incorporation in the integrated theory. There is a substantial risk that parsimony may be lost in this process. One way of avoiding that would be to concentrate on only the most important problems; not to attempt to fill in all or even most of the gaps, only certain key ones.

Still, constructing an integrated theory of any kind that does in fact tie together the four role motivation theories even loosely is going to take a lot of theoretical work. One could hope for some panacea, some universal set of constructs, to guide the gap filling process. Perhaps something of this kind will emerge. It could be that after some ten or fifteen gap problems are conquered, it will be possible to abstract out certain common factors or variables that will make it much easier to deal with subsequent problems. However, we are a long way from that point at the present time. In fact the real present need is to complete the validation of the four existing role motivation theories. As things stand currently it is only the gaps between the hierarchic, professional, and task theories that can be attacked at all. The group theory needs to be added into the calculus. But when it is, a great deal more space that must be covered is added as well. Many new and important problems in the space between the theories open up, such as how to effectively integrate autonomous work groups into hierarchic structures and how to utilize professional expertise in free standing voluntary groups. The agenda for future theorizing and research is long indeed.

PUTTING ROLE MOTIVATION THEORIES TO USE

There are many points in the preceding discussions where role motivation theories have been linked to matters of usefulness in application. In large part this involves promoting productivity through appropriate use of selection and development approaches; it may also involve the use of problem-solving assessments. We consider these procedures as they contribute to matters of usefulness and productivity in the following discussions.

Dealing with productivity problems

The central thesis of this book is that organizational effectiveness yields high levels of productivity and that effectiveness results from achieving a state variously referred to as integration (Lawrence and Lorsch, 1967; Lorsch and Morse, 1974; Stogdill, 1959), congruence (Argyris, 1957; 1964), concordance (McMahon and Ivancevich, 1976; McMahon and Perritt, 1973), or simply fit (Galbraith and Nathanson, 1978; Miles and Snow, 1984). Although these theorists, and others, elaborate this concept in somewhat different ways, there is a consistent emphasis on the importance of achieving integration between the type of organizational system, including structure and process, and the kind of people who fill the key positions in the system. Inherent in this approach is the view that organizational systems can vary substantially, and that individual differences are an important consideration for organization theory. Accordingly, it follows that understanding organizational productivity requires a combining of organizational structure and process (macro-level) theory with organizational behavior (micro-level) theory.

This kind of integration, congruence, concordance, or fit can be achieved either by varying the type of organization – its structure and its processes - or by making changes in the individual who enters the organization. This latter may involve selecting appropriate people who fit the structure or changing incumbents to move them in the direction of a more appropriate fit. Thus one can utilize either selection or training and development. Or one can resort to both. On this latter point Campbell has the following to say:

> ... asking whether training or selection is the more powerful intervention, for purposes of increasing performance, is not a useful question. In general, questions of this form ... are misleading and unhelpful.

Certainly, both are important, and it is both the sum of their main effects and their interaction that should be investigated.

(Campbell, 1989: 470)

One way for an organization to achieve high productivity is to recruit, select, and perhaps promote people whose motivational patterns are congruent with the requirements of the various types of systems contained in the organization. An essential requirement to this end is that reliable and valid measures exist to identify both the nature of the organizational system itself and the motivational patterns. This is the subject matter of Chapters 3–6.

Another approach to enhancing productivity is the use of some type of training or development procedure. There is ample evidence that people can be changed in accordance with the demands of the various organizational systems and that the necessary motives can be fostered. This appears to be true, however, only to a degree, and while some people are quite responsive to such training, others are not at all responsive. Changes are maintained best when the resulting motives are put directly to work in a matching system. Changing role motivation in this matter is the subject matter of Chapter 7.

Ideally, given the less than perfect nature of both selection and development, the two procedures would be combined in the hope that organizational fits not achieved by one approach would be achieved by the other. Furthermore such a maximizing procedure should yield some individuals who, because of dual effects, are outstandingly suited to their organizational system.

Finally, another approach that might be introduced into the mix is some type of re-engineering of the organizational system. However, it is also true that unless one has a group of individuals who are relatively homogeneous in their possession of a motive pattern that matches some system other than that currently in effect, re-engineering the system will have to be combined with a certain amount of selection and/or training to fit the new system, if productivity gains are to be achieved. Given what is known regarding the wide range of individual differences (Tyler, 1978), it seems unlikely that the system-related homogeneity required by the pure re-engineering approach will be found frequently. Accordingly it appears that the widespread use of appropriate selection and educational procedures, possibly combined with system re-engineering in some contexts, offers the greatest prospects for major increases in the productivity of the society at the present time. (See Miner, 1974b for further discussion of this point.)

Conducting problem-solving assessments

Chapters 1 and 3 contained descriptions and test profiles of three individuals selected to provide examples of good organization–motivation fits. The objective here is to take this process a step further to show how the OODQ and the three MSCSs may be utilized in solving basic organizational problems. Normally, problem-solving assessments of this kind involve using an extensive battery of tests beyond these core instruments, as well as substantial data collection via interviewing, examination of personnel files, and the like (Miner, 1991). However, in order to serve the present purposes, the example that follows focuses on the OODQ and MSCS measures.

The problem to be solved through assessment is one of succession. The entrepreneur who founded the firm some 20 years previously says he wants to step down gradually and turn his firm over to new management. In fact he has already made certain moves in that direction without, in fact, picking a successor. The entrepreneur, Robert Lambert, appears to envisage a retirement process which follows the ambassador style as described by Sonnenfeld (1988). This style is described as follows:

> Ambassadors leave office quite gracefully and frequently serve as post-retirement mentors. They may remain on the board of directors for some time, but they do not try to sabotage the successor. The ambassadors provide continuity and counsel.
>
> (Sonnenfeld, 1988: 70–1)

> Unlike the monarchs (who leave via death or palace revolt) and the generals (who return as saviors after being forced out), the ambassador type of retiring leaders never wage war with their own organizations. They leave their positions feeling accomplished and appreciated.
>
> (Sonnenfeld, 1988: 180)

The company carries out roughly 10 million dollars' worth of business annually and has remained at that same level for a number of years. It has 160 employees. It operates in the electronics industry, and is fueled by the inventions of Robert Lambert and his two sons. Ever since its creation the company has been driven by a new product development strategy which has kept the firm afloat through difficult times and on occasion made it quite profitable. However, it has been some time since profits have been more than minimal. Without question the firm has plateaued.

Robert Lambert is best described as an inventor-entrepreneur (Miner, Smith, and Bracker, 1992). He has a PhD, and at one time worked as a university professor. He left to start his own company because he was having difficulty obtaining federal funding for his research and because he wanted to take his inventions all the way through into the market. At the time of assessment he was 65 years old.

There were three individuals who by virtue of their positions in the firm had to be considered as possible successors to Robert Lambert. All held the vice-presidential title. The preferred candidates were the two sons, because they had the technical know-how to spearhead a high technology firm of this kind and because they were family. However, there was a third person at the same level who was included in the assessment process because leaving her out might well alienate her, and because she was considered a very effective manager, which the firm needed.

Albert Lambert, the older son, also had a PhD. However, he had worked in the firm on and off throughout the period of his education and had joined it directly from school. He had a number of patents to his credit and had contributed almost as much as his father to the implementation of the firm's new product development strategy. He was outstanding at troubleshooting customers' technical problems, and in the process made a number of sales. Albert was 42 years old.

Ronald Lambert, the younger son, had earned an undergraduate degree in electrical engineering and worked for several years for a large corporation as an engineer while studying for an MBA at night. Ultimately he became disenchanted with the corporate world as one after another of his ideas was turned down. He joined the family firm short of completing the MBA. Like his brother he obtained a number of patents for his inventions. In addition he has taken primary responsibility for the financial affairs of the firm. Ronald was 39 years old.

Jane Walters was the company's human resource manager. She had joined the firm from another company at a time when turnover, especially among technical personnel, was so high that something had to be done. Jane was largely responsible for getting this situation under control, and keeping it that way. She had at one time been a graduate student in psychology. However, she had taken a position in industry after completing her coursework and never finished her dissertation. She was widely respected in the company as a peacemaker and a stabilizing force in what at times could be a rather turbulent environment. Jane was 54 years old.

The test score profiles that follow present the raw scores obtained by these four individuals and their percentile equivalents. As in Chapter 3 the OODQ percentiles are for the broad or balanced sample containing essentially equal numbers from each of the four domains, the Form H (free response) percentiles are for corporate managers, the Form P percentiles are for practicing professionals, and the Form T percentiles are for entrepreneurs. The instruments were given to each respondent immediately following a lengthy interview. They were to mail the completed forms directly to the author.

Test scores
Robert C. Lambert – inventor-entrepreneur

		Score	Percentile equivalent
OODQ –	H score	7	65th
	P score	7	68th
	T score	3	43rd
	G score	3	53rd
MSCS –	Total score	+3	40th
Form H	Authority figures	+3	89th
	Competitive games	−1	12th
	Competitive situations	0	63rd
	Assertive role	−2	12th
	Imposing wishes	+2	81st
	Standing out from group	0	30th
	Routine administrative functions	+1	59th
MSCS –	Total score	+11	74th
Form P	Acquiring knowledge	+2	74th
	Independent action	+2	50th
	Accepting status	−1	24th
	Providing help	+2	53rd
	Professional commitment	+6	99th
MSCS –	Total score	+22	96th
Form T	Self achievement	+6	93rd
	Avoiding risks	+3	78th
	Feedback of results	+1	67th
	Personal innovation	+6	89th
	Planning for the future	+6	96th

Test scores
Albert R. Lambert – older son

		Score	Percentile equivalent
OODQ –	H score	3	35th
	P score	1	10th
	T score	4	53rd
	G score	10	86th
MSCS –	Total score	+3	40th
Form H	Authority figures	+2	70th
	Competitive games	+1	43rd
	Competitive situations	0	63rd
	Assertive role	−1	25th
	Imposing wishes	0	31st
	Standing out from group	+2	77th
	Routine administrative functions	−1	18th
MSCS –	Total score	+17	92nd
Form P	Acquiring knowledge	+3	82nd
	Independent action	+3	65th
	Accepting status	+1	43rd

	Providing help	+7	99th
	Professional commitment	+3	86th
MSCS –	Total score	+8	56th
Form T	Self achievement	−1	16th
	Avoiding risks	0	34th
	Feedback of results	−1	35th
	Personal innovation	+6	89th
	Planning for the future	+4	82nd

Test scores
Ronald P. Lambert – younger son

		Score	Percentile equivalent
OODQ –	H score	4	41st
	P score	3	34th
	T score	5	62nd
	G score	8	79th
MSCS –	Total score	−4	7th
Form H	Authority figures	+1	45th
	Competitive games	+4	95th
	Competitive situations	−1	40th
	Assertive role	−3	4th
	Imposing wishes	−1	12th
	Standing out from group	−1	10th
	Routine administrative functions	−3	2nd
MSCS –	Total score	+2	32nd
Form P	Acquiring knowledge	−1	31st
	Independent action	+2	50th
	Accepting status	0	32nd
	Providing help	+2	53rd
	Professional commitment	−1	35th
MSCS –	Total score	+10	63rd
Form T	Self achievement	+3	64th
	Avoiding risks	−1	20th
	Feedback of results	+1	67th
	Personal innovation	+7	96th
	Planning for the future	0	32nd

Test scores
Jane V. Walters – human resource manager

		Score	Percentile equivalent
OODQ –	H score	3	35th
	P score	3	34th
	T score	4	53rd
	G score	10	86th
MSCS –	Total score	+8	75th
Form H	Authority figures	+3	89th

	Competitive games	+2	66th
	Competitive situations	0	63rd
	Assertive role	0	45th
	Imposing wishes	+1	59th
	Standing out from group	+1	54th
	Routine administrative functions	+1	59th
MSCS – Form P	Total score	+15	89th
	Acquiring knowledge	0	48th
	Independent action	+4	79th
	Accepting status	+5	93rd
	Providing help	+6	98th
	Professional commitment	0	49th
MSCS – Form T	Total score	+4	37th
	Self achievement	−2	9th
	Avoiding risks	−2	11th
	Feedback of results	+2	81st
	Personal innovation	+5	77th
	Planning for the future	+1	45th

Let us look at the test profiles from the viewpoint of the succession problem, starting with Robert Lambert. A striking finding is that his T score on the OODQ is not elevated at all. Here is an entrepreneur who does not view himself as in an entrepreneurial organization. Both the H score and P score are elevated, however. It is as if he has lost personal contact with his organization, with the result that an amalgam of hierarchic and professional scientific forms have taken control. In fact Robert Lambert has been devoting much of his time for the past three years to outside business interests; in many respects he has lost touch with his original firm, although he has continued to create new products in the laboratory.

On the motivational level Robert Lambert turns out to be not much of a manager. He has built up his firm, not by managing it, but by devoting his tremendous personal energy to putting out fires and grasping opportunities. The only Form H measure that is elevated involves positive attitudes to authority. Competitive Games and Assertive Role are rather low. Perhaps these factors have contributed to his distraction from the company and to other business interests. In any event the plateauing of the business is consistent with a rather limited managerial motivation; there is only so much one can accomplish on a face-to-face entrepreneurial basis.

Clearly, Robert Lambert is strongly professionally motivated. This fits with the OODQ results. He feels a very strong professional commitment consistent with his scientific training. He is a scientist contributing to the advancement of science. His outside business interests are, in fact, entirely consistent with this professional commitment; he is involved in a new start-up utilizing petrochemical products.

But above everything else Robert Lambert is an inventor-entrepreneur. He derives great satisfaction from doing things himself, he is strongly motivated to innovate as attested to by his inventions, and he likes to plan for the future. In many respects he is the prototype of a successful entrepreneur. One has to wonder whether he is the ambassador retiree he contends. Perhaps he will turn out to be more of a monarch or general; perhaps he really plans it that way. On a Form T item dealing with early retirement he rejects this possibility completely. The high Self Achievement and Personal Innovation scores do not suggest a person who wants to retire gracefully. Maybe he means to shift his energies completely to the petrochemical business; maybe he means to keep a hold on the original electronics company. One must assume from the high Planning for the Future score that he has already planned what he wants to do. Yet from a pragmatic viewpoint it is essential to come up with a recommendation regarding a successor, even if succession is in fact to be many years removed.

The leading candidate to replace his father is the older son, Albert. Albert, like his brother Ronald and Jane Walters, views the company as essentially a group system. All three have elevated G scores on the OODQ with no other score approximating the same level. It appears that the three have created a group system with a general sharing of decisions in the absence of the entrepreneurial system that must have existed when Robert Lambert was more fully involved.

Albert's Form H score is about at the level of the average first line supervisor; it is not high, and neither are any of the subscales. It is clear from the OODQ results that Albert has not moved into the gap as his father has become less involved in the business; rather he has merged himself into a group at the top. The Form H results are consistent with this behavior. Albert is not a 'take charge' person.

What he is is a highly dedicated professional. His Form P score is very high. This is consistent with his obtaining a PhD and becoming a practicing scientist. He has been a very successful professional in his field. The extremely high providing help score fits with Albert's troubleshooting skills; he wants to help customers solve their problems. On Form T the most pronounced finding is the high Personal Innovation score, something that one might expect from an inventor with numerous patents. If one discounts this innovation score, what appears to be a reasonably high Form T total score is not very high at all. Furthermore, the rather depressed Self Achievement score is not what one would expect from a true entrepreneur.

Clearly, the company needs to break out of its current plateau. It needs to be managed into a period of substantial growth. Albert can contribute to that growth through his inventions, but he does not look to be the one who should manage it. He is first and foremost a professional, not a manager, and he is likely to be most satisfied remaining in the professional mode.

If Albert is minimally motivated to assume a managerial role, Ronald is totally unmotivated. His total Form H score is very low and so are many of the subscale scores. There is an element of competitiveness manifest, but this is primarily in the games area. The lack of managerial motivation is consistent with Ronald's departure from the corporate world and his failure to complete the MBA. Ronald does not have the professional motivation that his brother has. Yet he is very high on the family trait of personal innovation – and he, like the others, has been a successful inventor. It is interesting to note that Ronald's proclivity for innovation is much more part of an overall entrepreneurial pattern than Albert's. Ronald is not low on Self Achievement and his T score on the OODQ is somewhat elevated.

Although Ronald does not appear to be the kind of person who could manage the company into growth, or even want to do so, he does have entrepreneurial potential; that is his most pronounced asset. Ideally, he would start his own firm or develop a side venture for the existing firm. If he were to take over the running of the company it almost surely would not grow further, and it might very well slip back a little. The company has grown already to a size where its entrepreneurial drive has been stretched to capacity.

On a motivational basis alone Jane Walters is the most qualified to head the company should Robert Lambert step aside. Her Form H score is good and she has the positive attitude toward authority that would make it possible for her to work with Robert Lambert in the ambassador role. Furthermore, her strong professional motivation fits well with the culture of a high technology firm such as this. In her case the need to provide help to others appears to be reflected in a penchant for defusing conflict. She would no doubt run a smooth ship, and derive considerable satisfaction from the status of her position. Jane is by no means the entrepreneur that the others are. Her Form T score is reduced by a lack of self achievement motivation and a tendency to take risks. This latter factor could become a problem were she to take complete control, but as an ambassador on the sidelines, Robert Lambert would be expected to provide a restraining influence.

The problem in Jane Walters' case is that motivational forces are not always the only determinant. This is a high technology firm fueled by invention. Much of the selling is to other companies and is done by the chief executive. Furthermore, the person at the top must be capable of evaluating the market potential of new inventions. Jane simply does not have the necessary knowledge in the area of the company's core technology; she does not match well with the predominant new product development strategy. Were the firm already much larger, this difficulty might not be such a matter for concern. But at this particular size it represents an almost insurmountable barrier.

What then should the recommendation be? One possibility is to stay with the group system and let the triumvirate manage the firm. Yet this is not a high motivation to manage group. The average Form H score is just over +2. Furthermore, to a considerable degree this is what has been happening for several years, and it has not resulted in either growth or profits. Given this situation, and the lack of a viable internal candidate, the best solution would appear to be to go outside the company and hire a general manager from within the industry. Such a person could then be moved up to chief executive upon Robert Lambert's retirement, whenever that might occur. It is unlikely that either Albert Lambert or Jane Walters would resist this move. Both have a major source of satisfaction inherent in their current activities. This is less true of Ronald Lambert, and his competitiveness might lead him to react to being passed over as if he had lost a race. Yet it seems likely that ultimately he would adjust to the situation.

This is one example of how problem solving assessments can be carried out. The process clearly suffers to some degree from the lack of an MSCS – Form G. Even so, it is a very powerful procedure, and it can provide insight into decisions that would be very difficult to make without it. It is important to remember, however, that the subscale scores are not as reliable as the total scores. Accordingly, they should be interpreted only if they are at one of the extremes.

CHAPTER SUMMARY AND CONCLUDING THOUGHTS

The looking back part of this chapter involves various criticisms and controversies that spanned the period from 1977 to 1988. In general the author's approach to critical hypotheses has been to undertake research that would provide an appropriate test of them. This approach has been applied to criticisms in the areas of construct validity, reliability, training, the decline, and gender effects. Without exception this research has vindicated the formulations related to role motivation theory. This does not mean that all the answers are in, but a goodly number are. It is a bit disconcerting to note how infrequently these criticisms have yielded a positive result. Some ought to have made a meaningful contribution to knowledge. However, this has not been the case. Perhaps if the criticisms had been grounded in adequate research initially, the record would have been better. Surely criticisms of this kind can help to build theory and extend it beyond its current formulations. In this instance that simply has not occurred. One recommendation that derives from this experience is that critics in science, or 'counterpunchers' as they are often termed, be required to submit sound and well-conceptualized research in behalf of their hypotheses, rather than shifting the entire burden of evidence to the theorists whom they attack. The intent in making this recommendation is to provide a possible guideline for journal editors.

The looking forward part of the chapter is concerned with two features. One is the matter of building a single integrated theory from the four parallel, limited domain theories. Examples of the types of efforts required to accomplish this goal are provided. It is evident that filling in the space between the four theories is a far more demanding task than constructing the original role motivation theories was. The movement from limited domain to general or comprehensive theory is not something that will occur in our generation.

A second aspect of looking forward is putting the role motivation theories to work for the practical purpose of improving productivity. A recent article in *Fortune* by Kupfer (1992) continues to demonstrate how important this is to the United States. The theories can contribute to selection and training or development activities, and to the conduct of problem solving assessments. An example of how the latter are conducted is provided. There appears to be a substantial potential here which accrues in large part because the theories concentrate on key positions within the various organizational forms. The theories, if effectively applied, can contribute to improved productivity.

Although certainly not to the exclusion of numerous other endeavors, the author has stayed with role motivation theory in some form throughout most of his professional career. This is to be contrasted with the course many major contributors to industrial/organizational psychology and organizational science have followed, which has involved substantial shifts in theoretical orientations, research thrusts, and even paradigm focuses. This difference deserves some explanation. First, by their very nature role motivation theories as they have evolved are extremely diverse, allowing for a wide range of theoretical and research activity. The author's devotion to diversity has been well documented (Miner, 1992a). The role motivation theories have provided an ideal outlet for this devotion.

Yet perhaps even more important is the fact that role motivation theory has continued to work. Anyone who goes back to look at the author's research in the 1950s and early 1960s will find a number of thrusts, with role motivation theory only one among many. All too often these thrusts simply 'ran out of gas,' for one reason or another. Role motivation theory never did. It kept providing meaningful results and raising new questions. You had to feel you were on the right track, even if others did not always feel the same way. Even today role motivation theory continues to generate both positive findings and new problems. It is a powerful and exciting approach. That is why I have devoted a career to it.

References

Abernathy, William J., Kim B. Clark, and Alan M. Kantrow (1981). 'The New Industrial Competition.' *Harvard Business Review*, 59:5, 68–81.

Adams, J. Stacy (1963). 'Toward an Understanding of Inequity.' *Journal of Abnormal and Social Psychology*, 67, 422–436.

Adams, J. Stacy (1965). 'Inequity in Social Exchange.' In Leonard Berkowitz, (ed.), *Advances in Social Psychology*, 2. New York: Academic Press, 267–299.

Adorno, Theodore W., Else Frenkel-Brunswik, Daniel J. Levinson, and R. Nevitt Sanford (1950). *The Authoritarian Personality*. New York: Harper & Row.

Albert, Michael (1977). *An Investigation of the Relationship Between Creative Ability and Managerial Motivation*. Ph.D. dissertation, Georgia State University, Atlanta, GA.

Albert, Michael (1981). 'A Comparison of the Managerial Motivation of Creative vs. Managerial Personnel.' *Proceedings, Southern Management Association*, 40–42.

Albert, Michael and Timothy M. Singleton (undated). 'The Effect of Managerial Motivation on Group Problem Solving.' Unpublished paper, San Francisco State University, San Francisco, Cal.

Aldag, Ramon J. and Arthur P. Brief (undated). 'The Miner Sentence Completion Scale: Further Clarification.' Unpublished paper, University of Wisconsin, Madison.

Alderfer, Clayton P. (1977). 'A Critique of Salancik and Pfeffer's Examination of Need-Satisfaction Theories.' *Administrative Science Quarterly*, 22, 658–669.

Al-Kelabi, Saad A. (1991). *A Multiple Level, Limited Domains Theory of Leadership: An Empirical Investigation of Leadership in Professional and Hierarchic Domains*. Ph.D. dissertation, State University of New York at Buffalo, Buffalo, NY.

Alper, Thelma G. (1974). 'Achievement Motivation in College Women: A Now-You-See-It-Now-You-Don't Phenomenon.' *American Psychologist*, 29, 194–203.

Ansoff, H. Igor (1983). 'Corporate Capability for Managing Change.' *Advances in Strategic Management*, 2, 1–30.

Argyris, Chris (1957). *Personality and Organization*. New York: Harper & Row.

Argyris, Chris (1962). *Interpersonal Competence and Organizational Effectiveness*. Homewood, IL: Irwin.

Argyris, Chris (1964). *Integrating the Individual and the Organization*. New York: Wiley.

Argyris, Chris (1973). 'Personality and Organization Theory Revisited.' *Administrative Science Quarterly*, 18, 141–167.

Arsan, Noyan, Frank R. Hunsicker, and Lloyd J. F. Southern (1983). 'A

Comparative Study of the Motivation to Manage of Turkish, South African, and U.S. Managers.' *Southern Management Association Proceedings*, 22, 114–116.

Arsan, Noyan, Frank R. Hunsicker, and Lloyd J. F. Southern (1983a). 'A Comparative Study of the Motivation to Manage of Turkish and U.S. Business Students.' *Southern Management Association Proceedings*, 22, 222–224.

Arvey, Richard D. and David A. Cole (1989). 'Evaluating Change Due to Training.' In Irwin L. Goldstein, (ed.), *Training and Development in Organizations*. San Francisco, CA: Jossey-Bass, 89–117.

Atkinson, John W. (1977). 'Motivation for Achievement.' In T. Blass, (ed.), *Personality Variables in Social Behavior*. Hillsdale, NJ: Erlbaum Associates, 25–108.

Atkinson, John W. (1982). 'Motivational Determinants of Thematic Apperception.' In A. Stewart, (ed.), *Motivation and Society*. San Francisco, CA: Jossey-Bass.

Baer, Donald (1988). 'Anxiety in America's Heartland.' *U.S. News and World Report*, 104:16, 24.

Baker, Sally H., Amitai Etzioni, Richard A. Hansen, and Marvin Sontag (1973). 'Tolerance for Bureaucratic Structure: Theory and Measurement.' *Human Relations*, 26, 775–786.

Barnett, Rosalind C. and Renato Tagiuri (1973). 'What Young People Think About Managers.' *Harvard Business Review*, 51:3, 106–118.

Barrick, Murray R. and Michael K. Mount (1991). 'The Big Five Personality Dimensions and Job Performance: A Meta-Analysis.' *Personnel Psychology*, 44, 1–26.

Bartol, Kathryn M., Carl R. Anderson, and Craig E. Schneier (1980). 'Motivation to Manage Among College Business Students: A Reassessment.' *Journal of Vocational Behavior*, 17, 22–32.

Bartol, Kathryn M., Carl R. Anderson, and Craig E. Schneier (1981). 'Sex and Ethnic Effects on Motivation to Manage Among College Business Students.' *Journal of Applied Psychology*, 66, 40–44.

Bartol, Kathryn M. and David C. Martin (1987). 'Managerial Motivation Among MBA Students: A Longitudinal Assessment.' *Journal of Occupational Psychology*, 60, 1–12.

Bartol, Kathryn M., Craig E. Schneier, and Carl R. Anderson (1985). 'Internal and External Validity Issues with Motivation to Manage Research: A Reply to Miner, Smith, and Ebrahimi.' *Journal of Vocational Behavior*, 26, 299=305.

Barton, Allen H. (1968). 'The Columbia Crisis: Campus, Vietnam, and the Ghetto.' *Public Opinion Quarterly*, 31, 333–351.

Bass, Bernard M. (1981, 1990). *Stogdill's Handbook of Leadership: A Survey of Theory and Research*. New York: Free Press.

Begley, Thomas M. and David P. Boyd (1987). 'Psychological Characteristics Associated with Performance in Entrepreneurial Firms and Smaller Businesses.' *Journal of Business Venturing*, 2, 79–93.

Behling, Orlando (1983). 'Review of Miner, John B. *Theories of Organizational Structure and Process*.' *Administrative Science Quarterly*, 28, 156–158.

Belasco, James A. and Harrison M. Trice (1969). *The Assessment of Change in Training and Therapy*. New York: McGraw-Hill.

Beldt, Sandra F. (1978). *An Analysis of Values in Traditional Organizations and Nontraditional Organizations Structured Using Socio-technical Systems Design*. Ph.D. dissertation, Georgia State University, Atlanta, GA.

Bellu, Renato R. (1988). 'Entrepreneurs and Managers: Are They Different?' *Frontiers of Entrepreneurship Research*, 8, 16–30.

Bellu, Renato R. (1992). 'Women Entrepreneurs and Managers: Are They Different?' Unpublished paper, Kingsborough College, City University of New York, New York.

Bellu, Renato R., Per Davidsson, and Connie Goldfarb (1990). 'Toward a Theory of Entrepreneurial Behavior: Empirical Evidence from Israel, Italy and Sweden.' *Entrepreneurship and Regional Development*, 2, 195–209.

Benham, Thomas W. (1972). 'What Are the People Thinking.' *Personnel Administrator*, 17:2, 17–18.

Bennis, Warren G. (1966). *Changing Organizations*. New York: McGraw-Hill.

Bennis, Warren G. and Philip E. Slater (1968). *The Temporary Society*. New York: Harper & Row.

Bentz, V. Jon (1967). 'The Sears Experience in the Investigation, Description, and Prediction of Executive Behavior.' In Frederic R. Wickert and Dalton E. McFarland, (eds), *Measuring Executive Effectiveness*. New York: Appleton-Century-Crofts, 147–205.

Bentz, V. Jon (1985). 'Research Findings from Personality Assessment of Executives.' In H. John Bernardin and David A. Bownas, (eds), *Personality Assessment in Organizations*. New York: Praeger, 82–144.

Berkshire, J. R. (1958). 'Comparisons of Five Forced-choice Indices.' *Educational and Psychological Measurement*, 18, 553–561.

Berman, Frederic E. (1979). *Managerial Role Motivation Among Top Executives*. Ph.D. dissertation, Georgia State University, Atlanta, GA.

Berman, Frederic E. and John B. Miner (1985). 'Motivation to Manage at the Top Executive Level: A Test of the Hierarchic Role Motivation Theory.' *Personnel Psychology*, 38, 377–391.

Bernardin, H. John and Richard W. Beatty (1984). *Performance Appraisal: Assessing Human Behavior at Work*. Boston, MA: Kent.

Biggadike, Ralph (1979). 'The Risky Business of Diversification.' *Harvard Business Review*, 57:3, 103–111.

Bird, Barbara J. (1989). *Entrepreneurial Behavior*. Glenview, IL: Scott, Foresman.

Black, Cameron H. (1981). *Managerial Motivation of Hospital Chief Administrators in Investor-Owned and Not-for-profit Hospitals*. Ph.D. dissertation, Georgia State University, Atlanta, GA.

Blake, Robert R. and Jane S. Mouton (1964). *The Managerial Grid*. Houston, TX: Gulf.

Block, Jeanne H., Norma Haan, and M. Brewster Smith (1968). 'Activism and Apathy in Contemporary Adolescents.' In James F. Adams, (ed.), *Understanding Adolescence – Current Developments in Adolescent Psychology*. Boston, MA: Allyn and Bacon, 198–231.

Bowin, Robert B. (1973). 'Attitude Change Toward a Theory of Managerial Motivation.' *Academy of Management Journal*, 16, 686–691.

Bowin, Robert B. (1978). 'Motivation to Manage: A Study of Change with Positive Implications for Women Managers.' *Psychological Reports*, 43, 355–362.

Bowin, Robert B. (1980). 'Comparison of the Miner Sentence Completion Scale and the Ghiselli Self-Description Index.' *Psychological Reports*, 47, 878.

Bracker, Jeffrey S., Barbara W. Keats, and John N. Pearson (1988). 'Planning and Financial Performance Among Small Firms in a Growth Industry.' *Strategic Management Journal*, 9, 591–603.

Bracker, Jeffrey S. and John N. Pearson (1986). 'Planning and Financial Performance of Small, Mature Firms.' *Strategic Management Journal*, 7, 503–522.

Bracker, Jeffrey S., John N. Pearson, Barbara W. Keats, and John B. Miner (1992). 'Entrepreneurial Intensity, Strategic Planning Process Sophistication, and Firm

Performance in a Dynamic Environment.' Unpublished paper, University of Louisville, Louisville, KY.

Braunstein, Daniel N. and George H. Haines (1971). 'Student Stereotypes of Business.' *Business Horizons*, 14:1, 73–80.

Bray, Douglas W., Richard J. Campbell, and Donald L. Grant (1974). *Formative Years in Business*: A Long-Term AT&T Study of Managerial Lives. New York: Wiley.

Brief, Arthur P., Ramon J. Aldag, and Thomas I. Chacko (1977). 'The Miner Sentence Completion Scale: An Appraisal.' *Academy of Management Journal*, 20, 635–643.

Brightman, Harvey J. (1975). 'Leadership Style and Worker Interpersonal Orientation: A Computer Simulation Study.' *Organizational Behavior and Human Performance*, 14, 91–122.

Brockhaus, Robert H. (1980). 'Risk Taking Propensity of Entrepreneurs.' *Academy of Management Journal*, 23, 509–520.

Brockhaus, Robert H. and Pamela S. Horwitz (1986). 'The Psychology of the Entrepreneur.' In Donald L. Sexton and Raymond W. Smilor, (eds), *The Art and Science of Entrepreneurship*. Cambridge, MA: Ballinger, 25–48.

Brody, Nathan (1980). 'Social Motivation.' *Annual Review of Psychology*, 31, 143–168.

Bucher, Rue and Joan G. Stelling (1977). *Becoming Professional*. Beverly Hills, CA: Sage.

Bureau of National Affairs (1969). 'ASPA – BNA Survey: Management and the Generation Gap.' *Bulletin to Management*, December.

Burgelman, Robert A. (1984). 'Designs for Corporate Entrepreneurship in Established Firms.' *California Management Review*, 26:3, 154–166.

Burns, Tom and G. M. Stalker (1961). *The Management of Innovation*. London, UK: Tavistock.

Butler, Richard P., Charles L. Lardent, and John B. Miner (1983). 'A Motivational Basis for Turnover in Military Officer Education and Training.' *Journal of Applied Psychology*, 68, 496–506.

Camealy, John B. (1968). *Management Development Training: Multiple Measurement of Its Effects When Used to Increase the Impact of a Long-Term Motivational Program*. Ph.D. dissertation, University of Washington, Seattle, WA.

Campbell, John P. (1989). 'The Agenda for Theory and Research.' In Irwin L. Goldstein and Associates, (eds), *Training and Development in Organizations*. San Francisco, CA: Jossey-Bass, 469–486.

Campbell, John P., Marvin D. Dunnette, Edward E. Lawler, and Karl E. Weick (1970). *Managerial Behavior, Performance, and Effectiveness*. New York: McGraw-Hill.

Carson, Kenneth P. and Debora J. Gilliard (1993). 'Construct Validity of the Miner Sentence Completion Scale: A Meta-Analytic Evaluation.' *Journal of Occupational and Organizational Psychology*, 66.

Cass, Eugene L. and Frederick G. Zimmer (1975). *Man and Work in Society*. New York: VanNostrand Reinhold.

Cattell, Raymond B., J. L. Horn, A. B. Sweney, and J. Radcliff (1964). *The Motivation Analysis Test*. Champaign, IL: Institute for Personality and Ability Testing.

Chandler, Alfred D. (1962). *Strategy and Structure: Chapters in the History of the American Industrial Enterprise*. Cambridge, MA: MIT Press.

Chandler, Alfred D. (1977). *The Visible Hand: The Managerial Revolution in American Business*. Cambridge, MA: Harvard University Press.

Churchill, Neil C. and Virginia L. Lewis (1983). 'The Five Stages of Small Business Growth.' *Harvard Business Review*, 61:3, 30–50.

Collins, Orvis F., David G. Moore, and Darab B. Unwalla (1964). *The Enterprising Man*. East Lansing, MI: Bureau of Business and Economic Research, Michigan State University.

Cornelius, Edwin T. (1983). 'The Use of Projective Techniques in Personnel Selection.' *Research in Personnel and Human Resources Management*, 1, 127–168.

Cox, Allan (1982). *The Cox Report on the American Corporation*. New York: Delacorte Press.

Crane, Donald P. (1971). 'How Blacks Become Managers in Atlanta, Georgia Companies.' *Training in Business and Industry*, 8:6, 21–26.

Crane, Donald P. and John B. Miner (1988). 'Labor Arbitrators' Performance: Views from Union and Management Perspectives.' *Journal of Labor Research*, 9, 43–54.

Crowne, D. P. and D. Marlowe (1960). 'A New Scale of Social Desirability Independent of Psychopathology.' *Journal of Counseling Psychology*, 24, 349–354.

Cyert, Richard M. and James G. March (1963). *A Behavioral Theory of the Firm*. Englewood Cliffs, NJ: Prentice-Hall.

Dalton, Dan R., William D. Todor, Michael J. Spendolini, Gordon J. Fielding, and Lyman W. Porter (1980). 'Organization Structure and Performance: A Critical Review.' *Academy of Management Review*, 5, 49–64.

Dansereau, Fred, George Graen, and William J. Haga (1975). 'A Vertical Dyad Linkage Approach to Leadership Within Formal Organizations: A Longitudinal Investigation of the Role Making Process.' *Organizational Behavior and Human Performance*, 13, 46–78.

Davidsson, Per (1989). *Continued Entrepreneurship and Small Firm Growth*. Stockholm, Sweden: Stockholm School of Economics.

Dawson, Leslie M. (1969). 'Campus Attitudes Toward Business.' *MSU Business Topics*, 17, 36–46.

Dayani, Mohammad H. (1980). *Academic Library Managers and Their Motivation to Manage*. Ph.D. dissertation, Rutgers, The State University of New Jersey, New Brunswick, NJ.

DeNisi, Angelo S. and George E. Stevens (1981). 'Profiles of Performance, Performance Evaluation, and Personnel Decisions.' *Academy of Management Journal*, 24, 592–602.

DeSalvia, Donald N. and Gary R. Gemmill (1971). 'An Exploratory Study of the Personal Value Systems of College Students and Managers.' *Academy of Management Journal*, 14, 227–238.

Dewey, John (1916). *Democracy and Education: An Introduction to the Philosophy of Education*. New York: Macmillan.

Digman, John M. (1990). 'Personality Structure: Emergence of the Five-Factor Model.' *Annual Review of Psychology*, 41, 417–440.

Driver, Michael J. (1988). 'Careers: A Review of Personal and Organizational Research.' *International Review of Industrial and Organizational Psychology*, 3, 245–277.

Dubin, Robert (1969). *Theory Building*. New York: Free Press.

Dunn, Dan T. (1977). 'The Rise and Fall of Ten Venture Groups.' *Business Horizons*, 20:5, 32–41.

Durand, Douglas E. (1975). 'Effects of Achievement Motivation and Skill Training on the Entrepreneurial Behavior of Black Businessmen.' *Organizational Behavior and Human Performance*, 14, 76–90.

Eagly, Alice H. and Blair T. Johnson (1990). 'Gender and Leadership Style: A Meta-Analysis.' *Psychological Bulletin*, 108, 233–256.

Eagly, Alice H., Steven J. Karau, John B. Miner, and Blair T. Johnson (1992). 'Gender and Motivation to Manage: A Meta-Analysis.' Unpublished paper, Purdue University, West Lafayette, IN.

Eagly, Alice H. and Wendy Wood (1990). 'Explaining Sex Differences in Social Behavior: A Meta-Analytic Perspective.' *Personality and Social Psychology Bulletin*,

Eberhardt, Bruce J., Choon K. Yap, and M. Tom Basuray (1988). 'A Psychometric Evaluation of the Multiple Choice Version of the Miner Sentence Completion Scale.' *Educational and Psychological Measurement*, 48, 119–126.

Ebrahimi, Bahman (1983). 'A Review of Cross-Cultural Research.' *Southern Management Association Proceedings*, 141–143.

Ebrahimi, Bahman (1984). *Measuring the Effects of Cultural and Other Explanatory Variables on Motivation to Manage of Potential Managers from Five Countries: A Case of Theory Building and Theory Testing in Cross-Cultural Research.* Ph.D. dissertation, Georgia State University, Atlanta, GA.

Ebrahimi, Bahman and John B. Miner (1991). 'The Cultural Dynamics of Managerial Motivation Among Students from Pan-Pacific Basin Countries.' *Journal of Global Business*, 2, 87–98.

Ehrenfeld, Tom (1989). 'Competitiveness Problem? HBR Readers Say Yes.' *Harvard Business Review*, 67:6, 222.

Emery, Fred E. (1959). *Characteristics of Socio-Technical Systems*. London, England: Tavistock Institute of Human Relations, Document No. 527.

Emery, Fred E. and Einar Thorsrud (1976). *Democracy at Work*. Leiden, Netherlands: Martinus Nijhoff.

Emery, Fred E. and Eric L. Trist (1965). 'The Causal Texture of Organizational Environments.' *Human Relations*, 18, 21–32.

Emery, Fred E. and Eric L. Trist (1973). *Toward a Social Ecology*. London, UK: Plenum.

England, George W. (1975). *The Manager and His Values*. Cambridge, MA: Ballinger.

England, George W., K. Olsen, and N. Agarwal (1971). *A Manual of Development and Research for the Personal Values Questionnaire*. Minneapolis: Industrial Relations Center, University of Minnesota.

Etzioni, Amitai (1964). *Modern Organizations*. Englewood Cliffs, NJ: Prentice-Hall.

Evans, Martin G. (1970). 'The Effects of Supervisory Behavior on the Path–goal Relationship.' *Organizational Behavior and Human Performance*, 5, 277–298.

Evans, Martin G. (1974). 'Extensions of a Path–goal Theory of Motivation.' *Journal of Applied Psychology*, 59, 172–178.

Fast, Norman D. (1977). *The Rise and Fall of Corporate New Venture Divisions*. Ann Arbor, MI: University Microfilms International Research Press.

Fayol, Henri (1949). *General and Industrial Management*. London, UK: Pitman.

Fernandez, John P. (1975). *Black Managers in White Corporations*. New York: Wiley.

Fiedler, Fred E. (1967). *A Theory of Leadership Effectiveness*. New York: McGraw-Hill.

Fiedler, Fred E. and Martin M. Chemers (1974). *Leadership and Effective Management*. Glenview, IL: Scott, Foresman.

Fiedler, Fred E. and Joseph E. Garcia (1987). *New Approaches to Effective Leadership: Cognitive Resources and Organizational Performance.* New York: Wiley.

Flacks, Richard (1970). 'Who Protests: The Social Bases of the Student Movement.' In Julian Foster and Durwood Long, (eds), *Protest: Student Activism in America.* New York: William Morrow, 134–157.

Fleishman, Edwin A. (1960). *Manual for Leadership Opinion Questionnaire.* Chicago, IL: Science Research Associates.

Fleishman, Edwin A., Edwin F. Harris, and Harold E. Burtt (1955). *Leadership and Supervision in Industry.* Columbus, OH: Bureau of Educational Research, Ohio State University.

Freedman, Mervin B. and Paul Kanzer (1970). 'Psychology of a Strike.' In Edward E. Sampson and Harold A. Korn, (eds), *Student Activism and Protest.* San Francisco, CA: Jossey-Bass, 142–157.

French, Wendell L. and Cecil H. Bell (1973). *Organization Development.* Englewood Cliffs, NJ: Prentice-Hall.

Freud, Sigmund (1930). *Civilization and Its Discontents.* London: Hogarth Press.

Fry, Louis W. and John W. Slocum (1984). 'Technology, Structure, and Workgroup Effectiveness: A Test of a Contingency Model.' *Academy of Management Journal,* 27, 221–246.

Fuller, Gerald B., Walker M. Parmelee, and James L. Carroll (1982). 'Performance of Delinquent and Nondelinquent High School Boys on the Rotter Incomplete Sentences Blank.' *Journal of Personality Assessment,* 46, 506–510.

Galbraith, Jay R. (1982). 'The Stages of Growth.' *Journal of Business Strategy,* 3:1, 70–79.

Galbraith, Jay R. and Robert K. Kazanjian (1986). *Strategy Implementation: Structure, Systems, and Process.* St. Paul, MN: West.

Galbraith, Jay R. and Daniel A. Nathanson (1978). *Strategy Implementation: The Role of Structure and Process.* St. Paul, MN: West.

Gantz, Benjamin S., Clara O. Erickson, and Robert W. Stephenson (1977). 'Measuring the Motivation to Manage in a Research and Development Population.' In John B. Miner, (ed.), *Motivation to Manage: A Ten-year Update on the 'Studies in Management Education' Research.* Buffalo, NY: Organizational Measurement Systems Press, 11–17 (originally published in APA Proceedings – 1971).

Gantz, Benjamin S., Clara O. Erickson, and Robert W. Stephenson (1977a). 'Some Determinants of Promotion in a Research and Development Population.' In John B. Miner, (ed.), *Motivation to Manage: A Ten-year Update on the 'Studies in Management Education' Research.* Buffalo, NY: Organizational Measurement Systems Press, 18–22 (originally published in APA Proceedings – 1972).

Ghiselli, Edwin E. (1971). *Explorations in Managerial Talent.* Pacific Palisades, CA: Goodyear.

Giegold, William C. (1982). 'Training Engineers to be Leaders: A Classical Management Approach.' *IEEE Transactions on Engineering Management,* 29:3, 94–101.

Ginzberg, Eli, John B. Miner, James K. Anderson, Sol W. Ginsburg, and John L. Herma (1959). *Breakdown and Recovery.* New York: Columbia University Press.

Goldner, Jane S. (1986). *Type A Behavior and the Motivation to Manage Among Postsecondary Vocational Educators in Georgia.* Ph.D. dissertation, Georgia State University, Atlanta, GA.

Goldstein, Irwin L. (1986). *Training in Organizations: Needs Assessment, Development, and Evaluation.* Monterey, CA: Brooks/Cole.

Golembiewski, Robert T. (1972). *Renewing Organizations: The Laboratory Approach to Planned Change*. Itasca, IL: F. E. Peacock.

Gooding, Judson (1971). 'The Accelerated Generation Moves Into Management.' *Fortune*, March, 101–104, 115–118.

Gordon, Leonard V. (1970). 'Measurement of Bureaucratic Orientation.' *Personnel Psychology*, 23, 1–11.

Gordon, Paul J. (1976). 'The Unfinished Business of Business Education.' *Conference Board Record*, 11:1, 60–64.

Gould, Sam and James D. Werbel (1983). 'Work Involvement: A Comparison of Dual Wage Earner and Single Wage Earner Families.' *Journal of Applied Psychology*, 68, 313–319.

Graen, George and James F. Cashman (1975). 'A Role-making Model of Leadership in Formal Organizations: A Developmental Approach.' In James G. Hunt and Lars L. Larson, (eds), *Leadership Frontiers*. Kent, OH: Kent State University Press, 143–165.

Greiner, Larry E. (1972). 'Evolution and Revolution as Organizations Grow.' *Harvard Business Review*, 50:4, 37–46.

Grimes, A. J. (1983). 'Review of Miner, John B. *Theories of Organizational Behavior.*' *Contemporary Psychology*, 28, 35–36.

Guion, Robert M. and Richard F. Gottier (1965). 'Validity of Personality Measures in Personnel Selection.' *Personnel Psychology*, 18, 135–164.

Gulowsen, Jon (1972). 'A Measure of Work Group Autonomy.' In Louis E. Davis and James C. Taylor, (eds), *Design of Jobs*. Baltimore, MD: Penguin, 374–390.

Guzzo, Richard A. (1981). 'Review of Miner, John B. *Theories of Organizational Behavior.*' *Industrial and Labor Relations Review*, 34, 468–469.

Hackman, J. Richard and Greg R. Oldham (1975). 'Development of the Job Diagnostic Survey.' *Journal of Applied Psychology*, 60, 159–170.

Hackman, J. Richard and Greg R. Oldham (1980). *Work Redesign*. Reading, MA: Addison-Wesley.

Hadden, Jeffrey K. (1969). 'The Private Generation.' *Psychology Today*, October, 32–35, 68–69.

Hadley, Galen D. and Warren R. Wilhelm (1980). 'A Profile of Business School Deans.' *Collegiate News and Views*, 33:3, 1–5.

Hall, Richard H. (1967). 'Some Organizational Considerations in the Professional-Organizational Relationship.' *Administrative Science Quarterly*, 12, 461–478.

Hall, Richard H. (1977). *Organizations: Structure and Process*. Englewood Cliffs, NJ: Prentice-Hall.

Harlan, Anne and Carol L. Weiss (1982). 'Sex Differences in Factors Affecting Managerial Career Advancement.' In Phyllis A. Wallace, (ed.), *Women in the Workplace*. Boston, MA: Auburn House, 59–100.

Harnett, Donald L. and Larry L. Cummings (1980). *Bargaining Behavior: An International Study*. Houston, TX: Dame.

Harrell, Thomas W. (1961). *Managers' Performance and Personality*. Cincinnati, OH: Southwestern.

Harrell, Thomas W. and Margaret S. Harrell (1973). 'The Personality of MBAs Who Reach General Management Early.' *Personnel Psychology*, 26, 127–134.

Harris, Edwin F., and Edwin A. Fleishman (1955). 'Human Relations Training and the Stability of Leadership Patterns.' *Journal of Applied Psychology*, 39, 20–25.

Harrison, Frank (1974). 'The Management of Scientists: Determinants of Perceived Role Performance.' *Academy of Management Journal*, 17, 234–241.

Hartigan, John A. and Alexandra K. Wigdor (1989). *Fairness in Employment*

Testing: Validity Generalization, Minority Issues, and the General Aptitude Test Battery. Washington, DC: National Academy Press.

HBR Editors (1987). 'Competitiveness Survey: HBR Readers Respond.' *Harvard Business Review*, 65:5, 8–12.

Hayes, Robert H. and William J. Abernathy (1980). 'Managing Our Way to Economic Decline.' *Harvard Business Review*, 58:4, 67–77.

Heller, Frank A. (1971). *Managerial Decision-making: A Study of Leadership Styles and Power Sharing Among Senior Managers.* London, UK: Tavistock.

Heller, Frank A. and Bernhard Wilpert (1981). *Competence and Power in Managerial Decision-making.* New York: Wiley.

Henry, William E. (1949). 'The Business Executive: The Psychodynamics of a Social Role.' *American Journal of Sociology*, 54, 286–291.

Herbst, P. G. (1976). *Alternatives to Hierarchies.* Leiden, Netherlands: Martinus Nijhoff.

Hermans, Hubert J. M. (1970). 'A Questionnaire Measure of Achievement Motivation.' *Journal of Applied Psychology*, 54, 353–363.

Herzberg, Frederick (1966). *Work and the Nature of Man.* Cleveland, OH: World.

Herzberg, Frederick (1976). *The Managerial Choice: To Be Efficient and To Be Human.* Homewood, IL: Dow-Jones-Irwin.

Herzberg, Frederick, Bernard Mausner, and Barbara S. Snyderman (1959). *The Motivation to Work.* New York: Wiley.

Hines, George H. (1973). 'Achievement Motivation, Occupations, and Labor Turnover in New Zealand.' *Journal of Applied Psychology*, 58, 313–317.

Hitschmann, Edward (1956). *Great Men: Psychoanalytic Studies.* New York: International Universities Press.

Hobson, Edwin L. and Richard M. Morrison (1983). 'How Do Corporate Start-Up Ventures Fare?' *Frontiers of Entrepreneurship Research*, 3, 390–410.

Hoffman, Robin W. (1983). *A Study of Motivation to Manage: Selected Post-Secondary Vocational Educators in Georgia.* Ph.D. dissertation, Georgia State University, Atlanta, GA.

Hofstede, Geert H. (1980). *Culture's Consequences: International Differences in Work-Related Values.* Beverly Hills, CA: Sage.

Hofstede, Geert (1981). 'Do American Theories Apply Abroad? A Reply to Goodstein and Hunt.' *Organizational Dynamics*, 10:1, 63–68.

Holland, Aprile M. (1980). *Comparative Analysis of Selected Predictors of Police Officer Job Performance.* Ph.D. dissertation, Georgia State University, Atlanta, GA.

Holland, Max (1981). 'Can Managerial Performance Be Predicted?' *Journal of Nursing Administration*, 11:3, 17–21.

Holland, Max G., Cameron H. Black, and John B. Miner (1987). 'Using Managerial Role Motivation Theory to Predict Career Success.' *Health Care Management Review*, 12:4, 57–64.

Hornaday, John A. and John Aboud (1971). 'Characteristics of Successful Entrepreneurs.' *Personnel Psychology*, 24, 141–153.

Hornaday, John A. and Charles S. Bunker (1970). 'The Nature of the Entrepreneur.' *Personnel Psychology*, 23, 47–54.

Horner, Matina S. (1974). 'The Measurement and Behavioral Implications of Fear of Success in Women.' In John W. Atkinson and Joel O. Raynor, (eds), *Motivation and Achievement.* Washington, DC: Winston, 91–117.

Horowitz, Irving L. and William H. Friedland (1970). *The Knowledge Factory: Student Power and Academic Politics in America.* Chicago, IL: Aldine.

House, Robert J. (1971). 'A Path–goal Theory of Leader Effectiveness.' *Administrative Science Quarterly*, 16, 321–338.

Howard, Ann and Douglas W. Bray (1981). 'Today's Young Managers: They Can Do It, But Will They?' *Wharton Magazine*, 5:4, 23–28.

Howard, Ann and Douglas W. Bray (1988). *Managerial Lives in Transition: Advancing Age and Changing Times*. New York: Guilford Press.

Howard, Ann and J. A. Wilson (1982). 'Leadership in a Declining Work Ethic.' *California Management Review*, 24:4, 33–46.

Howell, Jon P., Peter W. Dorfman, and Steven Kerr (1986). 'Moderator Variables in Leadership Research.' *Academy of Management Review*, 11, 88–102.

Hundal, P. S. (1971). 'A Study of Entrepreneurial Motivation: Comparison of Fast- and Slow-Progressing Small-Scale Industrial Entrepreneurs in Punjab, India.' *Journal of Applied Psychology*, 55, 317–323.

Inglehart, Ronald (1981). 'Value Change in the Uncertain 1970s.' In Gunter Dlugos and Klaus Weiermair, (eds), *Management Under Different Value Systems: Political, Social, and Economical Perspectives in a Changing World*. Berlin: Walter deGruyter, 75–107.

Inglehart, Ronald (1990). *Culture Shift in Advanced Industrial Society*. Princeton, NJ: Princeton University Press.

Jackson, Karl W. and Dennis J. Shea (1972). 'Motivation Training in Perspective.' In Walter Nord, (ed.), *Concepts and Controversy in Organizational Behavior*. Pacific Palisade, CA: Goodyear, 100–118.

James, Barrie G. (1973). 'The Theory of the Corporate Life Cycle.' *Long-Range Planning*, June.

Jenkins, C. D., S. J. Zyzanski and Ray Rosenman (1979). *Jenkins Activity Survey*. New York: Psychological Corporation.

Jourdan, Louis F. (1987). *Differentiation Between Successful and Unsuccessful Entrepreneurs*. Ph.D. dissertation, Georgia State University, Atlanta, GA.

Jung, Carl (1923). *Psychological Types*. London, UK: Routledge & Kegan Paul.

Kahn, Robert L. and Daniel Katz (1953). 'Leadership Practices in Relation to Productivity and Morale.' In Dorwin Cartwright and Alvin Zander, (eds), *Group Dynamics: Research and Theory*. Evanston, IL: Row, Peterson.

Kanter, Rosabeth (1985). 'Supporting Innovation and Venture Development in Established Companies.' *Journal of Business Venturing*, 1, 47–60.

Karmin, Monroe W. (1987). 'Will the U.S. Stay Number One?' *U.S. News and World Report*, 102:4, 18–22.

Katz, Daniel and Robert L. Kahn (1966, 1978). *The Social Psychology of Organizations*. New York: Wiley.

Katz, Robert L. (1955). 'Skills of an Effective Administrator.' *Harvard Business Review*, 33:1.

Kearns, D. T. (1981). 'Why the U.S. Economy Struggles in Reverse – and What to Do About It.' *Management Review*, 70, 29–31.

Keniston, Kenneth (1970). 'Sources of Student Dissent.' In Edward E. Sampson and Harold A. Korn, (eds), *Student Activism and Protest*. San Francisco, CA: Jossey-Bass, 158–190.

Kennedy, John K. (1982). 'Middle LPC Leaders and the Contingency Model of Leadership Effectiveness.' *Organizational Behavior and Human Performance*, 30, 1–14.

Kerr, Steven (1977). 'Substitutes for Leadership: Some Implications for Organizational Design.' *Organization and Administrative Sciences*, 8:1, 135–146.

Kerr, Steven and John M. Jermier (1978). 'Substitutes for Leadership: Their Meaning and Measurement.' *Organizational Behavior and Human Performance*, 22, 375–403.

Kiechel, William (1981). 'Oh Where, Oh Where Has My Little Dog Gone? Or My Cash Cow, or My Star?' *Fortune*, 104 (November 2), 148–154.

Kimberly, John R. and Robert H. Miles (1980). *The Organizational Life Cycle*. San Francisco, CA: Jossey-Bass.

Kinslinger, Howard J. (1966). 'Applications of Projective Techniques in Personnel Psychology Since 1940.' *Psychological Bulletin*, 66, 134–150.

Korman, Abraham K. (1968). 'The Prediction of Managerial Performance: A Review.' *Personnel Psychology*, 21, 295–322.

Kraus, William A. (1980). *Collaboration in Organizations: Alternatives to Hierarchy*. New York: Human Sciences Press.

Krell, Terence C. (1982). 'Humanism and the Decline of Traditional Organization Development.' *Journal of Applied Behavioral Science*, 18, 534–536.

Kupfer, Andrew (1992). 'How American Industry Stacks Up.' *Fortune*, 125(5), 30–46.

Lacey, Lynn (1974). 'Discriminability of the Miner Sentence Completion Scale Among Supervisory and Nonsupervisory Scientists and Engineers.' *Academy of Management Journal*, 17, 354–358.

Lah, Michael I. (1989). 'New Validity, Normative, and Scoring Data for the Rotter Incomplete Sentences Blank.' *Journal of Personality Assessment*, 53, 607–620.

Lardent, Charles L. (1979). *An Assessment of the Motivation to Command Among U.S. Army Officer Candidates*. Ph.D. dissertation, Georgia State University, Atlanta, GA.

Latham, Gary P. (1988). 'Human Resource Training and Development.' *Annual Review of Psychology*, 39, 545–582.

Lawler, Edward E. (1971). *Pay and Organizational Effectiveness: A Psychological View*. New York: McGraw-Hill.

Lawler, Edward E., Allan M. Mohrman, Susan A. Mohrman, Gerald E. Ledford, and Thomas G. Cummings (1985). *Doing Research That Is Useful for Theory and Practice*. San Francisco, CA: Jossey-Bass.

Lawrence, Paul R. and Jay W. Lorsch (1967). *Organization and Environment: Managing Differentiation and Integration*. Boston, MA: Graduate School of Business Administration, Harvard University.

Lawrence, Paul R. and Jay W. Lorsch (1973). 'A Reply to Tosi, Aldag, and Storey.' *Administrative Science Quarterly*, 18, 397–398.

Lee, Cynthia and P. Christopher Earley (1988). 'Comparative Peer Evaluations of Organizational Behavior Theories.' Unpublished manuscript, Northeastern University, Boston, MA.

Lehman, I. J. and W. H. Hill (1969). *Michigan State University 1958 and 1967 Freshman: A Contrast in Profiles*. East Lansing: Office of Evaluation Services, Michigan State University.

Leontiades, Milton (1980). *Strategies for Diversification and Change*. Boston, MA: Little, Brown & Co.

Lesser, Gerald S. (1973). 'Achievement Motivation in Women.' In David C. McClelland and Robert S. Steele, (eds), *Human Motivation*. Morristown, NJ: General Learning Press, 202–221.

Levenson, Hanna (1974). 'Activism and Powerful Others: Distinctions Within the Concept of Internal–External Control.' *Journal of Personality Assessment*, 38, 377–383.

Levitan, Sar A. and Diane Werneke (1984). *Productivity: Problems, Prospects, and Policies*. Baltimore, MD: Johns Hopkins University Press.

Lewin, Kurt (1952). 'Group Decision and Social Change.' In Guy E. Swanson, Theodore M. Newcomb, and Eugene L. Hartley, (eds), *Readings in Social Psychology*. New York: Holt, 459–473.

Lieberman, Seymour (1956). 'The Effects of Changes in Roles on the Attitudes of Role Occupants.' *Human Relations*, 9, 385–402.

Likert, Rensis (1961). *New Patterns of Management*. New York: McGraw-Hill.

Likert, Rensis (1967). *The Human Organization: Its Management and Value*. New York: McGraw-Hill.

Likert, Rensis and Jane G. Likert (1976). *New Ways of Managing Conflict*. New York: McGraw-Hill.

Lippitt, Gordon (1983). 'Learning: Doing What Can Come Naturally.' *Training and Development Journal*, 37:8, 70–73.

Lipset, Seymour M. (1967). *Student Politics*. New York: Basic Books.

Lipset, Seymour M. and Everett C. Ladd (1970). ' . . . And What Professors Think.' *Psychology Today*, November, 49–51, 106.

Livingston, J. Sterling (1971). 'Myth of the Well-Educated Manager.' *Harvard Business Review*, 49:1, 79–89.

Locke, Edwin A. (1968). 'Toward a Theory of Task Motivation and Incentives.' *Organizational Behavior and Human Performance*, 3, 157–189.

Locke, Edwin A. (1970). 'Job Satisfaction and Job Performance: A Theoretical Analysis.' *Organizational Behavior and Human Performance*, 5, 484–500.

Locke, Edwin A., Norman Cartledge, and Claramae S. Knerr (1970). 'Studies of the Relationship Between Satisfaction, Goal Setting, and Performance.' *Organizational Behavior and Human Performance*, 5, 135–158.

Locke, Edwin A. and Douglas Henne (1986). 'Work Motivation Theories.' *International Review of Industrial and Organizational Psychology*, 1, 1–35.

Locke, Edwin A. and Gary P. Latham (1984). *Goal Setting: A Motivational Technique that Works*. Englewood Cliffs, NJ: Prentice-Hall.

Locke, Edwin A. and Gary P. Latham (1990). *A Theory of Goal Setting & Task Performance*. Englewood Cliffs, NJ: Prentice-Hall.

London, Manuel (1981). 'Review of Miner, John B. *Theories of Organizational Behavior*.' *Personnel Psychology*, 34, 383–385.

Lord, Robert G., Christy L. DeVader, and George A. Alliger (1986). 'A Meta-Analysis of the Relation Between Personality Traits and Leadership Perceptions: An Application of Validity Generalization Procedures.' *Journal of Applied Psychology*, 71, 402–410.

Lord, Robert G. and Karen J. Maher (1991). *Leadership and Information Processing: Linking Perceptions and Performance*. Boston, MA: Unwin-Hyman.

Lorsch, Jay W. and John J. Morse (1974). *Organizations and Their Members: A Contingency Approach*. New York: Harper & Row.

Lowman, Rodney L. (1991). *The Clinical Practice of Career Assessment: Interests, Abilities, and Personality*. Washington, DC: American Psychological Association.

Lubell, Samuel (1968). 'Where the New Left Dissidents Come From.' *Boston Globe*, October 10.

McCaskey, Michael B. (1982). *The Executive Challenge: Managing Change and Ambiguity*. Boston, MA: Pitman.

McClelland, David C. (1961). *The Achieving Society*. Princeton, NJ: Van Nostrand.

McClelland, David C. (1962). 'Business Drive and National Achievement.' *Harvard Business Review*, 40:4, 99–112.

McClelland, David C. (1965). 'N Achievement and Entrepreneurship: A Longitudinal Study.' *Journal of Personality and Social Psychology*, 1, 389–392.

McClelland, David C. (1965a). Toward a Theory of Motive Acquisition.' *American Psychologist*, 20, 321–333.

McClelland, David C. (1975). *Power: The Inner Experience*. New York: Irvington.

McClelland, David C., John W. Atkinson, Russell A. Clark, and Edgar L. Lowell (1976). *The Achievement Motive*. New York: Irvington.

McClelland, David C. and Richard E. Boyatzis (1982). 'Leadership Motive Pattern and Long-Term Success in Management.' *Journal of Applied Psychology*, 67, 737–743.

McClelland, David C. and David H. Burnham (1976). 'Power is the Great Motivator.' *Harvard Business Review*, 54:2, 100–110.

McClelland, David C. and David G. Winter (1969). *Motivating Economic Achievement*. New York: Free Press.

McGregor, Douglas (1960). *The Human Side of Enterprise*. New York: McGraw-Hill.

McGregor, Douglas (1967). *The Professional Manager*. New York: McGraw-Hill.

McGuire, Joseph W. (1974). *Contemporary Management: Issues and Viewpoints*. Englewood Cliffs, NJ: Prentice-Hall.

McInnes, J. Morris (1984). 'Corporate Management of Productivity – An Empirical Study.' *Strategic Management Journal*, 5, 351–365.

Mackenzie, Kenneth D. (1991). *The Organizational Hologram: The Effective Management of Organizational Change*. Boston, MA: Kluwer.

Mackenzie, Kenneth D. and Robert House (1978). 'Paradigm Development in the Social Sciences: A Proposed Research Strategy.' *Academy of Management Review*, 3, 7–23.

McMahon, J. Timothy and John M. Ivancevich (1976). 'A Study of Control in a Manufacturing Organization: Managers and Nonmanagers.' *Administrative Science Quarterly*, 21, 66–83.

McMahon, J. Timothy and G. W. Perritt (1973). 'Toward a Contingency Theory of Organizational Control.' *Academy of Management Journal*, 16, 624–635.

Macmillan, Ian C., Zenos Block, and P. N. Subba Narasimha (1986). 'Corporate Venturing: Alternatives, Obstacles Encountered and Experience Effects.' *Journal of Business Venturing*, 1, 177–191.

Mahoney, Thomas A. (1980). 'Examples of Middle Range Theory: Discussion.' In Craig C. Pinder and Larry F. Moore, (eds), *Middle Range Theory and the Study of Organizations*. Boston, MA: Martinus Nijhoff, 326–333.

Mahoney, Thomas A., Thomas H. Jerdee, and Allan N. Nash (1960). 'Predicting Managerial Effectiveness.' *Personnel Psychology*, 13, 147–163.

March, James G. and Herbert A. Simon (1958). *Organizations*. New York: Wiley.

Marshak, R. J. (1983). 'Cognitive and Experiential Approaches to Conceptual Learning.' *Training and Development Journal*, 37:5, 72–77.

Maslow, Abraham H. (1954). *Motivation and Personality*. New York: Harper & Row.

Maslow, Abraham H. (1962). *Toward a Psychology of Being*. Princeton, NJ: Van Nostrand.

Matarazzo, Joseph D. (1972). *Wechsler's Measurement and Appraisal of Adult Intelligence*. Baltimore, MD: Williams and Wilkins.

Matteson, Michael T. and John M. Ivancevich (1982). *Managing Job Stress and Health*. New York: Free Press.

Mayer, Patricia A. (1987). *A Comparison of Entrepreneurial Traits in Staff Nurses and Head Nurses in a State Owned and a Church Affiliated Hospital*. MS thesis, University of Texas, Galveston, TX.

Mendick, S. A. (1962). 'The Associative Basis of the Creative Process.' *Psychological Review*, 69, 220–232.

Merton, Robert K. (1949). *Social Theory and Social Structure*. New York: Free Press.

Metropolitan Economic Development Association (1977). 'Business Leadership Training – What's Happening?' *MEDA Reports*, 5:1, 1–7.

Meyer, Herbert H., Emanual Kay, and John R. P. French (1965). 'Split Roles in Performance Appraisal.' *Harvard Business Review*, 43:1, 123–129.

Miles, Raymond E. and Charles C. Snow (1984). 'Fit, Failure and the Hall of Fame.' *California Management Review*, 26:3, 10–28.

Miller, Alex and Bill Camp (1985). 'Exploring Determinants of Success in Corporate Venturing.' *Journal of Business Venturing*, 1, 87–105.

Miller, Danny and Cornelia Droge (1986). 'Psychological and Traditional Determinants of Structure.' *Administrative Science Quarterly*, 31, 539–560.

Miner, John B. (1950). *A Study of the Alcoholic Personality Utilizing the Thematic Apperception Test*. AB Thesis, Princeton University, Princeton, NJ.

Miner, John B. (1952). *Illusory Motion: An Exploratory Study*. MA Thesis, Clark University, Worcester, MA.

Miner, John B. (1956). 'Motion Perception, Time Perspective, and Creativity.' *Journal of Projective Techniques*, 20, 405–413.

Miner, John B. (1960). 'The Effect of a Course in Psychology on the Attitudes of Research and Development Supervisors.' *Journal of Applied Psychology*, 44, 224–232.

Miner, John B. (1960a). 'The Concurrent Validity of the Picture Arrangement Test in the Selection of Tabulating Machine Operators.' *Journal of Projective Techniques*, 24, 409–418.

Miner, John B. (1960b). 'The Kuder Preference Record in Management Appraisal.' *Personnel Psychology*, 13, 187–196.

Miner, John B. (1961). 'The Validity of the Picture Arrangement Test in the Selection of Tabulating Machine Operators: An Analysis of Predictive Power.' *Journal of Projective Techniques*, 25, 330–333.

Miner, John B. (1961a). 'On the Use of a Short Vocabulary Test to Measure General Intelligence.' *Journal of Educational Psychology*, 52, 157–160.

Miner, John B. (1961b). 'Management Development and Attitude Change.' *Personnel Administration*, 24:3, 21–26.

Miner, John B. (1962). 'Conformity Among University Professors and Business Executives.' *Administrative Science Quarterly*, 7, 96–109.

Miner, John B. (1962a). 'Personality and Ability Factors in Sales Performance.' *Journal of Applied Psychology*, 46, 6–13.

Miner, John B. (1963). *The Management of Ineffective Performance*. New York: McGraw-Hill.

Miner, John B. (1963a). 'Evidence Regarding the Value of a Management Course Based on Behavioral Science Subject Matter.' *Journal of Business*, 36, 325–335.

Miner, John B. (1964). *Scoring Guide for the Miner Sentence Completion Scale*. Buffalo, NY: Organizational Measurement Systems Press (originally published by Springer Publishing Company).

Miner, John B. (1965). *Studies in Management Education*. Buffalo, NY: Organizational Measurement Systems Press (originally published by Springer Publishing Company).

Miner, John B. (1965a). 'The Prediction of Managerial and Research Success.' *Personnel Administration*, 28:5, 12–16.

Miner, John B. (1966). *Introduction to Industrial Clinical Psychology*. New York: McGraw-Hill.

Miner, John B. (1967). *The School Administrator and Organizational Character*. Eugene, OR: University of Oregon Press.

Miner, John B. (1968). 'The Managerial Motivation of School Administrators.' *Educational Administration Quarterly*, 4, 55–71.

Miner, John B. (1968a). 'The Early Identification of Managerial Talent.' *Personnel and Guidance Journal*, 46, 586–591.

Miner, John B. (1971). 'Personality Tests as Predictors of Consulting Success.' *Personnel Psychology*, 24, 191–204.

Miner, John B. (1971a). 'Changes in Student Attitudes toward Bureaucratic Role Prescriptions During the 1960s.' *Administrative Science Quarterly*, 16, 351–364.

Miner, John B. (1973). 'The Real Crunch in Managerial Manpower.' *Harvard Business Review*, 51:6, 146–158.

Miner, John B. (1973a). 'The Management Consulting Firm as a Source of High-Level Managerial Talent.' *Academy of Management Journal*, 16, 253–264.

Miner, John B. (1973b). *Intelligence in the United States*. Westport, CT: Greenwood Press (originally published by Springer Publishing Company).

Miner, John B. (1973c). 'The OD-Management Development Conflict.' *Business Horizons*, 16:6, 31–36.

Miner, John B. (1974). 'The Organization for Motivation.' In Joseph W. McGuire, (ed.), *Contemporary Management: Issues and Viewpoints*. Englewood Cliffs, NJ: Prentice-Hall, 575–578.

Miner, John B. (1974a). 'Motivation to Manage Among Women: Studies of Business Managers and Educational Administrators.' *Journal of Vocational Behavior*, 5, 197–208.

Miner, John B. (1974b). *The Human Constraint: The Coming Shortage of Managerial Talent*. Buffalo, NY: Organizational Measurement Systems Press (originally published by Bureau of National Affairs (BNA) Books).

Miner, John B. (1974c). 'Student Attitudes Toward Bureaucratic Role Prescriptions and the Prospects for Managerial Talent Shortages.' *Personnel Psychology*, 27, 605–613.

Miner, John B. (1974d). 'Motivation to Manage Among Women: Studies of College Students.' *Journal of Vocational Behavior*, 5, 241–250.

Miner, John B. (1975). 'The Uncertain Future of the Leadership Concept: An Overview.' In James G. Hunt and Lars L. Larson, (eds), *Leadership Frontiers*. Kent, OH: Kent State University Press, 197–208.

Miner, John B. (1975a). *The Challenge of Managing*. Philadelphia, PA: W. B. Saunders.

Miner, John B. (1975b). *Case Analyses and Description of Managerial Role Motivation Training to Accompany The Challenge of Managing*. Philadelphia, PA: W. B. Saunders.

Miner, John B. (1976). 'Levels of Motivation to Manage Among Personnel and Industrial Relations Managers.' *Journal of Applied Psychology*, 61, 419–427.

Miner, John B. (1976a). 'Relationships Among Measures of Managerial Personality Traits.' *Journal of Personality Assessment*, 40, 383–397.

Miner, John B. (1977). *Motivation to Manage: A Ten-year Update on the 'Studies in Management Education' Research*. Buffalo, NY: Organizational Measurement Systems Press (Stoess, Alfred W., p. 173; Korman, Abraham K., p. 172).

Miner, John B. (1977a). *Scoring Guide for the Miner Sentence Completion Scale – Form H – 1977 Supplement*. Buffalo, NY: Organizational Measurement Systems Press.

Miner, John B. (1977b). 'Motivational Potential for Upgrading Among Minority and Female Managers.' *Journal of Applied Psychology*, 62, 691–697.

Miner, John B. (1977c). 'Implications of Managerial Talent Projections for Management Education.' *Academy of Management Review*, 2, 412–420.

Miner, John B. (1978). 'The Miner Sentence Completion Scale: A Reappraisal.' *Academy of Management Journal*, 21, 283–294.

Miner, John B. (1978a). 'Twenty Years of Research on Role Motivation Theory of Managerial Effectiveness.' *Personnel Psychology*, 31, 739–760.

Miner, John B. (1979). 'The Role of Organizational Structure and Process in Strategy Implementation: Commentary.' In Daniel E. Schendel and Charles W. Hofer, (eds), *Strategic Management: A New View of Business Policy and Planning*. Boston, MA: Little, Brown & Co, 289–302.

Miner, John B. (1979a). 'Managerial Talent in Personnel.' *Business Horizons*, 22:6, 10–20.

Miner, John B. (1979b). 'Leadership: Our Nation's Most Critical Shortage.' In Frank E. Kuzmits, (ed.), *Leadership in a Dynamic Society*. Indianapolis, IN: Bobbs-Merrill, 1–13.

Miner, John B. (1980). 'Limited Domain Theories of Organizational Energy.' In Craig C. Pinder and Larry F. Moore, (eds), *Middle Range Theory and the Study of Organizations*. Boston, MA: Martinus Nijhoff, 273–286.

Miner, John B. (1980a). 'A Rationale for the Limited Domain Approach to the Study of Motivation.' In Craig C. Pinder and Larry F. Moore, (eds), *Middle Range Theory and the Study of Organizations*. Boston, MA: Martinus Nijhoff, 334–336.

Miner, John B. (1980b). *Theories of Organizational Behavior*. Hinsdale, IL: Dryden.

Miner, John B. (1980c). 'The Role of Managerial and Professional Motivation in the Career Success of Management Professors.' *Academy of Management Journal*, 23, 487–508.

Miner, John B. (1981). 'Theories of Organizational Motivation.' In George W. England, Anant R. Negandhi, and Bernhard Wilpert, (eds), *The Functioning of Complex Organizations*. Cambridge, MA: Oelgeschlager, Gunn, and Hain, 75–110.

Miner, John B. (1981a). *Scoring Guide for the Miner Sentence Completion Scale – Form P*. Buffalo, NY: Organizational Measurement Systems Press.

Miner, John B. (1982). 'The Uncertain Future of the Leadership Concept: Revisions and Clarifications.' *Journal of Applied Behavioral Science*, 18, 293–307.

Miner, John B. (1982a). *Theories of Organizational Structure and Process*. Hinsdale, IL: Dryden.

Miner, John B. (1983). 'The Unpaved Road from Theory, Over the Mountains to Application.' In Ralph H. Kilmann, Kenneth W. Thomas, Dennis P. Slevin, Raghu Nath, and S. Lee Jerrell, (eds), *Producing Useful Knowledge for Organizations*. New York: Praeger, 37–68.

Miner, John B. (1984). 'The Validity and Usefulness of Theories in an Emerging Organizational Science.' *Academy of Management Review*, 9, 296–306.

Miner, John B. (1985). 'Sentence Completion Measures in Personnel Research: The Development and Validation of the Miner Sentence Completion Scales.' In H. John Bernardin and David A. Bownas, (eds), *Personality Assessments in Organizations*. New York: Praeger, 145–176.

Miner, John B. (1985a). *People Problems: The Executive Answer Book*. Buffalo, NY: Organizational Measurement Systems Press (originally published by Random House).

Miner, John B. (1986). *Scoring Guide for the Miner Sentence Completion Scale – Form T.* Buffalo, NY: Organizational Measurement Systems Press.

Miner, John B. (1986a). 'Managerial Role Motivation Training.' *Journal of Managerial Psychology*, 1:1, 25–30.

Miner, John B. (1988). *Organizational Behavior: Performance and Productivity.* New York: McGraw-Hill (originally published by Random House).

Miner, John B. (1989). *Scoring Guide for the Miner Sentence Completion Scale – Form H – 1989 Supplement.* Buffalo, NY: Organizational Measurement Systems Press.

Miner, John B. (1990). 'The Role of Values in Defining the Goodness of Theories in Organizational Science.' *Organization Studies*, 11, 161–178.

Miner, John B. (1990a). 'Entrepreneurs, High-Growth Entrepreneurs, and Managers: Contrasting and Overlapping Motivational Patterns.' *Journal of Business Venturing*, 5, 221–234.

Miner, John B. (1991). 'Psychological Assessment in a Developmental Context.' In Curtiss P. Hansen and Kelley A. Conrad, (eds), *A Handbook of Psychological Assessment in Business.* Westport, Conn.: Quorum, pp. 225–236.

Miner, John B. (1991a). 'Individuals, Groups, and Networking: Experience with an Entrepreneurship Development Program.' *International Council for Small Business Proceedings*, 2, 82–90.

Miner, John B. (1992). *Industrial-Organizational Psychology.* New York: McGraw-Hill.

Miner, John B. (1992a). 'Pursuing Diversity in an Increasingly Specialized Organizational Science.' In Arthur G. Bedeian, (ed.), *Management Laureates: A Collection of Autobiographical Essays.* Greenwich, Conn.: JAI Press.

Miner, John B. and J. Frank Brewer (1976). 'The Management of Ineffective Performance.' In Marvin D. Dunnette, (ed.), *Handbook of Industrial and Organizational Psychology.* Chicago: Rand McNally, 995–1029.

Miner, John B., Chao-chuan Chen, and K. C. Yu (1991). 'Theory Testing Under Adverse Conditions: Motivation to Manage in the People's Republic of China.' *Journal of Applied Psychology*, 76, 343–349.

Miner, John B. and Donald P. Crane (1977). 'The Continuing Effects of Motivational Shifts Among College Students.' In John B. Miner, (ed.), *Motivation to Manage: A Ten-year Update on the 'Studies in Management Education' Research.* Buffalo, NY: Organizational Measurement Systems Press, 146–148.

Miner, John B. and Donald P. Crane (1981). 'Motivation to Manage and the Manifestation of a Managerial Orientation in Career Planning.' *Academy of Management Journal*, 24, 626–633.

Miner, John B., Donald P. Crane, and Robert J. Vandenberg (1992). 'Congruence and Fit in Professional Role-Motivation Theory.' *Organization Science*, 3.

Miner, John B. and John E. Culver (1955). 'Some Aspects of the Executive Personality.' *Journal of Applied Psychology*, 39, 348–353.

Miner, John B. and H. Peter Dachler (1973). 'Personnel Attitudes and Motivation.' *Annual Review of Psychology*, 24, 379–402.

Miner, John B. and Susan S. Doe (1992). 'Effects of "Teaching the Theory" on Managerial Role Motivation Training Outcomes.' Unpublished paper, State University of New York at Buffalo, Buffalo.

Miner, John B. and Mary G. Miner (1976). 'Managerial Characteristics of Personnel Managers.' *Industrial Relations*, 15, 225–234.

Miner, John B. and Mary G. Miner (1979). *Employee Selection Within the Law.* Washington, DC: BNA Books.

Miner, John B., John R. Rizzo, Dorothy N. Harlow, and James W. Hill (1974).

'Role Motivation Theory of Managerial Effectiveness in Simulated Organizations of Varying Degrees of Structure.' *Journal of Applied Psychology*, 59, 31–37.

Miner, John B. and Norman R. Smith (1969). 'Managerial Talent Among Undergraduate and Graduate Business Students.' *Personnel and Guidance Journal*, 47, 995–1000.

Miner, John B. and Norman R. Smith (1981). 'Can Organizational Design Make Up for Organizational Decline?' *The Wharton Magazine*, 5:4 29–35.

Miner, John B. and Norman R. Smith (1982). 'Decline and Stabilization of Managerial Motivation Over a Twenty-Year Period.' *Journal of Applied Psychology*, 67, 297–305.

Miner, John B., Norman R. Smith, and Jeffrey S. Bracker (1989). 'Role of Entrepreneurial Task Motivation in the Growth of Technologically Innovative Firms.' *Journal of Applied Psychology*, 74, 554–560.

Miner, John B., Norman R. Smith, and Jeffrey S. Bracker (1992). 'Defining the Inventor-Entrepreneur in the Context of Established Typologies.' *Journal of Business Venturing*, 7, 103–113.

Miner, John B., Norman R. Smith, and Jeffrey S. Bracker (1992a). 'Predicting Firm Survival from a Knowledge of Entrepreneur Task Motivation.' *Entrepreneurship and Regional Development*, 4, 145–153.

Miner, John B., Norman R. Smith, and Bahman Ebrahimi (1985). 'Further Considerations in the Decline and Stabilization of Managerial Motivation: A Rejoinder to Bartol, Anderson, and Schneier (1980).' *Journal of Vocational Behavior*, 26, 290–298.

Miner, John B., Jeffrey M. Wachtel, and Bahman Ebrahimi (1989). 'The Managerial Motivation of Potential Managers in the United States and Other Countries of the World: Implications for National Competitiveness and the Productivity Problem.' *Advances in International Comparative Management*, 4, 147–170.

Mintzberg, Henry (1973). *The Nature of Managerial Work*. New York: Harper & Row.

Mintzberg, Henry (1983). *Power In and Around Organizations*. Englewood Cliffs, NJ: Prentice-Hall.

Mintzberg, Henry (1984). 'Power and Organization Life Cycles.' *Academy of Management Review*, 9, 207–224.

Mintzberg, Henry (1985). 'The Organization as Political Arena.' *Journal of Management Studies*, 22, 133–154.

Miron, David and David C. McClelland (1979). 'The Impact of Achievement Motivation Training on Small Business.' *California Management Review*, 21:4, 13–28.

Mitchel, James O. (1983). 'Review of Miner, John B. *Theories of Organizational Structure and Process*.' Personnel Psychology, 36, 162–164.

Mitroff, Ian L. and Richard O. Mason (1981). 'The Metaphysics of Policy and Planning: A Reply to Cosier.' *Academy of Management Review*, 6, 649–651.

Morris, Charles and Linwood Small (1971). 'Changes in Conceptions of the Good Life by American College Students from 1950 to 1970.' *Journal of Personality and Social Psychology*, 20, 254–260.

Morrow, Paula C. and Joe F. Goetz (1988). 'Professionalism as a Form of Work Commitment.' *Journal of Vocational Behavior*, 32, 92–111.

Morrow, Paula C. and Rosemary E. Wirth (1989). 'Work Commitment among Salaried Professionals.' *Journal of Vocational Behavior*, 34, 40–56.

Mowday, Richard T., Lyman W. Porter, and Richard M. Steers (1982). *Employee–Organization Linkages: The Psychology of Commitment, Absenteeism, and Turnover*. New York: Academic Press.

Muczyk, Jan P. and Randall S. Schuler (1976). 'The Management Motive Among Male College Students.' *Academy of Management Proceedings*, 36, 311–315.

Muczyk, Jan P. and Randall S. Schuler (1978). 'The Will to Manage, Validity of Its Measurement, and Possible Moderating Variables.' No. 78–14, Ohio State University, College of Administrative Science Working Paper Series, 22 pages.

Myerchin, Thomas S. (1980). *The Comparative Effectiveness of Two Short-Term Supervisory Management Development Courses – Individualized and Motivation Theory Based vs. Nonindividualized and Traditional – In a U.S. Defense Department Organization*. Ph.D. dissertation, Georgia State University, Atlanta, GA.

Nadler, David A. and Michael L. Tushman (1988). *Strategic Organization Design*. Glenview, IL: Scott, Foresman.

Nash, Allan N. (1966). 'Development of an SVIB Key for Selecting Managers.' *Journal of Applied Psychology*, 50, 250–254.

Nathan, Barry R. and Ralph A. Alexander (1985). 'An Application of Meta-Analysis to Theory Building and Construct Validation.' *Academy of Management Proceedings*, 45, 224–228.

Nellen, Eugene H. (1986). *Motivation to Manage of Black College Students Aspiring to Careers in Business Management: An Application of Miner's Role Motivation Theory*. D.P.S. dissertation, Pace University, New York, NY.

Nunnally, J.C. (1978). *Psychometric Theory*. New York: McGraw-Hill.

Nystrom, Paul C. (1986). 'Comparing Beliefs of Line and Technostructure Managers.' *Academy of Management Journal*, 29, 812–819.

O'del, John N. (1990). 'An Examination of Differences Between Canadian and American Students in Entrepreneurial Programs.' *Eastern Academy of Management Proceedings*, 27, 92.

Oliver, John E. (1981). *Scoring Guide for the Oliver Organization Description Questionnaire*. Buffalo, NY: Organizational Measurement Systems Press.

Oliver, John E. (1982). 'An Instrument for Classifying Organizations.' *Academy of Management Journal*, 25, 855–866.

Oliver, John E. and William B. Fredenberger (1987). 'Factor Structure of an Organizational Taxonomy.' Unpublished paper, School of Business Administration, Valdosta (GA) State College.

Ondrack, Daniel A. (1971). 'Examining the Generation Gap – Attitudes Toward Authority.' *Personnel Administration*, 34:3, 8–17.

Ondrack, Daniel A. (1973). 'Emerging Occupational Values: A Review and Some Findings.' *Academy of Management Journal*, 16, 423–432.

Opinion Research Corporation (1980). *Strategic Planning for Human Resources: 1980 and Beyond*. Princeton, NJ: ORC.

Overstreet, James S. (1980). *Managerial Motivation of Government Managers: A Comparison of Business and State Government Managers Using Miner's Role-Motivation Theory*. DBA dissertation, Florida State University, Tallahassee, FL.

Pandey, Janek and N. B. Tewary (1979). 'Locus of Control and Achievement Values of Entrepreneurs.' *Journal of Occupational Psychology*, 52, 107–111.

Papaloizos, Antoine (1962). 'Personality and Success of Training in Human Relations.' *Personnel Psychology*, 15, 423–428.

Pearson, John N. and Jeffrey S. Bracker (1983). 'Professional and Managerial Motivation Among Business Students: An Exploratory Empirical Investigation.' *Southern Management Association Proceedings*, 180–182.

Pelz, Donald C. (1952). 'Influence: A Key to Effective Leadership in the First-Line Supervisor.' *Personnel*, 29, 209–217.

Perham, Roy G. (1989). *The Effect of Relevant and Irrelevant Information on*

Miner Sentence Completion Scale Scoring Accuracy. Ph.D. dissertation, Stevens Institute of Technology, Hoboken, NJ.

Perrow, Charles (1967). 'A Framework for the Comparative Analysis of Organizations.' *American Sociological Review*, 32, 194–208.

Pilgrim, Martha S. (1986). *Development of a Professional Role-Motivation Training Package for Special Educators.* Ph.D. dissertation, Georgia State University, Atlanta, GA.

Pinder, Craig C. and Larry F. Moore (1980). *Middle Range Theory and the Study of Organizations.* Boston, MA: Martinus Nijhoff.

Pines, Ayala and Elliott Aronson (1988). *Career Burnout: Causes and Cures.* New York: Free Press.

Piotrowski, Zygmunt A. and Milton R. Rock (1963). *The Perceptanalytic Executive Scale.* New York: Grune & Stratton.

Porter, Charles G. (1991). 'Role Motivation in a Rapidly-Growing, Privately-Held Manufacturing Company.' Unpublished paper, State University of New York at Buffalo, Buffalo.

Porter, Lyman W. and Edward E. Lawler (1968). *Managerial Attitudes and Performance.* Homewood, IL: Irwin.

Porter, Lyman W. and Lawrence E. McKibbin (1988). *Management Education and Development: Drift or Thrust into the 21st Century.* New York: McGraw-Hill.

Porter, Michael E. (1990). 'The Competitive Advantage of Nations.' *Harvard Business Review*, 68:2, 73–93.

Porter, Michael E. (1990a). *The Competitive Advantage of Nations.* New York: Free Press.

Prentice-Hall, Inc. (1971). 'Business and the New Breed Employee.' *P-H Personnel Management: Policies and Practices*, 1971.

Price, James L. (1972). *Handbook of Organizational Measurement.* Lexington, MA: D. C. Heath.

Pugh, D. S. and David J. Hickson (1976). *Organizational Structure in Its Context: The Aston Programme I.* Lexington, MA: D. C. Heath.

Quigley, John V. (1979). *Predicting Managerial Success in the Public Sector: Concurrent Validation of Biodata and the Miner Sentence Completion Scale in the Georgia Department of Human Resources.* Ph.D. dissertation, Georgia State University, Atlanta, GA.

Quinn, James B. (1979). 'Technological Innovation, Entrepreneurship, and Strategy.' *Sloan Management Review*, 20:3, 19–30.

Raynor, Joel O. (1974). 'Future Orientation in the Study of Achievement Motivation.' In John W. Atkinson and Joel O. Raynor, (eds), *Motivation and Achievement*, New York: Wiley, 121–154.

Reilly, Richard R. and Georgia T. Chao (1982). 'Validity and Fairness of Some Alternative Employee Selection Procedures.' *Personnel Psychology*, 35, 1–62.

Rice, Robert W. (1978). 'Psychometric Properties of the Esteem for Least Preferred Coworker (LPC) Scale.' *Academy of Management Review*, 3, 106–117.

Richards, Max D. (1973). 'An Exploratory Study of Strategic Failure.' *Academy of Management Proceedings*, 33, 40–46.

Rind, Kenneth W. (1981). 'The Role of Venture Capital in Corporate Development.' *Strategic Management Journal*, 2, 169–180.

Robinson, Peter B. and H. Keith Hunt (1989). 'Entrepreneurial Research on Student Subjects May Not Generalize to Real World Entrepreneurs.' *Frontiers of Entrepreneurship Research*, 9, 491–492.

Roethlisberger, Fritz J. (1945). 'The Foreman: Master and Victim of Double Talk.' *Harvard Business Review*, 23:5, 283–298.

Rogers, Carl and Fritz J. Roethlisberger (1952). 'Barriers and Gateways to Communication.' *Harvard Business Review*, 30:4, 28–34.

Ronstadt, Robert (1988). 'The Corridor Principle.' *Journal of Business Venturing*, 3, 31–40.

Rootes, Mary D., Karla Moras, and Rana Gordon (1980). 'Ego Development and Sociometrically Evaluated Maturity: An Investigation of the Validity of the Washington University Sentence Completion Test of Ego Development.' *Journal of Personality Assessment*, 44, 613–619.

Roseman, Edward (1982). *Managing the Problem Employee*. New York: AMACOM.

Rotter, Julian B. (1966). 'Generalized Expectancies for Internal Versus External Control of Reinforcement.' *Psychological Monographs*, 80 (1, Whole No. 609).

Rotter, Julian B. (1971). 'Generalized Expectancies for Interpersonal Trust.' *American Psychologist*, 26, 443–452.

Rotter, Julian B. (1971a). 'External Control and Internal Control.' *Psychology Today*, June, 37–42, 58–59.

Rowe, Alan J. and Richard O. Mason (1987). *Managing with Style*. San Francisco, CA: Jossey-Bass.

Ryan, Thomas A. (1970). *Intentional Behavior: An Approach to Human Motivation*. New York: Ronald.

Satow, Roberta L. (1975). 'Value Rational Authority and Professional Organizations: Weber's Missing Type.' *Administrative Science Quarterly*, 20, 526–531.

Saydjari, Cheryl A. (1987). *Entrepreneurial Task Motivation in Graduate Nursing Students*. MS thesis, University of Texas, Galveston, TX.

Scherer, J. J. (1984). 'How People Learn: Assumptions for Design.' *Training and Development Journal*, 38:1, 64–65.

Schmidt, Warren H. (1970). *Organizational Frontiers and Human Values*. Belmont, CA: Wadsworth.

Schneider, Benjamin and Neal Schmitt (1986). *Staffing Organizations*. Glenview, Ill.: Scott, Foresman.

Schoonhoven, Claudia B. (1981). 'Problems with Contingency Theory: Testing Assumptions Hidden within the Language of Contingency Theory.' *Administrative Science Quarterly*, 26, 349–377.

Scott, Bruce R. (1973). 'The Industrial State: Old Myths and New Realities.' *Harvard Business Review*, 51:2, 133–148.

Scott, Bruce R. (1987). 'Competitiveness: 23 Leaders Speak Out.' *Harvard Business Review*, 65:4, 106–123.

Scott, Bruce R. (1989). 'Competitiveness: Self-Help for a Worsening Problem.' *Harvard Business Review*, 67:4, 115–121.

Seashore, Stanley E., Edward E. Lawler, Philip H. Mirvis, and Cortlandt Cammann (1982). *Observing and Measuring Organizational Change: A Guide to Field Practice*. New York: Wiley.

Sekaran, Uma (1983). 'Methodological and Theoretical Issues and Advancements in Cross-cultural Research.' *Journal of International Business Studies*, 14:2, 61–74.

Shouval, Ron, Edmund Duek, and Avital Ginton (1975). 'A Multiple Choice Version of the Sentence Completion Method.' *Journal of Personality Assessment*, 39, 41–49.

Shure, G. H. and J. P. Meeker (1967). 'A Personality Attitude Schedule for Use in Experimental Bargaining Studies.' *Journal of Psychology*, 65, 233–252.

Silver, Allan (1969). 'Who Cares for Columbia?' *New York Review of Books*, January, 15–19, 22–24.

Simon, Herbert A. (1947). *Administrative Behavior: A Study of Decision-Making Processes in Administrative Organizations*. New York: Free Press.

Simon, Herbert A. (1973). 'Organization Man: Rational or Self-Actualizing.' *Public Administration Review*, 33, 346–353.

Singh, Satvir (1979). 'Relationships Among Projective and Direct Verbal Measures of Achievement Motivation.' *Journal of Personality Assessment*, 43, 45–49.

Singleton, Timothy M. (1976). *A Study of Managerial Motivation Development Among College Student Leaders*. Ph.D. dissertation, Georgia State University, Atlanta, GA.

Singleton, Timothy M. (1977). 'Managerial Motivation Development: College Student Leaders.' In John B. Miner, (ed.), *Motivation to Manage: A Ten-Year Update on the 'Studies in Management Education' Research*. Buffalo, NY: Organizational Measurement Systems Press, 175–180.

Singleton, Timothy M. (1978). 'Managerial Motivation Development: A Study of College Student Leaders.' *Academy of Management Journal*, 21, 493–498.

Singleton, Timothy M. and Linda M. Calvert (1977). 'Fear of Flying or Will an Executive Development Seminar for Women Fly?' Unpublished Paper, University of Houston, Clear Lake City, TX.

Singleton, Timothy M. and Linda M. Calvert (1978). 'Testing the Effects of Management Development Training for Nursing Managers.' Unpublished Paper, University of Houston, Clear Lake City, TX.

Singleton, Timothy M., Aaron Kelley, Ester Yao, and Louis P. White (1987). 'Motivation to Manage: People's Republic of China and Hong Kong.' *Southern Management Association Proceedings*, 34–36.

Skinner, B. F. (1938). *The Behavior of Organisms*. New York: Appleton-Century-Crofts.

Skinner, B. F. (1953). *Science and Human Behavior*. New York: Macmillan.

Skinner, B. F. (1963). 'Operant Behavior.' *American Psychologist*, 18, 503–515.

Skinner, B. F. (1971). *Beyond Freedom and Dignity*. New York: Knopf.

Skinner, B. F. (1974). *About Behaviorism*. New York: Knopf.

Slevin, Dennis P. (1989). *The Whole Manager: How to Increase Your Professional and Personal Effectiveness*. New York: AMACOM.

Slocum, John W. and Don Hellriegel (1983). 'A Look at How Managers' Minds Work.' *Business Horizons*, 26:4, 58–68.

Smith, Norman R. (1967). *The Entrepreneur and His Firm: The Relationship Between Type of Man and Type of Company*. East Lansing, MI: Bureau of Business and Economic Research, Michigan State University.

Smith, Norman R., Jeffrey S. Bracker, and John B. Miner (1987). 'Correlates of Firm and Entrepreneur Success in Technologically Innovative Companies.' *Frontiers of Entrepreneurship Research*, 7, 337–353.

Smith, Norman R., K. G. McCain, and John B. Miner (1976). 'The Managerial Motivation of Successful Entrepreneurs.' *Oregon Business Review*, 34, 3.

Smith, Norman R. and John B. Miner (1983). 'Type of Entrepreneur, Type of Firm, and Managerial Motivation: Implications for Organizational Life Cycle Theory.' *Strategic Management Journal*, 4, 325–340.

Smith, Norman R. and John B. Miner (1984). 'Motivational Considerations in the Success of Technologically Innovative Entrepreneurs.' *Frontiers of Entrepreneurship Research*, 4, 488–495.

Smith, Norman R. and John B. Miner (1985). 'Motivational Considerations in the

Success of Technologically Innovative Entrepreneurs: Extended Sample Findings.' *Frontiers of Entrepreneurship Research*, 5, 482–488.

Sonnenfeld, Jeffrey (1988). *The Hero's Farewell: What Happens When CEOs Retire*. New York: Oxford University Press.

Sorensen, James E. and Thomas L. Sorensen (1974). 'The Conflict of Professionals in Bureaucratic Organizations.' *Administrative Science Quarterly*, 19, 98–105.

Southern, Lloyd J. F. (1976). *An Analysis of Motivation to Manage in the Tufted Carpet and Textile Industry of Northwest Georgia*. Ph.D. dissertation, Georgia State University, Atlanta, GA.

Southern, Lloyd J. F. and Peter Pih (1987). 'A Comparative Study of the Motivation to Manage of Taiwanese, Turkish, and U.S. Business Students.' Paper presented at the 26th Southern Management Association Meetings, New Orleans, LA.

Spock, Benjamin M. (1946). *Baby and Child Care*. New York: Pocket Books.

Stahl, Michael J. (1986). *Managerial and Technical Motivation: Assessing Needs for Achievement, Power and Affiliation*. New York: Praeger.

Stahl, Michael J., David W. Grigsby, and Anil Gulati (1985). 'Comparing the Job Choice Exercise and the Multiple Choice Version of the Miner Sentence Completion Scale.' *Journal of Applied Psychology*, 70, 228–232.

Steers, Richard M. and Daniel N. Braunstein (1976). 'A Behaviorally-Based Measure of Manifest Needs in Work Settings.' *Journal of Vocational Behavior*, 9, 251–266.

Steger, Joseph A., Winslow B. Kelley, Gregory Chouiniere, and Arnold Goldenbaum (1975). 'A Forced Choice Version of the MSCS and How It Discriminates Campus Leaders and Nonleaders.' *Academy of Management Journal*, 18, 453–460.

Stein, Aletha H. and Margaret W. Bailey (1973). 'The Socialization of Achievement Orientation in Females.' *Psychological Bulletin*, 80, 345–366.

Steiner, George A. and John B. Miner (1986). *Management Policy and Strategy*. New York: Macmillan.

Steinmetz, Lawrence L. (1969). *Managing the Marginal and Unsatisfactory Performer*. Reading, MA: Addison-Wesley.

Steinmetz, Lawrence L. (1969a). 'Critical Stages of Small Business Growth: When They Occur and How to Survive Them.' *Business Horizons*, 12:1, 29–36.

Stevens, George E. and O. C. Brenner (1990). 'An Empirical Investigation of the Motivation to Manage Among Blacks and Women in Business Schools.' *Educational and Psychological Measurement*, 50, 879–886.

Stewart, Valerie and Andrew Stewart (1982). *Managing the Poor Performer*. Aldershot, Hants, UK: Gower.

Stinchcombe, Arthur L. (1974). *Creating Efficient Industrial Administrations*. New York: Academic Press.

Stogdill, Ralph M. (1959). *Individual Behavior* and Group Achievement. New York: Oxford University Press.

Stogdill, Ralph M. and Alvin E. Coons (1957). *Leader Behavior: Its Description and Measurement*. Columbus, OH: Bureau of Business Research, Ohio State University.

Suojanen, Waino W. and Wayne W. Suojanen (1980). 'Management Theory, Managerial Work, and Graduate Education for Management.' *Finnish Journal of Business Economics*, 3, 155–173.

Swisher, Robert, Rosemary R. DuMont, and Calvin J. Boyer (1985). 'The Motivation to Manage: A Study of Academic Librarians and Library Science Students.' *Library Trends*, 34, 219–234.

Sykes, Hollister B. (1986). 'The Anatomy of a Corporate Venturing Program: Factors Influencing Success.' *Journal of Business Venturing*, 1, 275–293.

Tannenbaum, Arnold S. (1968). *Control in Organizations*. New York: McGraw-Hill.

Tannenbaum, Robert, Newton Margulies, and Fred Massarik (1985). *Human Systems Development: New Perspectives on People and Organizations*. San Francisco, CA: Jossey-Bass.

Tannenbaum, Robert and Warren H. Schmidt (1958). 'How to Choose a Leadership Pattern.' *Harvard Business Review*, 36:2, 95–101.

Tarnowieski, Dale (1973). *The Changing Success Ethic*. New York: American Management Association.

Thain, Donald H. (1969). 'Stages of Corporate Development.' *Business Quarterly*, 34, 32–45.

Thompson, James D. (1967). *Organizations in Action*. New York: McGraw-Hill.

Thurstone, Louis L. and Thelma G. Thurstone (1941). *Factorial Studies of Intelligence*. Chicago, IL: University of Chicago Press.

Timmons, Jeffry A. (1971). 'Black Is Beautiful – Is It Bountiful?' *Harvard Business Review*, 49:6, 81–94.

Tomkiewicz, Joseph, O. C. Brenner, and James Esinhart (1991). 'Hispanic Persons in Business: Is There Cause for Optimism?' *Psychological Reports*, 69, 847–852.

Tomkins, Silvan S. and John B. Miner (1957). *The Tomkins–Horn Picture Arrangement Test*. New York: Springer Publishing.

Tomkins, Silvan S. and John B. Miner (1959). *Picture Arrangement Test Interpretation: Scope and Technique*. New York: Springer Publishing.

Trist, Eric L. (1969). 'On Socio-Technical Systems.' In Warren G. Bennis, Kenneth D. Benne, and Robert Chin, (eds), *The Planning of Change*. New York: Holt, Rinehart and Winston, 269–282.

Trist, Eric L., G. W. Higgin, H. Murray, and A. B. Pollock (1963). *Organizational Choice: Capabilities of Groups at the Coal Face Under Changing Technologies*. London, UK: Tavistock.

Tuason, Ramon V. (1973). 'Corporate Life Cycle and the Evolution of Corporate Strategy.' *Academy of Management Proceedings*, 33, 35–40.

Turnbow, Karen and Richard H. Dana (1981). 'The Effects of Stem Length and Directions on Sentence Completion Scale Responses.' *Journal of Personality Assessment*, 45, 27–32.

Tyler, Leona E. (1978). *Individuality*. San Francisco, CA: Jossey-Bass.

Van de Ven, Andrew H. and Robert Drazin (1985). 'The Concept of Fit in Contingency Theory.' *Research in Organizational Behavior*, 7, 333–365.

Veroff, Joseph, Elizabeth M. Douvan, and Richard A. Kulka (1981). *The Inner American: A Self-portrait from 1957 to 1976*. New York: Basic Books.

Vollmer, Howard M. and Donald L. Mills (1966). *Professionalization*. Englewood Cliffs, NJ: Prentice-Hall.

Von Glinow, Mary Ann (1988). *The New Professionals: Managing Today's High-Tech Employees*. Cambridge, MA: Ballinger.

Vroom, Victor H. (1964). *Work and Motivation*. New York: Wiley.

Vroom, Victor H. and Philip W. Yetton (1973). *Leadership and Decision-making*. Pittsburgh, PA: University of Pittsburgh Press.

Wachtel, Jeffrey M. (1986). *A Cross-Cultural Comparative Management Study Measuring the Differences in Managerial Motivation and the Effects of Cultural and Other Explanatory Variables of Potential Managers from Mexico and the United States*. Ph.D. dissertation, Georgia State University, Atlanta, GA.

Wainer, Herbert A. and Irwin M. Rubin (1969). 'Motivation of Research and

Development Entrepreneurs: Determinants of Company Success.' *Journal of Applied Psychology*, 53, 178–184.

Ward, Lewis B. and Anthony G. Athos (1972). *Student Expectations of Corporate Life: Implications for Management Recruiting*. Boston: Graduate School of Business Administration, Harvard University.

Waugh, Mark H. (1981). 'Reliability of the Sentence Completion Test of Ego Development in a Clinical Population.' *Journal of Personality Assessment*, 45, 485–487.

Weber, Max (1968). *Economy and Society*. New York: Bedminster Press.

Weiss, Leo A. (1981). 'Start-up Businesses: A Comparison of Performances.' *Sloan Management Review*, 23:1, 37–53.

Wexley, Kenneth N. and Gary P. Latham (1981). *Developing and Training Human Resources in Organizations*. Glenview, IL: Scott, Foresman.

White, Kay S. (1974). *A Study of the Use of Management Training as a Change Agent*. Ph.D. dissertation, Georgia State University, Atlanta, GA.

White, Kay S. (1975). 'Evaluation of Laboratory Management Training.' *Health Laboratory Science*, 12, 347–350.

Wilderom, Celeste P. M., John B. Miner, and Anne Pastor (1991). 'Organizational Typology: Superficial Foursome of Organization Science?' Unpublished paper, Free University, Amsterdam, The Netherlands.

Wilderom, Celeste P. M. and John B. Miner (1991). 'Defining Voluntary Groups and Agencies Within Organization Science.' *Organization Science*, 2, 366–378.

Winer, B. J. (1971). *Statistical Principles in Experimental Design*. New York: McGraw-Hill.

Wittreich, Warren J. (1977). 'Managerial Motivation Development: Business Managers.' In John B. Miner, (ed.), *Motivation to Manage: A Ten-Year Update on the 'Studies in Management Education' Research*. Buffalo, NY: Organizational Measurement Systems Press, 181–183.

Wohlking, Wallace (1971). 'Management Training: Where Has It Gone Wrong?' *Training and Development Journal*, 25:12, 2–8.

Woodward, Joan (1965). *Industrial Organization: Theory and Practice*. London, UK: Oxford University Press.

Woodward, Joan (1970). *Industrial Organization: Behavior and Control*. London, UK: Oxford University Press.

Yankelovich, Daniel (1969). 'What They Believe.' *Fortune*, January, 70–71, 179–181.

Yukl, Gary A. (1981, 1989). *Leadership in Organizations*. Englewood Cliffs, NJ: Prentice-Hall.

Name index

Abernathy, William J. 238
Aboud, John 164
Adams, J. Stacy 44
Adorno, Theodore W. 122
Agarwal, N. 68
Albert, Michael 93, 95–7, 104, 122, 124, 125, 214, 263–5
Aldag, Ramon J. 76, 78, 109, 119, 120, 214, 289–91, 296
Alderfer, Clayton P. 289
Alexander, Ralph A. 109–11
Al-Kelabi, Saad A. 83, 84, 94, 105, 139, 255, 259, 260
Alliger, George A. 113
Allport, Gordon W. 112
Alper, Thelma 58, 154
Anderson, Carl R. 78, 210, 215, 270, 271, 276, 289, 291, 293–6
Anderson, James K. 176
Argyris, Chris 21, 44, 302
Aronson, Elliott 140
Arsan, Noyan 257, 279
Arvey, Richard D. 179
Athos, Anthony G. 221, 226, 295
Atkinson, John W. 19, 59, 82
Atwater, Bruce 4

Baer, Donald 239
Bailey, Margaret W. 154
Baker, Sally H. 72
Barnett, Rosalind C. 223
Barrick, Murray R. 123
Bartol, Kathryn M. 78, 83, 94, 98, 106, 124, 189, 198, 210, 215, 270, 271, 276, 279, 282, 283, 289, 291, 293–6
Barton, Allen H. 229
Bass, Bernard M. 108, 109, 233

Basuray, M. Tom 83, 85, 122, 289–91, 296
Beatty, Richard W. 28
Bedeian, Arthur G. 329
Begley, Thomas M. 166
Behling, Orlando 47
Belasco, James A. 199
Beldt, Sandra F. 67, 68
Bell, Cecil H. 21
Bellu, Renato R. 152–4, 170, 255
Benham, Thomas W. 223
Benne, Kenneth D. 336
Bennis, Warren G. 45
Bentz, V. Jon 112, 113
Berkshire, J. R. 70
Berman, Frederic E. 77, 93, 105, 146, 257, 263
Bernardin, H. John 28, 108
Biggadike, Ralph 299
Bird, Barbara J. 166
Black, Cameron H. 94, 263
Blake, Robert R. 195
Block, Jeanne H. 227, 228
Block, Zenos 299
Bowin, Robert B. 119, 178, 181, 182, 189, 214
Bownas, David A. 108
Boyatzis, Richard E. 114, 118, 197
Boyd, David P. 166
Boyer, Calvin J. 279
Bracker, Jeffrey S. 142, 143, 145, 147–51, 155, 156, 167, 170, 268, 304
Braunstein, Daniel N. 121, 165, 223
Bray, Douglas W. 113, 224–6, 295
Brenner, O. C. 83, 123, 272, 274, 279
Brewer, J. Frank 176
Brief, Arthur P. 76, 78, 109, 119, 120, 214, 289–91, 296

Subject index

131, 134–5, 137–40, 205–6, 267–8, 306–8
punishment 231, 234
P score 71–3, 86–9, 94, 105, 133–4, 136, 138, 160–1, 306–8
psychologists 57

race 262–87
rare scores 62, 65–7, 80
reliability 59–60, 90, 291–3, 311; internal consistency 82–5, 290; scorer 58, 75–80; test-retest 79–81, 90
Remote Association Test 122
Rensselaer Polytechnic Institute (RPI) 63–4, 92, 215–16
resistance to change 193, 195
restriction of range 97
retention of change 183–5
risk 19–20, 67–8, 158, 268
role conflicts 195
role requirements 9–14
Rorschach test 58, 291
Routine Administrative Functions subscale 14, 62, 64–5, 68–9, 77, 79, 81, 83, 85–9, 92, 95–101, 103–6, 110–11, 115, 117, 119–20, 126–8, 180–2, 185–6, 190, 192, 209–13, 218, 240–2, 247–8, 251–2, 254, 256, 263–5, 271–7, 279–80, 287, 306–8

St. Edwards University 246
sales representatives 3, 42–3, 58, 102–3, 162–3
San Bernardino State College 181
Saudi Arabia 83–4, 94, 105, 129, 139–40, 143, 255, 259–60
Scalar principle 36
The School Administrator and Organizational Character 108
school administrators 92, 103
school district, study of 73, 136–8
scientists 93, 102, 104, 122; organizational 143
Sears, Roebuck & Company 112–13
selection 302–3, 312
Self Achievement subscale 66–7, 77, 81, 84, 88–9, 148–54, 156, 159, 161–3, 166–8, 269, 306–10
self-actualization 6, 111, 120
self-assurance 111, 119–20
Self-Description Inventory (SDI) 111–12, 119–21, 141, 168, 290

self-report: indexes 117–18; items 125, 243–4, 249–50, 286; measures 114–15
sensitivity (T-group) training 21, 198
sentence completion measures 58, 60–1, 66, 76, 78, 82, 291
separation anxiety 174
sex differences see gender
skills 48, 68, 113, 194–5, 198, 200
sociotechnical: plants 67–8; systems 1; work groups 43, 67
sociotechnical systems theory 34
Solero, Andrew, case of 29, 86–7
South Africa 260
span of control 174
Spearman-Brown coefficient 71, 83–4
special education teachers 73, 129, 136–8, 143, 205, 266–7, 275
special education unit 74
Standing Out from Group subscale 13, 62, 64–5, 68–9, 77, 79, 81, 83, 85–9, 92, 95–6, 98–101, 103–6, 110–11, 115, 117, 119–20, 126–8, 130, 132, 142, 176, 180–2, 184–6, 190, 192, 208–13, 217–18, 241, 247–8, 251–4, 256, 270–4, 276, 280, 306–8
Stanford University 112
State University of New York at Buffalo (SUNY-Buffalo) 72, 74, 80–1, 83–4, 94, 155, 158, 166, 168–70, 182, 189, 217–18, 265–6, 268–9, 275; Center for Entrepreneurial Leadership 72, 74, 160
strategic planning 155
Strong Vocational Interest Blank 112, 122
students 37, 65, 78, 80–5, 92, 95, 98, 102, 106, 119, 122–4, 142–3, 165, 169–70, 198, 215–18, 220–32, 239, 243–4, 264–6, 268, 272–3, 278, 290; business 80–1, 92–4, 98, 106, 115, 147, 155–8, 180–2, 191, 207–14, 223, 236, 271, 275–7, 279, 281–2, 287, 293–4; Canadian 255; Chinese 250–2; education 80, 92; European 258–9, 283; Mexican 245–50, 265; Taiwanese 258; Turkish 257–8
Students for a Democratic Society 226
Studies in Management Education 108
subordinates 62, 175, 178, 193
success 68, 112, 135–7, 186–8, 228;